The Ten Bodhisattva Grounds

The Avataṃsaka Sūtra

Chapter 26

To refrain from doing any manner of evil,
to respectfully perform all varieties of good,
and to purify of one's own mind—
This is the teaching of all buddhas.

The Ekottara Āgama Sūtra
(T02 n.125 p.551a 13–14)

A Note on the Proper Care of Dharma Materials

Traditional Buddhist cultures treat books on Dharma as sacred. Hence it is considered disrespectful to place them in a low position, to read them when lying down, or to place them where they might be damaged by food or drink.

The Ten Bodhisattva Grounds

The Avataṃsaka Sūtra
Chapter 26

The Ten Highest Levels of Practice
On the Bodhisattva's Path to Buddhahood

As Translated From Sanskrit by Tripiṭaka Master Śikṣānanda
(699 CE)

An Annotated English Translation by Bhikshu Dharmamitra
Including the Entire P. L. Vaidya Sanskrit Text

Kalavinka Press
Seattle, Washington
www.kalavinkapress.org

Kalavinka Press
8603 39th Ave SW
Seattle, WA 98136 USA
(www.kalavinkapress.org)

Kalavinka Press is associated with the Kalavinka Dharma Association, a non-profit organized exclusively for religious educational purposes as allowed within the meaning of section 501(c)3 of the Internal RevenueCode. Kalavinka Dharma Association was founded in 1990 and gained formal approval in 2004 by the United States Internal Revenue Service as a 501(c)3 non-profit organization to which all donations are tax deductible.

Donations to KDA are accepted by mail and on the Kalavinka website where numerous free Dharma translations and excerpts from Kalavinka publications are available in digital format.

Edition: 10GSIK-EO-1019-1.0-English/Sanskrit
Kalavinka Buddhist Classics Book 12b

ISBN: 978-1-935413-12-7
Library of Congress Control Number: 2019029483

Library of Congress Cataloging-in-Publication Data

Names: Śikṣānanda, 652-710, translator. | Dharmamitra, Bhikshu, translator.
Title: The ten Bodhisattva grounds : the Avataṃsaka Sūtra, chapter 26 : the ten highest levels of practice on the Bodhisattva's path to Buddhahood / as translated from Sanskrit by Tripiṭaka Master Śikṣānanda (699 ce) ; an annotated English translation by Bhikshu Dharmamitra including the entire P. L. Vaidya Sanskrit text.
Description: 10gsik-eo-1019-1.0-english/sanskrit. | Seattle, Washington : Kalavinka Press, 2019. | Series: Kalavinka buddhist classics; book 12b | Includes bibliographical references. | Summary: ""The Ten Bodhisattva Grounds" is an annotated English Translation by Bhikshu Dharmamitra of Tripitaka Master Śikṣānanda's circa 699 ce Sanskrit-to-Chinese translation of the Avataṃsaka Sūtra, Chapter 26. This text describes in great detail the ten highest levels of bodhisattva practice on the path to buddhahood as taught in that sutra. This edition of the translation includes the P. L. Vaidya Sanskrit text. The Sanskrit section headings are inset in the English translation to facilitate easy correlation of the English translation with the Sanskrit text"-- Provided by publisher.
Identifiers: LCCN 2019029483 | ISBN 9781935413127 (paperback)
Subjects: LCSH: Tripiṭaka. Sūtrapiṭaka. Avataṃsakasūtra.--Criticism, interpretation, etc. | Bodhisattva stages (Mahayana Buddhism)
Classification: LCC BQ1622.A1 D432 2019 | DDC 294.3/55--dc23
LC record available at https://lccn.loc.gov/2019029483

Kalavinka Press books are printed on acid-free paper.
Cover and interior designed by Bhikshu Dharmamitra.
Printed in the United States of America

Dedication

Dedicated to the memory of the selfless and marvelous life of the Venerable Dhyāna Master Hsuan Hua, the Guiyang Ch'an Patriarch and the very personification of the bodhisattva's six perfections.

Dhyāna Master Hsuan Hua

宣化禪師

1918–1995

Acknowledgments

The accuracy and readability of this translation have been greatly improved by many corrections, preview comments, and editorial suggestions generously contributed by Bhikkhu Bodhi, Feng Ling, and Nicholas Weeks.

Expenses incurred in bringing forth this publication were underwritten by generous donations from Craig and Karen Neyman, Madalena Lew, Shuyu Yang, Jiajing Li, Kam Chung Wong, Loritta Chan, David Fox, Upasaka Guo Ke, Yuen-Lin Tan, the BDK English Tripiṭaka Project, and others. Sponsorship of Adobe Indesign book layout was provided by Anagarika Mahendra.

Use of the digital Sanskrit texts is by the kind permission of Dr. Miroj Shakya, Project Coordinator of the Digital Sanskrit Buddhist Canon Project.

Were it not for the ongoing material support provided by my late guru's Dharma Realm Buddhist Association and the serene translation studio provided by Seattle's Bodhi Dhamma Center, creation of this translation would have been impossible.

Additionally, it would have been impossible for me to produce this translation without the Dharma teachings and personal inspiration provided to me by my late guru, the awesomely wise and compassionate Dhyāna Master Hsuan Hua, the Guiyang Ch'an patriarch, Dharma teacher, and exegete.

Finally, I owe an immense debt of gratitude to the members of the liver care and transplant teams at Seattle's University of Washington Medical Center who cured me of liver cancer in 2010 and gave me a liver transplant several months later. In particular, if it weren't for over a decade of wonderfully attentive and compassionate care by Dr. Renuka Bhattacharya, medical director of UW's liver transplant program, the kindness and skill in three major surgeries by my transplant surgeon, Dr. Jorge Reyes, and the marvelous generosity of an anonymous liver donor, I would have died a half dozen years ago and thus never could have completed the scriptural translations I have produced in the last eight years.

Outlining in This Work

The ten chapter titles in this work are from the Taisho Chinese text. All other outline headings originate with the translator. Buddhist canonical texts are often so structurally dense that they are best navigated with the aid of at least a simple outline structure such as I have supplied here.

List of Abbreviations

AN	Aṅguttara Nikāya
BB	Buddhabhadra (T278)
BCSD	Hirakawa's *Buddhist Chinese-Sanskrit Dictionary*
BDK	Bukkyo Dendo Kyokai English Tripiṭaka
BHSD	Edgerton's *Buddhist Hybrid Sanskrit Dictionary*
BR	Bodhiruci (T1522)
CBETA	Chinese Buddhist Electronic Text Association's digital edition of the Taisho Chinese Buddhist canon.
DN	*Dīgha Nikāya*
DR	Dharmarakṣa (T278)
DSBC	Digital Sanskrit Buddhist Canon's digitized edition of *Daśabhūmikasūtram*, edited by P. L. Vaidya.
HH	Venerable Hsuan Hua
KB	Kumārajīva assisted by Buddhayaśas (T286)
KJ	Kumārajīva
LTX	Li Tongxuan (李通玄)
MDPL	*Materials for a Dictionary of the Prajñāpāramitā Literature*
MLDB	*The Middle Length Discourses of the Buddha*
MN	*Majjhima nikāya*
Mppu	*Mahāprajñāpāramitā upadeśa*
MW	Monier Williams' *A Sanskrit-English Dictionary*
N	Nāgārjuna
PDB	Princeton Dictionary of Buddhism
QL	Qing Liang (唐清涼山大華嚴寺沙門澄觀)
QLSC	Qing Liang's *Huayan Shuchao* (大方廣佛華嚴經疏鈔會本. L130 no. 1557)
SYMG	The Song, Yuan, Ming, Gong editions of the Chinese Buddhist canon.
SA	Śikṣānanda (T279)
SD	Śīladharma (T287)
T	Taisho Chinese Buddhist Canon via CBETA (Version 2004. ed.) Taibei)
VB	Venerable Bhikkhu Bodhi
XHYJL	*Xin huayanjing lun* (新華嚴經論 – T36, no. 1739) by Li Tongxuan.

General Table of Contents

Directory to Chapter Subsections

Translator's Introduction

Continuing my focus on translating bodhisattva path texts important in the history of Classic Indian and Chinese Mahāyana Buddhism, I present here my English translation of "The Ten Grounds" chapter of the *Greatly Expansive Buddha's Flower Adornment Sutra* (*Mahāvaipulya-buddha-avataṃsaka-sūtra*) as translated by Tripiṭaka Master Śikṣānanda some time between 695 and 699 CE. The subject of this six-fascicle 26th chapter, "The Ten Grounds," is the bodhisattva's ascent through ten "grounds," "planes," or "levels" of spiritual path cultivation transited by the bodhisattva as he progresses from the state of a common person toward that of a fully enlightened buddha.

There have been two relatively complete Chinese translations of the *Avataṃsaka Sutra* itself from Sanskrit, the first of which was an edition in 34 chapters and 60 fascicles completed by Tripiṭaka Master Buddhabhadra in 421 (T 278) and the second of which was an edition in 39 chapters and 80 fascicles completed by Tripiṭaka Master Śikṣānanda in 699 (T 280). My reasons for drawing this "Ten Grounds" chapter from the Śikṣānanda edition rather than the Buddhabhadra edition were two-fold. First, the Śikṣānanda edition is more complete and, outside of Japan, it has generally now regarded as the "standard" edition ever since the middle of the Tang Dynasty. Secondly, I had already been introduced to the Śikṣānanda edition by my guru, the Venerable Hsuan Hua, this in the context of his lectures on it which started in San Francisco in 1970 or '71.

In order to encourage a better understanding of these ten bodhisattva grounds and the bodhisattva path in general, I have also translated three other closely related works:

Kumārajīva's 4-fascicle *Ten Grounds Sutra* (T 286);
Nāgārjuna's 17-fascicle *Treatise on the Ten Grounds* (T 1521);
Śikṣānanda's 80-fascicle *Flower Adornment Sutra* (T 279).

The first two of these three related works are Kalavinka Press publications. Even though I finished the first draft of my *Flower Adornment Sutra* translation in early 2014, due to the inevitable delay imposed by editing, revising, and incorporating recommended improvements from colleagues, it could easily be a few more years before I release it to publication.

Regarding this "Ten Grounds" text itself, because it also circulated as an independent scripture known as the *Ten Grounds Sutra* (*Daśabhūmika-sūtra*), it does not exist only as a chapter of the *Avataṃsaka Sutra*. There is no real consensus on whether this text was, per the tradition, originally integral to the *Avataṃsaka Sutra* or was instead an independently circulating scripture later incorporated into the *Avataṃsaka Sutra*. In any case, in addition to the later Sanskrit, Tibetan, and Mongolian editions of this text, there are six relatively early surviving Chinese editions as follows:

Dharmarakṣa (*c.* 297 CE), T 283;
Kumārajīva assisted by Buddhayaśas (c. 408–412 CE),[1] T 286;
Buddhabhadra (*c.* 418–20 CE), as *Avataṃsaka Sutra* Ch. 22, T 278;
Bodhiruci (*c.* 508–511 CE), in Vasubhandu's commentary, T 1522;
Śikṣānanda (*c.* 695–699 CE), as *Avataṃsaka Sutra* Ch. 26, T 279;
Śīladharma (*c.* 790 CE), T 287.

In English, there have been several translations, as follows:

Megumu Honda from the Sanskrit of the *Daśabhūmika-sūtra*;[2]
Buddhist Text Translation Society (partial) of the Śikṣānanda edition's Chapter 26;
Thomas Cleary, supposedly (but not really) from Śikṣānanda's edition of the *Avataṃsaka Sutra,* this in Ch. 26 of his *Flower Ornament Scripture.*[3]

The Megumu Honda translation was done in 1961–62 when he was still a student at Yale, and, although perhaps useful for beginning students of Sanskrit, its utility is diminished by the author's early difficulties with both Sanskrit and English.

The BTTS translation is so far only a partial translation consisting of a translation of the first four of the ten grounds. I have been advised by a member of that translation team that, as of July, 2018, the tentative publication date for the remainder of the BTTS translation is still 2 or more years away.

Regarding this "Ten Grounds Chapter" itself, Thomas Cleary's translation is represented as a translation from the Chinese of the Śikṣānanda edition of the *Avataṃsaka Sutra*. However, it is no such thing. His translation of Chapter 26 which he calls "The Ten Stages" chapter appears to instead be a loose translation of the P. L. Vaidya Sanskrit edition of the *Daśabhūmika Sūtra*. Hence his supposed translation of this chapter has little if any relation to Śikṣānanda's Chinese edition.

Although there are other schemas describing the levels of cultivation through which one passes in cultivating the bodhisattva path, the "ten grounds" arrangement described in this text is really quite standard for the Classic Indian Mahāyana tradition. As listed in the introductory section of this chapter, these ten levels of progress along the bodhisattva path are as follows:

1) The Ground of Joyfulness (*pramuditā*);
2) The Ground of Stainlessness (*vimalā*);
3) The Ground of Shining Light (*prabhākarī*);
4) The Ground of Blazing Brilliance (*arciṣmati*);[4]
5) The Difficult-to-Conquer Ground (*sudurjayā*);
6) The Ground of Direct Presence (*abhimukhī*);
7) The Far-Reaching Ground (*dūraṃgamā*);
8) The Ground of Immovability (*acalā*);
9) The Ground of Excellent Intelligence (*sādhumatī*);[5]
10) The Ground of the Dharma Cloud (*dharma-megha*).

Each of these grounds is correlated with the practice of one of these ten perfections:

The perfection of giving (*dāna-pāramitā*);
The perfection of moral virtue (*śīla-pāramitā*);
The perfection of patience (*kṣānti-pāramitā*);
The perfection of vigor (*vīrya-pāramitā*);
The perfection of *dhyāna* meditation (*dhyāna-pāramitā*);
The perfection of wisdom (*prajñā-pāramitā*);
The perfection of skillful means (*upāya-pāramitā*);
The perfection of vows (*praṇidhāna-pāramitā*);
The perfection of powers (*bala-pāramitā*);
The perfection of knowledge (*jñāna-pāramitā*).

There are also other correlations between particular grounds and important bodhisattva skills and capacities. Examples include:

The four means of attraction on the first four grounds;
The thirty-seven enlightenment factors on the fourth ground;
The four truths on the fifth ground;
The twelve links of conditioned arising on the sixth ground;
The unproduced-dharmas patience on the eighth ground;
The four unimpeded knowledges on the ninth ground.

According to this text, as the bodhisattva moves from one level to another in his cultivation of the ten grounds, he sees more and more buddhas, manifests more and more bodhisattva transformation bodies attended by bodhisattva retinues, and appears as a bodhisattva king in higher and higher stations of existence. This bodhisattva kingship phenomenon begins with his appearance as a king over the continent of Jambudvīpa on the first ground after which he appears as a king over all four continents on the second ground, appears as a king of the Trāyastriṃśa Heaven on the third ground, and so forth, finally culminating with his appearance as a king of the Akaniṣṭha Heaven on the tenth ground.

There are a few technical difficulties that I encountered in translating this text from Chinese, most of which involve ambiguities in meaning introduced by the limitations of Chinese language in accurately reflecting Sanskrit technical term nuances. This problem is well evidenced by the particular Chinese-language technical term translations chosen by Śikṣānanda. (The challenges I encountered in translating Kumārajīva's *Ten Grounds Sutra* were nearly identical.)

Fortunately, because I could consult the surviving Sanskrit edition, it was for the most part possible to trace the antecedent Sanskrit terms and then choose somewhat more accurate English technical term translations than would have resulted from simply trying to translate Śikṣānanda's terms directly from Chinese. Relative clarity in this matter was aided somewhat by J. Rahder's *Glossary*.[6] Even though the P. L. Vaidya Sanskrit edition dates from roughly a millennium after the Śikṣānanda and Kumārajīva editions, I think it is still mostly valid to rely on it for this purpose because, even as aspects of meaning at the sentence and paragraph level of the Sanskrit manuscript morph over time with each recopying or transcription from memory, technical terms still tend to remain unchanged. The same cannot be said for the actual text of the scripture because we can readily observe very obvious differences between the Sanskrit edition and the very early Śikṣānanda and Kumārajīva editions.

The first and most obvious problem is the difficulty which the Chinese translations have in reliably reflecting the difference between technical terms such as *jñāna* (knowledge, cognition, etc.) and *prajñā* (wisdom). In an ideal translation world, Śikṣānanda and Kumārajīva would have very rigorously stuck with simply *zhi* (智)

for "*jñāna* / knowledge" and *zhihui* (智慧) for "*prajñā* / wisdom," but this is not the case, especially in the translation of verse lines where the need for extreme economy in composing Chinese 5- or 7-character verse lines where it often became necessary to shorten *zhihui* (智慧) to simply *zhi* (智), thereby accidentally obscuring for the Chinese reader the difference between "wisdom" and "knowledge." I found that this problem was fairly easily overcome through consulting the Sanskrit.

Other technical terms which initially produced difficulties due to the widely varying and sometimes deceptive Chinese translations were *adhyāsaya* (usually "higher aspirations," etc.), *āśaya* (usually "intentions," "resolute intentions," "dispositions," "inclinations," etc.), and *adhimukti* (usually "resolute beliefs," "resolute faith," "convictions," etc.). Had I not closely tracked the Sanskrit text, it would have been nearly impossible to accurately translate these terms and preserve their distinctions.

Due to the particular need of specialists and advanced students to closely track and distinguish technical terms and other issues such as these, at least in the multilingual editions of my translation, I am including under the same cover not only the facing-page Chinese simplified and traditional texts, but also (in the back of the book) the Sanskrit text.

Use of the digital Sanskrit text is by the kind permission of Dr. Miroj Shakya, Project Coordinator of the Digital Sanskrit Buddhist Canon Project. The Sanskrit text itself is the edition edited by P. L. Vaidya and published by The Mithila Institute of Post-Graduate Studies and Research in Sanskrit learning.To ease the reader's correlation of the Sanskrit text with both the English translation and the facing-page Chinese, I have embedded the alphabetical Sanskrit section headings within all versions of the text (Chinese, English, and Sanskrit).

These very helpful alphabetical section markers originate with Johannes Rahder who embedded them in his 1923 and 1926 editions of the *Daśabhūmika-Sūtra*.[7] In all cases I have placed these alphabetical section headings within the texts in bolded reduced-font "curly brackets" or "braces" as follows: **{A}**, **{B}**, **{AA}**, etc.

In bringing forth this translation, I making no claims to absolute accuracy. Though I have been assisted by critical comments from about a half dozen colleagues and have gone through the manuscript many times, there is probably room for improvement. I hope that readers who notice errors or infelicities will favor me with constructive email criticism via the Kalavinka website. I hope that this edition will at least serve to encourage a deeper study of this text by students of the Dharma.

Bhikshu Dharmamitra

Seattle,

July 9, 2018

Introduction Endnotes

1. Citing Kusugai, Richard Robinson (*Early Mādhyamika in India and China*, p. 76) says that Kumārajīva is said to have "procrastinated about starting work on the *Daśabhūmika* until Buddhayaśas joined him in the undertaking." Buddhayaśas arrived in Chang'an in 408, so the translation must date from around that time.

2. Sinor, D., Raghu Vira, Honda, Megumu, & Permanent International Altaistic Conference. (1968). *Studies in South, East, and Central Asia : Presented as a memorial volume to the late Professor Raghu Vira* (Śata-piṭaka series ; v. 74). New Delhi: International Academy of Indian Culture.

3. Cleary, T. (1984). The Flower Ornament Scripture : A Translation of the Avatamsaka Sutra. Boulder : [New York]: Shambhala Publications ; Distributed in the U.S. by Random House.

4. SA,SD, and Prajñā all translate the name of this *bhūmi* as "the Ground of Blazing Intelligence" (焰慧地). This appears to be the result of an error arising from misinterpreting the Sanskrit name (*arciṣmatī*) by mistaking a suffix indicating possession (*-mat* modified to agree with the feminine noun *bhūmi* to become *-matī*) for a completely unrelated word that means "intelligence," "intellect," "mind" (*mati*). (BB, BR, KB, and the Tibetan all recognize *–matī* as a possessive suffix and hence accord with the Sanskrit meaning.) I have chosen to "bridge" the problem by translating the name of this ground as "the Ground of Blazing Brilliance" in order to allow both meanings the be reflected in the word "blazing" and thus more or less accurately translate both the (seemingly erroneous) SA translation and the correct meaning of the Sanskrit.

5. There seem to be two distinctly different understandings of the meaning of this ground:

   DR, SA, BB, BR, SD, and Prajñā all translate the name of this *bhūmi* as "the Ground of Excellent Intelligence" (善慧地). DR translates that same meaning slightly differently: (善哉意). The Tibetan translation also corresponds to this with "the Ground of Excellent Insight" (*legs pa'i blo gros*). Strictly speaking, one could infer that most of these renderings appear be the result of an error arising from misinterpreting the Sanskrit name (*sādhumatī*) by mistaking a suffix indicating possession (*-mat* modified to agree with the feminine noun *bhūmi* to become *-matī*) for a completely unrelated word that means "intelligence," "intellect," or "mind" (*mati*).

Of all the Chinese and Tibetan translators, it appears that the Kumārajīva-Buddhayaśas translation team may have been the only one to render the name of this *bhūmi* more or less in accordance with the above-referenced "strictly correct" interpretation of the Sanskrit term as "the Ground of Sublime Goodness" (妙善地). The KB edition only employs the possibly erroneous Chinese and Tibetan default rendering once (in its initial listing of the ten bodhisattva grounds), but otherwise accords with the strictly grammatically correct interpretation of the term throughout its detailed discussion of the ninth *bhūmi* itself.

6. Glossary of the Sanskrit, Tibetan, Mongolian, and Chinese Versions of the Daśabhūmika-Sūtra. Compiled by J. Rahder. (Buddhica, Documents et Travaux pour l'Étude du Bouddhisme publiés sous la direction de J. Przyluski; Deuxième Série; Documents—Tome I). Paris: Librarie Orientaliste Paul Geuthner, 1928.

7. On page vii in his Introduction to his *Glossary of the Sanskrit, Tibetan, Mongolian and Chinese Versions of the Daśabhūmika-Sūtra,* Rahder says, "capital letters between brackets refer to the sections of the chapters as indicated in my edition (1926)." (They are also present in his 1923 edition of the *Daśabhūmikasutra* that was published together with the *Bodhisattvabhūmi* with only the minor oversight of having left out "A" and "B" at the very beginning of the first *bhūmi.*)

The Ten Bodhisattva Grounds

The Avataṃsaka Sūtra

Chapter 26: The Ten Grounds

(Taisho T10, no. 279, Fascicles 34–39, pp. 178b25–210c25)

Translated under Imperial Auspices by
Tripiṭaka Master Śikṣānanda from the State of Khotan[1]

Chinese to English Translation by Bhikshu Dharmamitra

Part One
The Joyfulness Ground[2]

I. The Introductory Section

A. The Setting and Audience

{A} At that time, the Bhagavat was residing in the Maṇi Jewel Treasury Palace of the Paranirmita Vaśavartin Heaven King, together with an assembly of great bodhisattvas. All of those bodhisattvas had already achieved irreversibility in their progression toward *anuttarasamyaksaṃbodhi*. They had all come to assemble there from the worlds of other regions.

B. The Great Bodhisattvas and Their Qualities

They dwelt in the realm of knowledge possessed by all bodhisattvas. They were tirelessly diligent in entering those places entered by the knowledge of all *tathāgatas*. They were well able to manifest many different sorts of endeavors accomplished by the spiritual superknowledges. They taught and trained all beings and, in doing so, never erred in their timing.

In order to fulfill all of the great vows of the bodhisattva, they remained diligent in the cultivation of all practices, doing so in all worlds, in all kalpas, and in all lands, never desisting even briefly. They had become completely equipped with the bodhisattva's merit and knowledge, the provisions assisting realization of the path, and were never deficient in benefitting beings everywhere. They had achieved the most ultimate perfection in all bodhisattvas' wisdom and skillful means.

They manifested entry into *saṃsāra* as well as nirvāṇa, and yet they still refrained from neglecting their cultivation of the bodhisattva practices. They were skillful in entering all of the bodhisattva's *dhyāna* concentrations, liberations, samādhis, *samāpattis*, spiritual superknowledges, and clear knowledges.[3]

They achieved sovereign mastery in all of their undertakings. They had already garnered all of the freely exercised spiritual powers of the bodhisattva such that, in but a moment, without moving in the slightest, they were all able to go forth to join the assemblies gathered at the *bodhimaṇḍas*[4] of all *tathāgatas* to serve therein as leaders for those congregations, and to request that the Buddhas expound the Dharma.

They served there as guardians of the wheel of the right Dharma[5] of all buddhas. With expansively magnanimous minds, they made offerings to and served all buddhas and were always diligent in their cultivation and implementation of all works performed by all bodhisattvas. Their bodies appeared everywhere in all worlds. Their voices reached everywhere throughout the ten directions of the Dharma realm.[6] Their minds and their knowledge were unimpeded. They everywhere saw all bodhisattvas of the three periods of time. They had already entirely cultivated and brought all meritorious qualities to perfect fulfillment. Even in an ineffable[7] number of kalpas, one would still be unable to entirely describe them all.

C. The Names of the Bodhisattvas in Attendance

Their names were:[8]

Vajragarbha Bodhisattva;
Jewel Treasury Bodhisattva;
Lotus Blossom Treasury Bodhisattva;
Treasury of Qualities Bodhisattva;
Treasury of Lotus Qualities Bodhisattva;
Solar Treasury Bodhisattva;
Sūrya Treasury Bodhisattva;
Stainless Moon Treasury Bodhisattva;
Treasury of Adornments Manifesting in All Lands Bodhisattva;
Treasury of Vairocana's Knowledge Bodhisattva;[9]
Treasury of Sublime Qualities Bodhisattva;
Treasury of Candana's Qualities Bodhisattva;
Treasury of Floral Qualities Bodhisattva;
Treasury of Kusuma's Qualities Bodhisattva;
Treasury of Utpala's Qualities Bodhisattva;
Treasury of Celestial Qualities Bodhisattva;
Treasury of Merit Bodhisattva;
Treasury of Unimpeded Pure Knowledge Qualities Bodhisattva;[10]
Treasury of Meritorious Qualities Bodhisattva;
Treasury of Nārāyaṇa's Qualities Bodhisattva;
Treasury of Stainlessness Bodhisattva;
Treasury of Defilement Transcendence Bodhisattva;
Treasury of Adornment with All Forms of Eloquence Bodhisattva;
Treasury of the Great Net of Light Rays Bodhisattva;

Treasury of the King of the Pure Light of Awesome Qualities Bodhisattva;
Treasury of the King of Great Qualities' Gold-Adorned Brilliance Bodhisattva;
Treasury of Pure Qualities Adorned with All the Marks Bodhisattva;
Treasury of Adornment with Flaming Vajra Radiance and the Marks of Merit Bodhisattva;
Treasury of Radiant Flames Bodhisattva;
Treasury of Constellation King's Radiance Bodhisattva;
Treasury of Spacious Unimpeded Knowledge Bodhisattva;[11]
Treasury of Unimpeded Sublime Sound Bodhisattva;
Treasury of Dhāraṇī Qualities and Vows Sustaining All Beings Bodhisattva;
Treasury of Oceanic Adornments Bodhisattva;
Treasury of Sumeru-Like Qualities Bodhisattva;
Treasury of All Qualities of Purity Bodhisattva;
Tathāgata Treasury Bodhisattva;
Treasury of Buddha Qualities Bodhisattva;
And Liberation Moon Bodhisattva.

An assembly of bodhisattva *mahāsattvas*,[12] such as these was present there in countless, measureless, boundless, matchless, innumerable, indescribable, inconceivable, immeasurable, and ineffable numbers.[13] Vajragarbha Bodhisattva served as their head.

D. Vajragarbha Enters Samādhi and Countless Buddhas Manifest

{B} At that time, Vajragarbha Bodhisattva, aided by the spiritual power of the Buddha, entered "the bodhisattva's great wisdom light samādhi."[14] {C} After he entered this samādhi, from beyond a number of worlds in each of the ten directions as numerous as the atoms in ten *koṭis*[15] of buddha lands, buddhas as numerous as the atoms in ten *koṭis* of buddha lands, all of them identically named "Vajragarbha," immediately appeared directly before him and uttered these words:

E. The Buddhas Praise Him and Encourage Him To Teach the Ten Grounds

It is good indeed, good indeed, Vajragarbha, that you have become able to enter this bodhisattva's great wisdom light samādhi.

Son of Good Family, these are a number of buddhas from each of the ten directions as numerous as the atoms in ten *koṭis* of buddha lands who have all joined in providing assistance to you here. This is due to the power of the original vows of Vairocana Tathāgata, Worthy of Offerings, of Right and Universal Enlightenment,[16] and because of his awesome spiritual powers. It is also because of your supreme powers of knowledge and because they wish to influence you to describe for all bodhisattvas the inconceivable Dharma light of all buddhas, in particular doing so:

{D} To cause their entry into the grounds of knowledge;
To bring about their gathering together of all roots of goodness;
To enable their skillful selective differentiation of all dharmas of the Buddha;
To bring about their vast knowing of all dharmas;
To enable their skillfulness in the ability to expound on Dharma;
To facilitate their purification of non-discriminating knowledge;
To ensure their non-defilement by any worldly dharma;
To facilitate their purification of roots of world-transcending goodness;
To facilitate their acquisition of the realm of inconceivable knowledge;
To cause their acquisition of the realm of knowledge of those possessed of all-knowledge;
To also cause their acquisition, from beginning to end, of the bodhisattva's ten grounds;
To bring about the reality-accordant explanation of the differentiating aspects of the bodhisattva's ten grounds;
To enable objectively focused mindfulness of all dharmas of the Buddha;
To facilitate their cultivation and differentiation of the dharmas that are free of the contaminants,[17]
To facilitate their skillful adornment through excellence in selection and contemplation employing the light of great wisdom;[18]
To cause their skillful entry into the gate of absolutely definitive knowledge;
To enable them to be fearless in providing sequential expositions wherever they may abide;
To facilitate their acquisition of the light of unimpeded eloquence;
To enable their abiding on the ground of great eloquence with skillful resolve;
To enable their bearing in mind the bodhisattva's resolve without ever forgetting it;
To bring about their ripening of beings in all realms of existence;
And to facilitate their realization of definitive awakening that reaches everywhere.

{E} Son of Good Family. You should eloquently explain the different skillful means dharmas associated with these Dharma gateways, doing so:

To receive the Buddha's spiritual power through being aided by the light of the Tathāgata's knowledge;
To facilitate the purification of one's own roots of goodness;
To everywhere purify the Dharma realm;
To everywhere draw forth beings;
To deeply enter the Dharma body and knowledge body;
To receive the Buddha's consecrating anointing of the crown;
To acquire the most supremely lofty and grand body in the entire world;
To step entirely beyond all worldly paths;
To purify roots of world-transcending goodness;
And in order to completely fulfill the cognition of all-knowledge.

F. The Buddhas Bestow Qualities and Abilities on Vajragarbha

{F} At that time, the Buddhas of the ten directions bestowed these things on Vajragarbha Bodhisattva:

They bestowed a body that none could outshine;
They bestowed the skill of unimpeded eloquent expression;
They bestowed skillfully differentiating pure knowledge;
They bestowed the power of skillful remembrance invulnerable to forgetfulness,
They bestowed thoroughly decisive and completely understanding intelligence;[19]
They bestowed awakened knowledge that extends to all places;
They bestowed the freely exercised powers associated with realization of the path;
They bestowed the fearlessnesses of the Tathāgatas;[20]
They bestowed the Omniscient Ones' eloquence and knowledges[21] that contemplate and distinguish all Dharma gateways;
And they bestowed the adornments of all Tathāgatas' supremely sublime and utterly perfected body, speech, and mind.

{G} Why did this occur?

Because acquisition of this samādhi dharma entails just such an occurrence;
Because this was generated by his original vows;
Because of his having well purified his resolute intentions;[22]
Because of his having well cleansed the sphere of knowledge;[23]

Because of his having well accumulated the provisions assisting realization of the path;[24]
Because of his having well cultivated and refined whatever he engaged in;
Because his mindfulness made him fit as a vessel able to contain measurelessly many dharmas;[25]
Because of the knowledge that he was possessed of pure resolute faith;[26]
Because of his having acquired the comprehensive retention *dhāraṇīs*[27] in which he was free of errors;
And because of his having been well-sealed by the seal of knowledge of the Dharma realm.[28]

G. Vajragarbha Emerges from Samādhi and Speaks of the Ten Grounds

{H} At that time, the Buddhas of the ten directions each extended their right hands and rubbed the crown of Vajragarbha Bodhisattva's head. {I} After they had rubbed the top of his head, Vajragarbha Bodhisattva emerged from samādhi and, {J} addressing everyone in that congregation of bodhisattvas, he informed them as follows:

Sons of the Buddha, the vows of the bodhisattva are excellent in their resolve, unmixed, imperceptible, as vast as the Dharma realm itself, and as ultimately far-reaching as empty space. They extend to the very bounds of future time and everywhere throughout all buddha lands. They serve to rescue and protect all beings, are carried out under the protection of all buddhas, and enter into the grounds of knowledge of all buddhas throughout the past, the future, and the present.

1. Vajragarbha Sets Forth the Names of the Ten Grounds

Sons of the Buddha, what then are the grounds of knowledge of the bodhisattva *mahāsattvas*? Sons of the Buddha, there are ten grounds of knowledge of the bodhisattva *mahāsattvas*. All buddhas of the past, the future, and the present have proclaimed them, will proclaim them, and do now proclaim them. In this same way, I too proclaim them here. What then are these ten? They are:[29]

First, the Ground of Joyfulness;
Second, the Ground of Stainlessness;
Third, the Ground of Shining Light;
Fourth, the Ground of Blazing Brilliance;[30]
Fifth, the Difficult-to-Conquer Ground;
Sixth, the Ground of Direct Presence;

Seventh, the Far-Reaching Ground;
Eighth, the Ground of Immovability;
Ninth, the Ground of Excellent Intelligence;[31]
Tenth, the Ground of the Dharma Cloud.

Sons of the Buddha, these ten bodhisattva grounds have been proclaimed by all buddhas of the three periods of time. They have proclaimed them in the past, will proclaim them in the future, and do proclaim them now.

Sons of the Buddha, I have never observed any among all the buddha lands in which the *tathāgata* therein failed to set forth an explanation of these ten grounds. Why is that? These constitute the bodhisattva *mahāsattvas'* most supreme path to the realization of bodhi as well as the gateway to the light of the pure Dharma. We refer here to the differentiation and explication of the bodhisattva grounds.

Sons of the Buddha, these stations are inconceivable. We refer here to all bodhisattvas' knowledge as it develops in accordance with their realizations.

2. Vajragarbha Bodhisattva Falls Silent

{K} Then, having set forth the names of these ten grounds of the bodhisattva, Vajragarbha Bodhisattva fell silent, remained in place, and did not then proceed to present a differentiating explanation of them.

H. The Congregation Is Caused to Wonder Why There Is No Explanation

At this time, having heard the names of the bodhisattvas' ten grounds without hearing any attendant explanation of them, that entire congregation of bodhisattvas gazed up at him with thirst-like anticipation as they thought to themselves, "Due to what causes and what conditions does Vajragarbha Bodhisattva merely set forth the names of the bodhisattvas' ten grounds while not then proceeding to explain them?"

I. Liberation Moon Bodhisattva's First Request for Dharma Teaching

Liberation Moon Bodhisattva, knowing the thoughts in the minds of those in that great assembly, thereupon employed verses with which he inquired of Vajragarbha Bodhisattva, asking:[32]

Why is it that you who are possessed of pure awakening
and are replete with the qualities of mindfulness and knowledge
speak of these supremely sublime grounds, but then,
even with the power to do so, still refrain from explaining them? {1}

All of those here are decisively resolute in all things,
valiantly brave, and entirely free of any timidity.
Why then would one set forth the names of the grounds
and yet still refrain from beginning to expound on them for us? {2}

As for the sublime meanings and import of the grounds,
the members of this congregation all wish to hear them.
Their minds are free of timidity.
Hence they wish you will differentiate and explain these for them. {3}

Those in this congregation are entirely pure,
have abandoned indolence, and are strict in their pristine purity.
They are able to remain solidly unmoving
and are replete with meritorious qualities and wisdom.[33] {4}

Looking at each other, they have all become filled with reverence
and have trained the focus of their gaze up at you.
In this, they are like bees when they bring to mind fine honey or
like one who is thirsty when he longs for the elixir of sweet-dew. {5}

J. Vajragarbha Explains His Silence

At that time, having heard him say this, the greatly wise and fearless Vajragarbha Bodhisattva, wishing to cause the assembled congregation to feel delighted in mind, spoke verses for the sake of all those sons of the Buddha: {6}

The matter of the bodhisattva's practices on the grounds
is the most supreme of all and is the origin of all buddhas.
To reveal them through a differentiating explanation
is the foremost of all rare and difficult endeavors. {7}

This is extremely subtle and difficult to perceive.
It transcends thought and steps beyond the mind ground.
It produces the domain realized by the Buddha.
Those who hear of it may all be thrown into confusion. {8}

It is those whose minds have a capacity for retention as solid as vajra,
who possess profound faith in the Buddha's supreme knowledge,
and who know the mind ground as devoid of any self
who are then capable of hearing this supreme Dharma. {9}

Like a mural painted in space
and like the appearance of wind in empty space—
The knowledge of the Muni is of this very sort,
for it is very difficult to see through differentiating explanations. {10}

As I call to mind the wisdom of the Buddha,
the most supremely inconceivable of matters,
I see that no one in the world would be able to accept it.
Hence I fall silent and no longer speak. {11}

K. Liberation Moon Bodhisattva's Second Request for Dharma Teaching

{L} At that time, having heard him declare this, Liberation Moon Bodhisattva then addressed Vajragarbha Bodhisattva, saying:

O Son of the Buddha. Those in this assembly that has gathered together here:

Have well purified their resolute intentions;[34]
Have well cleansed their thoughts;
Have well-cultivated all of the practices;
Have well-accumulated the provisions for realization of the path,[35]
Have been well able to draw close to hundreds of thousands of *koṭis* of buddhas;
Have perfected countless meritorious qualities and roots of goodness;
Have abandoned delusion;
Have become free of the defilements;
Are possessed of resolute intentions and resolute faith;
And, as they abide in the Buddha's Dharma, do not follow other sorts of teachings.

It would be good indeed, O Son of the Buddha, if, having here received the aid of the Buddha's spiritual powers, you would expound on these matters for their sakes. All of these bodhisattvas are able to achieve realization of such extremely profound stations as these.

At that time, Liberation Moon Bodhisattva, wishing to restate his meaning, spoke verses, saying:

Please speak on what is most conducive to peace and security,
these unsurpassable practices of the bodhisattva,
presenting a differentiating explanation of all of the grounds,
the purification of knowledge, and realization of right enlightenment.

Those in this congregation are free of all defilements,
are entirely bright and pristine in resolve and understanding,
have rendered service to countless buddhas,
and are able to realize the meaning of these grounds.

L. Vajragarbha Further Explains His Reticence to Teach This Dharma

{M} At that time, Vajragarbha Bodhisattva responded by saying:

O Son of the Buddha. Although those within this assembled congregation have well purified their thought, have abandoned delusion and doubts, and within the extremely profound Dharma, do not follow others' teachings, still, there are yet other beings possessed of only inferior understanding who, on hearing of these extremely profound and inconceivable matters, would then generate numerous doubts due to which they would consequently suffer all manner of ruin and torment for a long time. It is because I feel pity for those of this sort that I have therefore fallen silent.

At that time, Vajragarbha Bodhisattva, wishing to once again state his meaning, thereupon uttered verses, saying:

Although those in this congregation are pure, of vast wisdom,
of extremely deep and brilliant acuity in their selective abilities,
are possessed of minds as immovable as the king of mountains,
and are as invulnerable to overturning as the great oceans—

Still, others, not long-tenured in practice, not yet understanding,
acting in accord with consciousness and thus not with knowledge—
Hearing this, they will raise doubts and fall into wretched destinies.
It is due to pity for those of this sort that I therefore do not speak.

M. Liberation Moon Bodhisattva's Third Request for Dharma Teaching

{N} At that time, Liberation Moon Bodhisattva again addressed Vajragarbha Bodhisattva, saying:

O Son of the Buddha, aided by the spiritual powers of the Buddha, please do present here a differentiating exposition of these inconceivable dharmas. These persons will be afforded the protective mindfulness of the Tathāgatas and will consequently bring forth faith and acceptance.

And how could this be? Whenever an explanation of the ten grounds is set forth, the Dharma of all bodhisattvas is such that they should be afforded the protective mindfulness of the Buddhas in this way. Due to having been afforded the protective mindfulness of the Buddhas, they will then be able to bring forth heroic valor in cultivating these grounds of knowledge.

And why is this? This is because these constitute what the bodhisattvas practice from the very beginning and utilize in perfecting all dharmas of the Buddhas. This is analogous to the circumstance involved in the writing of words wherein everything in the realm of counting and description relies upon the alphabet[36] as its origin and also relies upon the alphabet in the end. There is not even the most minor increment of this that departs from the alphabet.

O Son of the Buddha. All dharmas of the Buddha in every case rely upon the ten grounds as their very origin and also rely upon the ten grounds in the end as they are cultivated and perfected and then culminate in all-knowledge.

Therefore, O Son of the Buddha, please expound on these matters for our sakes. These persons will most certainly be afforded the protection of the Tathāgatas through which they will be caused to bring forth faith and acceptance.

At that time, Liberation Moon Bodhisattva, wishing to restate his meaning, thereupon uttered verses, saying:

Good indeed it would be, O Son of the Buddha. Please do expound
on the practices taken up in progressing into bodhi's grounds.
Of all of the ten directions' sovereignly masterful Honored Ones,
none fail to hold these roots of knowledge in protective mindfulness.

These bases of establishment in knowledge are also ultimate,
for all the dharmas of the Buddha grow forth directly from them
just as all writing and counting are but expressions of their alphabets.
So too it is with Buddha's Dharma in its reliance on the grounds.

N. The Bodhisattva Congregation Joins in Requesting This Teaching

{O} At that time, that entire congregation of great bodhisattvas, simultaneously and with a single united voice, uttered verses to Vajragarbha Bodhisattva, saying:

[May it be that you] of supremely sublime and stainless knowledge
as well as boundless eloquence in differentiation
will expound with profound and exquisite phrases
that correspond to the supreme meaning. {12}

[May you] whose pure practice is maintained with mindfulness,
who has ten powers, and who has gathered the meritorious qualities
proceed to differentiate their meanings with eloquence
and present the exposition of these most supreme grounds. {13}

With concentration, moral precepts, and accumulated right thought,
as well as transcendence of arrogance and wrong views,
this congregation is entirely free of doubting thoughts
and hence wishes only to hear a skillful proclamation. {14}

We are like the thirsty thinking about cool water,
like the hungry recalling exquisite cuisine,
like the sick calling to mind an especially fine physician,
and like bees craving fine honey.
We are all just like these
in our wishing to hear this sweet-dew Dharma. {15}

Good indeed it would be, you of such vast knowledge.
We only pray that you will expound on the entry into the grounds,

on accomplishment of the ten powers' unimpeded realization,
and on all of the practices of the Well Gone Ones. {16}

O. {P} The Buddha Emits Brilliant Light From Between His Eyebrows

At that time, the Bhagavat emitted from between his eyebrows a pure light known as "the flaming light of bodhisattva powers," a brilliance attended by a retinue of a hundred thousand *asaṃkhyeyas*[37] of light rays. It everywhere illuminated all worlds of the ten directions, having none it failed to entirely pervade. The sufferings of the three wretched destinies then all subsided. It also illuminated the assemblies in attendance on all *tathāgatas*, revealed the inconceivable powers of the Buddhas, and also shone upon the bodies of all of the bodhisattvas in all worlds throughout the ten directions who were then being aided by all buddhas in the proclamation of Dharma. After it had done this, it then ascended into space, formed an immense terrace made of a net of light clouds, and then remained there.

P. All Buddhas Emit Light That Utters Verses Requesting Dharma

At that time, the Buddhas of the ten directions all proceeded in this very same manner, emitting a pure light from between their eyebrows wherein that light, its retinue of light rays, and its actions all manifested in just the same manner. In addition, they illuminated this Sahā World, the Buddha, and his great assembly, and then, after shining on the person of Vajragarbha Bodhisattva and his lion throne, those rays ascended up into empty space and formed an immense terrace made of a curtain of light clouds. Then, from within that terrace of light, through the awesome spiritual powers of the Buddhas, there then resounded the proclamation of verses, stating:

The Buddhas, the equals of the unequaled, are like empty space[38]
in their possession of the ten powers and countless supreme qualities.
They are the most superior of men, supreme in the entire world.
Here they augment the Dharma of the Lion of the Śākya Clan. {17}

Son of the Buddha, you should take on the powers of the Buddhas,
open forth the most supreme treasury of this Dharma king,
and employ Buddha's awesome powers to distinguish and explain
the supreme and sublime practices of the grounds' vast knowledge. {18}

Where one is afforded the assistance of the Well Gone Ones,
one will receive the entry of the Dharma jewel into one's mind. {19}

When one gains sequential fulfillment of the grounds' stainlessness,
he shall then also completely embody a *tathāgata*'s ten powers. {20}

Though residing amidst an ocean's waters or in kalpa-ending fires,
those able to accept this Dharma will certainly be able to hear it. {21}
Wherever someone doubts it or has no faith in it,
they will never be able to hear ideas such as these. {22}

You should expound on the grounds' path of supreme knowledge,
on their entry, abiding, and progressively sequential cultivation,
and on the birth of Dharma knowledge from the domains of practice,
doing so because this will provide benefit to all beings. {23}

Q. Vajragarbha's Preliminary Verses on the Difficulty of This Explanation

{Q} At that time, Vajragarbha Bodhisattva directed his contemplative regard to the ten directions and, wishing to cause those in that immense assembly to develop an increased degree of pure faith, thereupon uttered verses, saying:

The path of the Tathāgatas, the Great Rishis,
is subtle, sublime, and difficult to know.
It is not perceptible through thought nor by abandoning thought.
If one seeks to perceive it in that way, it cannot thereby be realized.
It is without either production or destruction
and is by nature pure and constantly quiescent. {24}

For those who abandon defilement and possess brilliant sagacity,
it is the place in which their knowledge is put into practice.
Its own nature is fundamentally empty, quiescently still,
devoid of duality, and endless.

It brings about liberation from all of the rebirth destinies
and the abiding in a state of uniform identity with nirvāṇa itself.
It has no beginning, has no middle, and has no end.
It cannot be described through words or phrases,
utterly transcends the three periods of time,
and, in character, is comparable to empty space. {25}

The quiescence in which the Buddha courses
cannot be reached through any verbal description.
The practices that are taken up on the grounds are also of this sort,
difficult to describe and difficult for one to be able to accept. {26}

The realm of the Buddha, produced through knowledge,
is not a path accessible through thought or by abandoning thought.
It is not a gate entered by aggregates, sense realms, or sense bases.
It is known by cognition, but not reached by the intellectual mind. {27}

Like the track of a bird through the air,
it is difficult to describe and difficult to show.
In this same manner, the meanings associated with the ten grounds
cannot be entirely fathomed by the mind's intellectual faculty. {28}

Kindness, compassion, and the power of vows
bring forth the practices through which one may enter the grounds
and sequentially realize perfect fulfillment of the mind.
The practices of knowledge are not the domain of mental reflection. {29}

This realm is difficult to perceive.
It can be known but cannot be described.
It is due to the powers of the Buddhas that one expounds on them.
You should all receive them in reverence. {30}

Such knowledge-entering practice as this
cannot be completely described even in a *koṭi* of kalpas.
Hence I shall now merely set forth a summarizing explanation
of their genuine meaning, leaving nothing unaddressed. {31}

Attend to this in single-minded reverence as,
aided by the Buddhas' powers, I speak
the subtle and sublime voice of the supreme Dharma
in a manner compatible with analogies' phrasings. {32}

The boundless spiritual powers of the Buddhas
all arrive here and enter my person.
Of this circumstance so difficult to proclaim,
I shall now describe but a minor measure. {33}

II. The Main Doctrinal Teaching Section

A. The First Ground: The Joyfulness Ground

1. Vajragarbha Lists the First Ground's Qualifications & Motivations

{R} Sons of the Buddha, suppose there is a being:

Who has deeply planted roots of goodness;
Who has well cultivated the practices;
Who has well accumulated the provisions facilitating realization of the path;[39]
Who has practiced well the making of offerings to the Buddhas;
Who has well accumulated the white dharmas of pristine purity;
Who has been skillfully drawn forth by the good spiritual guide;
Who has well purified his resolute intentions;
Who has established himself in the vast resolve;
Who has developed vast understanding;
And who has brought forth presently manifest kindness and compassion, [having done so]:

{S} For the sake of the quest to acquire the knowledge of the Buddha;
For the sake of gaining the ten powers;
For the sake of realizing the great fearlessnesses;
For the sake of gaining the Buddhas' dharma of uniformly equal regard for all;
For the sake of coming to the rescue of all worlds;
For the sake of purifying the great kindness and great compassion;
For the sake of gaining the knowledge that knows everything without exception throughout the ten directions;
For the sake of bringing about the unimpeded purification of all buddha lands;
For the sake of knowing all three periods of time in a single instant;
And for the sake of fearlessly turning the great wheel of Dharma.

2. The Qualities of the Bodhisattva's Resolve

{T} Son of the Buddha, the bodhisattva's generation of such resolve:

Takes the great compassion as foremost;
Takes wisdom as its predominant condition;
Is subsumed within skillful means;
Is sustained by the most superior resolute intentions;
[Is aided by] the measureless powers of the Tathāgata;

[Is accompanied by] skillful contemplation and assessment of beings' strength of courage and strength of knowledge;
[Is implemented with] the directly manifested unimpeded knowledge;
Is accordant with spontaneous knowledge;[40]
Is able to take on all dharmas of the Buddha in using wisdom in transformative teaching;
And is as vast as the Dharma realm, as ultimately extensive as empty space, and so enduring as to reach the very end of future time.

3. The Consequences of Generating the Bodhisattva Vow

{U} Son of the Buddha, when the bodhisattva first brings forth this resolve, he immediately:

Steps beyond the grounds of the common person;
Enters the station of the bodhisattva;
Takes birth into the clan of the Tathāgatas;
Becomes such that no one can claim his lineage is possessed of any fault;
Leaves behind worldly destinies;
Enters the world-transcending path;
Acquires the bodhisattva dharmas;
Abides in the bodhisattva abodes;
Equally enters the three periods of time;
And becomes definitely bound to realize the unexcelled bodhi in the lineage of the Tathāgatas.

{V} The bodhisattva who dwells in dharmas such as these is known as one who dwells on the Ground of Joyfulness, this on account of his being imperturbable.

Son of the Buddha, abiding on the Ground of Joyfulness, the bodhisattva is completely endowed with:

Abundant joy;
Abundant pure faith;
Abundant fond delight;
Abundant happiness;
Abundant exultation;
Abundant ebullience;
Abundant valiant fortitude;
Abundant disinclination to disputatiousness;
Abundant harmlessness;
And abundant disinclination to anger.[41]

4. The Bases For the First Ground Bodhisattva's Joyfulness

{W} Son of the Buddha, the bodhisattva dwelling on this Ground of Joyfulness:

Becomes joyful due to calling to mind the Buddhas;
Becomes joyful due to calling to mind the Dharma of the Buddhas;
Becomes joyful due to calling to mind the bodhisattvas;
Becomes joyful due to calling to mind the conduct practiced by the bodhisattvas;
Becomes joyful due to calling to mind the pure *pāramitās*;
Becomes joyful due to calling to mind the exceptional supremacy of the bodhisattva grounds;
Becomes joyful due to calling to mind the indestructibility of the bodhisattvas;
Becomes joyful due to calling to mind the Tathāgata's teaching of beings;
Becomes joyful due to calling to mind the ability to cause beings to acquire benefit;
And becomes joyful due to calling to mind entry into all *tathāgatas'* knowledge and skillful means.

{X} He also has this thought:

I become joyful due to turning away from and abandoning all worldly states;
I become joyful due to drawing close to all buddhas;
I become joyful due to departing far from the grounds of the common person;
I become joyful due to drawing near to the grounds of wisdom;[42]
I become joyful due to eternally cutting off any vulnerability to entering the wretched destinies;
I become joyful due to serving as a place of refuge for all beings;
I become joyful due to seeing all the Tathāgatas;
I become joyful due to being born into the domain of the Buddhas;
I become joyful due to becoming of the same nature as all bodhisattvas;
And I become joyful due to leaving behind the fear of all circumstances that would cause hair-raising terror.

5. The First Ground Bodhisattva's Five Kinds of Fearlessness

{Y} Why is it that, once this bodhisattva has gained the Ground of Joyfulness, he abandons all forms of fearfulness? In particular, they are:

The fear of failing to survive;
The fear of a bad reputation;
The fear of death;
The fear of rebirth in the wretched destinies;
And the fear of the awesomeness of great assemblies.[43]

He succeeds in forever leaving behind all such forms of fearfulness. And why is this? It is because this bodhisattva has abandoned any perception of a self. Thus he does not even cherish his own body. How much the less might he cherish any provisions or valuables it happens to possess. As a consequence, he is entirely free of any fear of failing to survive.

He does not hope for or seek out offerings from others. Rather, he devotes himself solely to providing for and making gifts to all beings. Consequently he has no fear of a bad reputation.

Because he has abandoned the view that conceives the existence of a self and because he does not perceive any existence of a self, he is therefore entirely free of any fear of death.

He realizes that once he dies, he will definitely not be reborn apart from the Buddhas and the bodhisattvas. Consequently he is entirely free of any fear of falling into the wretched destinies.

He thinks, "That to which I aspire is without equal anywhere in the world. How much the less might there be anything superior to it?" Consequently, he is entirely free of any fear of the awesomeness of great assemblies.

Thus it is that the bodhisattva leaves far behind all such circumstances that might otherwise cause fear and hair-raising terror.

6. The Bodhisattva's Grounds Purifying Practices

{Z} Son of the Buddha, this bodhisattva takes the great compassion as foremost. He is possessed of a vast aspiring resolve that no one could obstruct or destroy. Thus he redoubles his diligent cultivation of all roots of goodness, thereby achieving complete success in his aims, in particular doing so:

{AA} Through making faith predominant;
Through abundant pure faith;[44]
Through the purity of his resolute faith;[45]

Through the resolute decisiveness of his faith;
Through bringing forth compassionate pity;
Through perfecting the great kindness;
Through remaining free of any tendency to become weary or withdraw from his efforts;
Through being adorned with a sense of shame and dread of blame;
Through perfecting mental pliancy;
Through respectfully according with and venerating the Buddhas' teaching dharmas;
{BB} Through insatiably cultivating and accumulating roots of goodness day and night;
Through drawing near to good spiritual guides;
Through always cherishing and delighting in the Dharma;
Through insatiably pursuing extensive learning;
Through engaging in right contemplative investigation accordant with the Dharma he has learned;
Through ensuring that his mind remains free of dependent attachments;
Through not indulging any attachment to receiving offerings, becoming renowned, or receiving expressions of reverence from others;
Through not seeking for any life-supporting material possessions;
Through tirelessly bringing forth jewel-like resolve;[46]
{CC} Through seeking to reach the ground of all-knowledge;
Through seeking to gain the Tathāgata's powers, fearlessnesses, and dharmas exclusive to the Buddhas;
Through seeking proficiency in the *pāramitās* and the other dharmas assisting realization of the path;
Through abandoning all flattery and deceptiveness;
Through being able to practice in accordance with what has been taught;
Through always maintaining adherence to truthful speech;
Through never defiling the house of the Tathāgatas;
Through never relinquishing the moral precepts of the bodhisattvas;
Through bringing forth a resolve to gain all-knowledge that is as unshakeable as the king of mountains;
Through never relinquishing his endeavors in service to anyone in the world while still perfecting the world-transcending path;

Through insatiably accumulating those dharmas that comprise the factors assisting realization of bodhi;

And through always striving to gain ever more superior realization of the most supremely excellent path.

Son of the Buddha, the bodhisattva who completely develops such dharmas for purification of the grounds as these thereby becomes one who abides securely on the bodhisattva's Ground of Joyfulness.

7. The Bodhisattva's Ten Great Vows

{DD} Son of the Buddha, the bodhisattva who dwells on this Ground of Joyfulness is able to completely institute just such great vows entailing just such great heroic courage and just such great effective action. Specifically, they are:[47]

He brings forth a vast, pure, and resolute understanding through which he makes a vow to reverently present gifts of every form of offering to all buddhas without exception. His implementation of this vow is as vast as the Dharma realm and as extensive as empty space as it continues on incessantly until the end of future time and throughout all kalpas.

{EE} He also makes a great vow in which he vows to take on all buddhas' turning of the Dharma wheel, vows to take on [the realization of] all buddhas' bodhi, vows to protect all buddha's teaching, and vows to preserve all buddhas' Dharma. His implementation of this vow is as vast as the Dharma realm and as extensive as empty space as it continues on incessantly until the end of future time and throughout all kalpas.

{FF} He also makes a great vow in which he vows that, in all worlds, when the Buddhas come forth into the world, descend from the Tuṣita Heaven Palace, enter the womb, abide in the womb, first take birth, leave behind the home life, achieve realization of the path, proclaim the Dharma, and finally enter nirvāṇa, in every instance, he will go forth to visit them, will draw close to them and make offerings to them, will serve them as a leader within their congregations, will take on the practice of right Dharma, and will proceed then to simultaneously turn the Dharma wheel in all places. His implementation of this vow is as vast as the Dharma realm and as extensive as empty space as it continues on incessantly until the end of future time and throughout all kalpas.

{GG} He also makes a great vow in which he vows to explain in accordance with their reality all of the bodhisattva practices, so vast, so immeasurable, indestructible, unalloyed in their purity, and inclusive of all the *pāramitās*, vows to explain the purifying cultivation of the grounds, their general characteristics, their specific characteristics, their common characteristics, their differentiating characteristics, the characteristics conducing to success in them, and the characteristics leading to ruination, vowing too to teach these matters to everyone, thus influencing them thereby to take on these practices and bring forth increasing resolve. His implementation of this vow is as vast as the Dharma realm and as extensive as empty space as it continues on incessantly until the end of future time and throughout all kalpas.

{HH} He also makes a great vow in which he vows: "I will teach all realms of beings in a manner influencing them to enter into the Dharma of the Buddha, influencing them to eternally cut off coursing in any of the destinies of worldly rebirth, and influencing them to become established in the path to the cognition of all-knowledge,[48] teaching all of them, whether they be possessed of form or formless, whether they be possessed of perception, free of perception, or abiding in a state of neither perception nor non-perception, whether they be egg-born, womb-born, moisture-born, or transformationally born, teaching all of them, no matter how they are connected to the triple world, no matter in which of the six destinies of rebirth they abide, and no matter in which place they have taken birth, teaching all beings possessed of name-and-form, teaching all such classes of beings as these." His implementation of this vow is as vast as the Dharma realm and as extensive as empty space as it continues on incessantly until the end of future time and throughout all kalpas.

{II} He also makes a great vow in which he vows to directly know and perceive with utterly clear cognition all worlds in all their vastness and countless varieties, including the coarse, the subtle, the disordered, the inverted, and the upright, knowing them all, whether in entering them, coursing along within them, or emerging from them,[49] knowing them in their countlessly many different sorts of variations throughout the ten directions that are analogous [in their mutual relationship] to the net-like curtain of Indra. His implementation of this vow is as vast as the Dharma realm and as extensive as empty space as it continues on incessantly until the end of future time and throughout all kalpas.

{JJ} He also makes a great vow in which he resolves to bring about the complete purification of all the measurelessly many buddha lands wherein all lands enter a single land, a single land enters all lands, and they are all adorned with many radiant phenomena, wherein they all become filled with measurelessly many wise beings[50] who have left behind all afflictions and perfected the path of purification, and wherein he everywhere enters the vast realms of all buddhas, accords with the mental dispositions of beings, and thus appears for them in a manner that causes them all to be pleased. His implementation of this vow is as vast as the Dharma realm and as extensive as empty space as it continues on incessantly until the end of future time and throughout all kalpas.

{KK} He also makes a great vow in which he vows to unite with all other bodhisattvas in practices with a single determined aim, doing so in a manner that remains free of enmity or jealousy, proceeding in this with the accumulation of all forms of roots of goodness, engaging with all bodhisattvas toward a single objective with universally equal regard, always gathering together with them and never allowing there to develop any mutual estrangement, doing so with a freely exercised ability to manifest all sorts of different buddha bodies, being able by resort to the capacities of his own mind to know all the domains, awesome powers, and wisdom[51] of all *tathāgatas,* being able thus to gain realization of the irreversible psychic powers through which one freely roams throughout all worlds, manifesting his physical presence in all of their assemblies, everywhere entering into all of stations of rebirth, perfecting the inconceivable Great Vehicle, cultivating the practices of the bodhisattvas. His implementation of this vow is as vast as the Dharma realm and as extensive as empty space as it continues on incessantly until the end of future time and throughout all kalpas.

{LL} He also makes a great vow in which he vows to take up the irreversible turning of the wheel, to course in the bodhisattva practices, to cultivate the refinement of physical, verbal, and mental karmic actions, to never neglect his endeavors in these matters, vowing too that, if anyone sees him, even if only momentarily, then he will thereby become bound for definite success in the Buddha's Dharma, vows that, if anyone hears his voice, even if only momentarily, then he will thereby become bound to gain genuine wisdom,[52] vows that, if one merely brings forth thoughts of pure faith, then he will thereby become bound to eternally cut off the afflictions, vows that he will succeed in becoming like a personification of the great king of medicine trees, that he will become like a personification of a wish-fulfilling jewel, and vowing that he will cultivate all of the bodhisattva practices. His implementation of this vow is as vast as the Dharma realm and as extensive as empty space as it continues on incessantly until the end of future time and throughout all kalpas.

{MM} He also makes a great vow in which he vows that he will gain realization of *anuttarasamyaksaṃbodhi* in all worlds, that he will not abandon even any of those places manifesting within the tip of a hair, that he will appear even in all those places manifesting within the tip of a hair the actions of taking on human birth, leaving behind the home life, arriving at the *bodhimaṇḍa,* realizing the right enlightenment, turning the wheel of Dharma, and entering nirvāṇa, that he will acquire the Buddha's realms of awareness and powers of great wisdom,[53] that even in every successive instant, adapting to the minds of every being, he will manifest for them the realization of buddhahood and cause them to succeed in achieving quiescent cessation themselves, that he will, through a single *saṃbodhi,* gain the realization of all dharma realms as characterized by identity with nirvāṇa, that, employing a single voice in the proclamation of Dharma, he will be able to cause the minds of all beings to become joyful, that, even though he manifests the appearance of entering the great nirvāṇa, he will still never cut off his coursing in the practices of the bodhisattva, that he will reveal the grounds of great wisdom[54] and the establishment of all dharmas, and that, in accomplishing this, he will employ the superknowledges associated with the cognition of dharmas, the superknowledges associated with the foundations of spiritual power, the conjuration-like superknowledges, and sovereignly masterful transformations that fill up the entire Dharma realm. His implementation of this vow is as vast as the Dharma realm and as extensive as empty space as it continues on incessantly until the end of future time and throughout all kalpas.

Son of the Buddha, the bodhisattva dwelling on this Ground of Joyfulness is able to bring forth such great vows, great heroic courage, and great effective action. Taking these ten vow gateways as foremost, he brings about the complete fulfillment of a hundred myriads of *asaṃkhyeyas* of great vows.

{NN} Son of the Buddha, these great vows are able to achieve their perfect completion on the basis of ten propositions on the ending [of various phenomena]. What then are those ten? They are:

The end of the realms of beings;
The end of worlds;
The end of the realms of empty space;
The end of the Dharma realm;
The end of the realm of nirvāṇa;
The end of the realms where the Buddhas come forth and appear;
The end of the realm of the Tathāgata's knowledge;
The end of the realm of objects of mind;
The end of the realms of objective circumstances penetrated by the Buddha's cognition;
And the end of the realms of permutations of worlds, permutations of dharmas, and permutations of knowledge.

[Accordingly, he vows that]:

"If the realms of beings come to an end, only then might my vows finally come to an end. If the worlds come to an end...," and so forth on up to, "If the realms of the permutations of worlds, permutations of dharmas, and permutations of knowledge come to an end, only then might my vows finally come to an end.

"However, because the realms of beings cannot possibly ever come to an end," and so forth on up to, "Because the realms of the permutations of worlds, permutations of dharmas, and permutations of knowledge cannot possibly ever come to an end, therefore the roots of goodness associated with these great vows of mine will never have an end."

8. The Mental Qualities & Faith Gained by the 1st Ground Bodhisattva

{OO} Son of the Buddha, once the bodhisattva has brought forth such vows as these, he then succeeds in acquiring:[55]

The beneficent mind;
The gentle mind;
The adaptive mind;
The serene mind;
The subdued mind;
The quiescent mind;
The humble mind;

The harmoniously smooth mind;
The unmoving mind;
And the unsullied mind.

He thereby succeeds in becoming one possessed of pure faith and possessed of the functional uses of faith, whereby he is able:[56]

To have faith in the original practices entered by the Tathāgatas;
To have faith in the perfectibility of the *pāramitās*;
To have faith in the entry into the supreme grounds;
To have faith in the perfectibility of the powers;
To have faith in the complete fulfillment of the fearlessnesses;
To have faith in the production and development of the indomitable dharmas exclusive to the Buddhas;
To have faith in the inconceivable Dharma of the Buddhas;
To have faith in the generation of the Buddha's realm transcendent of either any middle or extremes;
To have faith in the entry into the Buddha's measureless domain;
And to have faith in the perfectibility of the resultant fruition.

To speak of the essentials, he has faith in all bodhisattva practices and the other related factors up to and including the Tathāgata's grounds of knowledge, proclamations, and powers.

9. The Bodhisattva's Reflective Contemplation on Dharma and Beings

{PP} Son of the Buddha, this bodhisattva has these additional thoughts:

The right Dharma of the Buddhas is characterized by:
Such extreme profundity;
Such serenity;
Such quiescence;
Such emptiness;
Such signlessness;
Such wishlessness;
Such non-defilement;
Such measurelessness;
And such vastness.[57]

{QQ} And yet common people:
Allow their minds to fall into wrong views;
Become covered over and blinded by ignorance;
Erect the lofty banner of arrogance;
Enter the net of craving;

Travel into the dense forest of flattery and deception and become unable to escape on their own;

Involve their minds in miserliness and jealousy, fail to relinquish them, and thus constantly create the causes and conditions conducing to rebirth in the various destinies;

Increase both day and night their accumulation of every sort of karmic activity based on greed, hatred, and delusion;

So set the wind of their anger and animosity blowing upon the flames of the mind's consciousness that they blaze incessantly.

Become such that whatever karmic actions they engage in are reflections of the inverted views;[58]

And become such that the flood of desire, the flood of becoming, the flood of ignorance, and the flood of views[59] continuously generate seeds associated with the mind and mental consciousness in the field of the three realms of existence that in turn grow forth the sprouts of suffering.

{RR} Specifically, this occurs as follows:

[The aggregates of] name-and-form[60] arise conjointly and inextricably.

This name-and-form develops and then produces the village of the six sense bases.[61]

In their corresponding pairings, these in turn produce contact.

As a result of the occurrence of contact, feelings then arise.

Because of feelings, there then follows the arising of craving.

Due to the growth of craving, there then occurs the generation of grasping.

Because of an increase in grasping, there then occurs the generation of becoming.

Because of becoming, there then follow birth, aging, death, worry, sorrow, suffering, and the afflictions.

It is in this manner that beings generate and proliferate a mass of suffering. In every case, everything therein is empty. Thus, absent the existence of any self or anything belonging to a self, there is no knowing, no awareness, nothing done, and nothing undergone. Thus these matters are all comparable to shrubs, trees, or a stone wall and are also comparable to mere reflected images. Still, beings remain unaware and unknowing of these circumstances.

10. The Bodhisattva's Resolve, Renunciation, & Grounds Purification

{SS} On observing all beings in this circumstance wherein they are unable to escape from such a mass of suffering, the bodhisattva straightaway brings forth wisdom in association with the great compassion and then has this additional thought: "I should rescue and pull forth all these beings and see to their being placed in a circumstance of ultimate happiness." He therefore immediately brings forth radiant wisdom in association with the great kindness.

{TT} Son of the Buddha, when, in accordance with just such great compassion and great kindness as this, the bodhisattva *mahāsattva* avails himself of deep and profound resolve and dwells on the first ground, he becomes free of any selfish cherishing for anything at all, pursues realization of the Buddha's great knowledge, and cultivates the great relinquishing through which he is able to bestow whatever he possesses as a gift. This includes his wealth, grain, the contents of his storehouses and granaries, gold, silver, *maṇi* jewels, true pearls, lapis lazuli, conch shells, jade, coral and other such things, precious jewels, necklaces, bodily adornments, elephants, horses, carriages, servants and workers, cities and villages, parks, forests, viewing terraces, wives, consorts, sons, daughters, members of his inner and outer retinue, and all other sorts of precious jewels and means of amusement. He is willing to also give even his head, eyes, hands, feet, blood, flesh, bones, marrow, and any other parts of his own body, bestowing all of these things without any selfish cherishing, and bestowing all these things in quest of the vast wisdom[62] of all buddhas. This is what constitutes the perfection of relinquishing carried out by the bodhisattva dwelling on the first ground.

{UU} Son of the Buddha, because of this mind of great giving imbued with kindness and compassion, the bodhisattva redoubles his quest to acquire every form of worldly and world-transcending beneficial means through which to facilitate the enactment of his aspiration to rescue and protect all beings. Through his tirelessness in this, he comes to perfect the tireless mind.

Having acquired the tireless mind, his mind then becomes entirely free of timidity with respect to pursuing the investigation of all scriptures and treatises. Because he is free of timidity in that regard, he then straightaway succeeds in acquiring the knowledge contained within all scriptures and treatises. Having acquired this knowledge, he is then well able to assess how he should and should not proceed in relating to all of the beings of superior, middling, and inferior capacities, adapting to what is appropriate for them, adapting to what suits their strengths, and adapting to whatever they are habitually accustomed to.

Due to proceeding in this manner, the bodhisattva succeeds in developing worldly wisdom. Having developed worldly wisdom, he then becomes aware of what constitutes correct timeliness and correct measure in those actions. Then, graced with a sense of shame and dread of blame, he diligently cultivates the path of simultaneously benefiting himself and benefiting others. Thus it is that he perfects the state of being graced by a sense of shame and dread of blame. As he engages in these practices, he diligently cultivates irreversible renunciation[63] and thus develops the power of enduring fortitude. Having developed the power of enduring fortitude, he then becomes diligent in making offerings to all buddhas and becomes able to practice in accord with the teaching dharmas proclaimed by the Buddha.

Son of the Buddha, thus it is that the bodhisattva perfects the ten dharmas employed in purifying the grounds, namely:[64]

Faith;
Compassion;
Kindness;
Renunciation;
Indefatigability;
Knowledge of the sutras and treatises;
Thorough comprehension of worldly dharmas;
A sense of shame and dread of blame;
The power of enduring fortitude;
The making of offerings to the Buddhas while cultivating in accordance with the teachings.[65]

11. The Bodhisattva's Seeing and Serving of Countless Buddhas

{VV} Son of the Buddha, having come to dwell on this Ground of Joyfulness, the bodhisattva, due to the power of his great vows, then becomes able to see many buddhas. That is to say that he becomes able to see many hundreds of buddhas, many thousands of buddhas, many hundreds of thousands of buddhas, many *koṭis* of buddhas, many hundreds of *koṭis* of buddhas, many thousands of *koṭis* of buddhas, many hundreds of thousands of *koṭis* of buddhas, many *koṭis* of *nayutas* of buddhas, many hundreds of *koṭis* of *nayutas* of buddhas, many thousands of *koṭis* of *nayutas* of buddhas, or many hundreds of thousands of *koṭis* of *nayutas* of buddhas, all of whom he reverently venerates with a magnanimous mind and resolute intentions as he serves them and makes offerings to them of robes, food and drink, bedding, medicines, and every sort of life-sustaining benefaction, all of which he offers up as gifts while also making offerings to all of the many members of the Sangha. He then dedicates all of the roots of goodness thereby created to the realization of the unsurpassable bodhi.

12. The Bodhisattva's Practice of Means of Attraction and Pāramitās

Son of the Buddha, on account of making offerings to the Buddhas, this bodhisattva acquires the dharmas by which one brings about the maturation of beings. Employing the first two of the means of attraction, namely "giving" and "pleasing words," he draws forth beings. As for the remaining two means of attraction,[66] he only employs them in a manner commensurate with his powers of resolute faith, for his practice of them has not yet reached a state of state of consummate skillfulness.

Among the ten *pāramitās*, this bodhisattva becomes especially superior in his practice of *dāna pāramitā*. It is not, however, that he does not cultivate the remaining *pāramitās* at all. Rather, he simply accords them an amount of emphasis corresponding to his own strengths and to what is fitting.[67]

This bodhisattva, in accordance with whatever he is diligently cultivating, whether it be making offerings to buddhas or teaching beings, in every case does so through cultivating the grounds-purifying dharmas. He dedicates all of the associated roots of goodness to the acquisition of the ground of all-knowledge. As he does so, they become ever more radiant, pure, and pliant to the point that he becomes freely able to put them to use however he wishes.

13. The Bodhisattva's Grounds Purification Compared to Refining Gold

Son of the Buddha, this circumstance is analogous to that of a goldsmith who, especially well skilled in the refinement of gold, introduces it into the fire again and again, with the result that it shines ever more brightly, becomes ever more pure, and becomes ever more pliant to the point that, once this process is completed, he can then freely put it to use however he wishes.

The bodhisattva is just like this. His making of offerings to the Buddhas and his teaching of beings is in every case done in the service of cultivating the dharmas employed in purification of the grounds. All of the roots of goodness thereby developed are dedicated to reaching the ground of all-knowledge. As he proceeds with this cultivation, they become ever more brightly shining, pure, and pliant to the point where he becomes freely able to put them to use.

14. The Bodhisattva's Acquisition of Further Knowledge of the Grounds

{WW} Son of the Buddha, the bodhisattva *mahāsattva* who dwells on the first ground should set forth searching questions in the presence of the Buddhas, the bodhisattvas, and his good spiritual guides, insatiably requesting from them clarification of this ground's characteristic aspects and acquired fruits, doing so wishing to completely develop this ground's dharmas.

So too should he set forth searching questions in the presence of the Buddhas, the Bodhisattvas, and his good spiritual guides, insatiably requesting from them clarification regarding the second ground's characteristic aspects and acquired fruits, doing so wishing to completely develop that ground's dharmas.

So too should he set forth searching questions insatiably requesting clarification of the characteristic aspects and acquired fruits associated with the third, fourth, fifth, sixth, seventh, eighth, ninth, and tenth grounds, doing so wishing to completely develop those grounds' dharmas.

This bodhisattva then:

Thoroughly knows the obstacles encountered on the grounds as well as the means for countering them;

Thoroughly knows the means of achieving success or falling into ruination on the grounds;

Thoroughly knows the characteristic aspects and fruits associated with the grounds;

Thoroughly knows the attainment and cultivation of the grounds;

Thoroughly knows the grounds' purification of dharmas;

Thoroughly knows the progression in the successively adopted practices used in advancing from ground to ground;

Thoroughly knows with respect to each successive ground what is and is not the correct station;

Thoroughly knows with respect to each successive ground the type of especially superior knowledge associated with it;

Thoroughly knows with respect to each successive ground the means by which to prevent retreating from it;

And thoroughly knows how to bring about the purifying cultivation of all of the bodhisattva grounds on through to the point of progression into the ground of the Tathāgata.

Son of the Buddha, in this way, the bodhisattva thoroughly knows the characteristic features of the grounds beginning with the first ground, knows how one takes up the practices and carries them forward without interruption in this manner until one finally enters the tenth ground, continuing on in this without any instance of the practice being cut off. It is on account of the light associated with the knowledge of the grounds that he succeeds in developing the light of the Tathāgata's wisdom.[68]

15. The Bodhisattva's Path Knowledge Compared to a Caravan Guide

Son of the Buddha, this circumstance is analogous to that of a leader of merchants who comes to know well the means employed when wishing to lead a group of merchants going off to some great city. Before embarking, he must first ask about the roads to be taken, inquiring about their fine qualities and their faulty aspects while also inquiring about the places where one might stop along the way, inquiring also as to whether the threats to security one might encounter along the way are surmountable or not. After doing this, he prepares the provisions to be used on the road and does all that one should do in preparing to embark.

Son of the Buddha, even though that great leader of merchants has not yet set foot on the road to be taken, he is nonetheless able to know all of the circumstances that might threaten their security along the path. He is skilled in applying his wisdom[69] in assessment and observation, in preparing whatever they will need, in ensuring that they will not run short of anything, and in safely leading the entire band of merchants all along the way until they reach that great city, doing so in a manner whereby he himself as well as that group of men will all be able to avoid encountering disastrous circumstances.

Son of the Buddha, so too it is with the bodhisattva in his acting like a leader of merchants. Even as he dwells on the first ground, he comes to know well the obstacles encountered on the grounds as well as the means for countering them. He comes to well know everything else as well, all the way on through to his knowing of the purifying cultivation of all of the bodhisattva grounds and the subsequent progression on forth into the ground of the Tathāgata. Having accomplished this, he next prepares the provisions of merit and knowledge with which he will be able to lead all beings through the hazardous and difficult regions within the vast wilderness of *saṃsāra*'s births and deaths so that they succeed in safely reaching the city of all-knowledge, all the while leading them along so neither he himself or those beings are forced to go through calamitous and difficult circumstances.

Therefore, the bodhisattva should never slacken in his diligent cultivation of the most especially superior purifying karmic deeds on all the grounds on through to the point where he enters the ground of the Tathāgata's knowledge.

16. Vajragarbha's Final Statements About the First Ground Bodhisattva

Son of the Buddha, this has been a summary discussion of the bodhisattva *mahāsattva*'s entry into the gateway of the first bodhisattva ground. Were one to present an extensive discussion of this, that would involve an incalculable and boundless number of hundreds of thousands of *asaṃkhyeyas* of differentiating factors.

a. The Bodhisattva's Station and Dharma Practice

{xx} Son of the Buddha, the bodhisattva *mahāsattva* dwelling on the first ground often becomes a monarch reigning over the continent of Jambudvīpa who is a member of the aristocratic nobility that, acting with sovereign freedom, is able to draw forth beings through great giving. He is skilled in doing away with beings' filth of miserliness as he always practices endless great giving.

b. The Bodhisattva's Four Means of Attraction and Mindfulness

Even while pursuing the practices of giving, pleasing words, beneficial actions, and joint endeavors, in all these works that he carries out:

He never departs from mindfulness of the Buddha;
He never departs from mindfulness of the Dharma;
He never departs from mindfulness of the Sangha;
He never departs from mindfulness of the bodhisattvas engaged in the same practices;
He never departs from mindfulness of the bodhisattva conduct;
He never departs from mindfulness of the *pāramitās;*
He never departs from mindfulness of the grounds;
He never departs from mindfulness of the powers;
He never departs from mindfulness of the fearlessnesses;
He never departs from mindfulness of the dharmas exclusive to the Buddha;
And so forth until we come to his never departing from mindfulness of his quest to achieve complete fulfillment of the knowledge of all modes and the cognition of all-knowledge.

c. The Bodhisattva's Aspiration to Serve Beings

He also has this thought: "I should become one who serves these beings as a leader, as one who is supreme, as one who is most especially supreme, as one who is marvelous, as one who is most subtly marvelous, as one who is excellent, as one who is unexcelled, as one who is a guide, as one who is a general, one who is a supreme leader," and so forth until we come to "as one who relies on the cognition of all-knowledge."

d. The Result of the Bodhisattva's Leaving the Household Life

If this bodhisattva wishes to relinquish the home life and take up the diligent practice of vigor in the Dharma of the Buddha, then he will be able to relinquish the household, his wife and children, and the five desires, and then rely on the teaching of the Tathāgata in his abandonment of the household and in his study of the path.

Having left behind the home life, if he diligently applies himself in the cultivation of vigor, in but a single moment:

He will be able to acquire a hundred samādhis, see a hundred buddhas, and know a hundred buddhas' spiritual powers;
He will be able to cause tremors in a hundred buddha worlds;
He will be able to travel across a hundred buddha worlds;
He will be able to illuminate a hundred buddha worlds;
He will be able to teach the beings in a hundred buddha worlds;
He will be able to remain for one hundred kalpas;
He will be able to know events occurring throughout a hundred kalpas of the past and future;
He will be able to enter a hundred Dharma gateways;
He will be able to manifest a hundred bodies;
And he will be able to manifest a hundred bodhisattvas to serve as the retinue for each and every one of those bodies.

{YY} Then, if he resorts to the power of the especially supreme vows of the bodhisattva, he will become freely able to bring forth manifestations beyond this number, such that one would never be able to count them even in a period of a hundred kalpas, a thousand kalpas, or a hundred thousand kalpas.

17. Vajragarbha Bodhisattva's Summarizing Verses

At that time, Vajragarbha Bodhisattva, wishing to once again proclaim his meaning, thereupon uttered verses, saying:

If someone accumulates the many sorts of good deeds,
perfects the hundred sorts of dharmas of purification,
makes offerings to those most honored among devas and men,
accords with the path of kindness and compassion,

possesses the most extremely vast sort of resolute faith,
and possesses resolve and delight that are pristinely pure,
then, for the sake of seeking the wisdom[70] of the Buddha,
he brings forth this unexcelled resolve. {1}

In order to pursue the purification of all-knowledge, the powers, and the fearlessnesses,
to achieve the perfection of all dharmas of the Buddha, and
to draws in and rescue the many sorts of beings,

And in order to acquire the great kindness and compassion,
set turning the wheel of the supreme Dharma,
and adorn and purify buddha lands,
he brings forth this utterly supreme resolve. {2}

In order, in a single moment, to know the three periods of time,
and still be free of discriminations about them,
in order, in all of the various eras, each different,
to manifest his presence within the world,

and, to state it briefly, in order to seek
all of the Buddhas' supreme meritorious qualities,
he brings forth the vast resolve
equal in its scope to the realm of empty space. {3}

Taking compassion as foremost and wisdom as primary,
adopting skillful means accordant with them,
being possessed of resolute faith and purified intentions,
availing himself of the Tathagata's measureless powers,

directly manifesting unimpeded knowledge,
bringing forth spontaneous understanding not reliant on others, and
gaining fulfillment herein that achieves parity with the Tathāgata,
he brings forth this most supreme resolve. {4}

When a son of the Buddha first brings forth
such a marvelous jewel-like resolve as this,
he then steps beyond the position of the common person
and enters into the station in which the Buddha courses.

He is thus born into the family of the Tathāgatas,
into that clan lineage utterly free of flaws, and
becomes one bound to become the equal of the Buddhas
who will definitely realize the unexcelled enlightenment. {5}

As soon as he brings forth such a resolve as this,
he straightaway succeeds in entering the first ground
and develops determination and delight as unshakeable
as the great king of the mountains.

He experiences abundant joy, abundant cherishing delight,
and abundant pure-minded faith as well,
marshals a great and heroically brave resolve,
and avails himself of celebratory and exhilarated thought. {6}

He abandons disputatiousness,
harmful behavior, and hatred,
and becomes humble, respectful, and straightforward in character
while also skillfully guarding the sense faculties.

Regarding those who are matchless in rescuing the world
and all of their many varieties of wisdom,[71]
he reflects: "This is the station that I am bound to realize,"
and, in bringing them to mind, he is filled with joy. {7}

On first gaining entry into the first ground,
he straightaway oversteps five types of fearfulness:
failure to survive, death, ill-repute,
the wretched destinies, and the awesome virtue of assemblies.

It is because they have no covetous attachment to a self
or to anything belonging to a self
that these sons of the Buddha
abandon all forms of fearfulness. {8}

They always practice great kindness and sympathy
and constantly possess faith and reverence.
Replete in a sense of shame, a dread of blame, and the qualities,
they strive day and night to increase in good dharmas.
They delight in the genuine benefit conferred by the Dharma,
and are not fond of indulgence in the desires. {9}

They contemplate the Dharma that they have learned
and leave far behind actions involving grasping and attachment.
They do not covet offerings or support,
only delight in the bodhi of the Buddha,

single-mindedly seek to acquire the Buddha's knowledge,
and focus intently on maintaining undistracted mindfulness.
They cultivate the *pāramitās*
and abandon flattery, falseness, and deception. {10}

They cultivate in accordance with what has been proclaimed,
and establish themselves in truthful speech.
They refrain from defiling the house of the Buddhas,
never relinquish the moral precepts of the bodhisattva,

do not delight in any sort of worldly matters,
and always benefit the world.
They are insatiable in the cultivation of what is good,
and strive ever more to reach increasingly superior paths. {11}

In this manner, they are fond of and delight in dharmas
associated with meritorious qualities and whatever is meaningful.
They constantly raise up the resolve of their great vows,
vow to go and see the Buddhas,

vow to guard and sustain all Buddhas' Dharma, and
vow to gather and preserve the Great Rishi's teachings on the path.
They always bring forth vows such as these,
vowing to cultivate the most supreme practices. {12}

They vow to bring all sorts of beings to maturation,
vow to carry forth the purifying adornment of the buddha lands,
vow to bring it about that, all buddha lands
shall become completely filled with sons of the Buddha,

vow that they shall maintain the same singular resolve as theirs,
vows that, whatever actions one does shall not have been in vain,
and vows that, even in those places within the tip of every hair,
they will, at once, manifest the realization of right enlightenment. {13}

They make such great vows as these
that are measurelessly vast and boundless in their reach.
They declare: "If there were an end to empty space or beings,
an end to the Dharma realm or nirvāṇa,
an end to the worlds or the appearance of buddhas in the world,
an end to the Buddhas' knowledge {14} or to objects of mind, {14}

an end to the realms entered by a *tathāgata's* knowledge
or to the three permutations [of worlds, dharmas, and knowledge]—
If all of these phenomena were to somehow come to an end,
my vows might then begin to come to an end.
But, just as all of those have no point at which they would end,
So too it is with these vows that I have made." {15}

Thus it is that they bring forth great vows
with minds that are gentle, subdued, and adaptive.
Through their ability to maintain faith in the Buddha's qualities
and contemplate the realms of beings,

they realize their circumstances arise due to causes and conditions,
and then let flourish their kindly and mindful resolve,
wherein they reflect thus: "Suffering beings of this sort
are such as I should now rescue and liberate." {16}

For the sake of these beings,
they then carry out the many different types of giving,
relinquishing the royal throne and jewels as well as
other possessions, including elephants, horses, and carriages,

their heads, eyes, hands and feet,
even to the point of giving their entire body, its blood and its flesh.
They are able to relinquish absolutely everything
while still remaining free of any distress or regret in this. {17}

They strive to study the many different scriptures
with minds tireless in this pursuit.
They skillfully comprehend their meaning and import,
and are able to adapt to the world in implementing their practices.

They grace themselves with a sense of shame and dread of blame
and become ever more solid in their cultivation.
They make offerings to countless buddhas,
doing so with respect and profound veneration. {18}

Thus it is that they are always devoted to cultivation,
carrying it forward tirelessly, both day and night.
Their roots of goodness become ever more bright and pure
just as with true gold when it is refined in fire.

The bodhisattva dwelling herein
engages in the purifying cultivation of the ten grounds
and remains free of obstacles in all endeavors he pursues,
bringing them to completion without interruption. {19}

In this, he is like a great leader of merchants
who, for the sake of benefiting an entire group of traders,
inquires about and learns the road's hazardous and easy conditions,
thus ensuring safe arrival at some great city.

The bodhisattva abiding on the first ground
should also be known as just like this.
Bringing heroic bravery to bear, he remains unimpeded
as he advances all the way to the tenth ground. {20}

When he abides on this first ground,
he may become a monarch possessed of great meritorious qualities
who employs the Dharma in teaching beings
and uses the mind of kindness to refrain from inflicting injury

as he unites and leads the residents of Jambudvīpa
in a way that there are none not reached by his transformative acts.
Thus they are all caused to abide in that great relinquishing
through which they perfect the Buddha's wisdom.[72] {21}

Then, wishing to pursue the most supreme of paths,
he relinquishes his position on the royal throne.
He becomes able in taking up the Buddha's teachings
to diligently pursue their cultivation with such heroic bravery

that he then succeeds in acquiring a hundred samādhis,
in seeing a hundred buddhas,
and in causing tremors throughout a hundred worlds.
His radiantly illuminating practices are also of this sort. {22}

Thus he teaches the beings in a hundred lands,
enters a hundred gateways into the Dharma,
knows the events occurring for a hundred kalpas,
manifests a hundred bodies therein,

and manifests a hundred bodhisattvas
to serve in each of their retinues.
If he avails himself of his sovereign mastery over the power of vows,
he may extend his capacities beyond this to incalculable numbers. {23}

I have provided here a summary description
of but a minor measure of this ground's meanings
If one wished to comprehensively distinguish them all,
he could never finish it even in a *koṭi* of kalpas.

The supreme path of the bodhisattva
benefits all of the many types of beings.
I have hereby now concluded the explanation of
such dharmas of the first ground as these. {24}

Part Two
The Stainlessness Ground

B. The Second Ground: The Stainlessness Ground

1. The Second Ground's Introductory Verses and Dharma Request

As the bodhisattvas listened to this description
of this especially superior and sublime ground,
their minds became entirely purified
and they were all filled with joy. {1}

All of them then rose from their seats,
ascended upward, stood in empty space,
scattered the most marvelous blossoms everywhere,
and then simultaneously uttered praises together, saying: {2}

"It is good indeed, Vajragarbha Bodhisattva,
that the greatly wise and fearless one
has so well described this ground
and the dharmas practiced by the bodhisattva." {3}

Then, Liberation Moon Bodhisattva,
knowing that the minds of those in the assembly were pure
and knowing they would delight in hearing of the second ground
and all of its characteristic aspects of practice, {4}

straightaway made a request of Vajragarbha Bodhisattva, saying:
"O You of Great Wisdom, we pray you will continue to expound,
for these sons of the Buddha would all delight in hearing
about the second of these grounds on which one may dwell." {5}

2. Vajragarbha Commences the Second Ground's Explanation

{A} At that time, Vajragarbha Bodhisattva informed Liberation Moon Bodhisattva, saying:

3. The Ten Resolute Intentions as Bases for Entering the Second Ground

Son of the Buddha. The bodhisattva *mahāsattva* who has already cultivated the first ground and then wishes to enter the second ground should bring forth ten types of resolute intentions.[73] What then are these ten? They are as follows:[74]

The resolute intention to be upright and straightforward;
The resolute intention to be gentle;
The resolute intention to be capable;

The resolute intention to be subdued;
The resolute intention to be serene;
The resolute intention to be thoroughly good;
The resolute intention to be unmixed [in moral purity];
The resolute intention to be unattached;
The resolute intention to be broadly inclusive;
And resolute intention to be magnanimous.

It is because of these ten types of resolute intentions that the bodhisattva succeeds in entering the second ground, the Ground of Stainlessness.

4. The Bodhisattva's Observance of 10 Courses of Good Karmic Action[75]

a. Avoidance of Killing

{B} Son of the Buddha, the bodhisattva dwelling on the Ground of Stainlessness has naturally abandoned all killing of beings He does not collect knives or staves, does not harbor feelings of animosity, is possessed of a sense of shame and dread of blame, is entirely complete in his humanity and consideration for others, and always brings forth thoughts of beneficial and kindly mindfulness for all beings including anything at all that is possessed of a life. This bodhisattva does not even produce evil thoughts envisioning his inflicting distress upon other beings, how much the less could it happen that he might, having formed the conception of the existence of a being, then proceed with deliberate intent to kill it.

b. Avoidance of Taking What Is Not Given

{C} He naturally refrains from stealing. As regards his own possessions and wealth, the bodhisattva is always easily satisfied. He feels kindness and consideration for others and so does not wish to appropriate what is theirs. If something belongs to someone else, he regards it as their property and hence never even thinks of stealing it. Hence, he will not take even a blade of grass or a leaf that has not been given. How much the less might he take anything else that serves to sustain another's life.

c. Avoidance of Sexual Misconduct

{D} He naturally refrains from sexual misconduct. The bodhisattva is satisfied with his own wife and hence does not seek after the wives of others. As for the wives or consorts of others, women under the protection of others, female relatives, women whose marriage has already been arranged, and those who are under the protection of the Dharma, he does not even produce any thoughts defiled by desire, how much the less would he actually engage in any such action, and how much the less might he engage in behaviors involving a wrong physical orifice.

d. Avoidance of False Speech

{E} He naturally refrains from false speech. The bodhisattva always practices truthful speech, genuine speech, and timely speech, and, even in dreams, does not countenance speech aimed at concealment. He does not even generate any thought of wishing to commit such actions, how much the less might he commit a deliberate transgression.

e. Avoidance of Divisive Speech

{F} He naturally refrains from divisive speech. The bodhisattva has no thought inclined toward instigating divisions between other beings, and has no thought to do harm to others. He does not report the words of this person to that one with the intention of breaking up that person's relationship with him, nor does he report to this person the words of that one with the intention of breaking up this person's relationship with him.

He does not cause the breaking apart of those who have not yet broken apart and, in the case of those who have already broken apart, he does not act in a way which might increase that schism. He does not rejoice in divisions that occur between others, does not delight in divisions between others, does not utter any speech that might create divisions between others, and does not pass on to anyone any talk that might create divisions between others, regardless of whether or not those reports might be truthful.

f. Avoidance of Harsh Speech

{G} He naturally refrains from harsh speech such as poisonous and injurious speech, coarse and ferocious speech, speech inflicting suffering on others whether as direct statements or indirect statements, speech inciting hatred, vulgar speech, base speech, speech that no one would enjoy hearing, displeasing speech, angry speech, speech that makes others feel as if burned by fire, speech generating animosity, aggravating speech, speech one cannot appreciate, speech in which one can find no happiness, speech that may bring harm to either oneself or others, or any other such forms of speech, all of which one should abandon.

He always engages in soothingly smooth speech, pliant speech, pleasing speech, speech that may inspire happiness in the hearer, speech that one would be happy to hear, speech that delights the hearer, speech that skillfully enters others' minds, refined and principled speech, speech loved by the many, speech that many would find pleasing, and speech tending to cause an upwelling of delight in body and mind.

g. Avoidance of Frivolous Speech

{H} He naturally refrains from frivolous speech. The bodhisattva always delights in thoughtful and reasoned speech, timely speech, genuine speech, meaningful speech, Dharma speech, speech accordant with principle, skillfully subdued speech, and speech that accords with the right time, is always rooted in careful reflection, and is definite in its clarity. This bodhisattva, even in humorous speech, still always imbues it with thoughtfulness. How much the less would he deliberately indulge scattered and chaotically confused speech.

h. Avoidance of Covetousness

{I} He naturally abstains from covetousness. The bodhisattva does not generate covetous thought, wishfulness, or craving to possess any of the wealth or possessions of others or anything others depend upon as a resource.

i. Avoidance of Ill Will

{J} He naturally abandons ill will. The bodhisattva constantly brings forth kind thoughts, beneficial thoughts, pitying thoughts, joyful thoughts, harmoniously smooth thoughts, and inclusively accepting thoughts toward all beings. He has eternally relinquished ill will, animosity, injuriousness, and behavior intending to vex or torment others. Rather, he always engages in thoughtful and agreeably adaptive actions while also being motivated toward humanity, kindness, helpfulness, and the desire to serve the benefit of others.

j. Avoidance of Wrong Views

{K} He also abandons wrong views. The bodhisattva abides in the path of what is right. Thus he does not practice divination and does not seize on wrongly conceived rules for one's conduct. His mental perspective is correct, straightforward, and free of motivations toward deceptiveness or flattery. He brings forth and maintains resolute and definite faith in the Buddha, in the Dharma, and in the Sangha.

Son of the Buddha, it is in this manner that the bodhisattva *mahāsattva* always and uninterruptedly guards and maintains his practice of the ten courses of good karmic action.

5. The Bodhisattva's Reflections on 10 Good and Bad Karmic Actions

{L} He also has this thought:

Of all of the beings who descend into the wretched destinies, there are none who do not accomplish this by resort to the ten types of unwholesome karmic actions. Consequently, I should cultivate right conduct myself while also encouraging this in others in a manner that causes them to cultivate right conduct as well. Why does one proceed in this way? It is because, if one were to remain incapable of cultivating right conduct oneself while attempting to cause others to cultivate it, it would be impossible to succeed in this.

a. Reflections on their Generation of the Six Rebirth Destinies

{M} Son of the Buddha, this bodhisattva *mahāsattva* also has this thought:

The ten courses of unwholesome karmic action constitute the causes of rebirth in the hells, among animals, and among hungry ghosts, whereas the ten courses of good karmic action constitute the causes for rebirth among humans and devas and the other rebirth stations on up to the station at the peak of existence.

b. Reflections on Generation of the Fruits of the 3 Vehicles' Paths

Additionally, among these superior classes of those who adhere to the ten courses of good karmic action, there are those who rely on wisdom in cultivating them. Among them, there are those who, due to narrow and inferior resolve, due to fear of the three realms of existence, due to deficiency in the great compassion, and due to having achieved their understanding based on hearing the spoken teachings of others, they then achieve success in the Śrāvaka-disciple Vehicle.

{N} Also, among these superior classes of those who adhere the ten courses of good karmic action, there are those whose cultivation is pure and who achieve self-awakening not derived from the teachings of others, but who, because of inadequacy in the great compassion and skillful means, and because they succeed in awakening through understanding the extremely profound dharma of causes and conditions, they then achieve success in the Pratyekabuddha Vehicle.

{O} Then again, among these superior classes of those who adhere to the ten courses of good karmic action, there are those whose cultivation is pure, and who, because their minds are immeasurably vast, because they are complete in their development of compassion and pity, because their practice is subsumed within skillful means, because they have brought forth great vows, because they have not forsaken beings, because they strive to acquire the great knowledge of the Buddhas, and because they carry out the purifying cultivation of the bodhisattva grounds, they then achieve success in the vast practices of the bodhisattva.

{P} Furthermore, these who are most superior among those who are superior in the practice of the ten courses of good karmic action—because they purify the knowledge of all modes and so forth on up to the point of gaining realization of the ten powers and the four fearlessnesses, they therefore succeed in perfecting all dharmas of the Buddha.

Therefore I should now engage in the equal practice of all ten of these good deeds and should cause them all to become perfectly purified.

The bodhisattva should train in just such skillful means as these.

c. Reflections on the 10 Transgressions' 10 Karmic Retribution

{Q} Son of the Buddha, this bodhisattva *mahāsattva* also has this thought:

The highest level of transgression in the ten courses of unwholesome karmic action constitutes the causal basis for rebirth in the hells. A middling level of such transgression constitutes the causal basis for rebirth as an animal. The lowest level constitutes the causal basis for rebirth as a hungry ghost.

Among these, the karmic offense of killing is able to cause beings to descend into the hell realms, animal realms, and hungry ghost realms. If they then achieve a human rebirth, they reap two types of retribution: First, a short lifespan. Second, extensive illness.

The karmic offense of stealing also causes beings to descend into the three wretched destinies. If they then achieve a human rebirth, they reap two types of retribution: First, poverty. Second, if they acquire any wealth, it is jointly held by others, thus preventing its independent use.

The karmic offense of sexual misconduct also causes beings to descend into the three wretched destinies. If they then achieve a human rebirth, they reap two types of retribution: First, their spouse is not virtuous. Second, they do not acquire a retinue responsive to their wishes.

The karmic offense of false speech also causes beings to descend into the three wretched destinies. If they then achieve a human rebirth, they reap two types of retribution: First, they are often slandered by others. Second, they are deceived by others.

The karmic offense of divisive speech also causes beings to descend into the three wretched destinies. If they then achieve a human rebirth, they reap two types of retribution: First, their retinue is fraught with mutually estranging divisions. Second, the members of their family and clan are corrupt and evil.

The karmic offense of harsh speech also causes beings to descend into the three wretched destinies. If they then achieve a human rebirth, they reap two types of retribution: First, they are always subjected to unpleasant sounds. Second, their conversation is characterized by abundant disputation.

The karmic offense of frivolous speech also causes beings to descend into the three wretched destinies. If they then achieve a human rebirth, they reap two types of retribution: First, nobody accepts their pronouncements. Second, their pronouncements fail to be clearly understood.

The karmic offense of covetousness also causes beings to descend into the three wretched destinies. If they then achieve a human rebirth, they reap two types of retribution: First, their minds are never satisfied. Second, they are extensively afflicted by insatiable desires.

The karmic offense of ill will also causes beings to descend into the three wretched destinies. If they then achieve a human rebirth, they reap two types of retribution: First, they are always subjected to others' criticism of their shortcomings. Second, they are constantly subjected to injurious torment by others.

The karmic offense of holding wrong views also causes beings to descend into the three wretched destinies. If they then achieve a human rebirth, they reap two types of retribution: First, they are always reborn into a household ruled by wrong views. Second, their own minds tend toward flattery and deviousness.

Son of the Buddha, the ten courses of unwholesome karmic action are able to generate such an aggregation of measurelessly and boundlessly many immense sufferings as these.

d. Renunciation of 10 Bad Actions & Rousing of 10 Altruistic Minds

{R, S} Consequently, the bodhisattva reflects thus: "I must entirely abandon the ten courses of unwholesome karmic action and instead take the ten courses of good karmic action as the gardens of the Dharma wherein I am delighted to abide, dwelling there myself while also encouraging others so that they too are caused to dwell therein."

{T} Son of the Buddha, with regard to all beings, this bodhisattva *mahāsattva* also brings forth:[76]

A mind resolved to serve their benefit;
A mind wishing to bring them peace and happiness;
A kind mind;
A compassionate mind;
An empathetically pitying mind;
A mind motivated to draw them forth;
A protective mind;
A mind that sees them as like oneself;
A mind that regards them as like teachers;
And a mind that regards them as like great teaching masters.

6. His Reflections on the Plight of Beings & Resolve To Rescue Them

{U} He reflects thus:

These beings are so pitiable. They have fallen into wrong views, into perverse knowledge, into perverse inclinations, and into the entangling thicket of the unwholesome courses of karmic action. I should cause them to abide in right views and practice the genuine path.

{V} He also thinks:

All beings differentiate "other" as opposed to "self" and thus engage in mutually destructive actions, disputatiousness, and hatred that blazes incessantly. I should cause them to abide in the unsurpassable great kindness.

{W} He also reflects thus:

All beings are inclined toward insatiable covetousness and thus only seek to obtain wealth and self-benefit even to the point that they pursue wrong livelihoods to sustain their lives. I should cause them to abide in the dharma of right livelihood characterized by pure actions of body, speech, and mind.

{X} He also thinks:

All beings always follow along with the three poisons and the many different varieties of afflictions and, on account of that, they are as if ablaze. They fail to understand this and fail to bring forth the determination to seek the essential means to escape their circumstances. I should cause them to extinguish that great blaze fed by all of their afflictions and to then become securely established in the station of nirvāṇa's clarity and coolness.

{Y} He also reflects:

Because the vision of all beings has been covered over by the deep darkness of delusion and the thick cataracts of false views, they have therefore strayed into a dark and dense thicket. Having lost the shining light of wisdom, they travel along on dangerous paths in a vast wilderness and bring forth all manner of wrong views. I should cause them to acquire the unimpeded purified wisdom eye with which they can know the true character of all dharmas in a manner not dependent upon the instruction of others.

{Z} He also thinks:

All beings abide on the hazardous road of cyclic births and deaths wherein they are bound to fall into the hell realms, the animal realms, and the realms of the hungry ghosts. They enter the net-trap of wrong views, become confused in the dense forest of delusions, and thus follow along with erroneous paths and pursue practices influenced by the inverted views. In this, they are like blind people with no guide. What is not a path of escape, they take to be a path of escape. They enter into Māra's realm, fall in with bands of evil thieves, follow the thoughts of Māra, and leave far behind the intentions of the Buddha. I should pull them out of these hazardous difficulties and cause them to abide in the fearless city of all-knowledge.

{AA} He also reflects:

All of these beings have become submerged in the waves of the great floods. They have been swept up by the flood of desire, the flood of existence, the flood of ignorance, and the flood of views and thus have become caught in the whirling currents of cyclic existence wherein they are tossed about and turned around in the river of craving as they are carried along in its racing rapids and bounding turbulence, finding no leisure in which to ponder their plight.

They are relentlessly driven along by desire-ridden thoughts, by thoughts motivated by hatred, and by thoughts intent on harming others. The *rākṣasa* of the view imputing the existence of a true self in association with one's body[77] seizes them and carries them off to dwell eternally within the dense forest of desire wherein they develop a deep defiling attachment for whatever they desire. They abide on the high plateau of arrogance and take up residence in the village of the six sense bases wherein they have no one well able to come to their rescue and no one who is able to liberate them.

I should bring forth the mind of great compassion for them, should employ roots of goodness as means of rescuing them, should thus prevent their encountering calamitous disasters, and should thus assist their abandonment of defilement, their abiding in quiescent stillness, and their coming to dwell on the jeweled isle of all-knowledge.

{BB} He also thinks:

All beings abide in the prison of worldly existence in which they are subjected to so much anguishing affliction. They always embrace love and hate and produce worries and fears for themselves. They are bound by the heavy shackles of desire, are covered over and obstructed by the dense forest of ignorance, and are stranded within the three realms of existence from which no one can escape on their own. I should cause them to abandon forever the three realms of existence so that they may come to dwell in the great nirvāṇa that is free of all obstacles.

{CC} He also reflects thus:

All beings are attached to the existence of a self and do not seek to escape from their residence within the cave of the aggregates. In their reliance upon the empty village of the six sense bases, they engage in actions influenced by the four inverted views, are assailed and tormented by the toxic serpents of the four great elements, are subjected to death and injury at the hands of the hostile insurgents of the five aggregates, and thus consequently undergo immeasurably great suffering. I should cause them to take up residence in the most extremely superior station in which they are free of all attachments, namely, in the unexcelled nirvāṇa where all obstacles have been entirely destroyed.

{DD} He also has this thought:

The minds of all beings are inferior and mean. They do not practice the most superior path, the path of all-knowledge. Although they might wish to make their escape, even then, they only delight in the vehicles of the Śrāvaka-disciples and the Pratyekabuddhas. I must cause them to dwell in the Buddha's vast Dharma and vast wisdom.

Son of the Buddha, through his guarding and upholding of the moral precepts, the bodhisattva becomes well able to achieve growth in the mind of kindness and the mind of compassion.

7. The Bodhisattva's Seeing and Serving of Countless Buddhas

{EE} Son of the Buddha, because of the power of his vows, the bodhisattva *mahāsattva* who abides on the Ground of Stainlessness becomes able to see many buddhas. That is to say that he is able to see many hundreds of buddhas, many thousands of buddhas, many hundreds of thousands of buddhas, many *koṭis* of buddhas, many hundreds of *koṭis* of buddhas, many thousands of *koṭis* of buddhas, many hundreds of thousands of *koṭis* of buddhas, and so forth in this manner on up to his being able to see even many hundreds of thousands of *koṭis* of *nayutas* of buddhas.

Wherever the buddhas dwell, by resort to his vast resolve and resolute intentions, he acts with reverence and extreme veneration in serving and making offerings to them of robes, food and drink, bedding, medicines, and every form of life-supporting benefaction, all of which he offers up as gifts while also making offerings to their entire assembly of Sangha members. He then dedicates the roots of goodness associated with this to the realization of *anuttarasamyaksaṃbodhi.*

In addition, in the presence of all buddhas, bringing forth a mind of profound veneration, he undertakes the cultivation of the dharma of the ten courses of good karmic action, persisting in what he has undertaken all the way to the point of reaching the realization of bodhi, never in all that time neglecting or failing in such practice.

8. The Bodhisattva's Grounds Purification Compared to Refining Gold

Because, for countless hundreds of thousands of *koṭis* of *nayutas* of kalpas, this bodhisattva has abandoned miserliness and any defilement arising from breaking the moral precepts, he achieves consummate purity in giving and the observance of the moral precepts. This is just as when one places real gold together with *kāsīsa*[78] and subjects it to standard refining processes, whereupon the gold leaves behind all impurities and becomes ever more radiant. So too it is in the case of this bodhisattva dwelling on the Ground of Stainlessness who, for countless hundreds of thousands of *koṭis* of *nayutas* of kalpas, in order to abandon miserliness and any defilement that would arise from breaking moral precepts, has practiced giving and upheld the moral precepts and has thus thereby achieved a state of consummate purity.

9. The Bodhisattva's Practice of Means of Attraction and Pāramitās

Son of the Buddha, among the four means of attraction, this bodhisattva focuses more strongly on "pleasing words" and, among the ten *pāramitās,* he focuses more strongly on upholding the moral precepts. It is not that he does not practice the others. Rather, he simply accords them an amount of emphasis corresponding to his own strengths and to what is fitting.

10. Vajragarbha's Final Statements About the 2nd Ground Bodhisattva

Son of the Buddha, this has been a summary discussion of the essentials of the bodhisattva *mahāsattva's* second ground, the Ground of Stainlessness.

a. The Bodhisattva's Station and Dharma Practice

The bodhisattva abiding on this ground often becomes a wheel-turning sage king who serves as a great Dharma sovereign possessed of an abundance of the seven precious things and sovereign powers through which he is able to cause beings to do away with their miserliness and precept-breaking defilements. He employs skillful means to cause them to abide securely in the ten courses of good karmic action. He serves as a great benefactor to all, endlessly supplying provisions to everyone.

b. The Bodhisattva's Mindfulness

In his practice of giving, pleasing words, beneficial actions, and joint endeavors, and in all other such works as these, he never departs from mindfulness of the Buddha, never departs from mindfulness of the Dharma, never departs from mindfulness of the Sangha, and so forth until we come to his never departing from mindfulness of his quest to achieve complete fulfillment of the knowledge of all modes and the cognition of all-knowledge.

c. The Bodhisattva's Aspiration to Serve Beings

He also has this thought: "I should become one who serves these beings as a leader, as one who is supreme, as one who is most especially supreme, as one who is marvelous, as one who is most subtly marvelous, as one who is excellent, as one who is unexcelled," and so forth until we come to "as one who relies on the cognition of all-knowledge."

d. The Result of the Bodhisattva's Leaving the Household Life

If this bodhisattva wishes to relinquish the home life and take up the diligent practice of vigor in the Dharma of the Buddha, then he will be able to relinquish the household, his wife and children, and the five desires, and having abandoned the home life, if he diligently applies himself in the practice of vigor, in but a single moment, he will acquire a thousand samādhis, will be able to see a thousand buddhas, will know the spiritual powers exercised by a thousand buddhas, will be able to cause tremors in a thousand world systems, and so forth until we come to his becoming able to manifest a thousand bodies and able to manifest a thousand bodhisattvas to serve in the retinue of each and every one of those bodies.

If he resorts to the power of the especially supreme vows of the bodhisattva, he will become freely able to bring forth a number of manifestations beyond even this such that one would never be able to count them even in a period of a hundred kalpas, a thousand kalpas, and so forth on up to a hundred thousand *koṭis* of *nayutas* of kalpas.

11. Vajragarbha Bodhisattva's Summarizing Verses

At that time, Vajragarbha Bodhisattva, wishing to again proclaim his meaning, thereupon uttered verses, saying:

The straightforward mind, the gentle mind, the capable mind,
the subdued mind, the serene mind, the mind of pure goodness,
the swift exits from *saṃsāra*, the broadly inclusive and great minds—
By employing these ten minds, one enters the second ground.[79] {6}

Abiding herein, one perfects the qualities of the moral precepts,
departs far from killing, refrains from vexing or harming others,
and also abandons stealing as well as sexual misconduct and
speech that is either false, harsh, divisive, or meaningless. {7}

He does not covet wealth, always feels kindness and pity,
walks the right path with a straight mind, has no flattery or falseness,
abandons treachery, forgoes arrogance, is utterly subdued and pliant,
accords with teachings in practice, and refrains from negligence. {8}

One thinks, "The many sufferings endured in the hells, as animals,
and as hungry ghosts who, burning, spew forth fierce flames—
All of these are caused by karmic offenses.
I must abandon them and instead abide in the true Dharma. {9}

Freely gaining rebirth among humans according to one's intentions,
and so on, up to *dhyāna* samādhi bliss in peak-of-existence heavens,
and the paths of Pratyekabuddha, Śrāvaka, and Buddha Vehicles—
All are gained with the ten good karmic actions as their cause." {10}

One contemplates in this manner and thus refrains from negligence,
upholds pure precepts oneself, instructs others in guarding them,
and also, observing the many sufferings undergone by beings,
one thus ever increases the mind of great compassion. {11}

"Foolish common people of faulty knowledge and wrong
understanding ever harbor hatred and engage in many disputes.
The objects of their covetousness never bring them satisfaction.
I should cause them to rid themselves of these three poisons. {12}

"They are enveloped and blanketed by stupidity's great darkness,
fall into the net of wrong views on extremely hazardous paths,
and are trapped by adversaries in the cage of birth and death.
I should cause them to utterly defeat Māra's marauders. {13}

"Swept away by the four floods, their minds become submerged.
They endure incalculable suffering as if burning in the three realms.
They conceive of the aggregates as a house in which a self abides.
Wishing to liberate them, I must diligently cultivate the path. {14}

"Where they might seek escape, their minds being inferior and mean,
they have cast aside the Buddha's supremely excellent wisdom.
I wish to cause them to abide in the Great Vehicle
and bring forth diligent and tireless vigor in this." {15}

The bodhisattva abiding herein accumulates meritorious qualities,
sees countless buddhas, presents offerings to them all,
and refines goodness to even greater brilliance for *koṭis* of kalpas
as if employing a fine elixir in refining real gold. {16}

A son of the Buddha dwelling herein becomes a wheel-turning king
everywhere teaching beings to practice the ten good karmic deeds
while also cultivating all of the other good dharmas
in order to perfect the ten powers and rescue those in the world. {17}

If he wishes to relinquish the royal throne, wealth, and jewels,
he thereupon abandons home life, accords with Buddha's teachings,
is valiant and energetic in diligence, and in a single moment,
acquires a thousand samādhis and sees a thousand buddhas. {18}

The bodhisattva abiding on this ground is able to manifest
all the many different powers of the superknowledges,
and, through power of vows, his capabilities extend even beyond this
as, in countless ways, he freely liberates the many classes of beings. {19}

As for these most supreme practices of the bodhisattva cultivated by
one who bestows benefit on everyone in the world,
all such meritorious qualities found on the second ground as these
have hereby been expounded on for the sake of the Buddha's sons. {20}

Part Three
The Shining Light Ground

C. The Third Ground: The Shining Light Ground

1. The Third Ground's Introductory Verses and Dharma Request

Of those sons of the Buddha hearing of this ground's practices
and of the inconceivable realms of the bodhisattva,
none failed to be moved to thoughts of reverence and delight.
Then, from the midst of space, they scattered blossoms as offerings. {1}

Uttering praises, they said, "It is good indeed, Great Mountain King,
that, with compassionate mind, you think of beings with pity.
You have so well described the dharmas of moral virtue of the wise
as well as the practices and characteristics of the second ground. {2}

"The sublime practices of these bodhisattvas,
true, real, free of irregularities, and unvarying—
Wishing to benefit the many classes of beings,
you have thus expounded upon their supreme purity. {3}

"You to whom all humans and devas make offerings here,
we pray you will now expound on the third ground for their sakes
and hope you will entirely explain in accordance with their states
the Dharma-accordant works of the wise. {4}

"All of the Great Rishi's dharmas of giving, moral virtue,
patience, vigor, *dhyāna*, and wisdom,
as well as the path of skillful means, kindness, and compassion—
All these pure practices of the Buddha—please explain them all." {5}

At that time, Liberation Moon repeated their request, saying:
"O fearless and greatly eminent master, Vajragarbha—
Please explain the manner of one's progression into the third ground
and all qualities of those there with pliant and harmonious minds." {6}

2. Vajragarbha Commences the Third Ground's Explanation

{A} At that time, Vajragarbha Bodhisattva informed Liberation Moon Bodhisattva, saying:

3. The Ten Resolute Intentions as Bases for Entering the Third Ground

Son of the Buddha. The bodhisattva who has already accomplished the purification of the second ground and then wishes to enter the third ground should bring forth ten types of resolute intentions.[80] What then are these ten? They are:[81]

The resolute intention set on purity;
The resolute intention set on stable abiding;
The resolute intention set on renunciation;
The resolute intention set on abandoning desire;
The resolute intention set on irreversibility;
The resolute intention set on solidity;
The resolute intention set on flourishing brilliance;
The resolute intention set on heroic bravery;
The resolute intention set on being broadly inclusive;
And the resolute intention set on magnanimity.

The bodhisattva employs these ten types of resolute intentions to acquire entry into the third ground.

4. The Bodhisattva's Contemplation of All Conditioned Dharmas

{B} Son of the Buddha, after the bodhisattva *mahāsattva* comes to abide on the third ground, he contemplates all conditioned dharmas in accordance with their true character, that is to say, they are characterized by:

Impermanence;
Suffering;
Impurity;
Instability;
Certainty of ruination;
Inability to long endure;
Production and destruction in each succeeding *kṣaṇa*;
Not coming forth from the past;
Not proceeding on to the future;
And not abiding in the present.

{C} He also contemplates these dharmas:

As affording no protection;
As devoid of any refuge;
As accompanied by worry, sorrow, and anguish;
As bound up with love and hate;
As proliferating worry and sorrow;
As involving ceaseless accumulation;
As ablaze with the fire of desire, hatred, and stupidity that blaze on incessantly;
As enveloped by the many sorts of calamities;
As increasing day and night;
And as like magical conjurations in their unreality.

5. The Bodhisattva's Renunciation & Quest For Buddha's Knowledge

{D} Having observed this, he doubly increases his renunciation of all conditioned things and progresses toward the wisdom of the Buddha. He perceives the wisdom of the Buddha:[82]

As inconceivable;
As unequaled;
As measureless;
As rarely encountered;
As unalloyed in its purity;
As beyond anguish;
As beyond worries;
As reaching all the way to the city of fearlessness;
As irreversible;
And as able to rescue countless beings beset with suffering and difficulty.

6. The Bodhisattva's Ten Sympathetic Mental Intentions Toward Beings

{E} Once the bodhisattva has in this way observed the immeasurable benefit of the Tathāgata's wisdom and has likewise observed the countless faults and calamitous qualities of all that is conditioned, he then brings forth ten types of sympathetic mental intentions[83] toward all beings. What then are these ten? They are:[84]

He brings forth sympathetic mental intentions on observing that beings abide in solitude with no one upon whom they can depend;
He brings forth sympathetic mental intentions on observing that beings are poverty-stricken and destitute;
He brings forth sympathetic mental intentions on observing that beings are engulfed in the flames of the three poisons;
He brings forth sympathetic mental intentions on observing that beings are confined in the prison of the states of existence;
He brings forth sympathetic mental intentions on observing that beings are constantly covered over and obstructed by the dense forest of afflictions;
He brings forth sympathetic mental intentions on observing that beings are not skilled in contemplative thought;
He brings forth sympathetic mental intentions on observing that beings have no desire for good dharmas;
He brings forth sympathetic mental intentions on observing that beings have lost the Buddhas' Dharma;

He brings forth sympathetic mental intentions on observing that beings flow along in the stream of cyclic births and deaths;
And he brings forth sympathetic mental intentions on observing that beings have lost the means of achieving liberation.

These are the ten.

7. The Bodhisattva's Generation and Practice of Great Vigor

{F} Having thus observed the immeasurable suffering and anguish of the realms of beings' existence, the bodhisattva brings forth great vigor and thinks:[85]

I should rescue these beings;
I should liberate them;
I should establish them in purity;
I should take them on across;
I should see that they become situated in a place of goodness;
I should cause them to abide securely;
I should cause them to be filled with joy;
I should cause them to acquire knowledge and vision;
I should cause them to become well trained;
And I should cause them to reach nirvāṇa.

{G} Having thus renounced all conditioned things, having thus become sympathetically mindful of all beings, having understood the supreme benefits of the cognition of all-knowledge, and wishing to rely on the Tathāgata's wisdom in rescuing beings, the bodhisattva reflects thus: "In this circumstance where all these beings have fallen into the great suffering of the afflictions, with what skillful means might I be able to extricate and rescue them so that they are caused to abide in the ultimate bliss of nirvāṇa?"

{H} He then thinks:

If one wishes to liberate beings and cause them to abide in nirvāṇa, this is inseparable from the unimpeded knowledge of liberation. The unimpeded knowledge of liberation is inseparable from awakening to all dharmas as they really are. The awakening to all dharmas as they really are is inseparable from the light of the practice wisdom that cognizes the non-existence of action and non-production. The light of the practice wisdom that is cognizant of the nonexistence of action and non-production[86] is in turn inseparable from *dhyāna* meditation's skillful and definitive knowledge arising from contemplative investigation. *Dhyāna* meditation's skillful and definitive knowledge arising from contemplative investigation is in turn inseparable from skillful extensive learning.

{I} Having contemplated and utterly realized this, the bodhisattva redoubles his diligent striving to cultivate right Dharma to the point that, day and night, he only wishes:[87]

To hear the Dharma;
To rejoice in the Dharma;
To delight in the Dharma;
To rely upon the Dharma;
To follow the Dharma;
To comprehend the Dharma;
To comply with the Dharma;
To arrive in the Dharma;
To abide in the Dharma;
And to practice the Dharma.

{J} As in this way he diligently pursues his quest to acquire the Dharma of the Buddha, the bodhisattva retains no miserly cherishing for any precious possessions or wealth, for he does not perceive that there is any such thing that is worthy of being esteemed as rare. Rather, it is only the person who is able to explain the Buddha's Dharma that he conceives of as but rarely encountered.

Consequently, for the sake of his quest to acquire the Dharma of the Buddha, the bodhisattva is able to give away all his inward and outward wealth. There is no expression of reverence he would be unable to carry out, no form of pride he would be unable to relinquish, no form of service he would be unable to perform, and no form of intensely bitter suffering he would be unable to endure. If he were to be able to hear but a single sentence of Dharma he has never heard before, he would be filled with immense joy more abundant than what he would experience on receiving an entire great trichiliocosm full of precious jewels.

Were he to be able to hear but a single stanza of right Dharma he has not heard before, he would be filled with immense joy even more abundant than that experienced on acquiring the position of a wheel-turning sage king. Were he to succeed in acquiring but a single stanza of Dharma he had not heard before through which he might be able to purify his cultivation of the bodhisattva conduct, he would regard that as superior to ascending to the station of Indra or Brahmā where he might be able to abide in that manner for countless hundreds of thousands of kalpas.

Were someone to tell him: "I possess a single sentence of the Dharma spoken by the Buddha through which you will be able to purify your cultivation of the bodhisattva conduct, but I will only give it to you if you will now be able to plunge into a huge fire pit in which you will undergo the most extreme suffering," the bodhisattva would reflect in this way:

> If I were able to purify the cultivation of the bodhisattva conduct by acquiring this one stanza of Dharma spoken by the Buddha, then, even if an entire great trichiliocosm were filled with a great conflagration, I would still wish to throw my body down into it from the height of the Brahma Heaven in order to be able to personally acquire it. How much the less might it be that I would be unable to enter some small fire pit in order to acquire it. Hence, for the sake of seeking the Dharma of the Buddha, I should now even be willing to undergo all the many sufferings of the hells. How much the less might I be unwilling to undergo any of the relatively minor sufferings encountered in the human realm.

In his practice of vigor in seeking the Buddha's Dharma, the bodhisattva brings forth just such diligence as this. He then implements the practice of contemplation and cultivation in accordance with whatsoever Dharma he has learned.

{K} Having been able to hear the Dharma, this bodhisattva then focuses his mind and takes up peaceful dwelling in a secluded place, thinking, "It is only through cultivating in accordance with what has been taught that one then acquires the Buddha's Dharma. Achieving purification in these matters is not something one can accomplish solely through the spoken word."

8. The Bodhisattva's Conquest of the Meditative Absorptions

Sons of the Buddha, when this bodhisattva comes to dwell on this Ground of Shining Light, he straightaway separates himself from desire and from evil and unwholesome dharmas. Still possessed of both ideation and mental discursion, he experiences the joy and the bliss arising from separation and abides in the first *dhyāna.*

Extinguishing both ideation and mental discursion, achieving inward purity, and anchoring the mind in a single place, he becomes free of ideation and free of mental discursion, experiences the joy and bliss generated through meditative concentration, and abides in the second *dhyāna.*

Separating himself from joy, abiding in equanimity, possessed of mindfulness and right knowing awareness, experiencing physical feeling of which the Āryas are able to state that one is able to maintain equanimity toward it, and possessed of mindfulness while experiencing such bliss, he abides in the third *dhyāna.*

Cutting off bliss, having earlier already done away with suffering, having extinguished joy and sorrow, experiencing neither suffering nor bliss, and maintaining equanimity and mindfulness that are pure, he abides in the fourth *dhyāna*.

He transcends all perceptions of physical form, extinguishes all perceptions of [sensory] impingement, does not attend to any perceptions of diversity, enters a state characterized by boundless space, and thus then abides in the station of boundless space.

He entirely transcends the station of boundless space, enters a state characterized by boundless consciousness, and thus then abides in the station of boundless consciousness.

He entirely transcends the station of boundless consciousness, enters a state characterized by nothing whatsoever, and thus then abides in the station of nothing whatsoever.

He entirely transcends the station of nothing whatsoever and thus then abides in the station of neither perception nor non-perception.

Because he accords with the Dharma, he carries forth his practice without having anything to which he retains a pleasure-based attachment.

9. The Bodhisattva's Development of the Four Immeasurables

{L} Son of the Buddha, this bodhisattva's mind pursues the cultivation of kindness to the point that it becomes vast, immeasurable, non-dual, free of enmity, free of any opposition, unimpeded, free of affliction, universally pervading everywhere throughout the Dharma realm and the realm of empty space, and extending universally to all worlds. His abiding in compassion, in sympathetic joy, and in equanimity are also just like this.

10. The Bodhisattva's Development of the Spiritual superknowledges

{M} Son of the Buddha, this bodhisattva acquires the power of measureless spiritual superknowledges by which:

He is able to cause the entire great earth to tremor;

He is able to create many bodies from a single body and is able to make those many bodies become a single body, either making them hidden or making them visible;

He is able to pass unimpededly through the obstructions of rock, walls, and mountains just as if moving through empty space;

He is able to travel through empty space while remaining in full lotus position, just like a flying bird;

He is able to enter into the earth as if it were water;

He is able to walk on water as if it were the earth;
He is able to emit smoke and flames like a great bonfire;
He is also able to rain down water like a great cloud;
He also possesses that great and awesome power by which he is able to reach up with his hand and stroke the sun and the moon where they reside in space;
And he is able to freely transport his person wherever he pleases, even up to the Brahma World.

11. The Bodhisattva's Heavenly Ear

This bodhisattva possesses the heavenly ear that is purified and surpasses the human ear. Thus he is able to entirely hear all of the sounds of both humans and devas, whether they be near or far. He is also able even to entirely hear all of the sounds emitted by mosquitoes, gnats, and the various sorts of flies.

12. The Bodhisattva's Knowledge of Others' Thoughts

Employing the knowledge of others' thoughts, this bodhisattva knows in accordance with reality the thoughts of other beings. Specifically, when they have thoughts of desire, he knows in accordance with reality that they have thoughts of desire and when they have abandoned thoughts of desire, he knows in accordance with reality that they have abandoned thoughts of desire. In all cases, he knows in accordance with reality when they have:

Thoughts of hatred or thoughts that have abandoned hatred;
Deluded thoughts or thoughts that have abandoned delusion;
Thoughts beset with afflictions or thoughts that are free of afflictions;
Thoughts that are small in scope or thoughts that are vast in scope;
Great thoughts or immeasurable thoughts;
Thoughts that are general in nature or thoughts not general in nature;
Scattered thoughts or thoughts that are not scattered;
Concentrated thoughts or thoughts that are not concentrated;
Liberated thoughts or unliberated thoughts;
Surpassable thoughts or unsurpassable thoughts;
Thoughts admixed with defilement or thoughts not admixed with defilement;
And vast thoughts or thoughts that are not vast.

So it is that the bodhisattva uses the knowledge of others' thoughts to know beings' thoughts.

13. The Bodhisattva's Recall of Past Lives

This bodhisattva remembers the details of countless past lives. Specifically, he remembers one life, two lives, three lives, four lives, and so forth on up to ten lives, twenty lives, thirty lives, and so forth on up to a hundred lives, countless hundreds of lives, countless thousands of lives, and countless hundreds of thousands of lives. He remembers the creation phase of the kalpa, the destruction phase of the kalpa, the creation and destruction phases of the kalpa, and remembers countless creation and destruction phases of kalpas. He remembers:

> I lived in such-and-such a place, was named this, was a member of this family, came from this caste, consumed these sorts of food and drink, lived a life of this length, dwelt for this amount of time, and experienced these sorts of suffering and happiness, after which I died in that place, was then reborn in such-and-such a place, after which I died in such-and-such a place, was then reborn in this place, possessed this sort of physical stature, was of this sort of appearance, and spoke with this sort of voice.

In this way, he entirely remembers countless details from his past.

14. The Bodhisattva's Heavenly Eye

This bodhisattva possesses the heavenly eye that is purified and surpasses the human eye. Thus he observes with respect to beings when they were born, when they died, whether they were of fine physical appearance or of hideous appearance, whether they dwelt in the destinies associated with goodness, whether they dwelt in the wretched destinies, and how they moved along in accordance with their karmic actions.

He is able as well to observe that, if some particular being had created bad physical karma, bad verbal karma, and bad mental karma, had slandered worthies and *āryas*, had become completely possessed of wrong views and the causes and conditions of karmic actions associated with wrong views, when his body perished and his lifespan came to an end, he then became bound for descent into the wretched destinies and was reborn into the hells.

He is also able to observe that, if yet some other being had created good physical karma, good verbal karma, and good mental karma, had refrained from slandering worthies and *āryas*, had become completely possessed of right views as well as the causes and conditions of karmic actions associated with right views, then, when his body perished and his lifespan came to an end, he then became bound for rebirth into the good destinies and for ascent into the heavens.

The bodhisattva's heavenly eye is able to observe all of these circumstances in accordance with the way they really are.

15. The Bodhisattva's Vow-Determined Rebirth Apart from the Dhyānas

This bodhisattva, though well able to enter and emerge from the *dhyāna* samādhis and *samāpattis,* nonetheless does not acquiesce in their power when taking rebirth, but rather only acquiesces in rebirth to locations conducing to his ability to achieve complete fulfillment of the factors leading to the realization of bodhi. In this, availing himself of his mind's power of vows, he thereby achieves rebirth in those sorts of circumstances.

16. The Bodhisattva's Seeing and Serving of Countless Buddhas

{N} Son of the Buddha, due to the power of his vows, this bodhisattva who abides on this Ground of Shining Light becomes able to see many buddhas. That is to say that he may see many hundreds of buddhas, many thousands of buddhas, many hundreds of thousands of buddhas, and so forth until we come to his seeing many hundreds of thousands of *koṭis* of *nayutas* of buddhas, all of whom he reveres, venerates, and serves. He presents offerings to them of robes, food and drink, bedding, medicines, and all things supporting their lives, offering up all of these things with a vast mind and a deep mind. He also makes offerings of such requisites to everyone in their sangha assemblies and then dedicates these roots of goodness to the realization of *anuttarasamyaksaṃbodhi.* He listens respectfully to the Dharma in the presence of the Buddhas. Having heard it, he retains it and cultivates it in a manner befitting his powers to do so.

17. The Bodhisattva's Purification and its Comparison to Refining Gold

This bodhisattva contemplates all dharmas as neither produced nor destroyed and as existing through the conjunction of causes and conditions.

{O} Having first destroyed the bonds of views, the bonds of desire, the bonds of form, the bonds of becoming, and the bonds of ignorance all become ever more attenuated. Because, for countless hundreds of thousands of *koṭis* of *nayutas* of kalpas, they are no longer accumulated, wrong desire, wrong hatred, and wrong delusion are all entirely cut off. All of his roots of goodness then become ever more radiant.

Son of the Buddha, this is analogous to skillfully refining real gold to the point where its weight no longer diminishes with smelting and it shines ever more brightly in its purity. So too it is with the bodhisattva who dwells on the Ground of Shining Light. Because he no longer accumulates them, wrongly generated covetousness, wrongly generated hatred, and wrongly generated stupidity are all entirely cut off and his roots of goodness then shine ever more brightly.

This bodhisattva's inclination to be patient, his inclination to be gently harmonious, his inclination to be congenially adaptive, his inclination to be pleasingly sweet, his inclination to refrain from anger, his inclination to remain imperturbable, his inclination to remain unconfused, his inclination to refrain from judgments as to "superior" or "inferior," his inclination to not long for expressions of gratitude, his inclination to repay kindnesses, his inclination to refrain from flattery, his inclination to refrain from deviousness, and his inclination to refrain from treachery—all of these become ever more purified.[88]

18. The Bodhisattva's Practice of Means of Attraction and Pāramitās

Among the four means of attraction, this bodhisattva focuses more strongly on the practice of "beneficial actions" and, among the ten *pāramitās*, he focuses more strongly on the practice of the patience *pāramitā*.[89] It is not that he does not practice the others. Rather, he simply accords them an amount of emphasis corresponding to his own strengths and to whatever is fitting.

19. Vajragarbha's Final Statements About the 3rd Ground Bodhisattva

Son of the Buddha, this is what constitutes the bodhisattva's third ground, the Ground of Shining Light.

a. The Bodhisattva's Station and Dharma Practice

{P} The bodhisattva dwelling on this ground often becomes a king of the Heaven of the Thirty-three who is able to employ skillful means to cause beings to abandon desire.

b. The Bodhisattva's Mindfulness

In his practice of "giving," "pleasing words," "beneficial actions," and "joint endeavors" and in all other such works as these, he never departs from mindfulness of the Buddha, never departs from mindfulness of the Dharma, never departs from mindfulness of the Sangha, and so forth until we come to his never departing from mindfulness of his quest to achieve complete fulfillment of the knowledge of all modes and the cognition of all-knowledge.

c. The Bodhisattva's Aspiration to Serve Beings

He also has this thought: "I should become one who serves these beings as a leader, as one who is supreme, as one who is most especially supreme, as one who is marvelous, as one who is most subtly marvelous, as one who is excellent, as one who is unexcelled," and so forth until we come to "as one who relies on the cognition of all-knowledge."

d. The Consequences of the Bodhisattva's Vigor and Vows

If he becomes diligent in the practice of vigor, then, in but a single moment, he will acquire a hundred thousand samādhis, will be able to see a hundred thousand buddhas, will know of the spiritual powers of a hundred thousand buddhas, will be able to cause tremors in a hundred thousand buddha worlds, and so forth until we come to his manifesting a hundred thousand bodies among which each and every one of those bodies manifests a hundred thousand bodhisattvas to serve as its retinue. If he uses the power of the bodhisattva's especially supreme vows, he will be freely able to bring forth manifestations beyond this number such that one could never count them all even in a hundred kalpas, a thousand kalpas, and so forth on up to a hundred thousand *koṭis* of *nayutas* of kalpas.

20. Vajragarbha Bodhisattva's Summarizing Verses

At that time, Vajragarbha Bodhisattva, wishing to again proclaim his meaning, thereupon uttered verses, saying:

The pure mind, stable abiding mind, mind of flourishing brilliance,
mind of renunciation, non-desiring mind, non-harming mind,[90]
the solid, valiant, broadly inclusive and magnanimous minds—
the wise resort to these in acquiring entry into the third ground. {7}

The bodhisattva dwelling on this Ground of Shining Light
contemplates formative factor dharmas as suffering, impermanent,
impure, bound to perish, rapidly bound to return to destruction,
as unenduring, as nonabiding, and as having no coming or going. {8}

He contemplates conditioned dharmas as like a grave disease,
as bound up with worry, lamentation, suffering and anguish,
as constantly ablaze with the fierce fire of the three poisons that,
from beginningless time onward, has continued without cease. {9}

He renounces the three realms, indulges no covetous attachment,
exclusively and without distraction pursues the Buddha's knowledge,
so difficult to fathom, difficult to conceive of, matchless,
immeasurable, boundless, and entirely free of torments. {10}

Having observed the Buddha's knowledge, he feels pity for beings,
abiding alone, with no one to rely on or to rescue and protect them,
burned by the blazing fire of the three poisons, ever poverty-stricken,
dwelling in the prison of existence, always undergoing sufferings, {11}

enveloped in and covered by the afflictions, blind, with no eyes,
aspiring to the inferior and mean, having lost the Dharma jewel,
swept along in cyclic births and deaths, frightened by nirvāṇa—
he thinks, "I should rescue them, being diligently vigorous in this. {12}

I shall seek the wisdom with which to benefit beings."
He reflects on which skillful means can cause their liberation and
realizes it is none other than the Tathāgata's unimpeded knowledge
that itself arises from the wisdom of non-production. {13}

He reflects, "This wisdom is acquired through learning."
Having considered it thus, he then assiduously urges himself on
so that, day and night, he listens and practices incessantly,
taking only right Dharma as what is worthy of his esteem. {14}

Whether it be countries, cities, wealth, the various precious jewels,
his wife, children, retinue, or even the royal throne—
for the sake of Dharma, the bodhisattva, with reverential mind,
is able to relinquish all such things. {15}

Even his head, eyes, ears, nose, tongue, and teeth,
his hands, feet, bones, marrow, heart, blood and flesh—
relinquishing even such things as these, he does not deem difficult,
but rather only esteems the hearing of Dharma as most rare. {16}

Should someone come and tell this bodhisattva,
"Whosoever is able to throw his body into a great bonfire—
I will bestow upon you a Dharma jewel of the Buddha,"
having heard this, he would feel no trepidation at leaping into it. {17}

He instead thinks, "Even were there a fire filling up a trichiliocosm,
I would leap down into it from the height of the Brahma world,
for, to do this in search of the Dharma is not to be seen as difficult,
how much the less might I shrink from minor human sufferings." {18}

Even all of the sufferings experienced in the Avīci Hells
from the time of his initial resolve until he achieves buddhahood—
he would be able to endure it all for the sake of hearing the Dharma.
How much the more would he endure all the sufferings of humans. {19}

Having heard it, by right contemplation that accords with principle,
he gains in sequence the four *dhyānas*, four formless absorptions,
four equally-regarding minds,[91] and five superknowledges,
yet does not acquiesce in their power to determine one's rebirths. {20}

The bodhisattva dwelling herein sees many buddhas,
makes offerings to them, listens to them, and, with resolute mind,
severs erroneous views and delusions and becomes ever more pure,
as when refining true gold, its substance remains undiminished. {21}

One who abides herein often becomes a Trāyastriṃśa Heaven King
teaching and guiding countless members of the assemblies of devas,
causing them to forsake the desire mind, abide in paths of goodness,
and proceed with singular devotion to seek the Buddha's qualities. {22}

A son of the Buddha abiding herein who is diligently vigorous
perfectly acquires a hundred thousand samādhis,
sees a hundred thousand buddhas' bodies adorned with the marks,
and, if resorting to the power of vows, exceeds even this. {23}

As for the universal benefiting of all beings
and all of those especially superior practices of the bodhisattvas
as well as all of the other such aspects of the third ground,
I have concluded their explanation according to their meaning. {24}

Part Four
The Blazing Brilliance Ground

D. The Fourth Ground: The Blazing Brilliance Ground

1. The Fourth Ground's Introductory Verses and Dharma Request

When those sons of the Buddha had heard of these vast practices
on this delightful, deeply sublime, and especially supreme ground,
their minds were exhilarated, they were filled with great joy, and
they scattered many flowers everywhere as offerings to the Buddha. {1}

When such sublime Dharma had been proclaimed there,
the great earth trembled, the ocean's waters roiled,
and all of the celestial nymphs became joyful,
whereupon they all joined their marvelous voices in singing praises. {2}

The Vaśavartin Heaven King, moved to immense celebratory delight,
rained down *maṇi* jewels as offerings to the Buddha,
and uttered praises: "The Buddha has come forth here for our sakes,
expounding the practices possessed of the foremost merit. {3}

"The meaning of the grounds taught by such a wise one as this
is extremely difficult to encounter in a hundred thousand kalpas.
We have now suddenly been able to hear this sublime Dharma voice
speak of a bodhisattva's supreme conduct. {4}

"We wish to additionally hear expounded the brilliantly wise one's
subsequent grounds on the definite path to the realm without residue
that bestows benefit on all devas and all humans.
All of these sons of the Buddha would delight in hearing this." {5}

Then the heroically valiant one of great resolve, Liberation Moon,
posed a request to Vajragarbha, saying, "O Son of the Buddha,
please explain here all aspects of the practice involved in
turning from here to enter the fourth ground." {6}

2. Vajragarbha Commences the Fourth Ground's Explanation

{A} At that time, Vajragarbha Bodhisattva informed Liberation Moon Bodhisattva, saying:

3. 10 Gateways to Dharma Light as Bases for Entering the 4th Ground

O Son of the Buddha. As for the bodhisattva *mahāsattva* who has already well purified his practice on the third ground and then wishes to enter the fourth ground, the Ground of Blazing Brilliance, he should cultivate ten gateways to the light of Dharma.[92] What are the ten? They are:

Contemplation of the realms of beings;
Contemplation of the Dharma realm;
Contemplation of the world realms;
Contemplation of the realms of empty space;
Contemplation of the realms of consciousness;
Contemplation of the desire realm;
Contemplation of the form realm;
Contemplation of the formless realm;
Contemplation of the realms of broadly inclusive resolute intentions and resolute convictions;[93]
And contemplation of the realms of magnanimous resolute intentions and resolute convictions.[94]

The bodhisattva employs these ten gateways to the light of Dharma to gain entry into the fourth ground, the Ground of Blazing Brilliance.

4. Ten Knowledge-Maturing Dharmas for Birth in the Buddhas' Clan

{B} Son of the Buddha, if a bodhisattva comes to dwell on this Ground of Blazing Brilliance, then, by employing ten types of knowledge-maturing dharmas,[95] he becomes able to acquire its inner dharmas[96] and achieve birth into the clan of the Tathāgatas. What then are those ten? They are:

Through possessing non-retreating resolute intentions;
Through bringing forth ultimately pure and indestructible faith in the Three Jewels;
Through contemplating the production and destruction of all karmic formative factors;
Through contemplating all dharmas as, by their very nature, unproduced;
Through contemplating the formation and destruction of worlds;
Through contemplating that it is on account of karmic actions that birth exists;
Through contemplating *saṃsāra* and nirvāṇa;
Through contemplating the karma associated with beings and lands;
Through contemplating the past and the future;
And through contemplating non-existence and complete destruction.

These are the ten.

5. The Bodhisattva's Practice of the 37 Enlightenment Factors

a. The Four Stations of Mindfulness

{C} Son of the Buddha, the bodhisattva dwelling on this fourth ground employs the body-examining contemplation that takes his own body as the objective focus, employing diligent and robust mindfulness and knowing awareness[97] in ridding himself of desire and distress associated with the world. He employs the body-examining contemplation taking others' bodies as the objective focus, employing diligent and robust mindfulness and knowing awareness in ridding himself of desire and distress associated with the world. And he employs the body-examining contemplation that takes both his own body and others' bodies as the objective focus, employing diligent and robust mindfulness and knowing awareness in ridding himself of desire and distress associated with the world.

In this same manner, he also applies such contemplation to his own feelings, to the feelings of others, and to the feelings of both himself and others, applying the feeling-examining contemplation to those objective conditions.

He also applies such contemplation to his own mind, to the minds of others, and to the minds of both himself and others, employing the mind-examining contemplation to those objective conditions.

And, finally, he also applies such contemplation to subjectively-related dharmas, to objectively-related dharmas, and to dharmas that are both subjectively related and objectively related, employing the dharma-examining contemplation to those objective conditions.

Thus it is that he employs diligent and robust mindfulness and knowing awareness in ridding himself of desire and distress associated with the world.[98]

b. The Four Right Efforts

Additionally, for the sake of not generating evil and unwholesome dharmas that have not yet arisen, this bodhisattva strives to bring forth diligently applied vigor and resolves to cut off their arising.

For the sake of severing already arisen evil and unwholesome dharmas, he strives to bring forth diligently applied vigor and resolves to cut them off.

For the sake of generating good dharmas not yet arisen, he strives to bring forth diligently applied vigor and resolves to proceed with their right practice.

And for the sake of ensuring that already-arisen good dharmas will continue and not be lost, and also in order to cultivate, increase and broaden them, he strives to bring forth diligently applied vigor and resolves to engage in right practice.[99]

c. The Four Bases of Psychic Power

Additionally, this bodhisattva cultivates the severance practice associated with zeal-based concentration, this in order to completely establish the spiritual powers, doing so based upon detachment, based upon dispassion, based upon cessation, and directed toward relinquishment.[100] He also cultivates the severance practices associated with vigor-based concentration, associated with mind-based concentration, and associated with contemplation-based concentration, this in order to completely establish the spiritual powers, doing so based upon detachment, based upon dispassion, based upon cessation, and directed toward relinquishment.[101]

d. The Five Roots

Additionally, this bodhisattva cultivates the root-faculty of faith, doing so based upon detachment, based upon dispassion, based upon cessation, and directed toward relinquishment, cultivates too the root-faculty of vigor, the root-faculty of mindfulness, the root-faculty of concentration, and the root-faculty of wisdom, in all cases doing so based upon detachment, based upon dispassion, based upon cessation, and directed toward relinquishment.[102]

e. The Five Powers

Additionally, this bodhisattva cultivates the power of faith, doing so based upon detachment, based upon dispassion, based upon cessation, and directed toward relinquishment, cultivates the power of vigor, the power of mindfulness, the power of concentration, and the power of wisdom, doing so based upon detachment, based upon dispassion, based upon cessation, and directed toward relinquishment.[103]

f. The Seven Limbs of Enlightenment

Additionally, this bodhisattva cultivates the mindfulness limb of enlightenment, doing so based upon detachment, based upon dispassion, based upon cessation, and directed toward relinquishment, cultivates the dharma-differentiation limb of enlightenment, the vigor limb of enlightenment, the joyfulness limb of enlightenment, the pliancy limb of enlightenment, the concentration limb of enlightenment, and the equanimity limb of enlightenment, doing so based upon detachment, based upon dispassion, based upon cessation, and directed toward relinquishment.[104]

g. The Eightfold Path

Additionally, this bodhisattva cultivates right views, doing so based upon detachment, based upon dispassion, based upon cessation, and directed toward relinquishment. So too, he cultivates right thought, right speech, right action, right livelihood, right effort, right mindfulness, and right concentration, doing so based upon detachment, based upon dispassion, based upon cessation, and directed toward relinquishment.[105]

h. The Bodhisattva's Ten Aims in Practicing the 37 Factors

{D} The bodhisattva cultivates such meritorious qualities as these, engaging in such cultivation:

In order to refrain from forsaking all beings;
In order to be sustained by his original vows;
In order to make the great compassion foremost;
In order to perfect the great kindness;
In order to reflect upon and bear in mind the cognition of all-knowledge;
In order to completely accomplish the adornment of buddha lands;
In order to completely realize the Tathāgata's powers, fearlessnesses, dharmas exclusive to the Buddhas, major marks, subsidiary signs, and voice;
In order to further his quest to acquire the most especially supreme path;[106]
In order to accord with what he has learned regarding the extremely profound liberation of the Buddha;
And in order to reflect upon greatly wise and good skillful means.

6. The Bodhisattva's Leaving of Wrong Views, Attachments, and Actions

{E} Son of the Buddha, the bodhisattva dwelling on the Ground of Blazing Brilliance, taking the view imputing the existence of a self associated with the body as chief among them, abandons all attachments that might be generated, including attachments to the existence of a self, to a person, to beings, to a lifespan, to the aggregates, to the sense realms, and to the sense bases, doing so because they arise and disappear in reliance on conceptual thought, because they are sustained through discursive thought, because they are but subsidiary to a self, because they are but its material possessions, and because they are but points of attachment. He entirely abandons them all.

{F} Whenever this bodhisattva sees that particular karmic actions have been censured by the Tathāgata as defiled by the afflictions, he abandons all of them. Whenever he sees that particular karmic actions accord with the bodhisattva path and have been praised by the Tathāgata, he cultivates all of them.[107]

7. Mental and Personal Qualities Gained in Path Cultivation

{G} Son of the Buddha, this bodhisattva cultivates the path and the provisions assisting realization of the path[108] in a manner that befits the skillful means and wisdom he has developed. Proceeding in this manner, he thus acquires:[109]

The harmoniously smooth mind;
The gentle mind;
The congenially adaptive mind;
The mind that benefits and provides happiness to others;
The mind unmixed with defilement;
The mind that seeks ever more superior dharmas;
The mind that seeks especially supreme wisdom;
The mind that seeks to rescue everyone in the world;
The mind that respects those of venerable virtue and does not go against their teaching instructions;
And the mind that thoroughly cultivates in accordance with the Dharma one has learned.

{H} This bodhisattva:[110]

Acknowledges kindnesses received;
Knows to repay kindnesses;
Has a mind that is extremely harmonious and good;
Dwells happily together with others;
Is endowed with a character that is straight-minded;
Is gentle and pliant;
Is free of behavior influenced by the dense forest [of afflictions];
Is free of arrogance;
Is one who skillfully accepts instruction;
And is one who well understands the intentions of those whose speech he hears.

It is in this way that this bodhisattva's patience becomes completely developed, in this way that his pliancy becomes completely developed, and in this way that his quiescence becomes completely developed. Having thus acquired completely developed patience, pliancy, and quiescence, he then purifies his karmic actions on the subsequent grounds.

8. The Bodhisattva's Acquisition of Ten Kinds of Vigor

{I} At this time, as he proceeds with well-considered cultivation, he acquires:[111]

Unresting vigor;
Vigor unmixed with defiling factors;
Non-retreating vigor;
Vast vigor;
Boundless vigor;
Blazing vigor;
Matchless vigor;
Invincible vigor;
Vigor aimed at maturing all beings;
And vigor that is well able to distinguish what is and is not the path.

9. Other Qualities Developed in the Bodhisattva's 4th Ground Practice

{J} This bodhisattva's aspirations have become purified, his resolute intentions never wane, his awakened convictions are brilliant and sharp, and his roots of goodness increase.[112] He abandons the world's defiling turbidities, cuts off all doubts and uncertainties, achieves perfected clarity in severance, and is filled with delight. He is one of whom the Buddhas are protectively mindful and his resolute intentions in relation to the immeasurable minds have become fully developed.[113]

10. The Bodhisattva's Seeing and Serving of Countless Buddhas

{K} Son of the Buddha, due to the power of his vows, the bodhisattva dwelling on this Ground of Blazing Brilliance is able to see many buddhas. That is to say that he can see many hundreds of buddhas, can see many hundreds of thousands of buddhas, and so forth until we come to his seeing of many hundreds of thousands of *koṭis* of *nayutas* of buddhas, all of whom he reveres, venerates, and serves, presenting offerings to them of robes, bedding, food and drink, medicines, and all amenities supporting their existence, offering up all of these things while also making offerings to those in all their sangha assemblies, proceeding then to dedicate the merit associated with these roots of goodness to *anuttarasamyaksaṃbodhi*.

So too does he then respectfully listen to the teachings on Dharma in the presence of those buddhas. Having heard these teachings, he takes them on, upholds them in practice, and entirely perfects their cultivation. Furthermore, during the Dharma reign of those buddhas, he leaves behind the home life to cultivate the path.

11. The Bodhisattva's Purification & Its Comparison to Refining Gold

He also purifies his resolute intentions and resolute faith[114] as he passes through countless hundreds of thousands of *koṭis* of *nayutas* of kalpas wherein he causes his roots of goodness to shine ever more brightly in their purity.

Son of the Buddha, this is analogous to a goldsmith's refining of real gold to create objects of adornment unmatched in their perfection by anything made from other grades of gold. So too it is with this bodhisattva *mahāsattva*. When he dwells on this ground, all of his roots of goodness are such that none of the roots of goodness of those on lower grounds could ever match them.

12. The Radiance of This Bodhisattva's Roots Like That of a Maṇi Jewel

This circumstance is analogous to a *maṇi* jewel's orb of pure radiant light that is able to emit radiance of the sort that no other jewel's radiance can even approach, radiance that not even the conditions of wind, rain, and so forth are able to ruin. So, too, the bodhisattva *mahāsattva* dwelling on this ground cannot be matched by any of the lower ground bodhisattvas, for he cannot be destroyed by any of the many sorts of *māras* or afflictions.

13. The Bodhisattva's Practice of Means of Attraction and Pāramitās

Among the four means of attraction, this bodhisattva most extensively devotes his practice to "joint endeavors," while, among the ten *pāramitās*, he most extensively practices the perfection of vigor. It is not that he does not practice the others. Rather, he simply accords them an amount of emphasis corresponding to his own strengths and to what is fitting.

14. Vajragarbha's Statements About the 4th Ground Bodhisattva

Sons of the Buddha, this has been a concise explanation of the bodhisattva *mahāsattva*'s fourth ground, the Ground of Blazing Brilliance.

a. The Bodhisattva's Station and Dharma Practice

The bodhisattva dwelling on this ground often becomes the heavenly king Suyāma in which capacity he is equipped with skillful means by which he can influence beings to rid themselves of the view imputing the existence of a real self in association with the body[115] and other such delusions, thereby causing them to abide in right views.

b. The Bodhisattva's Mindfulness

In his practice of giving, pleasing words, beneficial actions, and joint endeavors and all other such works that he pursues, he never departs from mindfulness of the Buddha, never departs from mindfulness of the Dharma, never departs from mindfulness of the Sangha, and so forth until we come to his never departing from mindfulness of his quest to achieve complete fulfillment of the knowledge of all modes and the cognition of all-knowledge.

c. The Bodhisattva's Aspiration to Serve Beings

He also has this thought: "I should become one who serves these beings as a leader, as one who is supreme, as one who is most especially supreme, as one who is marvelous, as one who is most subtly marvelous, as one who is excellent, as one who is unexcelled," and so forth until we come to "as one who relies on the cognition of all-knowledge."

d. The Consequences of the Bodhisattva's Vigor and Vows

If this bodhisattva brings forth diligently vigorous practice, then, in but a moment, he will become able to enter a *koṭi* of samādhis, will be able to see a *koṭi* of buddhas, will become aware of the spiritual powers as exercised by a *koṭi* of buddhas, will be able to cause tremors in a *koṭi* of worlds, and so forth until we come to his being able to manifest a *koṭi* of bodies wherein each and every one of those bodies will itself become able to manifest a *koṭi* of bodhisattvas serving in his retinue. If he resorts to the power of the especially supreme vows of the bodhisattva, he will become freely able to bring forth manifestations beyond this number such that one would never be able to count them even in a period of a hundred kalpas, a thousand kalpas, and so forth until we come to a hundred thousand *koṭis* of *nayutas* of kalpas.

15. Vajragarbha Bodhisattva's Summarizing Verses

At that time, Vajragarbha Bodhisattva, wishing to once again proclaim the meaning of his discourse, thereupon uttered verses, saying:

"The bodhisattva who has already purified the third ground
next contemplates beings, the worlds, the Dharma realm,
the realms of empty space and consciousness, the three realms,
intentions, and convictions. Fathoming these, he is able to enter.[116] {7}

On first ascending to the flaming ground, as he increases in strength,
he is born into the Tathāgatas' clan through never-retreating resolve,
indestructible faith in the Buddha, Dharma, and Sangha,
contemplating dharmas as impermanent and unproduced, {8}

contemplating worlds' rise and fall, karma as the basis for birth,
saṃsāra and nirvāṇa, the karma associated with lands and such,
contemplating past and future, and also contemplating destruction.
Through just such cultivation as this, he is born in Buddha's clan.[117] {9}

After acquiring these dharmas, his kindly sympathy increases,
he redoubles diligent cultivation of the four stations of mindfulness
and their inward and outward contemplation of body, feelings, mind,
and dharmas, thus expelling and banishing all worldly desires. {10}

The bodhisattva cultivates the four right efforts by which
bad dharmas are extinguished and good dharmas are increased.
Psychic power bases, faculties, and powers are all well cultivated.
So too it is with the seven limbs of bodhi and the eightfold path.[118] {11}

He cultivates those practices in order to liberate beings, to be guarded
by original vows, to perfect kindness, to make compassion foremost,
to aid his quest for all-knowledge and adornment of buddha lands,
and also to bear in mind acquisition of the Tathāgata's ten powers, {12}

four fearlessnesses, the dharmas exclusive to the Buddhas,
their special major marks, subsidiary signs, and fine voice.
He also cultivates those practices to pursue his quest for
the sublime path's stations of liberation and great skillful means.[119] {13}

As for seeing a self related to the body, chief of the sixty-two views
that include conceiving of a self, its possessions, and countless other
attachments to aggregates, sense realms, sense bases, and such,
he abandons all of these on this fourth ground. {14}

Because they are meaningless and unbeneficial, he cuts off all
affliction-ridden actions censured by the Tathāgata,
while, of the pure karmic actions cultivated by the wise,
there are none he fails to implement in order to liberate beings. {15}

The bodhisattva, assiduous in cultivating, refrains from indolence,
straightaway achieves perfect fulfillment of ten types of mind,
focuses intently on tirelessly pursuing the path to buddhahood,
is resolute in aspiring to receive the consecration and liberate beings, {16}

respectfully follows cultivation dharmas of the venerably virtuous,
acknowledges kindness, is easily taught, is free of enmity or temper,
forsakes pride, abandons flattery, has a subdued and pliant mind,
and increases in energetic diligence that then never retreats. {17}

As for the bodhisattva dwelling on this Ground of Blazing Brilliance,
his intentions are purified and never are lost.
His awakened convictions are definite, his goodness increases, and
he entirely abandons the net of doubts and all defiling turbidity. {18}

The bodhisattva on this ground, the most supreme of all men,
makes offerings to countless *nayutas* of buddhas,
listens to their right Dharma teaching, leaves the home life,
becomes impossible to impede, and becomes like real gold. {19}

The bodhisattva abiding herein is replete with meritorious qualities.
He employs knowledge and skillful means in cultivating the path.
His resolve cannot be turned back by the many sorts of *māras*.
In this he becomes like a marvelous jewel that no one can ruin. {20}

One abiding herein often becomes Suyāma, a king of the devas who,
masterfully adept in all dharmas and revered by the multitudes,
everywhere teaches all types of beings to be rid of wrong views and
focuses on seeking Buddha's knowledge and cultivating good karma. {21}

This bodhisattva who is diligent in applying the power of vigor
acquires samādhis and other achievements, each a *koṭi* in number,
and, if he avails himself of the power of vows and knowledge, his acts
go beyond this number and exceed even the range of knowability. {22}

Thus it is that the sublime path of the bodhisattva's fourth ground,
pure in its practices and mutually consistent with
the meritorious qualities, meaning, and knowledge,
has been explained by me for the Sons of the Buddha." {23}

Part Five
The Difficult-to-Conquer Ground

E. The Fifth Ground: The Difficult-to-Conquer Ground

1. The Fifth Ground's Introductory Verses and Dharma Request

On hearing of this ground's supreme practices,
the bodhisattvas awakened to this Dharma with joyous minds.
Blossoms rained down from the sky and praises resounded, saying:
"This is good indeed, O Great Eminence, Vajragarbha." {1}

The Vaśavartin Deva King and his celestial host,
having heard this Dharma teaching, leapt up, stood in space,
and everywhere released all sorts of marvelous light clouds
as offerings to the Tathāgata, and everyone was filled with joy. {2}

The celestial nymphs played heavenly music,
sang songs in praise of the Buddha,
and then, through the awesome spiritual power of the Bodhisattva,
from amidst the sounds of their voices, they uttered these words: {3}

"The Buddha's vows, made so long ago, are now fulfilled.
The path of the Buddha, so long in its course, is now realized.
Śākyamuni Buddha has arrived at the celestial palace where
he who benefits both devas and humans, after so long, is now seen. {4}

"The Great Sea, so ancient and vast, for the first time, now moves.
The Buddha's light, so ancient and far-reaching, now shines forth.
Beings, after a long and distant past, for the first time, are happy.
The voice of the great compassion, after so long, is now heard. {5}

"[After such a long time, the Great Muni is now met.]
The far shore of all perfected qualities has been reached.
The darkness of all arrogance and pride has been dispelled
[The Great Śramaṇa, worthy of reverence, is revered.] {6}[120]

"He who is possessed of utmost purity, like empty space,
undefiled by worldly dharmas, comparable to a lotus blossom,
the Great Muni, the Honored One, appears here in this world,
like Mount Sumeru rising up from the midst of the great ocean. {8}

"By making offerings to him, one becomes able to end all suffering.
By making offerings, one certainly acquires the Buddhas' knowledge.
In this place of one worthy of offerings, we offer to one without peer.
Hence, with delighted minds, we present offerings to the Buddha." {7}

After these countless daughters of the devas
had sung these phrases in praise,
everyone there was moved to reverence and was filled with joy.
They then gazed up at the Tathāgata who dwelt there in silence. {9}

At this time, the great eminence, Liberation Moon,
again presented a request to the fearless one, Vajragarbha,
"We only pray, O Son of the Buddha, that you will explain for us
the practices and characteristic aspects of the fifth ground." {10}

2. Vajragarbha Begins the Fifth Ground's Explanation

{A} At that time, Vajragarbha Bodhisattva informed Liberation Moon Bodhisattva, saying:

3. Ten Impartial Resolute Intentions Enabling 5th Ground Access

O Son of the Buddha. The bodhisattva *mahāsattva* who has already thoroughly and perfectly fulfilled the path of the fourth ground's practices and then wishes to enter the fifth ground, the "difficult-to-conquer" ground, should progress into it through the practice of ten kinds of equally regarding pure resolute intentions.[121] What then are these ten? They are:

Equally regarding pure resolute intentions toward the Dharma of the buddhas of the past;

Equally regarding pure resolute intentions toward the Dharma of the buddhas of the future;

Equally regarding pure resolute intentions toward the Dharma of the buddhas of the present;

Equally regarding pure resolute intentions toward the moral precepts;

Equally regarding pure resolute intentions toward the mind;[122]

Equally regarding pure resolute intentions toward ridding himself of views, doubts, and regretfulness;

Equally regarding pure resolute intentions toward the knowledge of what is the path and what is not the path;

Equally regarding pure resolute intentions toward the knowledge and vision associated with cultivating the practices;

Equally regarding pure resolute intentions toward ever more superior contemplations of all the dharmas constituting the limbs of bodhi;

And equally regarding pure resolute intentions toward teaching all beings.

The bodhisattva *mahāsattva* employs these ten types of equally regarding pure resolute intentions to achieve entry into the fifth bodhisattva ground.

4. The Bodhisattva's Bases for the Irreversible Bodhi Resolve

{B} Son of the Buddha, once the bodhisattva *mahāsattva* has come to dwell on this fifth ground, then:

Due to thoroughly cultivating the dharmas of the limbs of bodhi;
Due to thoroughly purifying the resolute intentions;[123]
Due to further redoubled efforts in seeking the most supreme stations on the path;
Due to according with true suchness,
Due to being sustained by the power of vows;
Due to never relinquishing kindness and pity for all beings;
Due to accumulating the merit and knowledge constituting the provisions for realization of the path;
Due to energetic and ceaseless diligence in cultivation,
Due to bringing forth skillful means;
Due to contemplating and illuminating ever higher grounds;
Due to being guarded by the Tathāgata's protective mindfulness;
And due to being sustained by the power of mindfulness and wisdom,

He then acquires the irreversible resolve.

5. The Bodhisattva's Knowledge of the Truths

{C} Son of the Buddha, this bodhisattva *mahāsattva* knows in accordance with reality: "This is the Āryas' truth of suffering, this is the Āryas' truth of the accumulation of suffering, this is the Āryas' truth of the cessation of suffering, and this is the Āryas' truth of the path to the cessation of suffering." He:

Knows well the conventional truth;[124]
Knows well the truth of the supreme meaning;[125]
Knows well the truth of characteristic signs;[126]
Knows well the truth of differentiating distinctions;[127]
Knows well the truth of establishment;[128]
Knows well the truth of phenomena;[129]
Knows well the truth of production;[130]
Knows well the truth of cessation with no further production;[131]
Knows well the truth of the knowledge associated with entering the path;[132]
Knows well the truth of the sequential and complete cultivation of all bodhisattva grounds, and so forth on up to his knowing well the truth associated with the complete cultivation of the Tathāgata's knowledge.[133]

This bodhisattva:

- Knows the conventional truth through adapting to beings' mental dispositions and thereby causing them to be delighted;[134]
- Knows the truth of the supreme meaning through achieving a penetrating comprehension of the one true character of all phenomena;[135]
- Knows the truth of characteristic signs through comprehending the individual and shared characteristics of dharmas;[136]
- Knows the truth of differentiating distinctions through completely comprehending the distinctions in dharmas' categorical differences;[137]
- Knows the truth of establishment through skillfully distinguishing the aggregates, sense realms, and sense bases;[138]
- Knows the truth of phenomena through being aware of the suffering and anguish inherent in body and mind;[139]
- Knows the truth of production through being aware of the factors involved in the continuity of rebirths within the rebirth destinies;[140]
- Knows the truth of complete cessation with no further production through the ultimate extinguishing of all inflaming afflictions;[141]
- Knows the truth of the knowledge associated with entering the path through bringing forth the realization of non-duality;[142]
- And knows well the truth of the sequential and continuous complete cultivation of all bodhisattva grounds on up to and including the complete cultivation of the Tathāgata's knowledge, accomplishing this through having become rightly aware of all aspects of the practices.[143]

It is through the power of knowledge associated with resolute faith[144] that he knows this, for this is not yet a case of knowing accomplished through the power of ultimately final knowledge.

6. The Bodhisattva's Resultant Generation of Compassion & Kindness

{D} Son of the Buddha, after this bodhisattva *mahāsattva* has acquired the knowledge associated with these truths, he knows in accordance with reality that all conditioned dharmas are false and deceptive and that they thereby delude the foolish common person. At this time, the bodhisattva increases even more his great compassion for beings and brings forth the light of the great kindness.

7. The Bodhisattva's Contemplation of Causality in Beings' Plight

{E} Son of the Buddha, the bodhisattva *mahāsattva* who has acquired such powers of knowledge never forsakes any being and always strives to acquire the Buddha's knowledge. He contemplates in accordance with reality all past and future conditioned actions and knows that it is from prior ignorance, existence, and craving that one therefore produces the flowing on and turning about in cyclic births and deaths wherein one is unable to move to escape the house of the aggregates and thus increases one's accumulation of suffering. He knows that there is no self, no entity possessed of a lifespan, no one who grows up, and no one who yet again repeatedly takes up bodies in subsequent rebirth destinies. He knows that this all occurs entirely apart from any self or anything possessed by a self and knows that, just as this has been the case in the past, so too does it continue to be so in the future, for, in every case, none of these exist at all. And he knows whether or not there is any complete cessation and escape to be had from this covetous attachment to what is empty and false. He knows all of these matters in accordance with reality.

{F} Son of the Buddha, this bodhisattva *mahāsattva* has this additional thought:

> These common people, so deluded and devoid of wisdom, are so very pitiable. They have countless bodies that have already destroyed, are now being destroyed, and will be destroyed in the future. In this way, their bodies are all entirely destroyed and yet they are unable to bring forth any thought of renunciation toward the body, but rather instead ever increase the matters that are the mechanisms for producing suffering. Hence they flow along, following the current of births and deaths and remain unable to turn back against it.
>
> They do not seek to escape from the house of the aggregates and never know to become concerned about or fear the poisonous snakes of the four great elements. They are unable to extricate the arrows of pride and views, are unable to extinguish the fires of desire, hatred, and delusion, are unable to destroy the darkness of ignorance, and are unable to dry up the great sea of desire. They do not seek to encounter the great *ārya* and guide who possesses the ten powers but instead enter the entangling thicket of resolute intentions influenced by *māras*.[145] They then become swept up and drowned in the crashing surf of ideation and mental discursion.[146]

{G} Son of the Buddha, this bodhisattva *mahāsattva* has yet another thought:

> In their undergoing of such suffering, these beings are alone, poverty-stricken, and distressed by difficulties. They have no one to rescue them and no one to rely on. They are without an island, without a shelter, without a guide, and without eyes. They are covered over by ignorance, and enveloped in darkness. For the sake of all those beings, I shall now cultivate merit and knowledge, the dharmas constituting provisions for the path. In doing so, I bring forth this resolve alone, not seeking any companions in this. Utilizing such meritorious qualities, I shall influence beings to achieve the ultimate purification and continue in this until they acquire the Tathāgata's ten powers and unimpeded wisdom.

8. The Bodhisattva's Compassionate Dedication of Roots of Goodness

{H} Son of the Buddha, this bodhisattva *mahāsattva* employing wisdom such as this, contemplates the roots of goodness that he cultivates as being dedicated entirely for the sake of:[147]

Rescuing and protecting all beings;
Benefiting all beings;
Bringing happiness to all beings;
Bringing forth sympathetic pity for all beings;
Bringing about the complete success of all beings;
Liberating all beings;
Drawing in all beings;
Causing all beings to abandon suffering and anguish;
Causing all beings everywhere to acquire purity;
Causing all beings to adopt the training;
And causing all beings to achieve entry into *parinirvāṇa*.

9. The Fifth Ground Bodhisattva's Qualities and Their Bases

{I} Son of the Buddha, regarding the bodhisattva dwelling on this fifth ground, the Difficult-to-Conquer Ground:

He is one who is mindful, for he never forgets any dharma;
He is one who is wise, for he is able to skillfully and resolutely bring forth complete understanding;
He is one who comprehends implications, for he realizes the purport of the ideas contained in the scriptures and understands their order and their connections;
He is one possessed of a sense of shame and a dread of blame, for he guards himself while also protecting others;

He is one who is possessed of solidity, for he never abandons his practice of the moral precepts;

He is one who is possessed of awakened awareness,[148] for he is able to assess what is and is not possessed of correct bases;

He is one who accords with knowledge,[149] for he does not accord with anything aside from that;

He is one who accords with wisdom,[150] for he knows well the distinctions between principled and unprincipled statements;

He is one possessed of the spiritual superknowledges, for he skillfully cultivates the *dhyāna* absorptions;

He is one possessed of skillful means, for he is able to adapt to the ways of the world;

{J} He is one possessed of insatiability, for he pursues the thorough accumulation of merit;[151]

He is one who is unresting, for he always seeks to acquire wisdom;[152]

He is one who is tireless, for he accumulates great kindness and compassion;[153]

He is one who pursues diligent cultivation on behalf of others, for he wishes to cause all beings to achieve entry into nirvāṇa;

He is one who is possessed of unrelenting diligence in the pursuit of his quest, for he seeks the Tathāgata's powers, fearlessness, and dharmas exclusive to the Buddhas;

He is one who is able to carry out whatever he decides to do, for he perfects the adornment of the buddha lands;

He is one who diligently cultivates every sort of good karmic work, for he is able to completely fulfil [the bases for acquiring] the major marks and the subsidiary signs;

He is one who always cultivates with diligence, for he seeks to acquire the physical, verbal, and mental qualities adorning the Buddha;

He is one who greatly venerates and reveres the Dharma, for he practices in accordance with the teachings wherever all bodhisattva Dharma teachers reside;

He is one possessed of unimpeded resolve, for he adopts great skillful means as he always implements his practice in the world;

And he is one who, both day and night, abandons any other sorts of intentions, for he always delights in teaching all beings.

10. The Methods Used by the Bodhisattva in his Teaching of Beings

{K} Son of the Buddha, as the bodhisattva *mahāsattva* diligently cultivates in this manner:

He uses giving in teaching beings;
He uses pleasing words, beneficial actions, and joint endeavors in teaching beings;
He manifests form bodies in teaching beings;
He expounds on all dharmas in teaching beings;
He opens up and reveals the bodhisattva conduct in teaching beings;
He displays the immensely awe-inspiring powers of the Tathāgata in teaching beings;
He reveals the transgressions associated with *saṃsāra* in teaching beings;
He praises the benefits of the Tathāgata's wisdom in teaching beings;
He manifests the power of great spiritual superknowledges in teaching beings;
And he uses all different sorts of practices involving skillful means in teaching beings.

Son of the Buddha, even as the bodhisattva *mahāsattva* is able in this fashion to diligently employ skillful means in teaching beings, his mind constantly progresses toward the Buddha's wisdom. He never turns back in his creation of roots of goodness, but rather always diligently cultivates and trains in the most especially supreme practice dharmas.

11. The Bodhisattva's Adoption of an Array of Means to Benefit Beings

{L} Son of the Buddha, in order to be of benefit to beings, there is no worldly skill or art that this bodhisattva *mahāsattva* does not comprehensively practice. In particular, this refers to writing, mathematical calculation, drawing, writing, printing, and all of the different sorts of treatises devoted to the elements of earth, water, fire, and wind, all of which he completely comprehends. He is also thoroughly skilled in medicinal prescriptions and the treatment of all diseases, including insanity, the wasting diseases, possession by ghosts, and poisoning at the hands of sorcerers, all of which he is able to dispel. He is thoroughly skilled in all such matters as literary compositions, praises, chants, singing, dance, musical performance, humor, and explanatory discussion.

He is also skilled in the placement and arrangement of states, cities, villages, palaces, homes, parks, gardens, springs, flowing waters, reservoirs, ponds, grasses, trees, flowers, and medicinal plants so that they each find their most appropriate location. He also knows the hidden locations of gold, silver, *maṇi* jewels, pearls, lapis lazuli, conch shells, jade, coral, and other such things that he brings forth and reveals for others.

He is also skilled in the contemplative assessment of all such things as the sun, the moon and stars, the cries of birds, earthquakes, the auspicious or inauspicious significance of dreams, and the good and bad fortune associated with physical features, never erring even once in his judgment on these matters.

In order to benefit them and gradually influence them to become securely established in the unsurpassed Dharma of the Buddha, he thoroughly explains and reveals for beings such matters such as the observance of moral precepts, entry into the *dhyāna* absorptions, the spiritual superknowledges, the immeasurables, and the four formless absorptions as well as all other sorts of other matters having to do with the world. In this, his sole concern is that he never act in a manner harmful or distressing to beings.

12. The Bodhisattva's Seeing and Serving of Countless Buddhas

{M} Son of the Buddha, due to the power of his vows, the bodhisattva dwelling on this Difficult-to-Conquer Ground becomes able to see many buddhas. Specifically, he becomes able to see many hundreds of buddhas, many thousands of buddhas, many hundreds of thousands of buddhas, and so forth until we come to his becoming able to see many hundreds of thousands of *koṭis* of *nayutas* of buddhas, to all of whom he offers up his reverence, veneration, service, and offerings of robes, food and drink, bedding, medicines, and all amenities facilitating their lives and also makes offerings to all their Sangha assemblies. He dedicates all the merit associated with these roots of goodness to *anuttarasamyaksaṃbodhi* and, wherever those buddhas dwell, he goes and reverently listens to their teachings on Dharma, whereupon, having heard them, he accepts and upholds those teachings and cultivates them in a manner befitting his powers to do so.

13. The Bodhisattva's Purification of His Roots of Goodness

Additionally, during the Dharma reign of those buddhas, he leaves the home life and, having left the home life, he listens to yet more teachings on Dharma, acquires *dhāraṇīs*, and becomes a master of the Dharma who, having heard the Dharma, upholds it and abides on this ground, passing through a hundred kalpas, passing through a thousand kalpas, and so forth up to the point that he even passes through countless hundreds of thousands of *koṭis* of *nayutas* of kalpas during which all of his roots of goodness shine forth with ever increasing brightness.

14. Good Roots Purification Like Refining Gold & Celestial Phenomena

Son of the Buddha, this is analogous to real gold that, as it is polished with *musāragalva*[154] to an ever more brilliant luster, shines forth with ever brighter purity. So too it is with all of the roots of goodness accumulated by this bodhisattva who dwells on this ground. As he employs his skillful means and wisdom in contemplative meditation, they shine forth with ever brighter purity.

Son of the Buddha, in the case of the bodhisattva who dwells on this Difficult-to-Conquer Ground, his use of skillful means and wisdom in perfecting meritorious qualities is such that the roots of goodness developed on lower grounds cannot even approach.

Son of the Buddha, this is just as with the sun, moon, stars, constellations, and the radiance of the celestial palaces wherein the wind-like forces supporting them are so irresistibly strong that none of the other winds could even slightly alter their course. So too it is with all the roots of goodness of the bodhisattva dwelling on this ground. Through his use of skillful means and wisdom in pursuing contemplative meditation, he becomes so invincible that he cannot be even slightly deflected from his path by anyone with only the roots of goodness of any *śrāvaka*-disciple, *pratyekabuddha*, or worldly being.

15. The Bodhisattva's Practice of the Pāramitās

Among the ten *pāramitās*, this bodhisattva most extensively practices the perfection of *dhyāna*. It is not that he does not practice the others. Rather, he simply accords them an amount of emphasis corresponding to his own strengths and to what is fitting.

16. Vajragarbha's Final Statements About the 5th Ground Bodhisattva

Son of the Buddha, this has been a general explanation of the bodhisattva *mahāsattva*'s, fifth ground, the Difficult-to-Conquer Ground.

a. The Bodhisattva's Station and Dharma Practice

The bodhisattva dwelling on this ground often becomes a Tuṣita Heaven king, one who in his interactions with other beings is possessed of sovereign mastery in all that he does. He utterly defeats in debate all proponents of the wrong views set forth by non-Buddhist traditions and he is able to influence other beings to abide in the real truth.

b. The Bodhisattva's Mindfulness

In his practice of giving, pleasing words, beneficial actions, joint endeavors, and all other such endeavors, he never departs from mindfulness of the Buddha, never departs from mindfulness of the Dharma, never departs from mindfulness of the Sangha, and so forth until we come to his never departing from mindfulness of his quest to achieve complete fulfillment of the knowledge of all modes and the cognition of all-knowledge.

c. The Bodhisattva's Aspiration to Serve Beings

He also has this thought: "I should become one who serves these beings as a leader, as one who is supreme, as one who is most especially supreme, as one who is marvelous, as one who is most subtly marvelous, as one who is excellent, as one who is unexcelled," and so forth until we come to "as one who relies on the cognition of all-knowledge."

d. The Consequences of the Bodhisattva's Vigor and Vows

If this bodhisattva brings forth diligently vigorous practice, then, in but a moment, he will become able to enter a thousand *koṭis* of samādhis, will be able to see a thousand *koṭis* of buddhas, will become aware of the spiritual powers as exercised by a thousand *koṭis* of buddhas, will be able to cause tremors in a thousand *koṭis* of worlds, and so forth until we come to his being able to manifest a thousand *koṭis* of bodies wherein each and every one of those bodies will itself be able to manifest a thousand *koṭis* of bodhisattvas serving in his retinue.

If he resorts to the power of the especially supreme vows of the bodhisattva, he will become freely able to bring forth manifestations beyond this number, such that one would never be able to count them even in a period of a hundred kalpas, a thousand kalpas, and so forth until we come to a hundred thousand *koṭis* of *nayutas* of kalpas.

17. Vajragarbha Bodhisattva's Summarizing Verses

At that time, Vajragarbha Bodhisattva, wishing to once again proclaim the meaning of his discourse, thereupon uttered verses, saying:

> The bodhisattva who has achieved the fourth ground's purification
> with equal dispositions contemplates the buddhas of the three times,
> precepts, the mind, riddance of doubt, what is and is not the path,
> and, through such contemplations, enters the fifth ground. {11}

With stations of mindfulness as bow, sharpness of roots as arrows,
the right efforts as steed, the bases of psychic powers as his chariot,
and the five powers as sturdy shield, he crushes hostile adversaries,
and, with unretreating heroic valor, he enters the fifth ground. {12}

With senses of shame and blame as robes, limbs of bodhi as garland,
pure moral precepts as incense, *dhyāna* meditation as perfume,
wisdom and skillful means as marvelous adornments,
he enters the *dhāraṇī* forest and the samādhi gardens. {13}

With psychic powers as his feet, right mindfulness as his neck,
kindness and compassion as his eyes, and wisdom as his teeth,
with the roar of "non-self," the lion among men
crushes the affliction adversaries, and then enters the fifth ground. {14}

The bodhisattva dwelling on this fifth ground
increases cultivation of the most supremely pure path,
is irreversible in his determined quest for the Buddha's Dharma, and
tireless in contemplative mindfulness of kindness and compassion. {15}

He gathers the supreme qualities of merit and wisdom, possesses
energetic diligence and skillful means, contemplates higher grounds,
is aided by Buddha's powers, embodies mindfulness and wisdom,
and utterly knows all four truths in accordance with reality. {16}

He knows well worldly truth, the truth of the supreme meaning,
the truths of characteristic signs, distinctions, and establishment,
the truths of phenomena, production, cessation, the path, and so on
up to the truth of what, for the Tathāgata, is unimpeded.[155] {17}

Although such contemplation of truths is subtle and marvelous,
he has not yet realized the unimpeded supreme liberation.
In this way, he is able to generate great meritorious qualities
and therefore steps entirely beyond the sphere of worldly wisdom. {18}

Having contemplated these truths, he realizes conditioned existence,
by its very nature, is false, deceptive, and devoid of solid reality.
He acquires the Buddha's radiant aspects of kindness and pity,
and seeks Buddha's knowledge in order to benefit beings. {19}

He contemplates prior and later periods in conditioned existence
as beset by the darkness of ignorance and bound by bonds of craving
by which one flows onward cyclically, abiding in a mass of suffering,
wherein there is no self, no person, and no entity with a lifespan. {20}

Craving and grasping are causes of their receiving future suffering
that, if one wished to seek its end, one could never find it.
"Confused by the false, they float on, never going against the flow.
Beings such as these are so pitiable. I should see to their liberation." {21}

In the house of aggregates, snakes of sense realms, arrows of views,
the mind's flames blaze fiercely and delusion's darkness is heavy.
They drift and swirl in love's river with no leisure to contemplate it,
and, bereft of a brilliant guide, sink in the sea of suffering's waters. {22}

Having realized such things as these, he becomes diligent in vigor
and dedicates all of his actions to the liberation of beings.
He becomes one possessed of mindfulness, possessed of wisdom,
and so on up to his becoming one aware of the means of liberation. {23}

He is insatiable in his cultivation of merit and wisdom,
tireless in his reverence for extensive learning,
and pursues adornment of all lands, the major marks, and the signs.
All such deeds are done for the sake of beings. {24}

For the sake of teaching everyone in the world,
he knows well methods of writing, mathematics, printing and such,
also well understands medicinal prescriptions
and the treatment of the many diseases, all of which he can cure, {25}

is marvelously skilled in all literary composition, songs, and dance,
assists secure placement of all palaces, homes, parks, and ponds,
shows others all locations of hidden jewels of not just a single sort,
and does all of this for the sake of benefiting countless beings. {26}

He interprets the omens of the sun, moon, stars, earthquakes,
and other such things, including even people's physical features,
and, in order to be of benefit to the world, reveals for them the
four *dhyānas,* formless absorptions, and spiritual superknowledges. {27}

Those wise ones who dwell on this Difficult-to-Conquer Ground
make offerings to *nayutas* of buddhas and listen to their Dharma.
Hence, just as when one uses a marvelous jewel to polish real gold,[156]
all of their roots of goodness shine ever more brightly in their purity. {28}

Just as the stars and constellations residing in space,
supported by wind-like forces, are not shaken out of place,
and just as the blooming lotus is not attached to its waters,
so too does this great eminence travel along in the world. {29}

Dwelling herein, he often becomes a Tuṣita Heaven King,
well able to utterly refute the wrong views of non-Buddhist paths.
The goodness he cultivates is done to acquire the Buddha's wisdom
and he vows to acquire the ten powers to thereby rescue beings. {30}

He redoubles his cultivation of great vigor
and so straightaway makes offerings to a thousand *koṭis* of buddhas,
gains absorptions and shakes lands just as numerous as they are,
and, through power of vows, surpasses even such numbers as these. {31}

Thus it is that, using the power of all different sorts of skillful means,
this Difficult-to-Conquer Ground, the fifth ground
within the most supreme and genuine of all paths for humans,
has been explained by me for the Sons of the Buddha. {32}

Part Six
The Direct Presence Ground

F. The Sixth Ground: The Direct Presence Ground

1. The Sixth Ground's Introductory Verses and Dharma Request

Having heard this teaching of supreme practices, the bodhisattvas'
minds were filled with joy, they rained down marvelous blossoms,
emanated pure light, sprinkled down precious jewels
as offerings to the Tathāgata, and praised his excellent discourse. {1}

A hundred thousand assembled devas, full of celebratory delight,
at once scattered down from space the many jewels as offerings,
together with floral garlands, strands of pearls, banners,
jeweled canopies, and perfumes, all offered there to the Buddha. {2}

The Vaśavartin Heaven King, together with his retinue,
all with minds filled with joyous delight, stood above in space,
scattered jewels forming a cloud holding their offerings, praised him,
and said, "O Buddha's Son, may you soon proclaim this teaching." {3}

Countless celestial nymphs residing above in space
together made offerings of music and song in praise of the Buddha
wherein one heard amidst their voicings such words as these:
"The Buddha's discourse can expel the disease of the afflictions. {4}

The nature of dharmas is originally quiescent, devoid of all signs,
and like empty space in that one makes no discriminations therein.
It transcends all attachments, reaches beyond the path of words,
and is genuine, uniformly equal, and eternally pure. {5}

If one can completely comprehend the nature of dharmas,
his mind is unmoved by what exists or by what does not exist
as he cultivates diligently to rescue the inhabitants of the world.
This is a true son of the Buddha, born from the Buddha's mouth. {6}

He does not seize on the various marks in his practicing of giving,
fundamentally cuts off all evil, and solidly upholds the precepts.
Knowing the Dharma, he is thus free of harming and always patient.
Knowing dharmas as by nature transcendent,[157] he is perfect in vigor. {7}

Having ended the afflictions, he enters the *dhyānas*, and, in making
distinctions about dharmas, knows well they are devoid of a nature.
Replete in wisdom power, he is able to extensively rescue beings and,
being rid of the many evils, he gains renown as a great eminence." {8}

Having used such marvelous voices of a thousand myriad sorts
in offering praises, they then fell silent and gazed up at the Buddha. {9}
Liberation Moon then set forth the request to Vajragarbha, "Through
which practice attributes does one enter the next ground?" {10}

2. Vajragarbha Commences the Sixth Ground's Explanation

{A} Vajragarbha Bodhisattva then informed Liberation Moon Bodhisattva, saying:

3. The Ten Dharmas of Identity Enabling Access to the Sixth Ground

O Son of the Buddha, the bodhisattva *mahāsattva* who has already completely fulfilled the fifth ground's practices and then aspires to enter the sixth ground, the Ground of Direct Presence, should then take up the contemplation of ten dharmas of identity.[158] What then are those ten? As follows, all dharmas:[159]

Are the same due to their signlessness;
Are the same due to their non-substantiality;
Are the same due to their being unproduced;
Are the same due to their being unborn;
Are the same due to their original purity;
Are the same due to their being beyond frivolous intellectual ideation;
Are the same due to their being beyond either grasping or relinquishing;
Are the same due to their quiescence.
Are the same due to their being like a conjured illusion, like a dream, like a shadow, like an echo, like the moon reflected on water, like an image in a mirror, like a mirage, and like a magical transformation; [160]
And are the same due to the non-duality in their existence and non-existence.

4. Sixth Ground Entry, Acquiescent Patience & Primacy of Compassion

The bodhisattva who contemplates all dharmas in this way realizes their nature is pure and practices in a manner that is consistent with this and that is free of anything that contradicts this. He thereby succeeds in entering the sixth ground, the Ground of Direct Presence, and acquires the acquiescent patience characterized by clarity and acuity.[161] Even so, he has not yet reached the realization of the unproduced-dharmas patience.

{B} Son of the Buddha, once this bodhisattva *mahāsattva* has come to contemplate in this manner, he then additionally takes the great compassion as what is foremost, the great compassion as what is to be made predominant, and the great compassion as what is to be brought to complete fulfillment.

5. The Bodhisattva's Contemplation of Causality in Cyclic Existence[162]

{C} He contemplates production and extinction as it takes place in the world, thinking, "Taking on rebirth in the world in every case arises through attachment to a self. Were one to abandon this attachment, then there would no longer be any basis for being reborn."

a. Contemplation of the Sequential Continuity of the Causal Factors

He additionally thinks:[163]

> Common people, so unknowing, are attached to a self, always seek existence or non-existence, engage in wrong thought, pursue falsely-based actions, and follow erroneous paths wherein they accumulate and increase offense-generating actions, merit-generating actions, or imperturbable actions.[164] Through all courses of actions, they plant mental seeds associated with the contaminants and with the *grasping* that further precipitates subsequent *becoming, birth, aging,* and *death*. This is a circumstance said to be one wherein one's karmic *volitional actions* serve as a field, one's *consciousness* serves as seeds, *ignorance* keeps them covered in darkness, the water of *cravings* moistens them, and pride in oneself irrigates them.
>
> As the net of views grows, the sprout of *name-and-form* is produced. As *name-and-form* develop, the five physical sense faculties are formed. With the oppositional impingement [of sense objects] on the sense faculties, *contact* is produced. This impingement-generated *contact* produces *feeling*. Subsequent wishing for further *feeling* produces *craving*. Increased *craving* brings about *grasping*. An increase in *grasping* produces *becoming*. Having produced *becoming*, it is one's generating of the five-aggregate bodies as one courses in the various destinies that constitutes *birth*, the deterioration following upon *birth* that constitutes *aging*, and the culmination of this process in mortality that brings about *death*. When *aging* and *death* arrive, one is seized by intense mental torment and, on account of this intense mental torment, one is then beset by distress, worry, sorrowful lamentation, and the accumulation of a multitude of sufferings.
>
> Because this is all simply a product of causes and conditions, there is no entity for whom this accumulation takes place, and, even as this process proceeds on to destruction, there is still no existent entity that is destroyed, either.

The bodhisattva pursues just such an investigative contemplation of the characteristic features of causally-based origination.

b. The Bodhisattva Contemplates the Definitions of Causal Links

{D} Son of the Buddha, this bodhisattva *mahāsattva* also thinks thus:

> It is the failure to utterly comprehend the ultimate truth that defines *ignorance*.
>
> It is the fruition of karmic actions one has done that constitutes *volitional actions*.
>
> The initial mental factor dependent on *volitional actions* is what constitutes *consciousness*.
>
> The additional four appropriated aggregates arising together with *consciousness* are what constitute *name-and-form*.
>
> The development of *name-and-form* creates *the six sense bases*.
>
> The conjunction of the three phenomena of *sense faculties*, *sense objects*, and *consciousnesses*, constitutes *contact*.
>
> Arising simultaneously with *contact*, there exists *feeling*.
>
> The forming of a defiled attachment for *feeling* is what constitutes *craving*.
>
> Based on an increase in *craving*, *grasping* then occurs.
>
> Those karmic actions associated with the contaminants that arise as a consequence of *grasping* are what constitute *becoming*.
>
> The arising of the aggregates resulting from such karmic actions is what constitutes *birth*.
>
> The progressive maturation of the aggregates is what constitutes *aging*.
>
> When the aggregates perish, this is what constitutes *death*.
>
> The confusion and fond attachment attendant on the separation occurring at the time of dying that then manifest as agitation and depression of the heart—this is what is meant by *worry*.
>
> Weeping and sniveling attended by regretful sighing—this is what is meant by *lamentation*.
>
> That which occurs based on the five physical sense faculties constitutes *pain*, whereas what occurs based on the intellectual mind faculty constitutes *distress*.
>
> As distress and pain increase they result in *mental torment*.
>
> In such circumstances as these, there is only a growing tree of suffering. There is no self in this, nothing belonging to a self, no agent of actions, and no entity undergoing experiences.

He has this additional thought: "If an agent of actions exists, then there exists an endeavor that is done. If no agent of actions exists, then there does not exist any endeavor that is done. From the perspective of ultimate truth, neither of them can even be found."

c. The Bodhisattva's Contemplation of Mind As the Basis of Existence

{E} Son of the Buddha, this bodhisattva *mahāsattva* has this additional thought:

> Everything throughout the three realms of existence is only mind. {F} Where the Tathāgata has, within this, distinguished and expounded upon these twelve factors comprising the bases of existence, they in every case rely on a single thought and are established on just such a basis. How is this the case?
>
> In accordance with particular circumstances, desire arises together with the mind. In this, the mind constitutes the *consciousness,* whereas the particular circumstances themselves constitute the basis of *volitional actions.* The confusion that exists regarding *volitional actions* constitutes *ignorance.* That which is produced from the cooperation of *ignorance* and the mind is *name-and-form.* That which develops from *name-and-form* is *the six sense bases.* The three-fold conjunction that occurs in association with *the six sense bases* constitutes *contact.* That which arises together with *contact* is *feeling.* Insatiability with respect to such *feeling* constitutes *craving. Craving* that becomes focused and is not relinquished culminates in *grasping.* That which all of these branches comprising existence produce is *becoming.* That which *becoming* brings forth is *birth.* The maturation of what has been born constitutes *aging.* The perishing brought on through *aging* is *death.*

d. The Contemplation of 2 Functions of Each Causal Chain Link

{G} Son of the Buddha, among these, *ignorance* has two types of karmic functions: First, it causes beings to be confused with respect to objective conditions. Second, it serves as a cause for the initiation of *volitional actions.*

Volitional actions also have two types of functions: First, they are capable of generating future retributions. Second, they serve as causes for the initiation of *consciousness.*

Consciousness also has two types of functions: First, it causes continuity of *becoming.* Second, it serves as a cause for the initiation of *name-and-form.*

Name-and-form also have two types of functions: First, they are mutually cooperative in their establishment. Second, they serves as the cause for the initiation of *the six sense bases.*

The six sense bases also have two types of functions: First, each of them clings to its own respective objective sense realm. Second, they serve as the cause for the initiation of *contact.*

Contact also has two types of functions: First, it is capable of touching its objective condition. Second, it serves as the cause for the initiation of *feeling.*

Feeling also has two types of functions: First it is capable of serving as the recipient of experiences that are craved, detested, and so forth. Second, it serves as the cause for the initiation of *craving.*

Craving also has two types of functions: First, it consists of a defiled attachment to whatsoever circumstances are deemed desirable. Second, it serves as the cause for the initiation of *grasping.*

Grasping also has two types of functions: First, it causes continuity of the afflictions. Second, it serves as the cause for the initiation of *becoming.*

Becoming also has two types of functions. First, it is capable of causing rebirth into the other destinies. Second, it serves as the cause for the initiation of *birth.*

Birth also has two types of functions. First, it is able to generate the aggregates. Second, it serves as the cause for the initiation of *aging.*

Aging also has two types of functions. First, it causes all of the sense faculties to undergo change. Second, it serves as the cause for the onset of *death.*

Death also has two types of functions. First, it is capable of destroying all actions. Second, because there is then no conscious awareness, it allows this process to continue on and not be cut off.

e. The Contemplation of Causal Chain Production and Destruction

{H} Son of the Buddha, in this circumstance wherein *ignorance* serves as a condition for *volitional actions,* and so on till we have *birth* serving as a condition for *aging-and-death,* it is because *ignorance* and so on up to *birth* serve as conditions that there then occurs the causation of *volitional actions* and so on up to *aging-and-death.* This occurs on account of [the prior conditions'] ceaseless facilitation of the establishment [of the subsequent conditions].

f. Contemplation of The 12 Links' association with inseparability.

In the circumstances wherein, "if *ignorance* is extinguished, then *volitional actions* will be extinguished," and so forth until we come to "if *birth* is extinguished, then *aging-and-death* will be extinguished," this occurs because, in those circumstances, *ignorance* and so forth on up to *birth,* do not then any longer serve as conditions causing the initiation of *volitional actions* and so on up to *aging-and-death.* This extinguishing through severance occurs because there no longer occurs the [prior condition's] facilitating establishment [of the subsequent condition].

g. The Twelve Links As Constituents of Three Paths

{I} Son of the Buddha, among these, ceaseless *ignorance, craving,* and *grasping* constitute *the path of the afflictions.* Ceaseless *volitional actions* and *becoming* constitute *the path of karmic actions.* The ceaseless occurrence of the remaining factors constitutes *the path of suffering.* Analytic extinguishing of these prior and subsequent factors facilitates severance of all three paths.[165] [The factors comprising] these three paths exist apart from any self or possessions of a self and exist only as a process of production and extinction wherein they are analogous to standing sheaves of mutually-supporting reeds.[166]

h. The Twelve Links' Correlation With the Three Periods of Time

{J} Additionally, where *ignorance* serves as the condition for the occurrence of *volitional actions,* this refers to past circumstances. The factors of *consciousness* on up to and including *feeling* refers to present circumstances. The factors of *craving* and so forth on up to and including *becoming* refer to future circumstances. Henceforth there occurs the unfolding of an ongoing continuity.

In those instances where the cessation of *ignorance* precipitates cessation of *volitional actions,* this is a case of severance occurring due to the dependency [of the latter conditions upon the prior conditions].

i. The Twelve Links' Correlation With the Three Kinds of Suffering

{K} Additionally, the twelve factors comprising the bases of existence are synonymous with *the three sufferings.* Among these, *ignorance, volitional actions,* and so forth on up to and including *the six sense bases* collectively constitute *the suffering associated with the karmic formative factors.*[167] *Contact* and feeling constitute *the suffering of suffering.*[168] The remaining factors constitute *the suffering of deterioration.*[169]

j. Contemplation of their arising & ceasing by causes and conditions

Where the cessation of *ignorance* brings about the cessation of *volitional actions,* these three types of suffering are then cut off.

{L} Additionally, in *ignorance*'s serving as a condition for the generation of *volitional actions,* ignorance is the cause and condition that can produce all manner of *volitional actions.* As for the circumstance wherein, once *ignorance* is extinguished, *volitional actions* are then extinguished, it is because, once there is an absence of *ignorance*, there are then no *volitional actions*, either. This same circumstance holds for all of the remaining factors as well.

k. Contemplation of their Creation and Destruction of the Bonds

Also, in *ignorance's* serving as a condition for the generation of *volitional actions*, this conduces to the generation of bondage. Where, with the extinguishing of *ignorance, volitional actions* are then extinguished, this then brings about the extinguishing of this bondage. This same principle holds for all of the remaining factors as well.

l. Contemplation of "Utter Nonexistence" and "Utter Cessation"

Then again, in *ignorance's* serving as a condition for the generation of *volitional actions*, this is a circumstance adaptable to the "nonexistence of anything whatsoever" contemplation. Where, with the extinguishing of *ignorance, volitional actions* are then extinguished, this is a circumstance adaptable to the "utter cessation of everything" contemplation. This same principle holds for all of the remaining factors as well.

m. A Summary Listing of 10 Contemplations of the 12 Causal Factors

{M} Son of the Buddha, the bodhisattva *mahāsattva* thus engages in ten types of sequential and counter-sequential contemplation of the factors involved in conditioned arising,[170] specifically:[171]

Contemplation of the sequential continuity in the existential factors.
Contemplation of their all being reducible to the one mind.
Contemplation of their each having their own distinct function.
Contemplation of their inseparability.
Contemplation of the non-severance of the three paths.[172]
Contemplation of their relationship to the past, the present, or the future.
Contemplation in terms of the accumulation of the three kinds of suffering.
Contemplation of their arising and ceasing through causes and conditions.
Contemplation in terms of the creation and destruction of bondage.
Contemplation in terms of "utter nonexistence" and "utter cessation."

6. The Bodhisattva's Acquisition of the Three Gates to Liberation

{N} Son of the Buddha, the bodhisattva *mahāsattva* contemplates everything within the realm of conditioned arising in accordance with these ten characteristics. Thus he realizes that there is no self, no person, and no lifespan, that there is an absence of any inherently existent nature, and that there is also no agent of actions or anyone who undergoes experiences. He then immediately acquires the direct manifestation of *the emptiness gate to liberation*.[173]

He contemplates all of the factors associated with becoming as having the nature of cessation, as ultimately synonymous with liberation, and as not having even the smallest dharma characteristic that they produce. He then immediately acquires the direct manifestation of *the signlessness gate to liberation*.[174]

Having thus gained entry into both emptiness and signlessness, he then becomes entirely free of anything at all that he seeks with the sole exception of taking the great compassion as foremost in the transformative teaching of beings. He then immediately acquires the direct manifestation of *the wishlessness gate to liberation*.[175]

Thus it is that, in his cultivation of *the three gates to liberation*, the bodhisattva abandons conceptions of the existence of either others or a self, abandons conceptions of either any agent of actions or anyone who undergoes experiences, and abandons the conceptions of anything as either existent or nonexistent.

7. The Bodhisattva's Compassionate Reluctance to Enter Final Nirvāṇa

{O} Son of the Buddha, this bodhisattva *mahāsattva*'s great compassion progressively increases. He is energetically diligent in his cultivation and, for the sake of bringing about the complete fulfillment of those factors facilitating bodhi he has not yet completely fulfilled, he reflects thus:

> All conditioned things possess an ongoing existence through a circumstance involving the conjunction of factors. Where there is no such circumstance involving the conjunction of factors, there is then no ongoing existence. When the conditions gather together, they may then possess an ongoing existence. When those conditions do not gather together, there is no ongoing existence.
>
> Thus I realize that, since conditioned dharmas are beset by many faults, I should cut off this conjunction of causes and conditions. However, for the sake of facilitating the successful

development of other beings, I shall nonetheless refrain from bringing about the ultimate extinguishing of all volitional actions.

Son of the Buddha, thus it is that the bodhisattva contemplatively investigates all conditioned things as possessed of many faults, as devoid of any inherently existent nature, as neither produced nor destroyed, and yet he nonetheless constantly generates the great compassion, refrains from abandoning beings, and then straightaway acquires the direct manifestation of the *prajñāpāramitā* known as the light of unimpeded wisdom.

Having successfully acquired such wisdom light, although he cultivates the causes and conditions related to the factors facilitating bodhi, he still refrains from abiding in the realm of conditioned things. And although he contemplates the nature of conditioned dharmas as that of quiescent cessation, he still does not abide in quiescent cessation either. This is because he has not yet achieved the complete fulfillment of the dharmas that lead to the realization of bodhi.

8. The Bodhisattva's Samādhis Related to the 3 Gates to Liberation

{P} Son of the Buddha, the bodhisattva who dwells on this Ground of Direct Presence succeeds in entering:[176]

The penetration of emptiness samādhi;
The emptiness of any inherently existent nature samādhi;
The emptiness of the supreme meaning samādhi;
The foremost emptiness samādhi;
The great emptiness samādhi;
The emptiness of unities samādhi;
The emptiness of production samādhi;
The reality-accordant non-discriminating emptiness samādhi;
The non-abandonment emptiness samādhi;
And the transcendent yet not transcendent emptiness samādhi.

With these ten emptiness samādhis as foremost among them, this bodhisattva acquires the direct manifestation of every one of a hundred thousand emptiness samādhis. In this same way, with ten signlessness samādhis and ten wishlessness samādhis as foremost, he also acquires the direct manifestation of every one of a hundred thousand signlessness and wishlessness samādhis.

9. The Bodhisattva's Ten Types of Resolute intentions

{Q} Son of the Buddha, the bodhisattva who dwells on this Ground of Direct Presence also cultivates and completely perfects:[177]

The indestructible resolute intention;[178]
The definitely certain resolute intention;
The resolute intention of pure goodness;
The especially profound resolute intention;
The non-retreating resolute intention;
The unrelenting resolute intention;
The vast resolute intention;
The boundless resolute intention;
The knowledge-seeking resolute intention;
And the resolute intention joining skillful means and wisdom.

In every case, he brings all of these to a state of perfect fulfillment.

10. 10 Consequences of the Bodhisattva's 10 Types of Resolute intentions

{R} Son of the Buddha, in availing himself of these types of resolute intentions, the bodhisattva:

Accords with the bodhi of the Buddhas;
Remains unfrightened by encounters with proponents of deviant doctrines;
Enters all the grounds of knowledge;
Abandons the paths of the Two Vehicles;
Progresses toward the knowledge of the Buddha;
Remains invulnerable to obstruction or ruination by any of the afflictions or *māras*;
Abides within the light of the bodhisattva's wisdom;
Skillfully cultivates and implements all the dharmas of emptiness, signlessness, and wishlessness;
In every case skillfully engages in the constantly conjoined practice of skillful means and wisdom;
And always implements and never relinquishes the dharmas assisting the realization of bodhi.

11. The Bodhisattva's Prajñāpāramitā Practice and Patience Acquisition

{S} Son of the Buddha, the bodhisattva abiding on this Ground of Direct Presence acquires an especially supreme degree of realization in the practice of *prajñāpāramitā* and acquires the third of the patiences, the clear and sharp acquiescent patience,[179] this because of acting in accordance with and not contrary to the true character of dharmas.

12. The Bodhisattva's Seeing and Serving of Countless Buddhas

Son of the Buddha, because of the power of his vows, the bodhisattva who has come to dwell on this Ground of Direct Presence succeeds in seeing many buddhas, that is to say, he can see many hundreds of buddhas and so forth until we come to his seeing of many hundreds of thousands of *koṭis* of *nayutas* of buddhas. In every instance, with a vast mind and a profound mind, he makes offerings to them, pays reverence to them, venerates them, praises them, and presents them with robes, food and drink, bedding, medicines, and all amenities supporting their existence, offering up all of these things while also making offerings to those within all their sangha assemblies. He then proceeds to dedicate the merit associated with these roots of goodness to *anuttarasamyaksaṃbodhi*.

So too does he then respectfully listen to the teachings on Dharma in the presence of those buddhas. Having heard these teachings, he takes them on and retains them, gains reality-concordant samādhis and the light of wisdom, and then accords with these in his cultivation, bearing them in mind and never relinquishing them.

13. Purifying Good Roots Like Polishing Gold & Moonlight's Coolness

He also gains access to the Buddhas' treasuries of extremely profound Dharma and, passing through a hundred kalpas, passing through a thousand kalpas, and so forth on up to incalculably many hundreds of thousands of *koṭis* of *nayutas* of kalpas, his roots of goodness shine ever more brightly in their purity just as when a goldsmith uses a lapis lazuli gem to repeatedly polish real gold, causing it to shine with ever more brilliant purity. So too it is with all the roots of goodness of the bodhisattva who dwells on this ground. Through his use of skillful means and wisdom, in a manner corresponding to his pursuit of meditative contemplation, they become ever brighter and ever more imbued with quiescence to the point where they cannot be outshone by anyone and become like the light of the moon that shines on the bodies of beings and causes them to experience a sense of pristine coolness that the four kinds of wind are incapable of diminishing.

So too it is with all the roots of goodness of the bodhisattva on this ground who is able to use them to extinguish the blazing fires of affliction burning in incalculably many hundreds of thousands of *koṭis* of *nayutas* of beings. In this, they remain invulnerable to destruction by the paths of any of the four kinds of *māras*.

14. The Bodhisattva's specialization in the Prajñāpāramitā

Among the ten *pāramitās*, this bodhisattva most extensively practices the *prajñā pāramitā*. It is not that he does not practice the others. Rather, he simply accords them an amount of emphasis corresponding to his own strengths and to what is fitting.

15. Vajragarbha's final Statements About the 6th Ground Bodhisattva

Sons of the Buddha, this has been a general explanation of the bodhisattva *mahāsattva*'s, sixth ground, the Ground of Direct Presence.

a. The Bodhisattva's Station and Dharma Practice

The bodhisattva dwelling on this ground often becomes a king of the Skillful Transformations Heaven[180] who, sovereignly masterful in all that he does, is one who cannot be driven into retreat or submission by any questioning challenge posed by any *śrāvaka*-disciple. He is able to influence beings to do away with arrogance and to deeply enter into a comprehension of conditioned origination.

b. The Bodhisattva's Mindfulness

In his practice of giving, pleasing words, beneficial actions, and joint endeavors, and in all such works that he pursues, he never departs from mindfulness of the Buddha, and so forth until we come to his never departing from mindfulness of his quest to achieve complete fulfillment of the knowledge of all modes and the cognition of all-knowledge.

c. The Bodhisattva's Aspiration to Serve Beings

He also has this thought: "I should become one who serves these beings as a leader, as one who is supreme," and so forth until we come to "as one who relies on the cognition of all-knowledge."

d. The Consequences of the Bodhisattva's Vigor and Vows

If this bodhisattva brings forth diligently vigorous practice, then, in but a moment, he will be able to enter hundreds of thousands of *koṭis* of samādhis, and so forth until we come to his becoming able to transformationally manifest a hundred thousand *koṭis* of bodhisattvas to serve as his retinue. If he resorts to the power of vows, he will become freely able to manifest them in numbers beyond even this, such that one would never be able to count them even in a period of hundreds of thousands of *koṭis* of *nayutas* of kalpas.

16. Vajragarbha Bodhisattva's Summarizing Verses

At that time, Vajragarbha Bodhisattva, wishing to once again proclaim the meaning of his discourse, thereupon uttered verses, saying:

After entirely fulfilling the fifth ground's practices, the bodhisattva
sees dharmas as the same due to their being signless, natureless,
unproduced, unborn, originally pure,
beyond frivolous ideation, beyond grasping or relinquishing, {11}

quiescent in substance and signs, and illusory, as well as
non-dual and beyond discrimination as existent or non-existent.
Thus contemplating in accordance with the nature of dharmas,
those with this knowledge succeed in entering the sixth ground. {12}

With clear and acute acquiescent patience and replete in knowledge,
he contemplates the world's aspects of production and destruction,
the world's production by the power of delusion's darkness, and sees,
if delusion's darkness were destroyed, the world would not exist. {13}

He contemplates all causes and conditions as, in reality, empty, yet
does not contradict artificial names' use in designating constructs.
Even as there is no doer, no recipient, and no thinker of thoughts,
all actions arise and spread forth everywhere like clouds. {14}

Failure to know the actual truth constitutes *ignorance*.
The *volitional actions* that are done are the fruit of delusion.
That which arises together with *consciousness* is *name-and-form*.
Thus it proceeds on forth until the manifold sufferings accumulate. {15}

He utterly comprehends the three realms exist dependent on mind,
that the same is true of the twelve causes and conditions,
that birth and death in every case are created because of mind,
and that, if the mind itself is extinguished, then birth and death end. {16}

That which *ignorance* brings about is in every case of two types:
Non-comprehension of conditions and the causes of *actions*,
This is so all the way through to *aging*'s end in *death*.
Suffering is generated endlessly from this. {17}

So long as *ignorance* serves as a condition, these cannot be cut off, but,
if that condition is brought to an end, then these are all extinguished.
Ignorance, craving, and *grasping* are the factors belonging to afflictions.
Actions and *becoming* form karma, and the rest are suffering. {18}

Ignorance up to *the six sense bases* relate to *formative-factor suffering*.
The proliferation of *contact* and *feeling* forms *the suffering of suffering*.
The rest of the existential factors relate to *the suffering of deterioration*.
If one sees non-existence of "self," all three sufferings are destroyed. {19}

Ignorance and *actions* both pertain to the past,
Consciousness on through to *feeling* continually unfold in the present.
Craving, grasping, and *becoming* generate future suffering.
If their interdependence is severed, such temporal phases all end. {20}

When *ignorance* serves as a condition, it is this that creates the bonds.
Through abandoning such conditions, the bonds are thus ended.
Effects are produced from causes, but if abandoned, they are cut off.
Closely contemplating this, one realizes they are, by nature, empty. {21}

Through following the course of *ignorance*, all existence arises.
If one but refrains from following its course, all existence is cut off.
If this exists, then that exists. So too it is for nonexistence as well.
Through the ten reflections, the mind abandons its attachments: {22}

Continuity of existential factors; traceability to a single thought;
individual karma; inseparability; non-severance of three paths;
three times, three sufferings; generation by causes and conditions;
the rising and passing of the fetters; nonexistence and cessation. {23}

Thus he universally contemplates the course of conditioned arising,
realizing that it is devoid of any actor, recipient, or reality,
that it is like a conjuration, like a dream, like shadows,
or like a circumstance wherein a fool chases after a mere mirage. {24}

Through just such analytic contemplation, he enters emptiness,
knows conditions as, by nature, separate, realizes signlessness,
utterly comprehends their falseness, and becomes free of any wish
with the sole exception of the desire to act with kindness for beings. {25}

Thus this great eminence cultivating the three gates to liberation
ever increases great compassion and his quest for Buddha's Dharma.
He realizes all conditioned things are created as an assemblage and,
with resolute fondness for it, resolves to diligently practice the path. {26}

He acquires a hundred thousand emptiness samādhi gateways and
gains the same number for signlessness and wishlessness as well.
His *prajñā* and acquiescent patience both become ever more superior,
and his liberations and wisdom reach complete fulfillment. {27}

With a deep mind, he also makes offerings to many buddhas
and cultivates the path through the instruction of those buddhas.
He gains Buddhas' Dharma treasuries enhancing roots of goodness
just as when gold is subjected to polishing with a lapis lazuli gem. {28}

Just as when the moon's pure and cool radiance shines on beings,
though the four winds may blow, none are able to interfere with it,
so too, this ground's bodhisattvas step over the paths of Māra
and extinguish the heat of all beings' afflictions. {29}

On this ground, he is often King of the Fine Transformations Heaven,
one who teaches and guides beings in doing away with pridefulness.
All endeavors he pursues are done to seek all-knowledge and they all
have already overstepped and become superior to the *śrāvaka* path. {30}

The bodhisattva on this ground who is diligent in practice of vigor
acquires hundreds of thousands of *koṭis* of samādhis
and is also able to see countlessly many buddhas
that appear to him like suns shining in the midsummer sky. (31)

This is extremely profound, sublime, and so difficult to know or see
that no *śrāvaka*-disciple or *pratyekabuddha* could ever fully fathom it.
So it is that I have here explained the bodhisattva's sixth ground
for the sake of the Sons of the Buddha. (32)

Part Seven
The Far-Reaching Ground

G. The Seventh Ground: The Far-Reaching Ground

1. The Seventh Ground's Introductory Verses and Dharma Request

Then the congregated devas, their minds filled with joy,
scattered jewels that formed a cloud hanging up in the sky,
whereupon they all sang with different sorts of sublime voices
addressed to The Most Supremely Pure One, saying: {1}

"Fully penetrating the supreme meaning with masterful knowledge
and perfected in a hundred thousand *koṭis* of fine qualities,
a lotus among men, entirely free of any attachments,
proclaims here the profound practices to benefit all beings." {2}

The Vaśavartin Heaven King, abiding there in space,
emanated a great light that illuminated the Buddha's body
and spread forth the most superior sorts of sublime incense clouds,
all presented as offerings to he who dispels worries and afflictions. {3}

Then, the entire congregation of devas, all of them joyful,
all sang beautiful sounds in a united chorus of praises:
"Having heard here of the qualities comprising this ground, we
have thence all reaped immense and fine benefit." {4}

Then the celestial nymphs, their minds full of celebratory delight,
vied in chorusing forth a thousand myriad musical sounds and then,
as all of them availed themselves of the Tathāgata's spiritual powers,
amidst all those sounds, they joined in uttering phrases like these: {5}

"With peerless awe-inspiring presence and quiescent stillness, he
can train those difficult to train, is worthy of the world's gifts,
and, though he has already transcended all worlds,
he still travels forth in the world, extolling the marvelous path. {6}

"Although he manifests incalculably many bodies of every kind,
he realizes each and every body is itself devoid of any existence.
He is skillful in the use of phrases in his explanation of all dharmas,
yet does not seize on any signs of words or sounds. {7}

"He goes forth to a hundred thousand buddha lands and
presents all the most supreme gifts as offerings to those buddhas.
Through sovereign mastery of knowledge, he is free of all attachment
and so does not generate any conception of 'my own buddha land.' {8}

"Although diligent in the teaching of all beings,
he does not have any thought conceiving of either 'other' or 'self.'
Although he has already cultivated vast goodness to perfection,
he still does not generate any attachment to good dharmas. {9}

"Because he perceives that all worlds are always fiercely ablaze
with the fires of desire, hatred, and stupidity,
he has utterly transcended all forms of thought even as
he still brings forth the great compassion and the power of vigor." {10}

After all of those devas and celestial nymphs
had finished presenting all different sorts of offerings and praises,
they all simultaneously fell silent and stood there,
gazing up at the most revered of men, wishing to hear the Dharma. {11}

At that time, Liberation Moon Bodhisattva again set forth a request:
"The minds of everyone in this assembly are pure.
We wish only, O Son of the Buddha, that you will explain for us
the practices and characteristic aspects of the seventh ground." {12}

2. Vajragarbha Commences the Seventh Ground's Explanation

At that time, Vajragarbha Bodhisattva addressed Liberation Moon Bodhisattva, saying:

3. 10 Types of Skillful Means & Wisdom Enabling 7th Ground Access

{A} O Son of the Buddha. The bodhisattva *mahāsattva* who has already completed the sixth ground's practices and then aspires to gain entry into the seventh ground, the Far-Reaching Ground, should proceed in the cultivation of ten kinds of skillful means and wisdom,[181] thereby bringing forth the most especially supreme path. What then are those ten? Specifically, they are:

Although he has skillfully cultivated the emptiness, signlessness, and wishlessness samādhis, through the practice of kindness and compassion, he refrains from forsaking beings;

Although he has acquired the Buddhas' dharma of uniform equality, he still delights in always making offerings to buddhas;

Although he has entered the gateway to wisdom of emptiness contemplation, he still diligently pursues the accumulation of merit;

Although he has become detached from the three realms of existence, he still engages in the adornment of the three realms of existence;

Although he has achieved the final extinguishing of the flames of all afflictions, he is still able for the sake of all beings to bring forth the means to extinguish the flames of their greed, hatred, and delusion;

Although he realizes that all dharmas are like conjurations, like dreams, like shadows, like echoes, like mirages, like transformations, like the moon reflected on water, and like images in a mirror, and realizes too that, in their essential nature, they are non-dual, he still accords with his resolve by performing works of countless different sorts;

Although he realizes that, by their very nature, all lands are like empty space, he is still able to use pure and sublime practices to adorn the buddha lands;

Although he realizes that the fundamental nature of all buddhas' Dharma body is free of any "body," he still adorns his own body with the major marks and subsidiary signs;

Although he realizes that, by its very nature, the voice of all buddhas is empty of inherent existence, quiescent, and ineffable, he is still able to accord with all beings by bringing forth for them many different sorts of pure voices;

And although he accords with all buddhas' complete fathoming of the three periods of time as reducible to but a single thought, he still accords with the differences in beings' minds and understandings by manifesting in many different sorts of appearances, many different temporal circumstances, and many different sorts of kalpas wherein he cultivates all the practices.

It is by resort to ten such types of skillful means and wisdom that the bodhisattva brings forth the especially supreme practices by which he leaves the sixth ground and enters the seventh ground. Once he has entered there, these practices always manifest directly before him and henceforth define his abiding on the seventh ground, the Far-Reaching Ground.

4. The Bodhisattva's Twenty Kinds of Penetrating Comprehension

{B} Son of the Buddha, after the bodhisattva *mahāsattva* has achieved entry into the seventh ground:

He acquires a penetrating comprehension of the measurelessly many realms of beings;

He acquires a penetrating comprehension of the measurelessly many works carried out by the Buddhas in their teaching of beings;

He acquires a penetrating comprehension of the measurelessly many networks of worlds;

He acquires a penetrating comprehension of the Buddhas' measurelessly many pure lands;

He acquires a penetrating comprehension of the measurelessly many different sorts of dharmas;[182]

He acquires a penetrating comprehension of the measureless knowledge manifested by the Buddhas' enlightenment;[183]

He acquires a penetrating comprehension of the enumeration of the measurelessly many kalpas;

He acquires a penetrating comprehension of the measureless knowledge of the three periods of time to which the Buddhas have awakened;

He acquires a penetrating comprehension of beings' measurelessly many different sorts of resolute convictions;

He acquires a penetrating comprehension of the measurelessly many different sorts of name-and-form bodies manifested by the Buddhas;[184]

He acquires a penetrating comprehension of the differences in beings' measurelessly many different mental dispositions and faculties;

He acquires a penetrating comprehension of the measurelessly many languages and voices through which the Buddhas' inspire delight in beings;

He acquires a penetrating comprehension of beings' measurelessly many different courses of thought;

He acquires a penetrating comprehension of the Buddhas' measurelessly many sorts of utterly complete understanding of vast knowledge;

He acquires a penetrating comprehension of the measurelessly many sorts of resolute convictions of adherents of the Śrāvaka-disciple Vehicle;

He acquires a penetrating comprehension of the measurelessly many proclamations of the path of wisdom set forth by the Buddhas in inspiring resolute faith;

He acquires a penetrating comprehension of the measurelessly many accomplishments of *pratyekabuddhas*;

He acquires a penetrating comprehension of the Buddhas' measurelessly many proclamations of gateways of extremely profound wisdom that cause others to enter therein;

He acquires a penetrating comprehension of the bodhisattvas' measurelessly many practices of skillful means;

And he acquires a penetrating comprehension of the measurelessly many works accumulated and accomplished in the Great Vehicle that, when described by the Buddhas, then influence bodhisattvas to enter into them.

5. His Adoption of Effortlessness, Non-Discrimination & Meditation

{C} This bodhisattva reflects thus: "Such measureless domains of the Tathāgatas as these could never be known even in a hundred thousand *koṭis* of *nayutas* of kalpas. I should therefore rather resort to the effortless and non-discriminating mind to succeed in achieving their perfect fulfillment."

{D} Son of the Buddha, employing deep wisdom, this bodhisattva engages in such contemplative meditations as these whereby he always diligently cultivates these forms of skillful means and wisdom and thus brings forth this especially supreme path wherein he becomes so securely and unshakably established in it that there is not so much as a single moment in which he rests or desists. While walking, standing, sitting, lying down, and even in the midst of sleep and dreams, he never even briefly involves himself with any of the hindrances and he never abandons thought such as this.

6. His Practice of 10 Pāramitās & Other Dharmas Leading to Bodhi

In each successive moment, this bodhisattva is always able to completely fulfill the ten *pāramitās*. And how is this the case? This is because he takes the great compassion as foremost in every successive mind-moment as he cultivates the Buddha's Dharma and proceeds toward realization of the Buddha's knowledge. In particular:

He bestows on beings all roots of goodness he develops in the course of seeking to acquire the Buddha's knowledge. This is what constitutes *dāna pāramitā.*

He is able to extinguish the heat of the afflictions. This is what constitutes *śīla pāramitā.*

Taking kindness and compassion as foremost, he refrains from inflicting harm on beings. This is what constitutes *kṣānti pāramitā.*

He is insatiable in seeking supremely good dharmas. This is what constitutes *vīrya pāramitā.*

He always keeps the path of all-knowledge directly present before him, never becoming scattered or distracted. This is what constitutes *dhyāna pāramitā.*

He is able to patiently acquiesce in all dharmas as neither produced nor destroyed. This is what constitutes *prajñā pāramitā.*

He is able to bring forth measureless knowledge. This is what constitutes the *pāramitā* of skillful means.

He is able to seek out higher and higher levels of knowledge. This is what constitutes the *pāramitā* of vows.

None of the deviant doctrines or hordes of *māras* are ever able to obstruct him or bring about his ruination. This is what constitutes the *pāramitā* of powers.

He utterly knows all dharmas in accordance with reality. This is what constitutes the *pāramitā* of knowledge.

Son of the Buddha, this bodhisattva is able to completely fulfill all of these ten *pāramitās* in every successive mind-moment. It is in this way that, in each successive mind-moment, he is able to completely fulfill the four means of attraction, the four types of retention,[185] the thirty-seven factors conducing to enlightenment, the three gates to liberation, and, to state it briefly, all dharmas assisting the realization of bodhi.

7. Vimukticandra Asks About Perfection of Bodhyaṅga Dharmas

{E} At that time, Liberation Moon Bodhisattva asked Vajragarbha Bodhisattva, saying, "O Son of the Buddha. Is it only on this seventh ground that the bodhisattva fulfills all dharmas assisting realization of bodhi?[186] Or is it rather that he is also able to completely fulfill them on all grounds?"

8. Vajragarbha on the Perfection of Bodhyaṅgas on All Grounds

Vajragarbha Bodhisattva then replied:

O Son of the Buddha. The bodhisattva is able to completely fulfill the dharmas facilitating realization of bodhi on all ten grounds. Still, it is on the seventh ground where this ability becomes most especially supreme in its implementation. How is this the case? This is because it is on this seventh ground that his effortfully implemented practice becomes complete, thereby enabling his entry into practice characterized by sovereign mastery in wisdom.[187]

O Son of the Buddha, on the first ground, it is because of his aspiration taking all Buddha dharmas as its object that the bodhisattva perfects the dharmas assisting realization of bodhi.

On the second ground, this occurs due to his abandonment of the mind's defilements.

On the third ground, this occurs due to the ever increasing strength of his vows and due to his acquiring the light of the Dharma.

On the fourth ground, this occurs through his entry into the path.

On the fifth ground, this occurs through his adaptation to the ways of the world.

On the sixth ground, this occurs through his entry into the extremely profound Dharma gateways.

On the seventh ground, it is due to bringing forth all Buddha dharmas and completely fulfilling all dharmas assisting realization of bodhi.

{F} How is this the case? From the first ground through the seventh ground, the bodhisattva achieves the complete development of the effortfully implemented preliminary practice factors conducive to knowledge. It is due to the power produced by this that, from the eighth ground to the tenth ground, all of his effortless practices then become completely developed.

Son of the Buddha, It is as if there were two worlds of which one is characterized by admixture with defilements whereas the other is entirely pure and it is difficult to pass between them, the sole exception being in the case of the bodhisattva who possesses the powers of great skillful means, spiritual superknowledges, and vows.

Son of the Buddha, so too it is with the grounds of the bodhisattva wherein there are those in which the practices are admixed with defilement and there are those in which the practices are pure. It is difficult for anyone to pass between these two with the sole exception of the bodhisattva possessed of great vow power, skillful means, and wisdom who only then is able to pass between them.

9. Vimukticandra Asks About Transcendence of Afflictions

Liberation Moon Bodhisattva then asked, "O Son of the Buddha. Does this seventh ground bodhisattva engage in defiled practices or does he instead engage in pure practices?"

10. Vajragarbha Explains the Transcendence of Afflictions

Vajragarbha Bodhisattva replied:

O Son of the Buddha. From the first ground to the seventh ground, all practices in which he engages involve abandoning affliction-related actions. This is because they are directed toward realizing unsurpassably supreme bodhi. However, because he has still only achieved a partial realization corresponding to the level of his position on the path, this still cannot be referred to as stepping completely beyond all affliction-related actions.

11. Vajragarbha's Cakravartin Sage King Analogy

Son of the Buddha, this circumstance is comparable to that of a wheel-turning sage king who mounts his precious heavenly elephant and roams the four continents. In doing so, he becomes well aware that there are poverty-stricken people in difficult straits who are afflicted with suffering, even as he himself remains unsullied by those many disastrous situations. In such a circumstance, he would still not qualify as having truly stepped entirely beyond the position of being human.

Suppose, however, that he were to relinquish the body in which he serves as a king and then take rebirth in the Brahma Worlds where he would mount a heavenly palace from which he could view a thousand worlds as he roams throughout a thousand worlds manifesting the radiance and awesome qualities of a Brahma Heaven deva. In such a case, he would only then truly qualify as having stepped entirely beyond the station of being human.

Son of the Buddha, so too it is with the bodhisattva. Beginning with the first ground and going on through to the seventh ground, he mounts the vehicle of the *pāramitās*. As he roams about in the world, he becomes well aware of all the world's afflictions, faults, and disastrous aspects. Because he rides along on the path of right conduct, he remains unsullied by the faults associated with the afflictions. Still, he does not yet truly qualify as having stepped entirely beyond actions associated with afflictions.

However, if he were to then relinquish all of the effortfully implemented preliminary practices, he would then go forth from the seventh ground and enter the eighth ground and would then travel through the world mounted on the pure vehicle of the bodhisattva wherein he would be cognizant of the faults associated with the afflictions and yet would still remain unsullied by them. It is only then that he would qualify as having truly stepped entirely beyond the practices associated with the afflictions, this due to his having successfully stepped beyond them all.

Son of the Buddha, in coming to abide on this ground, this seventh ground bodhisattva has stepped entirely beyond the many sorts of afflictions such as abundant desire and the other sorts of afflictions. Abiding on this ground, he is not designated as someone who possesses the afflictions and yet he is not designated as entirely devoid of the afflictions, either. How is this the case? This is because, since none of the afflictions directly manifest in his practice, he is not designated as possessing them. However, because he seeks to acquire the Tathāgata's knowledge and his intentions have not yet become completely fulfilled, he is not yet designated as entirely free of them, either.

{G} Son of the Buddha, through profound purified intentions, the bodhisattva abiding on the seventh ground perfects his physical karma actions, perfects his verbal karmic actions, and perfects mental karmic actions. He has already entirely abandoned all bad courses of karmic action criticized by the Tathāgata and he always thoroughly cultivates all good courses of karmic actions praised by the Tathāgata. As for everything related to the world's classical texts, skills, and arts, his actions here are as described earlier in relation to the fifth ground. He naturally practices all of these without having to expend any particular effort in doing so.

This bodhisattva serves as a greatly illustrious teacher for those throughout the worlds of a great trichiliocosm, one who, with the sole exceptions of the Tathāgatas and those on the eighth ground and above, is unmatched by any of the other bodhisattvas in his resolute intentions and the marvelousness of his practice. All of the *dhyāna* samādhis, *samāpattis*, spiritual superknowledges, and liberations become directly manifest for him. Still, their cultivation and development here is not like that occurring on the eighth ground wherein they become completely realized as a function of karmic reward. In every successive mind-moment, the bodhisattva on this ground completely cultivates the power of skillful means and wisdom as well as all dharmas assisting realization of bodhi, all of which become ever more supremely fulfilled herein.

12. The Conquest of Samādhis and Unproduced-Dharmas Patience

{H} Son of the Buddha, the bodhisattva abiding on this ground enters:[188]

The bodhisattva's skillful investigative contemplation samādhi;
The skillful consideration of meanings samādhi;
The most supreme intelligence samādhi;
The distinguishing of the treasury of meanings samādhi;
The distinguishing of meaning in accordance with reality samādhi;
The skillful abiding in solidly established roots samādhi;
The gateway to knowledge and spiritual superknowledges samādhi;
The works throughout the Dharma realm samādhi;
The supreme benefit of the Tathāgata samādhi;
And the samādhi of the treasury of many different meanings and the gateway to *saṃsāra* and nirvāṇa.

He enters hundreds of myriads of samādhis such as these that are gateways to complete fulfillment of great knowledge and spiritual superknowledges whereby he is able to carry out the purifying cultivation of this ground.

{I} Having acquired these samādhis, due to thoroughly purifying skillful means and wisdom and due to the power of the great compassion, this bodhisattva steps beyond the Two Vehicles' grounds and reaches the wisdom contemplation ground.[189]

{J} Son of the Buddha, because the bodhisattva dwelling on this ground well purifies countless signlessness practices related to physical karma, well purifies countless signlessness practices related to verbal karma, and well purifies countless signlessness practices related to mental karma, he consequently acquires the light of the unproduced-dharmas patience.

13. Vimukticandra: "Doesn't the 1st Ground Surpass the Two Vehicles?"

Liberation Moon Bodhisattva then asked, "O Son of the Buddha. How could it be that all of the measurelessly many physical, verbal and mental deeds performed by each of the bodhisattvas from the first ground onward have not already stepped entirely beyond the Two Vehicles' practices?"

14. Vajragarbha: "In Aspiration, Yes. By Virtue of Practice, Not Yet"

Vajragarbha Bodhisattva then replied:

Son of the Buddha, all of those bodhisattvas do step entirely beyond them, however, they do so only due to their aspiration to acquire the Dharma of all buddhas. It is not due to their own cognition's power of meditative contemplation.[190] Now, however, on this seventh ground, it itw, however, on this seventh ground, this occurs by virtue of their own power of wisdom.n.of the Buddhas. It is not by firtue os because of their own power of cognition that Two Vehicles practitioners are unable to even approach them.

15. Vajragarbha's Analogy of a Prince Not Yet Ascended to Power

This circumstance is analogous to that of a prince born of a queen into the house of a king entirely possessed of all of the marks of a king. Right at birth, he is immediately deemed superior even to all of the government ministers. This, however, is solely due to the power associated with kingship and not due to any power he as yet possesses himself. If as he grows to adulthood he becomes accomplished in the various sorts of skills, it will only then be due to his own powers that he steps entirely beyond everyone else.

So too it is with the bodhisattva *mahāsattva*. When he first brings forth the resolve, because he has established the great Dharma as the goal of his determination, he right then steps entirely beyond all *śrāvaka*-disciples and *pratyekabuddhas*. Now, in dwelling on this ground, it is due to the power of wisdom that he surpasses all adherents of the Two Vehicles.

16. This Bodhisattva's Unique Practice & Restraint From Final Nirvāṇa

{K} Son of the Buddha, the bodhisattva dwelling on this seventh ground acquires the ability to engage in extremely profound and secluded non-practice even as he still always practices deeds of body, speech, and mind through which he diligently pursues the supreme path, thus never abandoning that quest. Therefore, although the bodhisattva practices in accordance with ultimate reality,[191] he still refrains from bringing about its complete realization.

17. Vimukticandra: "When Can One Enter The Cessation Samādhi?"

{L} Liberation Moon Bodhisattva then asked, "O Son of the Buddha. Beginning with which ground can the bodhisattva enter the cessation concentration?"

18. Vajragarbha: "From the 6th Ground; Now He Enters & Arises at Will"

Vajragarbha Bodhisattva replied:

Son of the Buddha, it is from the sixth ground onward that the bodhisattva has the ability to enter the cessation concentration. Now, as he abides on this ground, he can enter it in each successive mind-moment and can also arise from it in each successive mind-moment and yet still refrain from bringing about its complete realization. So it is that this bodhisattva is known as one who has completely developed inconceivable deeds of body, speech, and mind.

19. Vajragarbha Likens Practice To Sailing on the Open Ocean

His practicing in accordance with ultimate reality even while still refraining from bringing about its complete realization is analogous to someone who sets sail in a boat out onto the open ocean and who then, by resorting to the power of his skillfulness, remains able to avoid disastrous difficulties out on those waters. So too it is with the bodhisattva dwelling on this ground. He sets sail in the ship of the *pāramitās* out onto the ocean of ultimate reality and, in doing so, through his reliance on the power of vows, he still refrains from bringing about the complete realization of cessation.

20. 10 Paradoxical Aspects of the 7th Ground Bodhisattva's Practice

{M} Son of the Buddha, having acquired powers of samādhi and knowledge such as these, he employs great skillful means by which:

Although he manifests within *saṃsāra*, he still constantly abides in nirvāṇa;

Although surrounded by a retinue, he still always delights in detachment;

Although, by resort to the power of vows, he takes birth in the three realms, he still remains undefiled by worldly dharmas;

Although he always abides in a state of quiescence, through the power of skillful means, he is as if ablaze, but, although ablaze, he remains unburned;

Although he proceeds in accordance with the knowledge of the Buddha, he may still manifest entry into the grounds of the Śrāvaka-disciples and the Pratyekabuddhas;

Although he has acquired the treasury of the Buddha's realms of cognition,[192] he may still manifest as dwelling in the realms of *māras*;[193]

Although he has stepped beyond the paths of the *māras*, he may still manifest as practicing the dharmas of *māras*;

Although he may manifest practices identical to those of non-Buddhist traditions, he still never relinquishes the Dharma of the Buddha;

Although he manifests in ways that adapt to those in all worlds, he still always practices all world-transcending dharmas;

And although all of his adorning phenomena[194] surpass anything possessed by any of the devas, dragons, *yakṣas*, *gandharvas*, *asuras*, *garuḍas*, *kinnaras*, *mahoragas*, humans, non-humans, Śakra Devānām-Indra, the Brahma Heaven King, the Four Heavenly Kings, or anyone else, he still never relinquishes the mind that delights in the Dharma.

{N} Son of the Buddha, the bodhisattva who has completely developed wisdom such as this abides on the Far-Reaching Ground.

21. The Bodhisattva's Seeing and Serving of Countless Buddhas

Due to the power of his vows he succeeds in seeing many buddhas, that is to say, he can see many hundreds of buddhas and so forth until we come to his seeing of many hundreds of thousands of *koṭis* of *nayutas* of buddhas. He goes forth wherever those buddhas dwell and then, with a vast mind and with an especially supreme mind, he makes offerings to them, pays reverence to them, venerates them, praises them, presents them with robes, food and drink, bedding, medicines, and all amenities supporting their existence, offering up all of these things while also making offerings to those within all of their sangha assemblies. He then dedicates the merit associated with these roots of goodness to *anuttarasamyaksaṃbodhi*. So too does he then respectfully listen to the teachings on Dharma in those places where those buddhas dwell. Having heard these teachings, he takes them on and retains them, gains reality-concordant samādhis and the light of wisdom, and then accords with these in his cultivation.

Wherever the Buddhas dwell, he guards and preserves right Dharma. He is always one whom the Tathāgatas praise and express delight in. No proponent of the Two Vehicles can cause him to retreat or prevail over him through questioning or challenging him. His benefiting of beings purifies his realization of the patience with respect to dharmas. He passes through incalculably many hundreds of thousands of *koṭis* of *nayutas* of kalpas in this way during which all of his roots of goodness achieve ever greater supremacy.

22. Good Roots Purification Likened to Gold Inlay and Sunlight

This circumstance is comparable to when one inlays in real gold many sorts of marvelous gems as adornments, thereby making it ever more superior in quality and thereby redoubling its radiance to the point that no other article of adornment can rival it in these respects. All of the roots of goodness of the bodhisattva who dwells on the seventh ground are of just this very sort. Employing the power of skillful means and wisdom, he brings them to a state of ever increasing brightness and purity unrivaled by any followers of the Two Vehicles.

Son of the Buddha, this circumstance is comparable to the light of the sun which the light cast by the stars, the moon, and other heavenly bodies cannot even approach it in its brilliance that is even able to dry up all of the marshes on the entire continent of Jambudvīpa. So too it is with the bodhisattva on this Far-Reaching Ground who cannot be rivaled by any follower of the Two Vehicles, for he is able to entirely dry up all of the marshes of delusion possessed by all beings.

23. The 7th Ground Bodhisattva's Focus on Skillful Means Pāramitā

Among the ten *pāramitās*, this bodhisattva most extensively practices the *pāramitā* of skillful means. It is not that he does not practice the others. Rather, he simply accords them an amount of emphasis corresponding to his own strengths and to what is fitting.

24. Vajragarbha's Final Statements About the 7th Ground Bodhisattva

Son of the Buddha, this has been a general explanation of the bodhisattva *mahāsattva*'s seventh ground, the Far-Reaching Ground.

a. The Bodhisattva's Station and Dharma Practice

The bodhisattva dwelling on this ground often becomes a Vaśavartin Heaven king who, through skillfully explaining for beings the means to achieve the realization of knowledge, thereby influences them to realize it and enter therein.

b. The Bodhisattva's Mindfulness

In his practice of giving, pleasing words, beneficial actions, and joint endeavors and in all such works that he pursues, he never departs from mindfulness of the Buddha, and so forth until we come to his never departing from mindfulness of his quest to achieve complete fulfillment of the knowledge of all modes and the cognition of all-knowledge.

c. The Bodhisattva's Aspiration to Serve Beings

He also has this thought: "I should become one who serves these beings as a leader, as one who is supreme," and so forth until we come to "as one who relies on the cognition of all-knowledge."

d. The Consequences of the Bodhisattva's Vigor and Vows

If this bodhisattva brings forth diligently vigorous practice, then, in but a moment, he will become able to enter hundreds of thousands of *koṭis* of samādhis, and so forth until we come to his becoming able to transformationally manifest hundreds of thousands of *koṭis* of bodhisattvas to serve as his retinue. If he resorts to the especially supreme power of the bodhisattva's vows, he will become freely able to manifest them in numbers beyond even this even to the point that one could never calculate their number even in a period of hundreds of thousands of *koṭis* of *nayutas* of kalpas.

25. Vajragarbha Bodhisattva's Summarizing Verses

At that time, Vajragarbha Bodhisattva, wishing to once again proclaim the meaning of his discourse, thereupon uttered verses, saying:

As, on the path of the supreme meaning's knowledge and samādhi,
his sixth ground mind cultivation reaches complete fullness,
he straightaway perfects skillful means and wisdom.
It is due to this that the bodhisattva enters the seventh ground. {13}

Though awakened to three liberations, he is kind and compassionate.
Though the same as *tathāgatas,* he is diligent in offerings to Buddhas.
Though contemplating emptiness, he still accumulates merit.
Through these things, a bodhisattva ascends to the seventh ground. {14}

He has become detached from the three realms yet still adorns them.
He's put out his own delusions' fires, yet douses others' fires as well.
He knows dharmas' non-duality and yet is diligent in doing works.
He fathoms all lands as empty, yet delights in adorning lands. {15}

Even knowing the body as unmoving, he embodies all of its signs.
Though aware voice's nature is transcendent, he is skilled in discourse.
Though he fathoms all as one thought, he distinguishes all matters.
It is due to this that the wise ascend to the seventh ground. {16}

Closely contemplating these dharmas, he gains utter illumination,
broadly brings forth benefit for the multitudes who are so confused,
and enters the boundlessly many realms of beings as well as
the Buddhas' acts of transformative teaching that are also countless. {17}

All lands, all dharmas, and all categories of kalpas,
beings' convictions and mental dispositions—he enters them all,
proclaiming Three Vehicles Dharma in a manner equally boundless,
carrying on in this way the teaching of all the multitudes of beings. {18}

The bodhisattva diligently pursues the supreme path
and, moving or still, never forsakes skillful means and wisdom.
He dedicates each and every act to gaining Buddha's bodhi,
and, in each successive mind-moment, he perfects the *pāramitās.* {19}

Generating the resolve and making dedications constitute giving.
Extinguishing delusions is moral virtue and non-harming is patience.
Insatiable pursuit of goodness—this is vigor's goad.
Being unshakable on the path is the cultivation of *dhyāna.* {20}

Patient acquiescence in the unproduced is what constitutes prajñā.
Dedicating merit constitutes skillful means. Aspirations form vows.
Invincibility is the mark of powers. Skillful fathoming is knowledge.
It is in this way that he develops all of these to complete fullness. {21}

On the first ground, grasping fine qualities' conditions is fulfilled.
On the second, one abandons defilement. The third: Disputes cease.
On the fourth, one enters the path. The fifth: Practice is compliant.
On the sixth, light shines from wisdom that fathoms the unproduced. {22}

On the seventh, merit from the bodhi practices becomes full
and all the different types of great vows become perfectly complete.
It is because of this that one is able to cause
everything one does on the eighth ground to become entirely pure. {23}

This ground is difficult to traverse. With wisdom, one steps beyond.
This is analogous to going between two worlds and
also like a sage king's degree of freedom from defiling attachment,
for it does not yet qualify as totally stepping beyond it. {24}

When he comes to abide on the eighth ground of knowledge
he then passes on beyond those domains of mind.
As Brahmā deva, viewing the world, steps beyond the human realm,
and like a lotus atop the water, he is free of defiling attachments. {25}

Although on this ground one oversteps the many sorts of afflictions,
one is not said either to have afflictions or to be free of afflictions.[195]
This is because there are no afflictions that are active therein even as
the mind seeking Buddha's knowledge has not yet become fulfilled. {26}

He entirely fathoms all of the many types of worldly skills,
the classical texts, books, literary skills, and polemics while, as for the
dhyāna concentrations, samādhis, and spiritual superknowledges,
he cultivates all such endeavors to the point of complete mastery. {27}

In cultivating and perfecting the path of the seventh ground,
the bodhisattva steps entirely beyond all Two Vehicles' practices.
First ground success arises from vows. Here it is from knowledge.
This is analogous to a prince whose powers are utterly perfected. {28}

Though perfect in the very profound, he still advances on the path.
His every moment is quiescent cessation, yet he forgoes realization.
It is just as when one goes forth in a boat out into the open ocean,
and yet still keeps from being capsized by its waters. {29}

His practice of skillful means and wisdom and perfection of qualities
are such that no one in the entire world can completely fathom.
By offerings to many buddhas and his mind's growing radiance
he becomes like gold that has been adorned with marvelous gems. {30}

The wisdom of this ground's bodhisattva is the most brilliant of all.
Like flourishing sunlight, it dries up the waters of craving.
He also serves as a lord of the Paranirmita Vaśavartin Heaven
who teaches and guides beings in the cultivation of right knowledge. {31}

If he resorts to the power of valiant and vigorous diligence,
he acquires numerous samādhis and sees multitudes of buddhas,
hundreds of thousands of *koṭis* of *nayutas* in number.
With freely exercised vow power, the number goes even beyond this. {32}

This is the bodhisattva's Far-Reaching Ground,
the path of the purification of skillful means and wisdom.
It is such that no deva, human, *śrāvaka*-disciple, or *pratyekabuddha*
anywhere in any world would be able to comprehend it. {33}

Part Eight
The Immovability Ground

H. **The Eighth Ground: The Immovability Ground**

1. The Eighth Ground's Introductory Verses and Dharma Request

At that time, the Deva King and those in the deva assembly,
hearing of these supreme practices, were filled with joyous delight.
Wishing to make offerings to the Tathāgata
and to that boundless congregation of great bodhisattvas, {1}

they rained down marvelous blossoms, banners, canopies,
incenses, floral garlands, necklaces, and jeweled robes,
measurelessly and boundlessly many, of a hundred thousand sorts,
all of which were adorned with *maṇi* jewels. {2}

Celestial nymphs simultaneously chorused forth heavenly music,
sending everywhere about many different sorts of sublime voices
as offerings to the Buddha as well to those sons of the Buddha there,
all together singing forth these words that they offered in praise: {3}

"The All Seeing One most revered among all two-legged beings,
out of kindly pity for these beings, manifests his spiritual powers,
causing these many sorts of celestial music and sublime sounds
to come forth from everywhere so that everyone is able to hear. {4}

On each hair tip, there are a hundred thousand *koṭis*
of *nayutas* of lands as numerous as atoms
wherein just such a measureless number of *tathāgatas*
abide there, proclaiming the sublime Dharma. {5}

Within each hair pore there are countless lands,
each of which has its four continents and great oceans
as well as Mount Sumeru and the Iron Ring Mountains,
all of which are seen therein without being cramped for space. {6}

Within the tip of each hair, there exist the six destinies of rebirth,
the three wretched destinies, as well as men and devas,
all of the multitudes of dragons and spirits, and the *asuras*, wherein
each undergoes retribution in accordance with his karma. {7}

In all of those lands, there are *tathāgatas*
expounding teachings with their marvelous voices,
adapting to the minds of all of the different sorts of beings
in order to turn the wheel of the supremely pure Dharma. {8}

In those lands, the beings have all different sorts of bodies.
Within their bodies, there are in turn many different types of lands.
Humans, devas, the other destinies—each is different from the others.
The Buddha, having fully known them, speaks Dharma for them all. {9}

Large lands, in response to thought, transform, becoming small.
Small lands, in response to thought, transform, becoming large.
He has such spiritual superknowledges that are so measureless that,
even if worldlings all described them at once, they could never finish."
{10}

Having sent forth everywhere these sublime sounds
praising the meritorious qualities of the Tathāgata,
those assembled there, filled with joyous delight, became silent
and then single-mindedly gazed up, wishing to hear an explanation.

At that time, Liberation Moon Bodhisattva again set forth a request:
"Everyone in this assembled congregation has become still and quiet.
We pray that you will describe the practice aspects
that one sequentially enters in reaching the eighth ground." {11}

2. Vajragarbha Commences the Eighth Ground's Explanation

{A} At that time, Vajragarbha Bodhisattva informed Liberation Moon Bodhisattva, saying:

3. Ten Accomplishments Associated With Entering the Eighth Ground

O Son of the Buddha. Here we have the bodhisattva *mahāsattva* who, on seven grounds:

Has well cultivated skillful means together with wisdom;
Has well purified the paths;
Has well accumulated the dharmas assisting realization of the path;
Has been sustained by the power of great vows;[196]
Has received the assistance of the Tathāgata's powers;[197]
Has been supported by the power of his own goodness;[198]
Has remained always mindful of the Tathāgata's powers, fearlessnesses, and dharmas exclusive to the Buddhas;[199]
Has well purified his higher aspirations and intentions;[200]
Has become able to completely develop merit and wisdom;[201]
And has practiced the great kindness and the great compassion by which he never forsakes any being. So it is that he enters the path of measureless knowledge.[202]

4. Ten Types of Comprehension Associated With 8th Ground Access

{B} He penetratingly comprehends all dharmas:[203]

As originally unproduced;
As non-arising;
As signless;
As neither created nor destroyed;
As inexhaustible and undergoing no transformation;
As having the nature of being devoid of any inherent nature;
As of uniformly equal character in the past, present, and future;
As being amenable to penetration by non-discriminating suchness-cognizing knowledge;
As being beyond the range of discriminating concepts associated with the mind or mind consciousness;
And as, in the manner of empty space, devoid of any basis for grasping or attachment.

This penetrating comprehension of all dharmas as comparable in their nature to empty space is synonymous with the realization of the unproduced-dharmas patience.

5. The Unproduced Dharmas Patience Basis for "Profound Practice"

{C} Son of the Buddha, when the bodhisattva acquires this patience, he immediately achieves entry into the eighth ground, the Ground of Immovability, and becomes a "profound practice" bodhisattva who is unfathomable and free of any discriminations, one who has transcended all signs, all conceptual thought, and all attachments, one who has reached a state that is immeasurable and boundless, one who cannot be matched by any *śrāvaka*-disciple or *pratyekabuddha,* one who has abandoned all contentiousness, and one in whom quiescence is directly manifest.

6. "Profound Practice" Like a Monk With Superknowledges & Dhyānas

This circumstance is comparable to that of a bhikshu who has perfected the spiritual superknowledges and whose mind has achieved sovereign mastery, one who has proceeded through the sequential development of the absorptions to the point of entering the absorption of complete cessation and has become one wherein all movement of the mind, all recollective thought, and all discriminations have entirely ceased.

In just such a way, when this bodhisattva *mahāsattva* comes to dwell on the Ground of Immovability, he immediately relinquishes all deliberately effortful practice and acquires the dharma of effortlessness. As for any undertakings of body, speech, and mind as well as any mental exertion, these all completely cease. He then abides in practice accomplished as the fruit of karmic rewards.[204]

7. 8th Ground Likened to Awakening From a River-Fording Dream

His situation is like that of a person who, in the midst of a dream, sees that he has tumbled into the waters of a great river, and then, wishing to get across, brings forth great bravery and pursues some means to accomplish this. Then, due to bringing forth great bravery and enacting some means to accomplish this, he suddenly wakes up. Having awoken, he then desists from everything he was doing.

So too it is with the bodhisattva. Having seen that beings are being swept along in the four floods,[205] he exerts himself with great bravery and brings forth great vigor to rescue them and bring them across. Due to his bravery and vigor, he then succeeds in reaching the Ground of Immovability. Then, having reached this station, there is none of his deliberate effortfulness that does not cease entirely. He then no longer manifests any duality-based practice or practice grounded in phenomenal characteristics.

8. 8th Ground Likened to the Brahma World's Absence of Afflictions

Son of the Buddha, this situation is comparable to what occurs when one is reborn into the Brahma World wherein, of all the afflictions associated with the desire realm, none of them fail to cease. So too it is when one comes to dwell on the Ground of Immovability. All activity associated with the mind or mind consciousness no longer manifests. This bodhisattva *mahāsattva* no longer even manifests the arising of any thought associated with being a bodhisattva, any thought associated with buddhahood, any thought associated with bodhi, or any thought associated with nirvāṇa, how much the less would he bring forth any sort of thought associated with the world.

9. The Buddhas' Manifestation Before the 8th Ground Bodhisattva

Son of the Buddha, on account of the power of his original vows, the Buddhas, the Bhagavats, personally manifest directly before the bodhisattva who dwells on this ground, bestowing on him the knowledge of the Tathāgatas, causing him to pass through the gateway leading into the flow of the Dharma.

10. The Buddhas' Praise & Instructions for the 8th Ground Bodhisattva

{D} They then speak as follows:

> This is good indeed, good indeed. Son of Good Family, this patience is the foremost among them all, one that accords with all dharmas of the Buddhas. Still, Son of Good Family, you have not yet acquired all of our ten powers, our fearlessnesses, and

our eighteen dharmas exclusive to the Buddhas. Hence, out of a desire to perfectly realize these dharmas, you should bring forth the diligent application of vigor even while, at the same time, you must never relinquish this gateway of patience.

{E} Furthermore, Son of Good Family, although you have indeed acquired this quiescent liberation, still, the foolish common people have not yet been able to acquire that realization. All of the different sorts of afflictions continue to manifest in them and all the different sorts of ideation and discursive thought always assail and injure them. Out of kindly pity, you should bear in mind the plight of these beings.

{F} Additionally, Son of Good Family, you should bear in mind your original vow to bestow great and universal benefit on all beings, in every instance causing them to enter the gateway of inconceivable wisdom.

{G} Also, Son of Good Family, this essential nature of all dharmas[206] always abides and never changes whether buddhas come forth into the world or do not come forth into the world. It is not through acquiring this dharma that they are designated as "*tathāgatas*." Even all those who pursue the Two Vehicles practice are equally able to acquire this dharma that is free of discriminating thought.

{H} Furthermore, Son of Good Family, you should behold the measurelessness of our physical signs, the measurelessness of our wisdom, the measurelessness of our lands, the measurelessness of our skillful means, the measurelessness of our light auras,[207] and also the measurelessness of our pure voices. It is only fitting that you should now perfect these phenomena yourself.

{I} Additionally, Son of Good Family, you have just now acquired this one Dharma light,[208] namely that all dharmas are unproduced and devoid of any differentiating distinctions.[209] Son of Good Family, the Dharma light that the Tathāgatas have acquired is possessed of so countlessly many circumstances it enters, so countlessly many implementations, and so countlessly many permutations that, even in hundreds of thousands of *koṭis* of *nayutas* of kalpas, one could still never succeed in knowing them all. You should cultivate and perfect this dharma.

{J} Also, Son of Good Family, as you contemplate throughout the ten directions the many different distinctions in the immeasurably many lands, the immeasurably many beings, and the immeasurably many dharmas, you should penetrate and comprehend them all in accordance with reality.

Son of the Buddha, the Buddhas, the Bhagavats, bestow upon these bodhisattvas just so countlessly many gateways to the generation of knowledge, thus enabling them to generate countlessly and boundlessly many different works arising from their knowledge.

11. The Importance of Buddhas' Appearing to 8th Ground Bodhisattvas

{K} Son of the Buddha, if the Buddhas did not bestow on these bodhisattvas these gateways to the generation of knowledge, they would otherwise straightaway enter final nirvāṇa and abandon all of their works carried out for the benefit of beings. It is because the Buddhas bestow on them just so countlessly and boundlessly many gateways for the generation of wisdom that the wisdom-implementing works these bodhisattvas then generate in but a single mind-moment become so numerous that all of the practices they have cultivated from the time of bringing forth their initial resolve all the way on through to the seventh ground could not even equal a hundredth part, and so forth until we come to their being in aggregate unable to equal even a single part in a hundred thousand *koṭis* of *nayutas* of parts and, in this same way, unable to equal even a single part in an *asaṃkhyeya* of parts, in a *kalā* of parts, in the highest number of parts reachable by calculation, in the highest number of parts describable by analogy, or even in an *upaniṣad*'s number of parts.

12. Why 8th Ground Bodhisattva's Practices Are So Measureless

And why is this? Son of the Buddha, this bodhisattva formerly employed but one single body in developing his practice. Now, in coming to dwell on this ground, he acquires countless bodies, countless voices, and measureless wisdom while also taking on countless rebirths whereby he engages in the purification of countless pure lands, teaches countless beings, makes offerings to countless buddhas, enters countless gateways into the Dharma, equips himself with countless sorts of spiritual superknowledges, becomes possessed of countless different *bodhimaṇḍa* congregations, abides in countless different sorts of physical, verbal, and mental deeds, and accumulates all of the bodhisattva practices, accomplishing all of this by relying on the dharma of immovability.

13. This Bodhisattva's Practices Likened to Sailing Out onto the Ocean

Son of the Buddha, in this, he is comparable to someone who boards a ship wishing to set sail out onto the great ocean. Before he has actually reached the ocean, he must tax his strength by devoting much deliberate effort to this end. If he manages to make his way out to sea, he then need only accord with the prevailing winds in continuing to travel along, doing so with no further requirement of human exertion.

Then, due to having finally reached the great ocean, the distance he can then travel in but a single day becomes so great that, were one to compare it with his progress before reaching the ocean, it could not be matched by even a hundred years of those previous methods.

Son of the Buddha, so too it is with bodhisattva *mahāsattva*. Once he has accumulated such a vast store of roots of goodness and sets sail in the ship of the Great Vehicle out onto the ocean of bodhisattva practices, then, in but a single mind-moment, he is able to employ effortlessly implemented knowledge to proceed so far into the realm of the cognition of all-knowledge that his progress then could not be rivaled by even countless hundreds of thousands of *koṭis* of *nayutas* of kalpas of his former deliberately effortful practices.

14. The Bodhisattva's Contemplation of Buddha's All-Knowledge

{L} Son of the Buddha, by using effortlessly manifest awakened intelligence produced by great skillful means and cleverly invoked knowledge, the bodhisattva dwelling on the eighth ground contemplates the realm in which the cognition of all-knowledge is implemented.

15. His Knowledge of the Arising and Destruction of Worlds

In particular, he contemplates the creation of worlds and the destruction of worlds and thus knows that they are created from the accumulation of these particular sorts of karmic deeds, that they are destroyed through the exhaustion of the effects of these particular sorts of karmic deeds, knows when their creation phase occurs, knows when their destruction phase occurs, knows how long their creation phase endures, and knows how long their destruction phase endures. He knows all of these things in accordance with reality.

16. His Knowledge of the Four Elemental Phases

He also knows with respect to the sphere of the earth-element its character on a small scale, its character on a large scale, its character when manifest on an immeasurable scale, and its character in its different manifestations. So too does he know of the spheres of the water, fire, and wind elements their character on a small scale, their character on a large scale, their character on an immeasurable scale, and their character in their different manifestations.

17. His Knowledge of Atoms' Manifestations in Worlds and Beings

So too does he know of the atoms their character as minutely manifest, their character in their different manifestations, and their character in their different manifestations when manifest on an immeasurable scale. He knows of whichever worlds what constitutes their entire accumulation of atoms as well as the character of those atoms' different manifestations, knowing all of these phenomena in accordance with reality.

So too does he know of whichever world, how many such atoms constitute each of its elemental spheres of earth, water, fire, and wind, how many such atoms form all of their precious things, how many such atoms constitute the bodies of all the beings there, and how many such atoms form the physical mass of those lands, knowing all of these phenomena in accordance with reality.

So too does he know of those beings, both of those who are physically large and of those who are physically small, how many such atoms collectively compose their bodies, knowing this as well of the bodies of the hell-dwellers, the bodies of the animals, the bodies of the hungry ghosts, the bodies of the *asuras*, the bodies of the devas, and the bodies of the humans, knowing of each of them of how many such atoms they are composed.

He acquires just such knowledge as this whereby he knows even of atoms their different sorts of manifestations.

18. His Knowledge of the Three Realms of Existence

So too, he knows of the desire realm, the form realm, and the formless realm the circumstances of their creation, knows of the desire realm, the form realm, and the formless realm the circumstances of their destruction, knows of the desire realm, the form realm, and the formless realm their character on a small scale, their character on a large scale, their character when manifest on an immeasurable scale, and their character in their different manifestations.

He acquires just such knowledge as this whereby he contemplates the different manifestations within the three realms of existence.

19. His Application of Knowledge in Adaptive Births To Teach Beings

Son of the Buddha, this bodhisattva also brings forth the light of knowledge by resort to which he teaches beings. In particular, he thereby becomes thoroughly aware of the different physical bodies of beings, thoroughly distinguishes the character of these beings' physical bodies, and thoroughly contemplates the stations of rebirth into which these beings are born. He then manifests bodies for them in ways adapted to what is appropriate for them, whereupon he then teaches them and brings them to maturation.

This bodhisattva employs his light of knowledge to manifest the taking on of rebirths everywhere throughout an entire great trichiliocosm, doing so in a manner adapted to the differences in beings' bodies and resolute convictions.

So too, everywhere throughout the worlds within two or three great trichiliocosms, within a hundred thousand great trichiliocosms, and even within ineffably many great trichiliocosms, he manifests this taking on of births in a manner adapted to the differences in beings' bodies and resolute convictions.

Because this bodhisattva has perfected wisdom such as this, even as his body remains motionless within a single buddha land, he manifests his bodies everywhere, doing so in the midst of assembled congregations in up to an ineffably great number of buddha lands.

{M} Son of the Buddha, this bodhisattva, adapting to all of the different variations in beings' bodies, minds, and resolute convictions, manifests his own bodies in the midst of the assembled congregations within those buddha lands. In particular, within assemblies of *śramaṇas*, he appears in the form of a *śramaṇa*, within assemblies of brahmins, he appears in the form of a brahmin, and within assemblies of *kṣatriyas*, he appears in the form of a *kṣatriya*. He appears in this same manner within assemblies of *vaiśyas*, within assemblies of *śūdras*, within assemblies of householders, within assemblies in the Heaven of the Four Heavenly Kings, within assemblies in the Heaven of the Thirty-three, within assemblies in the Yāma Heaven, within assemblies in the Tuṣita Heaven, within assemblies in the Transformation of Bliss Heaven, within assemblies in the Paranirmita Vaśavartin Heaven, within assemblies of *māras*, within assemblies in the Brahma Heaven, and so forth on up to his manifestations that appear within assemblies in the Akaniṣṭha Heaven. In each of these cases, he manifests in a form adapted to the particular sorts of beings there.

Also, for the sake of those who should most readily achieve liberation through someone manifesting in the form of a *śrāvaka*-disciple, he then manifests in the form of a *śrāvaka*-disciple. For the sake of those who should most readily achieve liberation through someone manifesting in the form of a *pratyekabuddha,* he then manifests in the form of a *pratyekabuddha.* For the sake of those who should most readily achieve liberation through someone manifesting in the form of a bodhisattva, he then manifests in the form of a bodhisattva. And for the sake of those who should most readily achieve liberation through someone manifesting in the form of a *tathāgata,* he then manifests in the form of a *tathāgata.*

Son of the Buddha, it is in this way that the bodhisattva manifests bodies in all of these ineffably many buddha lands, doing so in accordance with the distinct differences in beings' resolute convictions.

20. His Transcendence of Discriminations & Knowledge of 10 Body Types

{N} Son of the Buddha, this bodhisattva has completely abandoned all discriminations associated with the perceptions of bodies and abides in the awareness of uniform equality in such things.

This bodhisattva knows:

The bodies of beings;
The bodies of lands;
The bodies received as karmic retribution;
The bodies of *śrāvaka*-disciples;
The bodies of *pratyekabuddhas;*
The bodies of bodhisattvas;
The bodies of *tathāgatas;*
The knowledge body;
The Dharma body;
And empty space bodies.

a. The Bodhisattva's Manifestation of Different Bodies for Beings

This bodhisattva, knowing beings' resolute convictions, is able to use a being's body to form his own body. So too is he able to turn it into the body of a land, a body received as karmic retribution, or any of the other sorts of bodies, up to and including an empty space body.

He is also able, knowing beings' resolute convictions, to turn the body of a land into his own body. So too is he able to turn it into the body of a being, a body received as karmic retribution, or any of the other sorts of bodies, up to and including an empty space body.

He is also able, knowing what pleases the minds of beings, to turn a karmic retribution body into his own body. So too is he able to turn it into the body of a being, the body of a land, or any of the other sorts of bodies up to and including an empty space body.

He is also able, knowing beings' resolute convictions, to turn his own body into the body of another being, the physical body of a land, and so forth on up to and including an empty space body.

So it is that, adapting to beings' different resolute convictions, he then employs these sorts of bodies to manifest for them just these very sorts of physical forms.

b. The Bodhisattva's Knowledge of Beings' Bodies

This bodhisattva knows beings' bodies associated with the accumulation of karmic actions, their karmic retribution bodies, their bodies associated with the afflictions, their form-realm bodies, and their formless-realm bodies.

c. The Bodhisattva's Knowledge of the Bodies of Lands

He also knows with regard to the bodies of lands:

Their characteristics when small;
Their characteristics when large;
Their characteristics when immeasurable;
Their characteristics when defiled;
Their characteristics when pure;
Their characteristics when vast;
Their characteristics when inverted;
Their characteristics when upright;
Their characteristics when they are universally pervasive;
And their different sorts of characteristics when existing as parts of a spatially distributed network.

d. His Knowledge of Retribution, 2 Vehicles, and Bodhisattva Bodies

He knows with respect to bodies received as karmic retribution, the distinctions in the conventional names applied to them and knows with respect to the bodies of *śrāvaka*-disciples, the bodies of *pratyekabuddhas,* and the bodies of bodhisattvas, the distinctions in the conventional names applied to them.

e. The Bodhisattva's Knowledge of Tathāgatas' Bodies

He knows with respect to the bodies of *tathāgatas,* their possession of:

Bodhi bodies;
Bodies associated with vows;
Transformationally produced bodies;
Bodies sustained through their powers;
Bodies graced with the major marks and subsidiary signs;
Bodies possessed of awe-inspiring strength;
Mind-generated bodies;

Merit bodies;
The Dharma body;
And the knowledge body.

f. The Bodhisattva's Knowledge of the Knowledge Body

He knows with respect to the knowledge body:

Its characteristic of skillful deliberation;
Its characteristic of selective judgment accordant with reality;
Its characteristics associated with the practices leading to the fruits of the path;
Its characteristics associated with the distinctions between what is worldly and what is world-transcending;
Its characteristics associated with distinctions in the Three Vehicles;
Its characteristics when shared;
Its characteristics when exclusive;
Its characteristics when associated with emancipation;
Its characteristics when associated with an unemancipated state;
Its characteristics when associated with the stages of the learner;
And its characteristics when associated with the stage of those beyond learning.

g. The Bodhisattva's Knowledge of the Dharma Body

He knows with respect to the Dharma body its characteristic of uniform equality and its characteristic of indestructibility, knows the characteristics associated with the differentiation in conventional names when adapted to times and when adapted to mundane circumstances, knows the characteristic distinctions in the dharmas associated with beings as opposed to those associated with non-beings, and knows the characteristic distinctions in the dharmas associated with the Buddhas, the Dharma, and the Ārya Sangha.

h. The Bodhisattva's Knowledge of the Empty Space Body

He knows with respect to the empty space body its characteristic of immeasurability, its characteristic of universal pervasion, its characteristic of formlessness, its characteristic of non-differentiation, its characteristic of boundlessness, and its characteristic of revealing the existence of form bodies.

21. The Bodhisattva's Acquisition of Ten Kinds of Sovereign Mastery

{O} Son of the Buddha, having completely developed such knowledge with respect to bodies as this, this bodhisattva acquires:

Sovereign mastery in lifespan;
Sovereign mastery of mind;
Sovereign mastery in wealth;
Sovereign mastery in karmic deeds;
Sovereign mastery in births;
Sovereign mastery in vows;
Sovereign mastery in resolute faith;[210]
Sovereign mastery in psychic power;
Sovereign mastery in knowledge;
And sovereign mastery of the Dharma.

{P} Due to having acquired these ten types of sovereign mastery, he then becomes one whose knowledge is inconceivable, one whose knowledge is measureless, one whose knowledge is vast, and one whose knowledge is invincible.

22. Ten Characteristic Aspects of this Eighth Ground Bodhisattva

Having achieved just such penetrating comprehension as this and having achieved just such consummate realization as this, he thus becomes:

One who is absolutely free of fault in physical karmic actions, free of fault in verbal deeds, and free of fault in mental deeds;
One in whom all physical, verbal, and mental karmic acts are carried forth in accordance with knowledge;
One in whom the *prajñāpāramitā* is dominant;
One in whom the great compassion has become the foremost priority;
One whose expedient means are skillful;
One who is well able to make distinctions;
One who is excellent in bringing forth great vows;
One who is protected by the power of the Buddha;
One who always diligently cultivates knowledge directed toward benefiting beings;
And one who dwells everywhere throughout the boundlessly many different worlds.

Son of the Buddha, to state this in terms of the most essential point, the bodhisattva dwelling on this Ground of Immovability is able to gather all dharmas of the Buddha in all that he does through his physical, verbal, and mental deeds.

23. Ten Types of Power in Which This Bodhisattva Is Well Established

Son of the Buddha, the bodhisattva dwelling on this ground:

Becomes well established in the power of the resolute intentions[211] because none of the afflictions function in him;
Becomes well established in the power of the supreme mind through never departing from the path;
Becomes well established in the power of the great compassion through never relinquishing his benefiting of beings;
Becomes well established in the power of the great kindness through striving to rescue and protect everyone abiding in all worlds;
Becomes well established in power of the *dhāraṇīs* through never forgetting any dharma;
Becomes well established in power of eloquence through skillfully contemplating and distinguishing all dharmas;
Becomes well established in the power of the spiritual superknowledges through going forth everywhere throughout the boundlessly many worlds;
Becomes well established in the power of the great vows through never relinquishing any of the bodhisattva endeavors;
Becomes well established in the power of the *pāramitās* through perfecting all dharmas of the Buddha;
And acquires the power of being protected and borne in mind by the Tathāgatas through his being directed toward the knowledge of all modes and the cognition of all-knowledge.

This bodhisattva who has acquired such powers of knowledge as these is able to manifest all endeavors that are to be accomplished while remaining free of fault in all those endeavors.

24. The Ten Names of this Eighth Bodhisattva Ground

{Q} Son of the Buddha, this bodhisattva ground of knowledge:

Is known as the Ground of Immovability because no one is able to obstruct or overcome him;
Is known as the ground of irreversibility because his wisdom never retreats;
Is known as the ground that is difficult to acquire because no one in the world is able to fathom it;
Is known as the ground of the pure youth[212] because he has abandoned all faults;
Is known as the ground of birth because he possesses sovereign mastery in doing whatever he pleases;
Is known as the ground of completion because there is nothing more to be done;
Is known as the ultimate ground because his wisdom has become resolutely decisive;

Is known as the ground of transformations because he achieves complete success in whatever he wishes to do;
Is known as the ground of sustenance through power because others are unable to move him;
And is known as the ground effortlessness because, earlier on, he has already achieved complete development.

25. Additional 8th Ground Bodhisattva Qualities and Practice Aspects

{R} Son of the Buddha, the bodhisattva who has developed wisdom such as this gains entry into the domain of the Buddhas, becomes illuminated by the Buddha's merit, and accords with the Buddha's awe-inspiring deportment. With the directly manifestation of the realms of the Buddhas, he is always protected and borne in mind by the Tathāgatas. Brahmā, Śakra, the Four Heavenly Kings, and the Vajra-wielding protectors constantly follow and protect him. He never leaves the great samādhis and is able to manifest countless different sorts of bodies each and every one of which is possessed of immense strength. As karmically generated effects, he acquires spiritual superknowledges and samādhis in which he has sovereign mastery.[213] Wherever there are beings amenable to being taught, he manifests the realization of right enlightenment.

Son of the Buddha, it is in this way that the bodhisattva enters the assembly of those who abide in the Great Vehicle, acquires great spiritual superknowledges, emits immensely radiant light, and is unimpeded in entering the Dharma realm. He knows the different variations among the worlds. He manifests all of the magnificent meritorious qualities, has sovereign mastery in whatever he directs his mind to, is well able to bring forth an utterly penetrating comprehension of both the past and the future, and is able to everywhere overcome all of the paths of Māra's deviance. He deeply enters the realms in which the Tathāgatas course and cultivates the bodhisattva practices in countless lands. It is because he has been able to acquire the dharma of irreversibility that he is described as dwelling on the Ground of Immovability.

26. The Bodhisattva's Seeing and Serving of Countless Buddhas

{S} Son of the Buddha, having come to dwell on this Ground of Immovability, this bodhisattva, through the power of samādhi, is then always able to directly see measurelessly many buddhas. He never relinquishes his practice of serving and making offerings to them. In each and every kalpa and in each and every world, this bodhisattva sees measurelessly many hundreds of buddhas, measurelessly many thousands of buddhas, and so forth on up to measurelessly many hundreds of thousands of *koṭis* of *nayutas* of buddhas, all of whom he reveres, venerates, serves, and presents with offerings. He offers up and bestows upon them all amenities facilitating the sustenance of their lives.

27. The Bodhisattva's Further Acquisition of Buddhas' Dharma Light

Wherever the Buddhas dwell, he acquires the Tathāgatas' treasuries of extremely profound Dharma and receives from them measureless Dharma light pertaining to the differences among worlds and other such phenomena. Should anyone approach him and challenge him by posing difficult questions regarding any of the distinctions among worlds or other such matters, no one can prevail over him.

28. The Radiance of Good Roots Likened to a Sage King's Crown

He continues on in this way passing through a period of measurelessly many hundreds of kalpas, measurelessly many thousands of kalpas, and so on up to measurelessly many hundreds of thousands of *koṭis* of *nayutas* of kalpas during which his roots of goodness become ever more radiant in their purity like the real gold that is fashioned into a jeweled crown to be placed on the head of the sage king ruling over the continent of Jambudvīpa. It is of a sort that none of the adornments possessed by any of his government ministers or any of his people could ever rival it.

So too it is with all the roots of goodness possessed by the bodhisattva dwelling on this ground, for they are such that they could never be rivaled by any roots of goodness possessed by followers of the Two Vehicles or by bodhisattvas dwelling on any of the first seven grounds.

Due to dwelling on this ground, the light of his great wisdom is able to everywhere extinguish the darkness of beings' afflictions. This is because he is well able to open up and expound upon the gateways to wisdom.

29. This Bodhisattva's Radiance Like That of a Brahma Heaven King

Son of the Buddha, just as that lord of a thousand worlds, the king of the Great Brahma Heaven, is able to everywhere extend his mind of kindness and everywhere send forth light that fills up a thousand worlds, so too it is with the bodhisattva dwelling on this ground. He is able to send forth light that illuminates worlds as numerous as the atoms in hundreds of myriads of buddha lands that extinguishes the flames of afflictions of the beings therein and causes them to experience clarity and coolness.

30. The 8th Ground Bodhisattva's Focus on the Skillful Means Pāramitā

Among the ten *pāramitās*, this bodhisattva is especially superior in his practice of the *pāramitā* of vows. It is not that he does not practice the other *pāramitās*. Rather, he simply accords them an amount of emphasis corresponding to his own strengths and to what is fitting.

31. Vajragarbha's Final Statements About the 8th Ground Bodhisattva

This has been a summary discussion of all bodhisattva *mahāsattvas'* eighth ground, the Ground of Immovability. Were one to speak of it extensively, one could pursue the discussion for measurelessly many kalpas and yet still be unable to find the end of it.

a. The Bodhisattva's Station and Dharma Practice

Son of the Buddha, the bodhisattva *mahāsattva* dwelling on this ground often serves as a king of the Great Brahma Heaven, the lord over a thousand worlds, who, supreme in his sovereign mastery, is well able to discourse on any principle and is able to bestow the path of the *pāramitās* on *śrāvaka*-disciples, *pratyekabuddhas*, and bodhisattvas. Should anyone challenge his explanations of the differences in world realms, no one is able to prevail over him.

b. The Bodhisattva's Mindfulness

In his practice of giving, pleasing words, beneficial actions, and joint endeavors as well as any of the other such endeavors he pursues, he never departs from mindfulness of the Buddha, and so forth on up to his never departing from mindfulness of the knowledge of all modes and the cognition of all-knowledge.

c. The Bodhisattva's Aspiration to Serve Beings

He also has this thought: "I should become one who serves these beings as a leader, as one who is supreme," and so forth until we come to "as one who relies on the cognition of all-knowledge."

d. The Consequences of the Bodhisattva's Vigor and Vows

If this bodhisattva brings forth the power of great vigor, then, in but a moment, he acquires a number of samādhis as numerous as the atoms in the worlds contained within a hundred myriads of great trichiliocosms. And so it goes on up to his then being able to manifest a following of bodhisattvas serving in his retinue as numerous as the atoms in all the worlds in a hundred myriads of great trichiliocosms.

{T} If this bodhisattva chooses to avail himself of the power of his especially supreme vows, he becomes able then to freely manifest these phenomena in numbers well beyond these, such that one would never be able to count them even in hundreds of thousands of *koṭis* of *nayutas* of kalpas.

32. Vajragarbha Bodhisattva's Summarizing Verses

At that time, Vajragarbha Bodhisattva, wishing to proclaim his meaning once more, thereupon uttered verses, saying:

Having on seven grounds cultivated expedients and wisdom, having
thoroughly assembled path-assisting practices and great vow power,
having become supported by those most honored among men, and
seeking the supreme knowledge, he ascends to the eighth ground. {12}

He perfects meritorious qualities,[214] is constant in kindliness and pity,
possesses wisdom as vast as empty space, and is then able
by hearing Dharma, to initiate the power of resolute decisiveness and
enter the quiescent unproduced-dharmas patience. {13}

He knows dharmas as unproduced, unarisen, signless,
as uncreated, undestroyed, endless, not undergoing transformation,
as beyond existence, uniformly equal, cutting short discriminations,
as stepping beyond the range of thought, and as abiding like space. {14}

Having perfected this patience, he transcends frivolous theorizing,
abides in very deep, motionless, and constant quiescence
such as no one in the entire world could ever comprehend,
and such as abandons all thoughts, signs, grasping, and attachment. {15}

Dwelling on this ground, he makes no discriminations,
like the bhikshu who has entered the cessation absorption, like
one in a river-fording dream who, awakening, sees it is nonexistent,
and like one who, born in the Brahma Heaven, severs base desires. {16}

By power of original vows, he receives encouragement and guidance,
is praised for gaining supreme patience, is given a crown anointing,
and is told, "The many Buddha dharmas that we possess,
you have now still not acquired. You must bring forth diligent vigor. {17}

Although you have already extinguished the afflictions' fires,
the flaming afflictions of the world's beings still blaze on.
You must recall your original vow to help beings cross beyond,
and influence them all to cultivate the causes leading to liberation. {18}

True constancy of Dharmas' nature and separation from thoughts
are of the sort that even adherents of the Two Vehicles can realize.
Hence it is not due to this that we are the World Honored Ones,
rather it is solely due to extremely deep and unimpeded knowledge." {19}

In this way, those worthy of the offerings of men and devas
bestow this wisdom on him, causing him to deeply contemplate it.
Thus they completely develop boundlessly many buddha dharmas
and, in a single moment, step beyond their many previous practices. (20)

When the bodhisattva dwells on this ground of sublime knowledge,
he then acquires vast spiritual superknowledges' powers whereby,
in a moment, his transformation bodies pervade the ten directions
as he becomes like a ship gone out to sea, carried across by the wind. (21)

The mind effortlessly avails itself of the power of knowledge,
entirely knows the creation, destruction, and abiding of lands,
all of the differences in each of the different sorts of realms,
and is able to utterly know them when small, large, or boundless. (22)

The four great elements throughout the trichiliocosms' worlds,
the different sorts of bodies of the beings in the six rebirth destinies,
as well as even the atoms forming the many jewels—
with his knowledge, he contemplates all of these without exception. (23)

This bodhisattva is also able to know all of the types of bodies
and take on the same forms as theirs for the sake of teaching beings.
In the countless lands with their many different types, he manifests
his forms for them, with none wherein he is not everywhere present. (24)

Like the sun and moon that, abiding in space,
display their reflections in all of the bodies of water,
he abides in the Dharma realm, remaining motionless, even as,
adapting to beings' minds, he manifests reflections in this same way. (25)

Adapting to their minds' predilections[215] that differ in each case,
he manifests bodies in the presence of all beings,
doing so with bodies of *śrāvakas*, *pratyekabuddhas*, bodhisattvas,
or buddhas, having no type of body that he does not manifest. (26)

Bodies of beings, bodies of lands, karmic retribution bodies,
bodies of the various *āryas*, the knowledge body, the Dharma body,
and the space-like body, all uniformly equal in character—
he manifests them everywhere for the sake of beings. (27)

With ten *ārya* knowledges,[216] his contemplation extends everywhere.
He also adapts kindness and compassion to doing many works,
entirely develops all dharmas of a buddha and,
in upholding moral precepts, is as immovable as Mount Sumeru. (28)

Completely developed in ten powers, he cannot be moved or shaken,
cannot be turned back by any of Māra's hordes,
is held in mindfully protected by buddhas, is revered by deva kings,
and is constantly served and guarded by traceless vajra-bearers. (29)

The meritorious qualities of those on this ground are boundless,
indescribable even in thousands of myriads of *koṭis* of kalpas.
He continues by offerings to buddhas to skillfully gain in radiance
that becomes like that of a crown adorning the head of the King. {30}

The bodhisattva dwelling on this eighth ground
often serves as a Brahma Heaven king, lord of a thousand realms,
who expounds endlessly on the Three Vehicles, everywhere shines
forth his light of kindness, and dispels the afflictions of the many. {31}

The samādhis he acquires in but a single moment
equal in number the atoms in a hundred myriads of worlds.
So too is the number of endeavors that he accomplishes,
and yet, through vow power, he may even manifest yet more. {32}

The bodhisattva's eighth ground, the Ground of Immovability
has thus been summarily explained by me for the sake of all of you.
Were one to pursue a vast, sequentially presented analysis of this,
even speaking on it for a *koṭi* of kalpas, one still could never finish. {33}

Part Nine
The Excellent Intelligence Ground

I. The Ninth Ground: The Excellent Intelligence Ground

1. The Ninth Ground's Introductory Verses and Dharma Request

Once the eighth bodhisattva ground's explanation had concluded,
the Tathāgata manifested great spiritual superknowledges' powers,
causing tremors in an inconceivable and incalculable number of *koṭis*
of lands throughout the ten directions. {1}

The body of that all-knowing and seeing Supremely Honored One
then sent forth everywhere immensely radiant light
that illuminated with dazzling brilliance all those countless lands,
causing all beings therein to be filled with happiness. {2}

The incalculably many hundreds of thousands of *koṭis* of bodhisattvas
simultaneously ascended into space where they remained
and presented offerings superior even to the devas' marvelous gifts
to he whose proclamations are the most superior of all. {3}

The Great Vaśavartin Heaven King and the Vaśavartin devas
then all together and with unified minds felt measureless joy.
They each then presented all different sorts of the many types of gifts
as offerings to the extremely deep ocean of meritorious qualities. {4}

A thousand myriads *koṭis* of celestial nymphs were also present
who, filled with joyous exultation in body and mind,
each played measurelessly many kinds of music
as offerings to the great guiding teacher among humans. {5}

Then the many sorts of music played simultaneously
a hundred thousand myriads of *koṭis* of countless musical variations
that, by the awe-inspiring spiritual power of the Well Gone One,
uttered praises with sublime voices, saying: {6}

"The quiescent and pliant one free of defilements or injuriousness
skillfully cultivates whichever ground he enters.
Possessed of a mind like space, he goes forth to the ten directions,
broadly proclaiming the Buddha's path to awaken the many beings. {7}

"In all places throughout the heavens and among men,
he manifests incomparably marvelous adornments
arising from the meritorious qualities of the Tathāgata
that cause those who observe them to delight in Buddha's wisdom. {8}

"Without leaving that single land, he goes to visit the many lands.
In this, he is like the moon everywhere illuminating the entire world.
Even as his voice's conceptual thoughts have all become quiescent,[217]
like echoes in a valley, there is no place where they do not resound. {9}

"Where there are beings of lesser resolve,
he expounds for them the practices of *śrāvaka*-disciples.
If their minds are bright, sharp and pleased by the *pratyeka* vehicle,[218]
then he discourses for them on the path of that intermediate vehicle. {10}

"For the kind and compassionate who delight in beneficence,
he explains for them the deeds practiced by bodhisattvas.
For those with the resolve to acquire the most superior wisdom,
he shows them the unsurpassable Dharma of the Tathāgata. {11}

"In this, he is like a conjurer in his creation of many phenomena
wherein none of those forms or features are real.
So too it is with these conjurations born of this bodhisattva's wisdom.
Though showing all, they transcend existence and nonexistence." {12}

Having thus sung with a thousand myriad beautiful sounds
these songs praising the Buddha, they all then stood there in silence.
Liberation Moon then spoke, saying: "This congregation is now pure.
Please expound now on the path as practiced on the ninth ground." {13}

2. Vajragarbha Commences the Ninth Ground's Explanation

{A} At that time, Vajragarbha Bodhisattva informed Liberation Moon Bodhisattva, saying:

3. Ten Earnestly Pursued Endeavors Enabling Ninth Ground Access

O Son of the Buddha. Here we have the bodhisattva *mahāsattva* who, resorting to such immeasurably vast knowledge as this, has pursued reflective meditative contemplations and has additionally sought:

To seek out ever more supreme realizations of quiescent liberation;
To further cultivate the wisdom of the Tathāgata;
To access the secret dharmas of the Tathāgata;
To contemplate the nature of inconceivably great knowledge;
To purify all gateways to *dhāraṇīs* and samādhis;
To become equipped with the great spiritual superknowledges;
To enter the different sorts of worlds;
To cultivate the powers, fearlessnesses, and dharmas exclusive to the Buddhas;
To accord with all buddhas in turning the wheel of the Dharma;
And to never relinquish his greatly compassionate original vows.

It is he who then succeeds in entering the bodhisattva's ninth ground, the Ground of Excellent Intelligence.

4. This Bodhisattva's Ten Types of Reality-Based Knowledge of Karma

{B} Son of the Buddha, the bodhisattva *mahāsattva* dwelling on this Ground of Excellent Intelligence knows in accordance with reality:

The effects of practicing[219] dharmas that are good, bad, and karmically neutral;
The effects of practicing dharmas either associated with or free of the contaminants;
The effects of practicing worldly dharmas and world-transcending dharmas;
The effects of practicing dharmas that are conceivable and dharmas that are inconceivable;
The effects of practicing the dharmas that are definite and the dharmas that are indefinite;
The effects of practicing *śrāvaka* dharmas and dharmas of *pratyekabuddhas;*
The effects of practicing the bodhisattva practice dharmas;
The effects of practicing dharmas of the Tathāgata's ground;
The effects of practicing conditioned dharmas;
And the effects of practicing unconditioned dharmas.

5. His Ten Types of Reality-Based Knowledge of Entangling Thickets

{C} This bodhisattva uses such wisdom to know in accordance with reality the entangling thickets[220] in beings' minds, specifically knowing:[221]

The entangling thicket of the afflictions;
The entangling thicket of karmic actions;
The entangling thicket of the faculties;
The entangling thicket of resolute beliefs;[222]
The entangling thicket of the sense realms;[223]
The entangling thicket of resolute intentions;[224]
The entangling thicket of latent tendencies;[225]
The entangling thicket of births;[226]
The entangling thicket of the continuity of karmic propensities;[227]
And the entangling thicket associated with the differences among the three groups of beings.[228]

6. Ten Types of Reality-Based Knowledge of Beings' Mental Aspects

{C} This bodhisattva knows in accordance with reality all of the different sorts of characteristics of beings' minds, specifically knowing:

The characteristic of arising with diverse character;
The characteristic of swift transformation;
The characteristic of either being destroyed or undestroyed;
The characteristic of having no physical form;[229]
The characteristic of becoming boundless;[230]
The characteristic of purity;
The characteristic of being either defiled or undefiled;
The characteristic of being either held in bondage or freed of bondage;
The characteristic of being deceptive about its endeavors;
And the characteristic of manifesting in accordance with the destinies of rebirth.

So it is that he knows in accordance with reality such characteristics numbering in the hundreds of thousands of myriads of *koṭis*, knowing characteristics that in number extend to the point of incalculability.

7. His Reality-Based Knowledge of the Afflictions' Characteristics

{E} So too does he know all of the different characteristics of the afflictions, specifically knowing:

Their characteristic of following one long and far;
Their characteristic of possessing boundlessly many bases for their arising;
Their characteristic of accompanying [the mind] in their arising and thus not being abandoned;
Their characteristic of possessing the same quality in both their latent and arisen states;
Their characteristic of being either associated with mind or dissociated from mind;
Their characteristic of abiding in a manner corresponding to the destiny of rebirth one enters;
Their characteristic of differing in each of the three realms of existence;
The characteristic of craving, views, ignorance, and pride to be as calamitous as deeply penetrating arrows;
And their characteristic of uninterrupted continuity in serving as causes and conditions of the three categories of karmic actions.

Briefly stated, he knows in accordance with reality all such characteristics, thus knowing even up to eighty-four thousand such characteristics.

8. His Reality-Based Knowledge of Characteristics of Karmic Actions

{F} So too does he know the characteristics of all of the different sorts of karmic actions, specifically knowing:

Their characteristic of being either good, bad, or neutral;
Their characteristic of being either manifest or not manifest;
Their characteristic of arising in association with and not separate from mind;
Their characteristic of being, due to their very nature, extinguished in every *kṣaṇa* even as there occurs the sequential accumulation of karmic fruits that are never lost;
Their characteristic of involving or not involving karmic retribution;
Their characteristic of involving the undergoing of multiple sorts of karmic retributions as when black actions are rewarded with black retributions, and so forth;[231]
Their characteristic of being comparable to immeasurably vast farm fields [in which their karmic causes are planted];[232]
Their characteristic of possessing differences as performed by the foolish common people and by the Āryas;
Their characteristic of involving the undergoing of their retribution in the present life, in the immediately ensuing rebirth, or in some subsequent life;
And their characteristic of being either definite or indefinite as determined by their association with any of the Vehicles or non-association with any of the Vehicles.

Briefly stated, he knows in accordance with reality all such characteristics, thus knowing even up to eighty-four thousand such characteristics.

9. His Reality-Based Knowledge of Characteristics of Beings' Faculties

{G} So too does he know the characteristics of the various faculties, specifically knowing:

Their characteristic of being either weak, middling, or superb;
Their characteristic of possessing or not possessing distinct differences between the past and the future;
Their characteristic of existing in association with what is either superior, middling, or inferior;
Their characteristic of arising in association with and being inseparable from the afflictions;
Their characteristic of being either definite or indefinite as determined by their association with any of the Vehicles or non-association with any of the Vehicles;

Their characteristic of being entirely ripened and trained to the point of pliancy;

Their characteristic of vulnerability, as befits the state of the individual web of faculties, to transformation and destruction;

Their characteristic of becoming so especially superb that they are insuperable by anyone;

Their characteristic of differing as regards their reversibility or irreversibility;

And their characteristic of possessing differences in the degree to which they continue even distantly to accompany one in their arising.

Briefly stated, he knows in accordance with reality all such characteristics, thus knowing even up to eighty-four thousand such characteristics.

10. His Knowledge of Beliefs, Sense Realms, and Resolute Intentions

So too does he know:

With respect to resolute beliefs,[233] the degree to which they may be either weak, middling, or superior;

With respect to sense realms,[234] the degree to which they may be either weak, middling, or superior;

With respect to resolute intentions,[235] the degree to which they may be either weak, middling, or superior.

With respect to all of these matters, briefly stated, he knows all of their associated characteristics, thus knowing of each of them even up to eighty-four thousand such characteristics.

11. His Knowledge of the Latent Tendencies' Characteristics

{H} He also knows with respect to the latent tendencies,[236] all of their different sorts of characteristics, specifically knowing:

Their characteristic of arising in association with resolute intentions;[237]

Their characteristic of arising in association with thought;

Their characteristic of differing when concomitant with mind or not concomitant with mind;

Their characteristic of following one long and far;

Their characteristic of having existed beginninglessly and thus never having been extricated;

Their characteristic of running counter to the realization of any and all of the *dhyāna* absorptions, liberations, samādhis, *samāpattis*, and spiritual superknowledges;

Their characteristic of being what holds one in bondage to continuous rebirth within the three realms;
Their characteristic of causing the boundlessly continuous manifestation of mind;
Their characteristic of opening the gateway to all of the sense bases;
Their characteristic of possessing such solidity as to be difficult to counteract;
Their characteristic of determining success or failure in acquisition of any of the grounds as stations of the path;
And their characteristic of being only such as may be extricated through the path of the Āryas.

12. His Knowledge of the Characteristics Associated With Births

{I} He also knows with respect to the taking on of rebirths, all of their different sorts of characteristics, specifically knowing:

The characteristic of taking on rebirths in accordance with one's karmic deeds;
The characteristics associated with differences in the six rebirth destinies;
The characteristics associated with differences between form realm and formless realm rebirth;
The characteristics associated with differences between rebirths with perception and rebirths without perception;
The characteristics associated with karmic action acting as a field, craving as moistening water, ignorance as sheltering darkness; and consciousness as a seed giving birth to the sprout of subsequent becoming;
The characteristics of simultaneous arising and inseparability of name and form;
The characteristic of delusion and craving to seek continued existence;
The characteristic of beginningless desirous attachment to desire feelings and to desire rebirth;
And the characteristic of erroneously thinking one has already escaped the desires involved in existence within the three realms.

13. His Knowledge of Characteristics of Habitual Karmic Propensities

{J} He also knows with respect to the habitual karmic propensities,[238] all their different sorts of characteristics, specifically knowing:

The characteristic of differing when active or inactive;
The characteristic of their imbued impressions to follow into the rebirth destinies;

The characteristic of their imbued impressions to accord with beings' actions;

The characteristic of their imbued impressions to accord with karma and afflictions;

The characteristic of their imbued impressions to accord with what is karmically good, bad, or neutral;

The characteristic of their imbued impressions to follow one into subsequent existences;

The characteristic of their creation of imbued impressions to occur in a sequential manner;

The characteristic of their imbued impressions to be associated with ceaseless afflictions that follow one afar and are not relinquished;

The characteristic of their imbued impressions to be associated with what is substantially true or associated with what is not substantially true;

And the characteristic of their imbued impressions to be associated with observing, listening to, and drawing close to either *śrāvaka*-disciples, *pratyekabuddhas*, bodhisattvas, or *tathāgatas*.

14. His Knowledge of Those Fixed in Right, in Wrong, or Unfixed

{K} He also knows with respect to beings the characteristics of being fixed in what is right, fixed in what is wrong, or unfixed, specifically knowing:[239]

The characteristic of being fixed in what is right through the possession of right views;

The characteristic of being fixed in what is wrong through the possession of wrong views;

The characteristic of being unfixed in both of these respects;

The characteristic of being fixed in what is wrong through the five heinous karmic offenses;[240]

The characteristic of being fixed in what is right through the five root faculties;

The characteristic of being unfixed in both of these respects;

The characteristic of being fixed in what is wrong through following the eight-fold wrong path;

The characteristic of being fixed in what is right through following what right by its very nature;

The characteristic of being unfixed in either respect by no longer engaging in either [what is right or what is wrong], thus separating from both;

The characteristic of being fixed in what is wrong through being deeply attached to wrong dharmas;

The characteristic of being fixed in what is right through habitual practice of the path of the Āryas;
And the characteristic of being unfixed in either respect through abandoning both [what is right and what is wrong].

15. His Knowledge-Based Adaptive Teaching and Liberation of Beings

{L} Son of the Buddha, the bodhisattva who accords with knowledge such as this is said to dwell on the Ground of Excellent Intelligence. Having come to dwell on this ground, he completely knows all the different aspects of beings' actions, teaches and trains them, and thereby causes them to gain liberation.

Son of the Buddha, this bodhisattva is well able to expound on the dharmas of the Śrāvaka-disciple Vehicle, the dharmas of the Pratyekabuddha Vehicle, the dharmas of the Bodhisattva Vehicle, and the dharmas of the ground of the Tathāgata.

Because, in all aspects of practice, he acts in accordance with such knowledge, he is able to adapt to variations in beings' faculties, natures, desires, understandings, and practices as well as to differences in their groups.[241] He also accords with whichever destiny they have been born into as well as with their particular afflictions, latent tendencies, karmic bonds, karmic actions and habitual karmic propensities. Having done so, he then explains the Dharma for them accordingly, thereby causing them to develop resolute belief,[242] to increase their wisdom, and to then achieve liberation through whichever vehicle is appropriate for them.

16. The Bodhisattva's Command of Four Types of Unimpeded Knowledge

{M} Son of the Buddha, the bodhisattva who dwells on this Ground of Excellent Intelligence becomes a great expounder of the Dharma[243] thoroughly equipped with the practice appropriate to an expounder of the Dharma. He is thus well able to preserve and protect the Dharma treasury of the Tathāgata.

{N} Availing himself of immeasurably vast knowledge, he brings forth the four types of unimpeded knowledge and uses the bodhisattva's command of phrasing to expound the Dharma. This bodhisattva always accords with permutations of the four kinds of unimpeded knowledge[244] and never abandons them even briefly. What then are those four? They are:

Unimpeded knowledge of Dharma;
Unimpeded knowledge of meaning;
Unimpeded knowledge of language;
And unimpeded knowledge of eloquence.

a. Ten Permutations of Expertise in the Four Unimpeded Knowledges

{O} It is through unimpeded knowledge of Dharma that this bodhisattva knows the specific characteristics of individual dharmas, through unimpeded knowledge of meaning that he knows the differentiating characteristics of dharmas, through unimpeded knowledge of language that he remains free of errors in his discourse, and through unimpeded knowledge of eloquence that his discourse is neither interrupted or exhausted.

{P} Additionally, it is through unimpeded knowledge of Dharma that he knows the nature of dharmas, through unimpeded knowledge of meaning that he knows the production and destruction of dharmas, through unimpeded knowledge of language that he establishes [the conventional designations of] all dharmas and discourses on them continuously,[245] and through unimpeded knowledge of eloquence that he presents boundless discourses that accord with and do no violence to [those conventional designations] he has established.

{Q} Also, it is through unimpeded knowledge of Dharma that he knows the distinctions among present dharmas, through unimpeded knowledge of meaning that he knows the distinctions among past and future dharmas, through unimpeded knowledge of language that he discourses without error on past, future, and present dharmas, and it is through unimpeded knowledge of eloquence that he discourses completely and with boundless Dharma light on each of the periods of time.

{R} Then again, it is through unimpeded knowledge of Dharma that he knows the differences among dharmas, through unimpeded knowledge of meaning that he knows the differences among meanings, through unimpeded knowledge of language that he accords with others' language in his discourse, and through unimpeded knowledge of eloquence that he adapts to others' mental dispositions.

{S} Additionally, it is through unimpeded knowledge of Dharma that he uses Dharma knowledge to know differentiating and non-differentiating aspects. It is through unimpeded knowledge of meaning that he employs comparative knowledge to know differences in accordance with reality. It is through unimpeded knowledge of language that he uses worldly knowledge to discourse on differentiating aspects. And it is through unimpeded knowledge of eloquence that he uses the knowledge of ultimate truth to discourse skillfully.

{T} Also, it is through unimpeded knowledge of Dharma that he knows dharmas' singular and indestructible character. It is through unimpeded knowledge of meaning that his knowing of the aggregates, the sense realms, the sense bases, the truths, and conditioned origination is skillful. It is through unimpeded knowledge of language that he is able to employ in his discourse a beautifully sublime voice and choice of phrasing that are easily and completely understood by all inhabitants of the world. And it is through unimpeded knowledge of eloquence that he becomes ever more supremely able to discourse with boundless Dharma light.

{U} Then again, it is through unimpeded knowledge of Dharma that he knows the uniformly equal nature of the One Vehicle, through unimpeded knowledge of meaning that he knows the different natures of all the vehicles, through unimpeded knowledge of language that he expounds on the absence of differences among all of the vehicles, and through unimpeded knowledge of eloquence that he expounds on each and every one of the vehicles with boundless Dharma [light].[246]

{V} Also, it is through unimpeded knowledge of Dharma that he knows the practices of all bodhisattvas, the practice of knowledge, the practice of the Dharma, and the realizations following from knowledge. It is through unimpeded knowledge of meaning that he knows the differences in meaning associated with the stations on ten grounds. It is through unimpeded knowledge of language that he discourses on the aspects of the path of the grounds that do not differ. And it is through unimpeded knowledge of eloquence that he expounds on the boundless practice aspects of each and every one of the grounds.

{W} Then again, it is through unimpeded knowledge of Dharma that he knows the realization of the right enlightenment in but a single mind-moment as achieved by all Tathāgatas. It is through unimpeded knowledge of meaning that he knows the individual distinctions in the many different times, the many different places, and so forth. It is through unimpeded knowledge of language that he expounds on the different aspects associated with the realization of right enlightenment. And it is through unimpeded knowledge of eloquence that he may discourse on each and every sentence of Dharma for measurelessly many kalpas and yet still not come to the end of it.

{X} Also, it is through unimpeded knowledge of Dharma that he knows the corresponding realizations associated with all

Tathāgatas' proclamations, powers, fearlessnesses, dharmas exclusive to buddhas, great kindness, great compassion, eloquence, skillful means, turning of the Dharma wheel, and cognition of all-knowledge. It is through unimpeded knowledge of meaning that he knows the means by which the Tathāgata's voice adapts to beings' eighty-four thousand different implementations of resolute intentions,[247] different faculties, and different resolute beliefs.[248] It is through unimpeded knowledge of language that, adapting to all of the courses of action engaged in by beings, he uses the voice of the Tathāgata to present different explanations to them. And it is through unimpeded knowledge of eloquence that, adapting to beings' resolute convictions,[249] he uses the Tathāgata's knowledge and perfectly pure practice to discourse for them.

17. His Acquisition of Dhāraṇīs & Further Receipt of Buddhas' Dharma

{Y} Son of the Buddha, the bodhisattva dwelling on the ninth ground acquires just such skill in the unimpeded knowledges, acquires the Tathāgata's treasury of sublime Dharma, becomes a great master of the Dharma, and also acquires the meanings *dhāraṇī*, the Dharma *dhāraṇī*, the wisdom *dhāraṇī*, the radiant illumination *dhāraṇī*, the good intelligence *dhāraṇī*, the manifold wealth *dhāraṇī*, the awe-inspiring virtue *dhāraṇī*, the unimpeded gateway *dhāraṇī*, the boundless *dhāraṇī*, and the variety of meanings *dhāraṇī*. He acquires in their fullness a hundred myriads of *asaṃkhyeyas* of *dhāraṇī* gateways and he employs a hundred myriads of *asaṃkhyeyas* of gateways of skillfulness in voice and eloquence with which he expounds the Dharma.

Having acquired hundreds of myriads of *asaṃkhyeyas* of *dhāraṇīs* such as these, this bodhisattva, appearing before each and every one of measurelessly many buddhas wherever those buddhas dwell, then uses hundreds of myriads of *asaṃkhyeyas* of *dhāraṇī* gateways such as these in listening to their teachings of right Dharma. Then, having heard them, he never forgets them. He then takes up those measurelessly many different gateways and expounds on them for others.

{Z} When this bodhisattva first enters the presence of a buddha, he bows, head to the ground, in reverential obeisance, and then, straightaway, in their very presence, acquires measurelessly many gateways into the Dharma. These dharmas that he acquires are so extensive that, even in a hundred thousand kalpas, none of the great *śrāvaka*-disciples who are skillful in learning and retention could ever be able to absorb them.

18. His Expounding on Dharma Throughout a Great Trichiliocosm

Having acquired such *dhāraṇīs* and such unimpeded knowledges as these, even as this bodhisattva sits on the Dharma throne and expounds on Dharma, he is just then explaining it for the beings abiding throughout the worlds of a great trichiliocosm, doing so in a manner adapted to their different mental dispositions.[250] With the sole exception of the Buddhas and those bodhisattvas who have already received the consecration, there is no one in any other assembly whose awe-inspiring virtue and brilliant radiance could ever rival that which he manifests.

19. This Bodhisattva's 10 Types of Voice-Like Expression in Teaching

When this bodhisattva sits on the Dharma throne:

He may wish to use but a single voice to cause everyone within a great assembly to gain complete comprehension, whereupon they will immediately acquire complete comprehension.

He may wish to employ many different sorts of voices to cause everyone in an entire great assembly to equally develop an understanding.

He may at times wish, by emanating great radiant light, to thereby proclaim gateways to the Dharma.

He may at times wish for the sound of Dharma to be proclaimed from each and every single hair pore on his body.

He may at times wish to cause all things with and without form throughout the worlds of a great trichiliocosm to simultaneously send forth the sublime sounds of Dharma.

He may at times wish to utter the sound of a single word that will then pervade the entire Dharma realm, causing all within it to achieve complete comprehension.

He may at times wish for the sounds of all words to emanate the sound of the Dharma, doing so in a way that constantly endures and never fades away.

He may at times wish for all musical sounds throughout all worlds, including those of flutes, pipes, bells, drums, songs, and chants, to proclaim in unison the sounds of the Dharma.

He may at times wish for but a single word to become entirely replete in itself with all of the words contained in all utterances of Dharma.

He may at times wish to cause each and every one of the finest atoms comprising the four great elements of earth, water, fire, and wind throughout an ineffable and measureless number of worlds to each proclaim an ineffable number of Dharma gateways.

In just this way, whatever he brings to mind comes to pass in accordance with his intentions so that none of them do not do so.

20. His Independent Command of Countless Simultaneous Voices

Son of the Buddha, even if all the beings within the worlds of a great trichiliocosm all came before this bodhisattva, and each and every one of them, using measurelessly many words, let flourish questions wherein each and every one of those questions was different from the others, this bodhisattva would still be able in but a single mind-moment to absorb them all and then, employing but a single voice, he would be able to explain and resolve every one of those questions, thereby causing each individual to become delighted in a manner accordant with whatever suits his mental disposition.

In this same way, even if each and every one of all the beings in an inexpressibly great number of worlds were, in but a single *kṣaṇa,* to use measurelessly many words as they let flourish questions wherein each and every one of those questions was different from the others, in but a single mind-moment, this bodhisattva would be able to absorb them all and, employing but a single voice, he would be able to explain and resolve every one of them, thereby causing each individual to become delighted in a manner accordant with his mental disposition.

So, too, even were this to be the case with all the beings filling up an ineffably great number of ineffably many worlds, this bodhisattva would still be able to explain the Dharma for each of them, in every case according with whatever suits each being's mental disposition, suits his faculties, and suits his resolute beliefs.

So it is that, receiving the assistance of the Buddhas' spiritual powers, he engages on a vast scale in accomplishing the Buddha's works, everywhere serving as someone upon whom everyone can rely.

21. The Bodhisattva's Vigor in Quest of the Light of Knowledge

Son of the Buddha, this bodhisattva redoubles his application of vigor in order to perfect the light of knowledge, doing so even to this degree: Suppose that on the tip of every single hair there were buddha assemblies as numerous as the atoms in an ineffably great number of worlds. Suppose as well that, in every one of those assemblies, there were beings as numerous as the atoms in an ineffably great number of worlds, each and every one of which beings possessed individual dispositions as numerous as the atoms in an ineffably great number of worlds. Suppose also that all of those buddhas bestowed on those beings a gateway into the Dharma suited to those beings' individual dispositions. And suppose too that this circumstance obtaining with this one single place on the tip of a single hair was also true of all other places throughout the entire Dharma realm. Even so, this bodhisattva would still be able in but a single mind-moment to take in and never forget even all of those measurelessly many gateways to the Dharma as have been described herein.

Son of the Buddha, the bodhisattva dwelling on this ninth ground is intensely focused in the diligence of his practice both day and night, never indulging any other thought other than his aspiration that is solely devoted to entering the realm in which the Buddha courses,[251] to drawing close to the Tathāgata, and to entering the extremely profound liberations of all bodhisattvas. He always abides in samādhi, constantly sees the Buddhas, and never relinquishes this circumstance.

22. The Bodhisattva's Seeing and Serving of Countless Buddhas

In each and every kalpa, he sees measurelessly many buddhas, measurelessly many hundreds of buddhas, measurelessly many thousands of buddhas, and so forth on up to his seeing of measurelessly many hundreds of thousands of *koṭis* of *nayutas* of buddhas. He pays reverence to, venerates, renders service to, and presents offerings to those buddhas. He also presents inquiries to them on many different sorts of difficult topics and acquires the *dhāraṇīs* facilitating the proclamation of Dharma.

23. His Good Roots' Purity Like the Gold of a Cakravartin's Crown

All of his roots of goodness become ever more bright in the radiance of their purity in a manner comparable to the real gold that would be crafted by a skillful goldsmith into a jeweled crown made to adorn the head of a wheel-turning sage king, one that could never be rivaled by any adornment in the possession of any of the lesser kings, ministers, or citizens anywhere else on the four continents. Just so are the roots of goodness of this bodhisattva dwelling on the ninth ground, for they are such that none of the roots of goodness of any *śrāvaka*-disciple, *pratyekabuddha*, or bodhisattva dwelling on a lesser ground could ever rival.

24. His Good Roots' Purity Like a Brahma Heaven King's Radiance

Son of the Buddha, this circumstance is comparable to that of a king of the Great Brahma Heaven, a lord of two thousand worlds, whose body emanates such radiant light that it illuminates with dazzling brilliance even the most dark and distant places throughout those two thousand worlds, thus dispelling all darkness therein. So too it is with all the roots of goodness of the bodhisattva dwelling on this ground, for he is thereby enabled to emanate such brilliant light that it illuminates the minds of beings and thus causes all the darkness of their afflictions to become entirely extinguished.

25. The Ninth Ground Bodhisattva's Focus on the Powers Pāramitā

Among the ten *pāramitās*, this bodhisattva has become most supreme in his perfection of the powers *pāramitā*. It is not that he does not practice the others. Rather, he simply accords them an amount of emphasis corresponding to his own strengths and to what is fitting.

26. Vajragarbha's Final Statements About the 9th Ground Bodhisattva

Son of the Buddha, this has been a general explanation of the bodhisattva *mahāsattva*'s, ninth ground, the Ground of Excellent Intelligence. Were one to discourse on this extensively, then one would remain unable to finish the discussion of it even if one carried it forth for measurelessly many kalpas.

a. The Bodhisattva's Station and Dharma Practice

Son of the Buddha, the bodhisattva dwelling on this ground often becomes a king of the Great Brahma Heaven, a lord ruling over two thousand worlds who is well able to govern and liberally serve the benefit of others with sovereign mastery. He is able to differentially expound on the practice of the *pāramitās* for the sake of all *śrāvaka*-disciples, *pratyekabuddhas*, and bodhisattvas. In this, he adapts to beings' mental dispositions[252] and, in addressing all of their challenging questions, there is no one who can prevail over him.

b. The Bodhisattva's Mindfulness

In his practice of giving, pleasing words, beneficial actions, and joint endeavors, and, in all such works that he pursues, he never departs from mindfulness of the Buddha, and so forth until we come to his never departing from mindfulness of the knowledge of all modes and the cognition of all-knowledge.

c. The Bodhisattva's Aspiration to Serve Beings

He also has this thought: "I should become one who serves these beings as a leader, as one who is supreme," and so forth until we come to "as one who relies on the cognition of all-knowledge."

d. The Consequences of the Bodhisattva's Vigor and Vows

If this bodhisattva brings forth diligently vigorous practice, then, in but a moment, he will become able to enter samādhis as numerous as the atoms in hundreds of myriads of *asaṃkhyeyas* of lands, and so forth until we come to his becoming able to transformationally manifest bodhisattvas to serve as his retinue that are as numerous as the atoms in hundreds of myriads of *asaṃkhyeyas* of lands. If he resorts to the power inherent in the bodhisattva's especially supreme vows, he becomes able then to freely manifest numbers beyond even this, such that one would never be able to count them even in a period of hundreds of thousands of *koṭis* of *nayutas* of kalpas.

27. Vajragarbha Bodhisattva's Summarizing Verses

At that time, Vajragarbha Bodhisattva, wishing to restate his meaning, thereupon uttered verses, saying:

Through skillful meditation with measureless wisdom power
that is the most supremely subtle and difficult for the world to know,
he everywhere enters the Tathāgata's secret places,
and, serving the benefit of beings, enters the ninth ground. {14}

Exercising sovereign mastery in both *dhāraṇis* and samādhis and
gaining great spiritual superknowledges, he enters the many lands.
Equipped with the powers, wisdom, fearlessness, exclusive dharmas,
vow power, and compassionate mind, he enters the ninth ground. {15}

Dwelling on this ground he preserves the treasury of Dharma
and utterly knows: what is good, bad, or neutral; what possesses
or is free of the contaminants; what is worldly or world-transcending;
and what is conceivable or inconceivable. He well knows them all. {16}

As for whether any dharma is definite or indefinite as well as what
Three Vehicle's adherents do, he meditatively contemplates it all.
Regarding the differences in conditioned and unconditioned actions,
he knows them just as they are and thus enters the worlds. {17}

If he wishes to know beings' minds, he can use knowledge to know
as they truly are their many characteristics including whether
they are diversely arising, swiftly transformed, deteriorating,
not deteriorating, insubstantial, boundless, and so forth. {18}

He knows afflictions as boundless, as in constant accompaniment, as
of the same quality, latent or arising, as continuing in the destinies,
knows karmic actions' varying natures, each different, destruction of
of causes, and accrual of effects. He is able to know all of these. {19}

All the different faculties, inferior, middling, or superior,
their past and future differences, countless other distinctions,
resolute beliefs, sense realms, and resolute intentions—
of eighty-four thousand aspects, there are none he does not know. {20}

[He knows] beings' afflictions and views that ever follow and bind,
their beginningless entangling thickets, never yet cut down, the
[latent tendencies] arising with intentions and together with mind,
and their always restraining and binding them, never being severed. {21}

He knows they are merely erroneous thought, are unreal phenomena,
are inseparable from the mind, are devoid of dwelling place, are
still able to cause retreat after being dispelled by *dhyāna* samādhis,
and are extinguished on the vajra path and then are finally ended. {22}

He knows that taking birth in the six destinies, each case differs,
that karma is the field, cravings are moisture, ignorance is covering,
consciousness is the seed, name-and-form are the sprout, and these
cause beginningless ever continuous becoming in the three realms. {23}

He knows afflicted acts and mental habits cause birth in the destinies,
knows that, if one abandons these, there will be no further births,
and knows beings as all existing within one of three groupings,[253]
and as either drowning among views or else as practicing the path. {24}

Dwelling on this ground, he is skillful in meditative contemplation,
adapts to their dispositions, faculties, and resolute beliefs, and,
always employs the unimpeded knowledges and sublime eloquence
by which he teaches each differently as befits what is appropriate. {25}

As he sits on the Dharma throne, he is like a lion,
also is like the king of bulls, the king of jewel mountains,
or a king of dragons who spreads forth dense clouds,
showers down the sweet dew rain, and thus fills the great oceans. {26}

He knows well the nature of dharmas and their abstruse meanings,
is able with concordant verbal expressions to expound eloquently,
and with a hundred myriad *asaṃkhyeyas* of *dhāraṇīs*, he retains all
just as the great ocean takes in the many showers of rain. {27}

With *dhāraṇīs* and samādhis that are all pure,
he is able in but a single mind-moment to see the many buddhas,
listens to the Dharma in the presence of each and every buddha,
and then in turn expounds on it with a sublimely wondrous voice. {28}

Whenever he wishes, throughout the worlds of a great trichiliocosm,
he teaches all of the many classes of beings, becoming in this
like a vastly spreading cloud that has no place it fails to reach as he
adapts to their faculties and predilections, causing all to feel joyful. {29}

Even with countless buddha assemblies on the tips of every hair
and even with beings' mental predilections also being endless,
they respond to all their minds in the bestowing of Dharma gates,
doing so in this same manner throughout the entire Dharma realm.

The bodhisattva diligently applies the power of vigor and thereby
gains yet more meritorious qualities, ever more supremely refined.
His hearing and retaining of so very many Dharma gateways as this
is comparable to the earth's ability to retain all seeds. {30}

If the countless beings throughout the ten directions
all came and drew close to where he sits in the midst of an assembly,
in but a moment, he would adapt to their minds as each poses queries
and then, with a single voice, he would respond and satisfy them all. {31}

Dwelling on this ground, he serves as a king of Dharma, adapting
to beings' potentials, tirelessly providing teaching and inducement.
Day and night, he sees the Buddhas, never relinquishes that vision,
and enters deeply quiescent knowledge and liberation. {32}

He makes offerings to buddhas, skillfully refines his brilliance
so that it shines like the Sage King's marvelously bejeweled crown
and also causes the darkness of beings' afflictions to be extinguished
just as when the Brahma Heaven King's light shines on every place. {33}

Dwelling herein, he often becomes king of a Great Brahma Heaven
who employs the Dharma of the Three Vehicles to teach beings.
The good works he does are everywhere and liberally beneficial
all the way on to his future realization of all-knowledge. {34}

The samādhis he enters in but a single mind-moment
number as the atoms comprising an *asaṃkhyeya* of lands.
So too is the number of buddhas he sees proclaiming the Dharma.
By the power of vows these extend in number even beyond this. {35}

This has been the ninth, the Ground of Excellent Intelligence,
the station in which bodhisattvas of great knowledge practice,
one that is extremely profound, sublime, and recondite.
I have now finished its explanation for the Sons of the Buddha. {36}

Part Ten
The Dharma Cloud Ground

J. The Tenth Ground: The Dharma Cloud Ground

1. The Tenth Ground's Introductory Verses and Dharma Request

Having heard of the supreme practices carried out on this ground,
the *nayutas* of Pure Dwelling Heaven devas
who were up in the sky sprang up in delight and then,
united in deep sincerity, presented offerings to the Buddha. {1}

That inconceivably vast assembly of bodhisattvas
that was also there in the sky was immensely delighted.
They all lit the most supremely mind-pleasing incenses
that everywhere permeated that assembly, causing it to be purified. {2}

The Paranirmita Vaśavartin Heaven King with his heavenly host
of countless *koṭis* of devas that were there in the sky scattered
everywhere heavenly raiment as offerings to the Buddha which
floated down in a profusion of a hundred thousand myriad sorts. {3}

Of the heavenly nymphs there in measureless numbers,
none failed to then joyfully present offerings to the Buddha
as they each played all sorts of sublime music and
all together used these phrases in offering their praises: {4}

"Even as this body of the Buddha sits securely in a single land,
he manifests bodies in all worlds, wherein, in stately adornment,
countless *koṭis* of his physical appearances are seen,
entirely filling the Dharma realm in all its vastness. {5}

Within a single hair pore, he emanates light
that everywhere extinguishes the darkness of the world's afflictions.
Though one might be able to know a land's number of atoms,
one could still never measure these light rays' number. {6}

One may see the Tathāgata there replete with all his many signs,
turning the unsurpassable wheel of right Dharma.
One may see him roaming forth to all of the buddha lands,
or one may see him still, at peace, unmoving. {7}

Or he may manifest as dwelling in the Tuṣita Heaven Palace,
or may manifest as descending into his mother's womb,
or may appear as dwelling in the womb or emerging from the womb,
in all such cases causing this to be observable in countless lands. {8}

He may manifest as leaving home, cultivating the path in the world,
as appearing in the *bodhimaṇḍa,* and as realizing right enlightenment.
He may appear as proclaiming the Dharma and as entering nirvāṇa,
everywhere causing there to be none in ten directions not seeing this. {9}

Just as a master conjurer skilled in the techniques of conjuration
performs his many feats in the midst of a great crowd,
so too it is in the case of the Tathāgata's wisdom by which
he manifests his bodies everywhere throughout the worlds. {10}

The Buddha dwells within dharmas' extremely profound true nature
that is quiescent, signless, and like space
even as, from within ultimate truth,
he manifests the many different deeds that he performs. {11}

All those endeavors performed for the benefit of beings,
come into existence in dependence upon the very nature of dharmas.
That possessed of signs and the signless have no differentiation,
for, with entry into the ultimate, they are all signless. {12}

If one wishes to acquire the knowledge of the Tathāgata,
one should abandon all false discriminations, utterly comprehend
existents and non-existents all abide in a state of uniform equality,
and thus swiftly become a great guide for humans and devas." {13}

Having offered up these praises with many different phrases,
this countless and boundlessly vast assemblage of celestial nymphs
fell silent in both body and mind, and, united in their happiness,
gazed up at the Tathāgata as they stood there quietly. {14}

Then Liberation Moon Bodhisattva,
aware that everyone in the great assembly was now still and silent,
straightaway addressed Vajragarbha Bodhisattva, saying:
"O, Great Fearless One, True Son of the Buddha." {15}

"We pray that you who possess such intelligence and wisdom
will expound here on all the meritorious qualities, aspects of practice,
spiritual superknowledges, and transformational deeds involved
in advancing from the ninth ground into the tenth ground." {16}

2. Vajragarbha Commences the Tenth Ground's Explanation

{A} At that time, Vajragarbha Bodhisattva Mahāsattva informed Liberation Moon Bodhisattva, saying:

3. The Ten Categories of Practice Before Entering the Tenth Ground

O Son of the Buddha. From the first ground through the ninth ground, having employed such measureless wisdom as this in meditative contemplation and awakening, the bodhisattva *mahāsattva*:

Engages in thorough meditative contemplation on cultivation;[254]
Thoroughly fulfills the pristinely white dharmas;
Assembles boundlessly many dharmas constituting the provisions for the path;
Increases his immense stock of merit and wisdom;
Cultivates the great compassion on a vast scale;
Comes to know the aspects distinguishing the worlds;
Penetrates the entangling thickets of the realms of beings;[255]
Enters the domain in which the Tathāgata courses;
Accords with the Tathāgata's quiescence practices;
And always carries on meditative contemplations focused on the Tathāgatas' powers, fearlessnesses, and dharmas exclusive to the Buddhas.

Having done so, he is then said to have reached the station wherein one receives the consecration of imminent acquisition of the knowledge of all modes and the cognition of all-knowledge.

4. This Bodhisattva's Subsequent Acquisition of Samādhis

{B} Son of the Buddha. Once this bodhisattva *mahāsattva* has employed wisdom such as this to enter the ground of consecration, he straightaway acquires:[256]

The bodhisattva's stainless samādhi;
The entering the distinctions within the dharma realm samādhi;
The adornment of the *bodhimaṇḍa* samādhi;
The radiance of every kind of flower samādhi;
The oceanic treasury samādhi;
The oceanic reflection samādhi;
The vastness of empty space samādhi;
The contemplation of the nature of all dharmas samādhi;
The knowledge of the minds and actions of all beings samādhi;
And the direct manifestation of all buddhas samādhi.

A hundred myriads of *asaṃkhyeyas* of other samādhis such as these also all manifest directly before him. In all of these samādhis, the bodhisattva, whether entering them or arising from them, in all cases achieves a state of consummate skillfulness while also comprehending well the differences in the functional uses to which all of these samādhis are devoted. The very last samādhi to manifest for him is the one known as "the station of the acquisition of the supreme consecration of all-knowledge."[257]

5. This Final Samādhi's Manifestation of an Immense Radiant Lotus

{C} When this samādhi manifests directly before him, an immense bejeweled lotus flower suddenly emerges, one whose blossom is so immense that it equals in volume the breadth of a hundred myriad great trichiliocosms. It is inlaid and adorned with the many sorts of marvelous precious gems and presents an appearance that surpasses any realm of objective phenomena observed in any world. This is a phenomenon that comes forth from his world-transcending roots of goodness and that is perfected by his many practices utilizing the knowledge that all dharmas are by nature like mere illusions.

It constantly radiates brilliant light that everywhere illuminates the Dharma realm. This is a phenomenon that is not found even in any of the celestial abodes. Its stem is made of beryl and *maṇi* jewels. Its dais consists of *candana* incense. Emeralds composes its floral pistils and its petals are made of *jambunada* gold. Its blossom always emanates countless light rays. The many sorts of precious jewels compose its inner chamber, and it is covered over by a bejeweled net canopy. Lotus blossoms as numerous as the atoms in ten great trichiliocosms make up its retinue.

6. This Bodhisattva Sits Atop a Lotus Encircled by Retinue Bodhisattvas

At this time, as the bodhisattva then sits atop the flower throne, the scale of his physical appearance precisely matches that of the throne itself. Measurelessly many bodhisattvas serve as his retinue, with each of them sitting upon one of the other lotus blossoms completely encircling him. Each and every one of them, having thereupon acquired a hundred myriad samādhis, then single-mindedly gazes up at this great bodhisattva.

{D} Son of the Buddha. When this great bodhisattva together with his retinue are all sitting there on their lotus thrones, all of those light rays as well as the sound of his words then everywhere fill all ten directions of the Dharma realm, those worlds all quake, the wretched destinies become stilled, and all lands then became adorned and purified. Of all the bodhisattvas engaged in the same practices, none of them do not then come and assemble there.

The musical sounds of men and devas then simultaneously resound as all of those beings experience feelings of happiness and then present offerings of inconceivable gifts to all the Buddhas. All of the assemblies of the Buddhas then became visibly manifest.

7. His Body Emanates Light Illuminating Ten Realms of Beings

Son of the Buddha. As this bodhisattva sits there atop that immense lotus blossom throne, from the bottom of his two feet, he releases a hundred myriads of *asaṃkhyeyas* of light rays that everywhere illuminate all the great hell realms throughout the ten directions and extinguish the sufferings undergone by the beings dwelling in them.

From his two knee caps, he releases a hundred myriads of *asaṃkhyeyas* of light rays that everywhere illuminate all the ten directions' animal rebirth destinies and extinguish the sufferings of the beings dwelling in them.

From the center of his navel, he releases a hundred myriads of *asaṃkhyeyas* of light rays that everywhere illuminate the ten directions' realms of King Yama and extinguish the sufferings of the beings residing in them.[258]

From his left and right sides, he releases a hundred myriads of *asaṃkhyeyas* of light rays that everywhere illuminate all the realms of the human destinies throughout the ten directions and extinguish the sufferings of the beings residing in them.

From his two hands, he releases a hundred myriads of *asaṃkhyeyas* of light rays that everywhere illuminate all the palaces of the devas and *asuras* throughout the ten directions.

From atop his two shoulders, he releases a hundred myriads of *asaṃkhyeyas* of light rays that everywhere illuminate all the *śrāvaka*-disciples throughout the ten directions.

From the back of his neck, he releases a hundred myriads of *asaṃkhyeyas* of light rays that everywhere illuminate the bodies of all the *pratyekabuddhas* throughout the ten directions.

From his face, he releases a hundred myriads of *asaṃkhyeyas* of light rays that everywhere illuminate the bodies of all the bodhisattvas throughout the ten directions, inclusive of those who have newly brought forth the initial resolve on up to all those dwelling on the ninth ground.

From between his eyebrows, he releases a hundred myriads of *asaṃkhyeyas* of light rays that everywhere illuminate all the bodhisattvas throughout the ten directions who had received the consecration while also causing the palaces of the *māras* to no longer appear.

From the crown of his head, he then releases light rays as numerous as the atoms in a hundred myriads of *asaṃkhyeyas* of great trichiliocosms that everywhere illuminate the assemblies attending upon the *bodhimaṇḍas* of all the Buddhas, the Tathāgatas, throughout all worlds of the ten directions.

8. The Light Rays Form a Canopy That Makes Offerings to All Buddhas

Those rays then circle around them ten times in a rightward direction and, having ascended into the midst of space, they dwell there and form a netlike canopy of bright light known as "Flaming Radiance" that then sends forth all sorts of different offerings to the Buddhas.

Those offerings are so numerous that the offerings of all the other bodhisattvas from those who have but newly brought forth the resolve on through to those who dwell on the ninth ground could not compare to even a hundredth part and so forth until we come to their being unable to compare at all even by resort to calculation or analogy.

That canopy of brilliant light rains down offerings before each and every one of the Tathāgatas and their assemblies everywhere throughout the ten directions, raining down the many sorts of marvelous incenses, floral garlands, raiment, banners, bejeweled canopies, various *maṇi* jewels, and other sorts of adornments, all of which are presented there as offerings. In every case, these offerings issue from world-transcending roots of goodness and surpass anything found in any worldly realm. Were there to be any being at all who might observe this occurrence, they would all be those who had already reached the stage of irreversibility with respect to the realization of *anuttarasamyaksaṃbodhi.*

9. The Light Rays Circle Around All Buddhas and Enter Their Feet

Son of the Buddha. Once this immense aggregation of light rays has finished these acts of offering, it then once again circles around each and every one of the *bodhimaṇḍa* assemblies of all buddhas throughout all worlds of the ten directions. After it has finished circling around them ten times, it then enters the bottoms of the feet of all *tathāgatas.*

It is at this time that all buddhas and bodhisattvas realize that, in this particular world system, a particular bodhisattva *mahāsattva* has been able to perform such immensely expansive practices and has thus reached the stage of receiving the consecration.

10. The 10 Regions' Bodhisattvas Come, Make Offerings & Enter Samādhi

Son of the Buddha. At this time, the congregation of all the measurelessly and boundlessly many bodhisattvas throughout the ten directions inclusive of those who have reached the ninth ground then arrives there. They circumambulate him, reverently present offerings, and then enter a state of single-minded meditative contemplation. At the very time when they enter into this state of meditative contemplation, each of these bodhisattvas acquires a myriad samādhis.

11. They Emanate Light from Their Chests That Enters His Chest

Just at that very time, all the bodhisattvas throughout the ten directions who have already received the consecration emanate from their chests' vajra adornment meritorious-qualities symbol an immense beam of bright light known as "able to destroy Māra's enmity," one attended by a hundred myriads of *asaṃkhyeyas* of light rays that form its retinue. It everywhere illuminates all of the ten directions and manifests incalculably many permutations of the spiritual superknowledges. After it has finished carrying out these actions, it then comes and enters the vajra adornment virtuous-qualities mark on this bodhisattva's chest. After that light has entered, it then causes all of the wisdom and powers of this bodhisattva to increase more than a hundred thousand fold.

12. All Buddhas Send Forth Light That Enters This Bodhisattva's Crown

{E} At that time, all buddhas throughout the ten directions put forth a pure beam of light from between their eyebrows known as "enhancer of all-knowledge's superknowledges," one attended by countless light rays that form its retinue. It everywhere illuminates all worlds throughout the ten directions, circling them ten times in a rightward direction, manifesting the Tathāgatas' vast powers of sovereign mastery and instigating the awakening of a congregation of incalculably many hundreds of thousands of *koṭis* of *nayutas* of bodhisattvas, everywhere causing the quaking of all buddha lands, extinguishing the sufferings in all the wretched destinies, covering over and hiding the palaces of the *māras*, and revealing the adornments and awe-inspiring qualities in all the assemblies at those *bodhimaṇḍas* wherein the Buddhas have achieved realization of bodhi.

After having everywhere illuminated all worlds even to the ends of empty space and throughout the entire Dharma realm, it then comes and, arriving in the assembly of this bodhisattva, circles ten times around in a rightward direction, revealing all of the different sorts of adornments there. After having revealed these phenomena, it then enters into the crown of this great bodhisattva. Its retinue light rays also each enter the crowns of those other bodhisattvas in attendance there.

13. This Bodhisattva Acquires Samādhis and All Buddhas' Consecration

At that very time, this bodhisattva acquires a hundred myriad samādhis he has never before acquired and becomes known[259] as one who has reached the station of consecration and has entered the realm of the Buddhas wherein, having completely developed the ten powers, he joins the ranks of the Buddhas.

14. The Simile of the Consecration of the Wheel Turning Sage King's Son

Son of the Buddha. In this circumstance he is comparable to a crown prince born to a wheel-turning sage king whose mother is the chief queen and who is himself completely endowed with the physical marks. That wheel-turning king orders this prince to sit on the throne of marvelous gold atop his white elephant treasure, raises the great canopy, plants the great banner, burns incense, scatters flowers, plays all sorts of music, takes up water from each of the four great seas, and places it into the vase of gold.

The King then takes up this vase and pours the liquid out over the crown of the prince's head. From this very moment on he is known as one who has reached the stage of receiving royal consecration at which point he then joins the ranks of the consecrated *kṣatriyan* kings. He then straightaway becomes able to completely fulfill the ten courses of good karmic action and is then also able to become known as a wheel-turning sage king.

So too it is in the case of this bodhisattva who has received the consecration. Because the waters of all buddhas' knowledge have been poured onto the crown of his head, he is then known as one who has received the consecration. It is on account of his complete development of the Tathāgata's ten powers that he then joins the ranks of the Buddhas.

15. The Capacities Arising From This Bodhisattva's Consecration

Son of the Buddha. This is what is what is known as the bodhisattva's great knowledge consecration. It is because of this great knowledge consecration that this bodhisattva is then able to engage in incalculably many hundreds of thousands of myriads of *koṭis* of *nayutas* of difficult-to-practice practices and increase his growth in incalculably many sorts of wisdom and meritorious qualities. So it is that he is then known as one who abides securely on the Dharma Cloud Ground.

16. This Bodhisattva's Knowledge of Attainments

{F} Son of the Buddha. The bodhisattva *mahāsattva* dwelling on this Dharma Cloud Ground knows in accordance with reality:

Attainment as it takes place in the desire realm;[260]
Attainment as it takes place in the form realm;
Attainment as it takes place in the formless realm;
Attainment as it takes place within the worldly realms;
Attainment as it takes place within the Dharma realm;
Attainment as it takes place within the conditioned realm;
Attainment as it takes place within the unconditioned realm;
Attainment as it takes place within the realms of beings;
Attainment as it takes place within the realms of consciousness;
Attainment as it takes place within the realm of empty space;
And attainment as it takes place within the realm of nirvāṇa.

This bodhisattva also knows in accordance with reality:

The attainment of karmic actions associated with the views and the afflictions;
Knows attainment as it takes place in the production and destruction of worlds;
Knows the attainment of *śrāvaka*-disciple practices;
Knows the attainment of *pratyekabuddha* practices;
Knows the attainment of bodhisattva practices;
Knows attainment as it takes place in a *tathāgata*'s powers, fearlessnesses, form bodies, and Dharma body;
Knows attainment of the knowledge associated with the knowledge of all modes and all-knowledge;
Knows attainment as it occurs in the manifestation of the appearance of realizing bodhi and turning the Dharma wheel;
And knows attainment as it takes place in entering the knowledge that is decisive in its distinguishing of all dharmas.

To speak of what is essential in this, he employs all-knowledge to know all processes of attainment.

17. This Bodhisattva's Knowledge of Transformation

Son of the Buddha. This bodhisattva *mahāsattva* resorts to just such supremely awakened wisdom to know in accordance with reality:

Transformation as it takes place in beings' karmic actions;
Transformation as it takes place in the afflictions;
Transformation as it takes place in the views;
Transformation as it takes place in the worlds;
Transformation as it takes place in the Dharma realm;
Transformation as it takes place among *śrāvaka*-disciples;
Transformation as it takes place among *pratyekabuddhas*;

Transformation as it takes place among bodhisattvas;
Transformation as it takes place among *tathāgatas;*
And transformation as it takes place in the presence and absence of differences.

He also knows in accordance with reality all of the other such sorts of transformations.

18. This Bodhisattva's Knowledge of Sustaining Bases

So too does he know in accordance with reality:

The sustaining bases[261] of the Buddha.
The sustaining bases of the Dharma;
The sustaining bases of the Sangha;
The sustaining bases of karma;
The sustaining bases of the afflictions;
The sustaining bases of time;
The sustaining bases of vows;
The sustaining bases of offerings;
The sustaining bases of practices;
The sustaining bases of kalpas;
And the sustaining bases of knowledge.

He also knows in accordance with reality all of the other such sorts of phenomena.

19. This Bodhisattva's Knowledge of Subtleties of Practice

So too does he know in accordance with reality all buddhas', all *tathāgatas'*, knowledge that enters into all sorts of subtlety, specifically knowing:

Their knowledge regarding the subtleties involved in cultivation;
Their knowledge regarding the subtleties involved in the ending of a lifetime;[262]
Their knowledge regarding the subtleties involved in the taking on of birth;
Their knowledge regarding the subtleties involved in abandoning the home life;
Their knowledge regarding the subtleties involved in the manifesting of the spiritual superknowledges;
Their knowledge regarding the subtleties involved in achieving realization of the right enlightenment;
Their knowledge regarding the subtleties involved in turning the wheel of Dharma;

Their knowledge regarding the subtleties involved in abiding throughout a lifespan;

Their knowledge regarding the subtleties involved in [passing into] nirvāṇa;

And their knowledge regarding the subtleties involved in the endurance of their teaching Dharma.

He also knows all of the other such sorts of phenomena in accordance with reality.

20. This Bodhisattva's Knowledge of the Tathāgatas' Secrets

So too does he enter into the Tathāgatas' secrets, specifically entering:

Their secrets associated with the body;

Their secrets associated with speech;

Their secrets associated with the mind;

Their secrets associated with the assessment of timeliness and non-timeliness;

Their secrets associated with the bestowing of predictions upon bodhisattvas;

Their secrets associated with the attraction of beings;

Their secrets associated with the many different sorts of vehicles;

Their secrets associated with the root faculties and practices of all beings;

Their secrets associated with the functioning of karmic actions;

And their secrets associated with acquisition of the practices associated with bodhi.

He also knows all other such sorts of phenomena in accordance with reality.

21. This Bodhisattva's Knowledge of the Interpenetration of Kalpas

So too does he know all of the knowledge of the Buddhas with regard to the interpenetration of kalpas [and other such measures of time], specifically knowing:

How a single kalpa may enter into an *asaṃkhyeya* kalpa;

How an *asaṃkhyeya* kalpa may enter into a single kalpa;

How an enumerated number of kalpas may enter into innumerable kalpas;

How innumerable kalpas may enter into an enumerated number of kalpas;

How a single mind-moment may enter into a kalpa;

How a kalpa may enter into a single mind-moment;

How a kalpa may enter into what does not constitute a kalpa;
How what does not constitute a kalpa may enter into a kalpa;
How a kalpa in which there is a buddha may enter into a kalpa in which there is no buddha;
How a kalpa with no buddha may enter into a kalpa in which there is a buddha;
How past and future kalpas may enter into the present kalpa;
How the present kalpa may enter into past and future kalpas;
How past kalpas may enter into future kalpas;
How future kalpas may enter into past kalpas;
How long kalpas may enter into short kalpas;
And how short kalpas may enter into long kalpas.

He also knows all the other such sorts of phenomena in accordance with reality.

22. This Bodhisattva's Knowing of the Buddha's Penetrating Knowledge

So too does he know all of the types of penetrating knowledge that the Tathāgata possesses, specifically knowing:

The penetrating knowledge[263] that knows the realms of ordinary common people;[264]
The penetrating knowledge that knows atoms;
The rightly enlightened penetrating knowledge that knows [buddha] land bodies;[265]
The rightly enlightened penetrating knowledge that knows the beings' bodies;
The rightly enlightened penetrating knowledge that knows beings' minds;
The rightly enlightened penetrating knowledge that knows beings' actions;
The rightly enlightened penetrating knowledge that knows adaptation to all places;
The penetrating knowledge that knows the manifestation of universally pervasive practices;
The penetrating knowledge that knows the manifestation of adaptive practices;
The penetrating knowledge that knows the manifestation of contrary practices;
The penetrating knowledge that knows the manifestation of conceivable and inconceivable practices and knows the manifestation of practices either completely comprehensible to the world or not completely comprehensible to the world;

And the penetrating knowledge that knows the manifestation of the practices of *śrāvaka*-disciples, *pratyekabuddhas*, bodhisattvas, and *tathāgatas*.

Son of the Buddha. In every case, the bodhisattva dwelling on this ground is able to have penetrating knowledge of all the vast and measureless wisdom possessed by all buddhas.

23. This Bodhisattva's Acquisition of Countless Liberations

{G} Son of the Buddha. The bodhisattva *mahāsattva* dwelling on this ground immediately acquires:

The bodhisattva's inconceivable liberation;
The unimpeded liberation;
The pure contemplation liberation;
The universal illumination liberation;
The *tathāgata* treasury liberation;
The compliance with the unimpeded wheel liberation;
The penetrating comprehension of the three periods of time liberation;
The Dharma realm treasury liberation;
The circle of liberation's light liberation;
And the realm of remainderless totality liberation.

These ten are those that are chief among them. There are incalculably many hundreds of thousands of *asaṃkhyeyas* of other such gateways to liberation that are all acquired on this tenth ground.

24. This Bodhisattva's Samādhis, Dhāraṇīs, and Superknowledges

In this same way, there are also even as many as measurelessly many hundreds of thousands of *asaṃkhyeyas* of samādhi gateways, measurelessly many hundreds of thousands of *asaṃkhyeyas* of *dhāraṇī* gateways, and measurelessly many hundreds of thousands of *asaṃkhyeyas* of spiritual superknowledge gateways that, in every case, he also succeeds in completely developing.

25. This Bodhisattva's Limitless Memory Power

{H} Son of the Buddha. This bodhisattva *mahāsattva* develops a penetrating comprehension of wisdom such as this that accords with measureless bodhi. He also develops such powers of skillful memory that, in a single mind-moment, he is in every case able to accommodate, able to take in, able to absorb, and is able to retain all of the measureless great Dharma light, great Dharma illumination, and great Dharma rain of all of the measurelessly many buddhas throughout the ten directions.

26. His Limitless Memory Compared to the Ocean's Limitless Capacity

Just as it is the case that, with the sole exception of the great ocean, all other places are in every case unable to accommodate, unable to take in, unable to absorb, and unable to retain the great rains poured down by Sāgara, the dragon king, so too it is with the great Dharma light, the great Dharma illumination, and the great Dharma rain coming forth from the secret treasury of the Tathāgata. With the sole exception of the tenth ground bodhisattvas, all other beings including *śrāvaka*-disciples, *pratyekabuddhas,* and bodhisattvas up through the ninth ground are all unable to accommodate it, unable to take it in, unable to absorb it, and unable to retain it.

Son of the Buddha. In this, he is comparable to the great ocean that is able to accommodate, able to take in, able to absorb, and able to retain those great rains poured down by one of the great dragon kings, two of them, three of them, and so forth on up to the rains poured down by countless dragon kings. In but a single mind-moment, it is able to accommodate, able to take in, able to absorb, and able to retain all the rain that they all simultaneously pour down. And why is it able to do this? It is because it is a vessel possessed of an immeasurably vast capacity.

So too it is with this bodhisattva who dwells on the Dharma Cloud Ground who is himself able to accommodate, able to take in, able to absorb, and able to retain the Dharma light, the Dharma illumination, and the Dharma rain brought forth by one buddha, two, three, and so forth on up to measurelessly many buddhas, being able to take it all in in this very same manner, even if it were all to be simultaneously expounded to him in but a single mind-moment. It is for this very reason that this ground is known as the Dharma Cloud Ground.

27. Vimukticandra Asks About the Limits of This Bodhisattva's Memory

Liberation Moon Bodhisattva then asked, "O Son of the Buddha. From how many Tathāgatas' is the bodhisattva dwelling on this ground able in but a single mind-moment to accommodate, take in, absorb, and retain their great Dharma light, their great Dharma illumination, and their great Dharma Rain?"

28. Vajragarbha's Analogy Describing This Bodhisattva's Memory Power

Vajragarbha Bodhisattva replied:

O Son of the Buddha. This is something that cannot be known merely by resort to numerical calculations. I shall provide an analogy for you.

Son of the Buddha. Suppose for instance that there existed in each of the ten directions worlds as numerous as the atoms in ten ineffably numerous hundreds of thousands of *koṭis* of *nayutas* of buddha lands, and in each of those worlds each and every one of the beings residing therein had all acquired the "hearing-and-retaining" *dhāraṇī*, had served as a buddha's attendant, was foremost in learning among everyone within the assembly of *śrāvaka*-disciples, was one comparable to Great Supremacy Bhikshu[266] residing in the dwelling place of Vajra Lotus Blossom Supremacy Buddha,[267] while the Dharma received by each of these beings was not the same as that received by any of the others.

Son of the Buddha. What do you think? Is all of the Dharma received by all of these beings measurable or immeasurable?

Liberation Moon Bodhisattva replied, "That is an exceedingly great amount, one that is measureless and boundless."

Vajragarbha Bodhisattva then said:

Son of the Buddha. I will explain this matter for you in a manner that will cause you to comprehend it.

Son of the Buddha. That great Dharma light, great Dharma illumination, and great Dharma rain constituting the Dharma treasury of the three periods of time that this Dharma Cloud Ground bodhisattva is able to accommodate, take in, absorb, and retain from but one single buddha in just a single mind-moment is such that all the Dharma heard and retained by all of those beings in those previously described world systems could not even compare to a hundredth part of it and is such that one could not adequately compare the two even by resort to analogy.

And just as this is the case with the Dharma taken in from but a single Buddha, so too it is for all those other buddhas as numerous as the atoms in all those previously described worlds throughout the ten directions wherein this number is exceeded immeasurably and boundlessly, for this bodhisattva is able in every case to accommodate, able to take in, able to absorb, and able to retain all of their Dharma light, Dharma illumination, and Dharma rain that constitute the Dharma treasury of the three periods of time as it is brought forth by each and every one of those *tathāgatas*. It is for this reason that this is known as the Dharma Cloud Ground.

29. The Dharma Cloud Bodhisattva's Great Dharma Rain

Son of the Buddha. Through the power of his own vows, the bodhisattva dwelling on this ground spreads forth the clouds of the great compassion, brings on the quaking of the great Dharma thunder, uses his superknowledges, clarities, and fearlessnesses as the flashing of his lightning, and brings forth his merit and wisdom as dense rain clouds. He manifests all different kinds of bodies that circulate everywhere, going forth and returning, and, in but a single mind-moment, they everywhere pervade the ten directions, going forth to a number of lands as numerous as the atoms in hundreds of thousands of *koṭis* of *nayutas* of worlds wherein they expound the great Dharma and utterly defeat Māra's hordes.

In yet greater numbers than these, in lands as numerous as the atoms in measurelessly many hundreds of thousands of *koṭis* of *nayutas* of worlds, he adapts to the dispositions of the beings therein and pours down the rain of sweet-dew *amṛta*, thus extinguishing the smoke and flames of beings' afflictions. It is for this reason that this is known as the Dharma Cloud Ground.

Son of the Buddha. From the time he descends from a particular world's Tuṣita Heaven on through to the time he enters nirvāṇa, the bodhisattva dwelling on this ground adapts to the minds of the beings he should bring to liberation and then manifests the works of a buddha. So too does he carry this out in the same way in two worlds, three worlds, and so forth on up to his doing so in lands as numerous as the above-described atoms, even doing so in a number of lands beyond even these, in even up to lands as numerous as the atoms in measurelessly many hundreds of thousands of *koṭis* of *nayutas* of worlds. It is for this reason that this ground is known as the Dharma Cloud Ground.

30. This Bodhisattva's Use of Spiritual Powers in Transforming Worlds

(I) Son of the Buddha. The bodhisattva dwelling on this ground is possessed of such brightly penetrating wisdom and sovereign mastery of the spiritual superknowledges that he is able in accordance with whatever he wishes to transform a narrow world into a broad world, transform a broad world into a narrow world, transform a defiled world into a pure world, transform a pure world into a defiled world, and is able, too, to mutually transform every type of world into the other, including those that are chaotically arranged, those that are arranged in an orderly fashion, those that are upside down, those that are right-side up, and those that are of countless other different varieties.

Or it may also be that, in accordance with whatever he wishes, he may also place within a single atom an entire world with its

Mount Sumerus as well as all of its other mountains and rivers, doing so even while keeping the appearance of an atom just as it was before and while also ensuring that world is not reduced in scale.

Or then again, it may also be that, within but a single atom, he may place two, place three, or place even up to an ineffably great number of worlds with their Mount Sumerus and other such mountains and rivers, doing so even while the physical appearance of that atom remains just as it originally was and doing so even while the world system within it is able to remain entirely and clearly manifest.

Or it may also be that, in accordance with whatever he wishes, he may manifest in a but a single world the adornments of two worlds, and so forth until we come to his placing the adornments of an ineffably great number[268] of worlds into the adornments of but a single world.

Or it may also be that, in the adornment of a single world, he may manifest two worlds and so forth on up to an ineffably great number of worlds.

Or it may also be that, in accordance with whatever he wishes, he may place the beings from an ineffably great number of worlds into but a single world.

Or it may also be that, in accordance with whatever he wishes, he places the beings from a single world into an ineffably great number of worlds and yet does so without disturbing or harming any of those beings in any way.

Or it may also be that, in accordance with whatever he wishes, he manifests in a single hair pore all the adornments associated with the realms of all buddhas.

31. His Use of Powers in Manifesting Bodies & Supernatural Phenomena

Or it may also be that, in accordance with whatever he wishes, in but a single mind-moment, he manifests bodies as numerous as the atoms in an ineffably great number of worlds, each and every one of those bodies then manifests hands as numerous as that same number of atoms, and each and every one of those hands holds a Ganges' sands number of trays of flowers, cases of incense, floral garlands, canopies, flags, and banners that are then presented as offerings to the Buddhas everywhere throughout the ten directions.

Additionally, each and every one of those bodies may manifest with a number of heads matching this same number of atoms as each and every one of those heads manifests a number of tongues matching this same number of atoms and, in each and every mind-moment, their utterances reach everywhere throughout the ten directions with praises of the Buddhas' meritorious qualities.

Or it may also be that, in accordance with whatever he wishes, in but a single mind-moment, he thus manifests everywhere throughout the ten directions the appearances of realizing the right enlightenment and the other associated events on through to the nirvāṇa along with the associated lands and their adornments.

Or it may be that he manifests bodies everywhere throughout the three periods of time while revealing within each of his bodies an incalculably great number of buddhas as well as their buddha lands, their adornments, and the creation and destruction of worlds, revealing all of these things in a manner whereby none of these phenomena fail to completely manifest therein.

Or it may also be that, from a single hair pore in his own body, he sends forth every variety of wind that, even so, does no harm to any being.

Or it may also be that, in accordance with whatever he wishes, he transformationally manifests therein boundlessly many worlds forming a single great sea and then manifests in the middle of this sea's waters a great lotus blossom that, with its radiance and graceful adornment, everywhere covers measurelessly and boundlessly many worlds as he manifests therein a great bodhi tree with all its adornments, and so forth on through to his manifestation of the realization of the knowledge of all modes.

Or it may also be that, even within his own body, he manifests every sort of light, including that of precious *maṇi* pearls, the sun, the moon, the stars, lightning in the clouds, and so forth, so that there are none that do not manifest therein.

Or it may also be that, employing the breath from his mouth, he is able to move the incalculably many worlds throughout the ten directions and yet still not cause any of the beings therein to give rise to thoughts of terror.

Or it may also be that he manifests the appearance of the wind disasters, fire disasters, and water disasters throughout the ten directions.

Or it may also be that, adapting to beings' predilections, he manifests form bodies that are entirely replete in their adornment.

Or it may also be that, even within his own body, he manifests the body of a buddha or else manifests his own body within the body of a buddha. Or it may also be that, within the body of a buddha, he manifests his own land, or else, within his own land, manifests the body of a buddha.

Son of the Buddha. This bodhisattva dwelling on the Dharma Cloud Ground is able to manifest such phenomena as these as well as measurelessly many other hundreds of thousands of *koṭis* of *nayutas* of such appearances produced through his sovereign mastery of the spiritual powers.

32. The Congregants Wonder: "What More Could Even a Buddha Do?"

{J} At that time, the bodhisattvas within the assembly as well as the devas, dragons, *yakṣas, gandarvas, asuras,* the Four World-Protecting kings, Śakra Devānām Indra, the Brahma Heaven devas, and the devas' sons of the Pure Dwelling Heavens and Maheśvara Heavens all had this same thought: "If a bodhisattva is able to employ the power of spiritual superknowledges and the power of his knowledge in ways such as this, what more in addition to that could be done even by a buddha?"

33. Liberation Moon Asks Vajragarbha for an Explanation

At that time, Liberation Moon Bodhisattva, aware of the thoughts in the minds of everyone within that assembly, then addressed Vajragarbha Bodhisattva, saying: "O Son of the Buddha. Having heard of this bodhisattva's power of spiritual superknowledges and wisdom, the members of this great assembly have now fallen into a net of doubts. It would be good indeed, O Humane One, if, for the sake of cutting off their doubts, one were to briefly reveal those phenomena associated with the spiritual powers and adornments of the bodhisattva."

34. Vajragarbha Enters "The Nature of All Buddha Lands' Samādhi"

At this time, Vajragarbha Bodhisattva immediately entered "the nature of the physical form of all buddha lands samādhi."[269] When he entered this samādhi, the bodhisattvas as well as the entire great assembly all viewed their own bodies residing within the body of Vajragarbha Bodhisattva and, within it, they observed all the many different sorts of adornments within the great trichiliocosm that were such that, even were one to attempt to describe them for an entire *koṭi* of kalpas, one would never be able to come to the end of them.

They also observed therein a bodhi tree, the trunk of which had the circumference of ten myriads of great trichiliocosms and a height that reached to a hundred myriads of great trichiliocosms. The span of the shade cast by its branches and leaves was of the same scale, matching the shape and size of the tree.

There was a lion throne there upon which sat a buddha named King of Omniscience and Superknowledges.[270] The entire great assembly observed that buddha sitting there beneath the bodhi tree on a lion throne adorned with many different characteristics that were such that, even in a *koṭi* of kalpas, one could never completely describe them.

Having manifested such great powers of spiritual superknowledges as these, Vajragarbha Bodhisattva caused each individual in the assembly to return to his original place. At that time, that great assembly, having experienced what it never experienced before, brought forth thoughts of amazement at the rarity of what they had experienced and then remained there quietly, single-mindedly gazing up at Vajragarbha Bodhisattva.

35. Liberation Moon Asks About This Samādhi's Name and Capacity

At that time, Liberation Moon Bodhisattva said, "O Son of the Buddha. This samādhi is extremely rare and possessed of immense power. What is its name?"

Vajragarbha Bodhisattva replied, "This samādhi is known as "the nature of the physical form of all buddha lands samādhi."

He also asked, "What is the range of this samādhi's objective domain?"

Vajragarbha Bodhisattva then replied:

> Son of the Buddha. If a bodhisattva were to cultivate this samādhi, then in accordance with whatever he wishes, he would be able to manifest within his own body a number of buddha lands as numerous as the atoms in a Ganges' sands number of worlds or even a number yet greater than this extending up to a measurelessly and boundlessly great number.
>
> Son of the Buddha. The bodhisattva dwelling on the Dharma Cloud Ground acquires measurelessly many hundreds of thousands of other great samādhis such as these. Consequently this bodhisattva's body and his physical deeds are impossible to completely fathom. So too, his speech, his verbal deeds, his mind, his mental deeds, his sovereign mastery of the spiritual superknowledges, his contemplation of the three periods of time, the objective domains of his samādhis, the objective domains of his wisdom, his wandering and sporting in all the gates to liberation, the

transformations he performs, what he accomplishes through the use of spiritual powers, the works his rays of light perform and, to state it briefly, everything he does up to and including every raising up and setting down of his feet—absolutely everything he does all the way along cannot be known by any bodhisattva up to and including those who have reached the Ground of Excellent Intelligence who dwell therein at the station of the Dharma Prince.

Son of the Buddha. To state it briefly, all of the objective domains of this bodhisattva dwelling on the Dharma Cloud Ground are of this very sort. If one were to attempt an extensive explanation of it, one would still be unable to finish it even in measurelessly many hundreds of thousands of *asaṃkhyeyas* of kalpas.

36. He Asks: "What More Might a Buddha's Powers Accomplish?"

Liberation Moon Bodhisattva said, "O Son of the Buddha. If the objective domains of this bodhisattva's spiritual superknowledges are of this sort, then what additional factors must characterize the powers of a buddha's spiritual superknowledges?"

37. Vajragarbha Contrasts a Few Clumps of Earth to All Worlds

Vajragarbha Bodhisattva replied:

O Son of the Buddha. By way of comparison, suppose there was someone who picked up a clump of soil from somewhere on the four continents and asked, 'Which is of greater volume? Is it all of that soil that comprises all the great earths in the boundlessly many worlds, or is it instead this clump of earth that I am holding here?' I see this question you have asked as of this very sort. The Tathāgata's wisdom is boundless and unequaled by anyone. How then could it possibly be compared to that of a bodhisattva?

Additionally, Son of the Buddha, it is just as when one picks up a small clump of earth from somewhere on the four continents and what remains is incalculable in volume. Were one to attempt to describe the spiritual superknowledges and wisdom of this bodhisattva on the Dharma Cloud Ground, even if one were to attempt to describe them for measurelessly many kalpas, one could only succeed in describing a minor portion of them. How much the more so then would this be the case if one were to attempt to describe them as they relate to one who abides on the ground of the Tathāgata?

38. Vajragarbha Compares Many Bodhisattvas' Wisdom to One Buddha's

Son of the Buddha. I will now bring forth a circumstance for you that will attest to the truth of this matter and thereby cause you to be able to understand the realm of the Tathāgata. Son of the Buddha. Suppose that in each and every one of the ten directions there were buddha lands as numerous as the atoms in boundlessly many worlds, and suppose too that each and every one of those lands was so completely filled with bodhisattvas abiding on this ground that they could be compared to dense thickets of sugar cane stalks, bamboo, reeds, paddy rice, or hemp. Even all the wisdom arising from the bodhisattva practices cultivated by all of those bodhisattvas across the course of hundreds of thousands of *koṭis* of *nayutas* of kalpas could not compare to even a hundredth part of that possessed by a single *tathāgata*, and so forth until we come to its inability to equal even the smallest fraction of an *upaniṣad* when compared with the wisdom possessed by a single *tathāgata*.

39. The Nature of This Bodhisattva's Practice and Wisdom Light

Son of the Buddha. Abiding in wisdom of this sort, this bodhisattva is no different from the Tathāgata in his actions of body, speech, and mind. He never relinquishes the power of any of the bodhisattva samādhis. Across the course of countless kalpas, he renders service to and makes offering to all buddhas and, in each and every kalpa, he presents every sort of gift to them as offerings. He is aided by the spiritual powers of all buddhas. The light of his wisdom becomes ever more supremely bright. Hence he is able to skillfully resolve all the difficult challenging questions throughout the Dharma realm, becoming one over whom no one can prevail even if they were to challenge him for a hundred thousand *koṭis* of kalpas.

40. The Light of His Wisdom Compared to That of Real Gold

Son of the Buddha. It is as if there was a goldsmith who, using the most supremely fine real gold, created articles of physical adornment to be personally worn by the Vaśavartin Heaven King,[271] adornments in which he inlaid large *maṇi* jewels, thereby creating adornments that could not be rivaled by those worn by any of the other devas.

So too it is in the case of the bodhisattva dwelling on this ground. His wisdom is such that it cannot be rivaled by all of the wisdom-based conduct of all bodhisattvas dwelling on the first ground through the ninth ground. The wisdom light of the bodhisattva dwelling on this ground is even able to cause beings to reach all the way through to the point of entering the cognition of all-knowledge. None of the wisdom light of those others is able to compare to this.

41. This Bodhisattva's Wisdom Light Compared to Maheśvara's Light

Son of the Buddha. This is analogous to the light of the Maheśvara Heaven King[272] that is able to cause the bodies and minds of beings to become clear and cool and, as such, is of a sort that cannot be rivaled by the light of any other beings.

So too it is with the wisdom light of the bodhisattva dwelling on this ground. It is able to cause all beings to acquire clarity and coolness and progress on through to the point where they themselves dwell in the cognition of all-knowledge. As such, it is of a sort that it cannot be rivaled by the wisdom light of any *śrāvaka*-disciple, *pratyekabuddha*, or bodhisattva on any ground up to and including the ninth ground.

42. The Buddhas' Ongoing Teaching of This Bodhisattva

Son of the Buddha. Though this bodhisattva *mahāsattva* already possesses the ability to be established in wisdom such as this, the Buddhas, the Bhagavats, additionally expound for his sake on the "the knowledge of the three periods of time," "the knowledge of the Dharma realm's distinctions," the knowledge that extends to all worlds," the knowledge that illuminates all worlds," "the knowledge that bears all beings in mind with kindness," and, to speak of what is essential, they expound for his sake on all the types of knowledge up to and including that culminates in gaining the cognition of all-knowledge.

43. The Tenth Ground Bodhisattva's Focus on the Knowledges Pāramitā

Among the ten *pāramitās*, this bodhisattva has become most especially superior in his perfection of the *pāramitā* of knowledges, though it is not the case that he does not cultivate the others.

44. Vajragarbha's Final Statements About the 10th Ground Bodhisattva

Son of the Buddha. This has been a summary explanation of the bodhisattva *mahāsattva*'s, tenth ground, the Ground of the Dharma Cloud. Were one to discourse on it extensively, even if one were to do so for measurelessly many *asaṃkhyeyas* of kalpas, one would still be unable to come to the end of it.

45. The Bodhisattva's Station and Dharma Practice

Son of the Buddha. The bodhisattva *mahāsattva* dwelling on this ground often becomes a Maheśvara Heaven King who possesses sovereign mastery of the Dharma and who is able to transmit on to beings the practices of *śrāvaka*-disciples and *pratyekabuddhas* as well as the practice of the bodhisattvas' *pāramitās*. Even if challenged with all the difficult questions from throughout the entire Dharma realm, there would still be no one able to prevail over him.

46. The Bodhisattva's Mindfulness

In his practice of giving, pleasing words, beneficial actions, joint endeavors, and all other such karmic works he pursues, he never departs from mindfulness of the Buddha, and so forth until we come to his never departing from mindfulness of his quest to achieve complete fulfillment of the knowledge of all modes and the cognition of all-knowledge.

47. The Bodhisattva's Aspiration to Serve Beings

He also has this thought: "I should become one who serves these beings as a leader, as one who is supreme," and so forth until we come to "as one who relies on the cognition of all-knowledge."

48. The Consequences of the Bodhisattva's Vigor and Vows

If he applies himself diligently to the practice of vigor, then, in but the instant of a single mind-moment, he succeeds in acquiring samādhis as numerous as the atoms in ineffably many hundreds of thousands of *koṭis* of *nayutas* of buddha lands. And so it goes on up to his then being able to manifest the acquisition of a following of bodhisattvas serving in his retinues as numerous as just that many atoms.

If this bodhisattva chooses to avail himself of the power of his especially supreme vows, he becomes able then to freely manifest such phenomena in numbers well beyond these, even to the point that, whether we speak of his cultivation, the adornments he creates, his resolute faith, what he accomplishes through physical or verbal actions, his light, his faculties, his spiritual transformations, his voice, or the domain of his practices, one would still be unable to enumerate them even if one were to attempt to do so for a hundred thousand *koṭis* of *nayutas* of kalpas.

III. The Final Summarizing Discussion of the Ten Grounds[273]

A. His Eventual All-Knowledge Likened to Rivers' Flow Into the Sea

{A} Son of the Buddha. This bodhisattva *mahāsattva*'s aspects of practice on the ten grounds are such that, so long as he causes them to become directly and sequentially manifest, he will thereby become able to progress into the cognition of all-knowledge.

This circumstance is analogous to Lake Anavatapta that sends forth the four great rivers, the flowing waters of which circulate throughout the continent of Jambudvīpa. Because these waters are never exhausted, they ever increase in volume until they enter the ocean and cause it to become full.

Son of the Buddha. So too it is with this bodhisattva. From the point of his initial resolve to realize bodhi, he continually streams forth the waters of his roots of goodness and great vows, employing the four means of attraction to completely fulfill the needs of beings. Not only are these waters inexhaustible, they are moreover ever increasing until they ultimately pour forth into the ocean of all-knowledge and cause it to become full.

B. The 10 Grounds' Differences Likened to Those of 10 Mountain Kings

{B} Son of the Buddha. Due to the Buddha's knowledge, the ten grounds of the bodhisattva have distinct differences. This is just as when, due to the great earth, there exist the ten kings of mountains. What then are those ten? They are: the Snow Mountain King, the Fragrance Mountain King, the Vaidharī Mountain King, the Rishi Mountain King, the Yugaṃdhara Mountain King, the Horse Ear Mountain King, the Nimindhara Mountain King, the Cakravāḍa Mountain King, the Ketumat Mountain King, and the Sumeru Mountain King.

1. The First Ground Compared to the Snow Mountain King

Son of the Buddha. Just as on the Snow Mountain King, every sort of herb grows there so abundantly that one could never harvest them all, so too it is on the bodhisattva's Ground of Joyfulness, for all the world's classical texts, skills and arts, literature, verses, mantras and other occult techniques—these are all so completely present therein that one could never exhaustively describe them all.

2. The Second Ground Compared to the Fragrance Mountain King

Son of the Buddha. Just as on the Fragrance Mountain King, every sort of incense is all accumulated there and is so abundantly present there that one could never harvest it all, so too it is on the bodhisattva's Ground of Stainlessness, for the bodhisattva's moral precept practices and standards of awesome deportment are all so completely present therein that one could never exhaustively describe them all.

3. The Third Ground Compared to the Vaidharī Mountain King

Son of the Buddha. Just as the Vaidharī Mountain King is so entirely composed of jewels that all the many different kinds of precious jewels are so abundantly present therein that one could never extract them all, so too it is on the bodhisattva's Ground of Shining Light, for the world's *dhyāna* absorptions, spiritual superknowledges, liberations, samādhis, and *samāpattis* are all so completely present therein that one could never exhaustively describe them all.

4. The Fourth Ground Compared to the Rishi Mountain King

Son of the Buddha. Just as the Rishi Mountain King composed entirely of jewels has rishis possessed of the five spiritual superknowledges in such abundance that they are endlessly numerous, so too it is with the bodhisattva's Ground of Blazing Brilliance, for the forms of especially supreme wisdom from all paths are so completely present therein that one could never exhaustively describe them all.

5. The Fifth Ground Compared to the Yugaṃdhara Mountain King

Son of the Buddha. Just as on the Yugaṃdhara Mountain King composed entirely of jewels, the *yakṣas,* those great spirits, live there in such abundance that one could never come to the end of them, so too it is on the bodhisattva's Difficult-to-Conquer Ground, for all types of sovereign masteries and psychic powers, and spiritual penetrations are so completely present therein that one could never exhaustively describe them all.

6. The Sixth Ground Compared to the Horse Ear Mountain King

Son of the Buddha. Just as on the Horse Ear Mountain King composed entirely of jewels, all the various fruits are so abundantly present there that one could never harvest them all, so too it is on the bodhisattva's Ground of Direct Presence, for those who have penetrated the principle of conditioned arising corresponding to the realizations of *śrāvaka* disciples' fruits of the path are all so completely present therein that one could never exhaustively describe them all.

7. The Seventh Ground Compared to the Nimindhara Mountain King

Just as on the Nimindhara Mountain King composed entirely of jewels, all the greatly powerful dragon spirits are so abundantly present there that one could never come to the end of them, so too it is on the bodhisattva's Far-Reaching Ground, for the skillful means, wisdom, and realizations corresponding to the fruits of a *pratyekabuddha*'s path are all so completely present therein that one could never exhaustively describe them all.

8. The Eighth Ground Compared to the Cakravāda Mountain King

Just as on the Cakravāda Mountain King composed entirely of jewels, the congregation of those possessed of sovereign mastery is so abundantly present that one could never come to the end of them, so too it is on the bodhisattva's Ground of Immovability, for all bodhisattvas' sovereign masteries in traveling to different worlds are all so completely present therein that one could never exhaustively describe them all.

9. The Ninth Ground Compared to the Ketumat Mountain King

Just as on the Ketumat Mountain King composed entirely of jewels, all the *asura* kings possessed of great awe-inspiring virtue who dwell there are so abundantly present that one could never come to the end of them, so too it is on the bodhisattva's Ground of Excellent Intelligence, for all forms of knowledge and practice pertaining to the creation and destruction of worlds are all so completely present therein that one could never exhaustively describe them all.

10. The Tenth Ground Compared to the Sumeru Mountain King

Just as on the Sumeru Mountain King that is entirely composed of precious jewels, the devas possessed of greatly awe-inspiring virtue are so abundantly present there that one could never come to the end of them, so too it is on the bodhisattva's Dharma Cloud Ground, for the Tathāgata's powers, fearlessnesses, exclusive dharmas, and matters pertaining to buddhahood are all so completely present therein along with their abundantly present facility in questions, answers, and proclamations that one could never come to the end of them all.

11. The Ten Grounds in All-Knowledge Likened to Mountains in the Sea

Son of the Buddha. These ten jeweled mountain kings all identically reside within the great ocean and achieve their names based on their differences. So too it is with the bodhisattva's ten grounds. They all identically reside within all-knowledge and acquire their names based on their differences.

C. The Ten Grounds Compared to Ten Aspects of the Great Ocean

{C} Son of the Buddha. [These ten bodhisattva grounds] are comparable to the great ocean that, on the basis of ten characteristic features, acquires the inalterably exclusive designation "great ocean."[274] What then are those ten? They are:

First, it progresses gradually from its shallows to its depths;
Second, it refuses to accept dead bodies;

Third, upon flowing into it, all other waters thereby lose their original names;
Fourth, it is everywhere of the same singular flavor;
Fifth, it holds incalculably many truly precious jewels;
Sixth, nobody is able to go all the way down to its bottom;
Seventh, it is incalculably vast;
Eighth, it is a place in which beings with huge bodies reside;
Ninth, its tides do not reach beyond its shoreline;
Tenth, it everywhere takes in the great rains without overflowing.

So too it is with the practices of the bodhisattva that on the basis of ten characteristic features acquire the inalterably exclusive designation "bodhisattva practices." What then are those ten? They are:

On the Ground of Joyfulness this is because it is therein that the production of great vows gradually and sequentially deepens;
On the Ground of Stainlessness this is because it refuses to accept the dead bodies of those who break the precepts;
On the Ground of Shining Light this is because that is where one relinquishes the world's false designations;
On the Ground of Blazing Brilliance this is because it is of the same singular flavor as the Buddha's meritorious qualities;
On the Difficult-to-Conquer Ground this is because this is where one produces incalculably many skillful means and spiritual superknowledges whereby what one does in the world constitutes a multitude of precious jewels;
On the Ground of Direct Presence this is because that is where one contemplates the extremely profound principles of conditioned arising;
On the Far-Reaching Ground this is because that is where one employs vast enlightened intelligence in skillful investigative contemplation;
On the Ground of Immovability this is because that is where one manifests vast works of adornment;
On the Ground of Excellent Intelligence this is because that is where one acquires profound liberation and, in one's practice within the world, one's awareness accords with reality and never extends beyond boundaries;
And on the Dharma Cloud Ground this is because that is where one becomes able to insatiably take on all the rain of the Buddha's, the Tathāgata's, great Dharma light.

D. The Ten Grounds Compared to a Large Maṇi Jewel

{D} Son of the Buddha. This circumstance is analogous to that of a large *maṇi* jewel that by virtue of possessing ten characteristic qualities surpasses all the many other sorts of jewels. What then are those ten? They are:

First, it comes forth from the great ocean;
Second, it is enhanced by the refinements of a skilled artisan;
Third, it is perfect and entirely free of flaws;
Fourth, it is possessed of stainless purity;
Fifth, its brightly penetrating brilliance shines both inwardly and outwardly;
Sixth, it has been skillfully drilled through;
Seventh, it is strung with precious thread;
Eighth, it is mounted at the very tip of a tall flagpole made of lapis lazuli;
Ninth, it shines forth everywhere with all the many different kinds of light;
Tenth, it is able to rain down the many sorts of precious things in response to the wishes of the King and is able to fulfill the wishes arising in beings' minds.

Son of the Buddha. So too it is with the bodhisattva who, in this same manner, by virtue of possessing ten characteristic features, surpasses the qualities of the many other *āryas*. What then are these ten?

First, he has brought forth the resolve to gain all-knowledge;
Second, in his observance of the moral precepts and his cultivation of the *dhūta* practices, he is possessed of radiantly pure right practice;
Third, he is possessed of perfectly full and flawless practice of all the *dhyāna* samādhis;
Fourth, his path practices are pure white and free from all stains and defilements;
Fifth, his skillful means and spiritual superknowledges are possessed of a penetrating brilliance that shines both inwardly and outwardly;
Sixth, his wisdom with respect to the process of conditioned arising has the capacity to be skillfully penetrating;
Seventh, [his practice] is strung through with the thread of the many different applications of skillful means and wisdom;
Eighth, he is placed high atop the pillar of the sovereign masteries;

Ninth, he contemplates beings' actions and emanates the light of learning and retention;

Tenth, having received the Buddhas' consecration of his knowledge, he then falls in among those counted as buddhas and thus becomes able, for the sake of beings, to carry out on a vast scale the works of the Buddhas.

E. The Prerequisite Conditions for Hearing The Ten Grounds Teachings

{E} Son of the Buddha. As for this chapter on the bodhisattva practice gateways by which one accumulates the meritorious qualities associated with the knowledge of all modes and all-knowledge, if any being had not himself already planted roots of goodness, he would be unable to even obtain a hearing of it.

F. Liberation Moon Asks: "How Much Merit by Hearing This Teaching?

Liberation Moon Bodhisattva then asked, "How much merit might one acquire due to having heard [this chapter that describes] these Dharma gateways?"

G. Vajragarbha Explains Merit and Importance Ten Grounds Teaching

Vajragarbha Bodhisattva replied:

The merit associated with simply hearing these Dharma gateways is of the same sort as the merit of all-knowledge. How could that be? It could not be that one might have resolute faith in, accept, uphold, study and recite these Dharma gateways to the meritorious qualities if one had not heard them. How much the less might one then proceed to vigorously pursue their cultivation in accordance with the way they were explained. Therefore, one should realize that it is essential that one gain a hearing of these Dharma gateways to the accumulation of the meritorious qualities associated with all-knowledge in order to then be able to have resolute faith in them, accept them, uphold them in practice, and thus later succeed in reaching the ground of all-knowledge.

H. The Auspicious Signs Occurring When This Sutra's Teaching Ended

At that time, because of the spiritual powers of the Buddha and because of the very nature of the Dharma, in each of the ten directions, worlds as numerous as the atoms in ten *koṭis* of buddha lands underwent the six types and eighteen varieties of characteristic movements, namely: movement, universal movement, equal-and-universal movement, rising, universal rising, equal-and-universal rising, upward thrusting, universal upward thrusting, equal-and-universal upward thrusting, shaking, universal shaking, equal-and-universal shaking, roaring, universal roaring, equal-and-universal roaring, striking, universal striking, and equal-and-universal striking. This was accompanied by the raining down of the many sorts of heavenly flower blossoms, heavenly floral garlands, heavenly raiment, and also heavenly jewels, articles of adornment, flags, banners, silken canopies, the playing of heavenly instruments and singing in which the sounds were harmonious and refined and accompanied by the simultaneous sounding of voices in praise of all the meritorious qualities of the ground of all-knowledge.

I. The 10 Directions' Bodhisattvas Attest to the Teaching's Universality

Just as this proclamation of this Dharma was taking place in the palace of this world's Paranirmita Vaśavartin Heaven, so too was it also taking place in this very fashion in all worlds of the ten directions.

Additionally, at that time, again on account of the spiritual powers of the Buddha, there came to this assembly from beyond worlds as numerous as the atoms in ten *koṭis* of buddha lands bodhisattvas as numerous as the atoms in ten *koṭis* of buddha lands who then spoke these words:

> It is good indeed, good indeed, O Vajragarbha, that you have discoursed so directly on this dharma. We too carry the name "Vajragarbha" and the worlds in which we dwell with all their differences, are all named, "Vajra Qualities." Our buddha is called "Vajra Banner." All of us, receiving the benefit of the spiritual powers of the Tathāgata, proclaim this very Dharma in those worlds in which we dwell and from which we come. Our assemblies are all also entirely identical. The language, the phrases, and the meanings are also neither enhanced nor reduced in comparison to what is set forth here.
>
> That all of us have come to this assembly is entirely because of the Buddha's spiritual powers through which we have come to offer this certifying corroboration. Just as we have now come and entered this world, so too is it the case that, in this same manner, we go forth to all the worlds of the ten directions to offer just such certifying corroboration there as well.

J. Vajragarbha's Summarizing Verses Augmented by the Buddha's Powers

At that time, Vajragarbha Bodhisattva regarded that entire congregation that had assembled from the ten directions throughout the entire Dharma realm and, wishing to praise the generation of the resolve to gain realization of the cognition of all-knowledge, wishing to reveal the realms of the bodhisattvas, wishing to reveal the purification of the practices and powers of the bodhisattva, wishing to discourse on the acquisition of the path to the knowledge of all modes, wishing to discourse on the extinguishing of all forms of worldly defilement, wishing to bestow all-knowledge, wishing to reveal the adornments associated with inconceivable knowledge, wishing to reveal all the meritorious qualities of all bodhisattvas, and wishing to cause such meanings associated with the grounds to become yet more clearly revealed, he availed himself of the spiritual power of the Buddha and then proceeded to utter verses, saying:

With a mind abiding in quiescence, forever tamed,
and as uniformly the same and unobstructed as space itself,
he abandons the turbidity of all defilements and abides in the path.
You should listen to such especially supreme practices as these. {17}

For a hundred thousand *koṭis* of kalpas, he cultivates every good,
presents offerings to incalculably and boundlessly many buddhas,
and to *śrāvaka*-disciples and *pratyekabuddhas* as well
and, in order to benefit beings, brings forth the great resolve. {18}

He diligently upholds moral precepts, is always pliantly patient,
is replete in senses of shame and blame and merit and knowledge,
resolutely seeks Buddha's knowledge, cultivates vast intelligence,
and, vowing to acquire the ten powers, brings forth the great resolve. {19}

He makes offerings to all Buddhas of the three periods of time,
adorns and purifies all lands,
utterly realizes all dharmas' uniform equality,
and, for the sake of benefiting beings, brings forth the great resolve.[275] {20}

Dwelling on the first ground, he brings forth this resolve,
forever abandons the many evils, and always abides in joyfulness.
Through the power of vows, he vastly cultivates all good dharmas,
and, through compassionate empathy, enters the next station.

Entirely replete in precepts and learning and mindful of beings,
he washes away defilements, his mind becomes radiantly pristine,
he contemplates the world's fires of the three poisons,
and, with vast comprehension, proceeds on to the third ground.

Seeing the three realms of existence as entirely impermanent,
as ablaze with sufferings akin to when an arrow is shot into the body,
he renounces all that is conditioned, pursues the Buddha's Dharma,
and, as one with great wisdom, enters the Blazing Ground.

Fully replete in mindfulness and wisdom, he gains path knowledge,
makes hundreds of thousands of offerings to countless buddhas,
and always contemplates all of the most supreme qualities,
whereupon this person then enters the Difficult-to-Conquer Ground.

Employing wisdom and skillful means, he skillfully contemplates,
brings forth all different sorts of manifestations to rescue beings,
again makes offerings to the unexcelled Honored One of ten powers,
and enters the unproduced and the Direct Presence Ground.

He becomes able to know what is difficult for a worldling to know,
does not accept any self, transcends existence and non-existence,
knows dharmas' basic stillness, adapts to conditions' transformations,
and, having gained these sublime states, enters the seventh ground.

With wisdom, skillful means, and a vast mind, [he masters] what is
hard to practice, hard to overcome, and hard to entirely know.
Though he has realized quiescent cessation, he cultivates diligently
and is able to enter the space-like Ground of Immovability.

Encouraged by Buddha, he is caused to rise from quiescent cessation,
takes up vast cultivation of many different deeds rooted in wisdom.
Equipped with ten sovereign masteries, he contemplates the world,
and, due to this, ascends to the Ground of Excellent Intelligence.

With subtle and marvelous wisdom, he contemplates beings'
thickets of mental actions, karmic actions, afflictions, and such,
and, wishing to teach them and cause them to enter the path,
he then expounds on all Buddhas' treasury of the supreme meaning.

He sequentially cultivates to completion the many forms of goodness,
accumulates merit and wisdom up through the ninth ground,
always pursues all buddhas' most supreme dharmas, and gains
the consecration with Buddha's wisdom waters poured on his crown.

He acquires measurelessly many samādhis and
also thoroughly and completely understands their functions.
The very last samādhi is known as "Receiving the Consecration"
wherein he dwells in a vast realm, forever unmoving.

When this bodhisattva acquires this samādhi,
an immense bejeweled lotus blossom suddenly appears,
whereupon, with a body of matching size, he sits down in its middle,
surrounded by those buddha's sons, all in the same contemplation.

He emanates a hundred thousand *koṭis* of great light beams
that extinguish the sufferings of all beings
and also emanates beams of light from his crown that
everywhere enter the assemblies of the buddhas of the ten directions.

They all remain there in space, forming a net-like canopy of light
that, after making offerings to the Buddhas, then enters their feet.
The Buddhas all then immediately know,
"This Buddha's son has now ascended to the consecration stage."

The bodhisattvas from the ten directions come to observe
this great consecration-receiving eminence pour forth illumination.
The Buddhas then also release light from between their eyebrows
that, after producing illumination everywhere, then enter his crown.

All worlds of the ten directions are then beset with tremors
and all the sufferings experienced in the hells are extinguished.
It is at this very time that the Buddhas confer their consecration
just as a wheel-turning king confers a consecration on his eldest son.

When one receives this anointing of the crown by the Buddhas, then
this is what is known as ascending to the Dharma Cloud Ground.
His wisdom continues to grow boundlessly to include
[the means of] awakening everyone in all worlds.

The desire realm, the form realm, the formless realm,
the Dharma realm, the worldly realms, and the realms of beings.
Whether calculable, incalculable, or in the realms of empty space,
he acquires a penetrating comprehension of all such things as these.

In all his transformations, he employs greatly awe-inspiring powers
and receives the Buddhas' augmenting support in subtle knowledge.
As for the esoteric, kalpa enumerations, ordinary beings, and such,
he can contemplate them all in accordance with reality.

He takes on birth, leaves the home life, realizes right enlightenment,
turns the wheel of the wondrous Dharma, and enters nirvāṇa.
Everything up to the dharma of quiescent liberation as well as
what has not yet been taught—he is able to completely fathom it all.

The bodhisattva dwelling on this Dharma Cloud Ground,
entirely perfect in mindfulness power, retains the Buddha's Dharma.
Just as the great ocean takes in the dragon's rains,
so too is his ability to take in and retain the Dharma on this ground.

Compared to all buddha dharmas countless beings in ten directions
who had the hearing-and-retaining [samādhi] could retain,
the Dharma that he hears [and retains] in the place of a single buddha
exceeds that number by a measurelessly great amount.

Using the power of wisdom, past vows, and awesome spiritual might,
in but a single mind-moment, he pervades the ten directions' lands,
pours down the rain of sweet-dew elixir, and extinguishes afflictions.
Hence the Buddha referred to this as "the Dharma Cloud."

What his superknowledges manifest throughout the ten directions
so surpasses matters in the worldly sphere of humans and devas,
exceeding their number so incalculably many *koṭis* of times, assessing
them with worldly knowledge, one is sure to become bewildered.

Even everyone up through the ninth ground cannot know how
much knowledge and merit is involved in his merely raising his foot.
How much less might this be known by any ordinary being
or even by any *śrāvaka*-disciple or *pratyekabuddha*.

The bodhisattva dwelling on this ground makes offerings to buddhas
in the lands throughout the ten directions
while also making offerings to all present-era assemblies of *āryas*
and completely fulfilling his adornment with a buddha's qualities.

As he dwells on this ground, they additionally discourse for him
on unimpeded knowledge of the three times, the Dharma realm,
and in the same manner, on beings, on lands,
and so forth on up to all of the Buddha's meritorious qualities.

The wisdom light of the bodhisattva dwelling on this ground
is able to reveal to beings the road of right Dharma.
As the Maheśvara Heaven King's light dispels worldly darkness,
so too this light of his dispels darkness in just that same manner.

Dwelling herein, one often becomes a king within the three realms
well able to expound on Dharma according to the Three Vehicles.
Incalculably many samādhis are acquired in but a mind-moment
and the number of buddhas he sees is of that same order.

I have now concluded a summary explanation of this ground.
If one wished to discourse on it extensively, it would be endless.
Just so, the grounds exist in reliance on the Buddha's wisdom just as
the ten mountain kings, towering, abide [in reliance on the earth].

Culturally supportive works done on the first ground are endless,
comparable to the density of the many herbs on Snow Mountain.
Second ground precepts and learning are like Incense Mountain.
The third is like the fine flowers that come forth on Vaidharī.

The jewels of the path on the "Blazing Brilliance" ground are endless,
comparable to the worthies skillfully dwelling on Rishi Mountain.
The spiritual powers on the fifth ground are like on Yugaṃdhara.
The many fruits on the sixth are like on Horse Ear Mountain.

The seventh ground's great wisdom is analogous to Nimindhara.
The sovereign masteries on the eighth ground are like Cakravāda.
The ninth is like Ketumat in its gathering of unimpeded knowledge.
The tenth is like Sumeru in its repletion with the manifold virtues.

The first ground is chief in vows, the second in upholding precepts,
the third ground in virtues, the fourth in singular focus,
the fifth ground in sublimity, the sixth in extreme profundity,
the seventh in vast wisdom, and the eighth in adornment.

The ninth is foremost in the contemplation of sublime meanings
in a manner that surpasses that of all the world's paths.
On the tenth ground, one takes on and preserves Buddha dharmas.
It is in this way that the ocean of practices is inexhaustible.

Ten practices overstep the worldly, the first is generating the resolve,
upholding precepts is second, *dhyāna* is third,
purification of practices is fourth, fulfillment is fifth, conditioned
arising is sixth, his threading of [means and wisdom] is seventh,

the eighth is placement atop the vajra pillar,
the ninth is contemplation of the beings' thickets,
the tenth is the anointing of the crown according to the King's intent.
It is in this way that the jewel of virtue gradually becomes purified.

Even if, having crushed the ten directions' lands to dust,
one could know in but a single mind-moment their number of dusts,
and, even if one could measure the size of space with a hair tip, still,
one could not finish describing [the grounds] even in a *koṭi* of kalpas.

End of the Ten Grounds Chapter

Translation Endnotes

1. Khotan was a Buddhist state located on the branch of the Silk Road that ran along the Southern periphery of the Taklamakan Desert and which corresponds to modern Xinjiang Province, China.
2. Because the Chinese translator only titled the sections of this text with section numbers ("Chapter 26: The Ten Grounds: Part One," "... Part Two," etc., I have elected to provide more specific titling for each part of the text as in "The Joyfulness Ground," "The Stainlessness Ground," etc.
3. "Clear knowledges" refers here to the "three knowledges" (*trividyā*): 1) The remembrance of previous lives (*pūrvavanivāsānusmṛti*); 2) Knowledge of beings' rebirth destinies (*cyutyupapattijñāna*); and 3) Knowledge of the destruction of the contaminants or "taints" (*āsravakṣaya*).
4. A *bodhimaṇḍa* is the "site of enlightenment" wherein enlightenment is cultivated and fully realized. It may be used as a general reference to Buddhist temples, though it often refers specifically to the site beneath the bodhi tree where a buddha gains complete realization of the utmost, right, and perfect enlightenment.
5. The "wheel of Dharma" or "Dharma wheel" (*dharmacakra*) refers to the eight-spoked wheel emblematic of the Buddha's teaching of the eight-fold path of the Āryas or "Noble Ones" consisting of right views, right thought or intention, right speech, right physical action, right livelihood, right effort, right mindfulness, and right meditative absorption (*samādhi*).
6. As a Buddhist technical term, "Dharma realm" or "dharma realm," *dharma-dhātu*, has at least several levels of meaning, of which this refers to the second of the three listed below:
   1) At the most granular level, "dharma realm" refers to the objective contents of one of the eighteen sense realms, dharmas as "objects of mind" (*dharma-āyatana*);
   2) In the most cosmically and metaphysically vast sense, "Dharma realm" refers in aggregate to all conventionally-existent phenomena and the universally pervasive noumenal "true suchness" (*tathatā*) that is the nature of all of those phenomena. In this sense, it is identical with the "Dharma body" (*dharma-kāya*);
   3) As a classifying term, "dharma realm" is used to distinguish realms of existence (as in "the ten dharma realms" that consist of the realms of buddhas, bodhisattvas, *śrāvaka* disciples, *pratyekabuddhas*, devas, *asuras*, humans, animals, hungry ghosts, and hell-dwellers) or metaphysical modes of existence (as in the "four dharma realms" of the Huayan hermeneutic tradition

that speaks of: a] the dharma realm of the "noumenal" [synonymous with emptiness or *śūnyatā*]; b] the dharma realm of the "phenomenal"; c] the dharma realm of the unimpeded interpenetration of the phenomenal and the noumenal; and d] the dharma realm of the unimpeded interpenetration of all phenomena with all other phenomena in a manner that resonates somewhat with quantum entanglement and non-locality).

7. An "ineffable"(*anabhilāpya*) is a specific nearly unimaginably large number that is the 120th of 123 numbers described in Chapter Thirty of the Flower Adornment Sutra wherein each of those numbers is defined as being the square of the immediately previous number the first of which is a *lakṣa* (100,000).

8. Per DSBC, the Sanskrit names of these bodhisattva *mahāsattvas*, (37 in BB and KB, 38 in BR, 39 in SA, SD and the Sanskrit) are:

   Vajragarbha, Ratnagarbha, Padmagarbha, Śrīgarbha, Padmaśrīgarbha, Ādityagarbha, Sūryagarbha, Kṣitigarbha, Śaśivimalagarbha, Sarvavyūhālaṃkārapratibhāsasaṃdarśanagar bha, Jñānavairocanagarbha, Ruciraśrīgarbha, Candanaśrīgarbha, Puṣpaśrīgarbha, Kusumaśrīgarbha, Utpalaśrīgarbha, Devaśrīgarbha, Puṇyaśrīgarbha, Anāvaraṇajñānaviśuddhigarbha, Guṇaśrīgarbha, Nārāyaṇaśrīgarbha, Amalagarbha, Vimalagarbha, Vicitrapratibhānālaṃkāragarbha, Mahāraśmijālāvabhāsagarbha, Vimalaprabhāsaśrītejorājagarbha, Sarvalakṣaṇapratimaṇ ḍitaviśuddhiśrīgarbha, Vajrārciḥśrīvatsālaṃkāragarbha, Jyotirjvalanārciḥśrīgarbha, Nakṣatrarājaprabhāvabhāsagar bha, Gaganakośānāvaraṇajñānagarbha, Anāvaraṇasvaramaṇ ḍalamadhuranirghoṣagarbha, Dhāraṇīmukhasarvajagatpraṇ idhisaṃdhāraṇagarbha, Sāgaravyūhagarbha, Meruśrīgarbha, Sarvaguṇaviśuddhigarbha, Tathāgataśrīgarbha, Buddhaśrīgarbha, and Vimukticandra.

9. Jñānavairocanagarbha.

10. Anāvaraṇajñānaviśuddhigarbha.

11. Gaganakośānāvaraṇajñānagarbha.

12. A *mahāsattva* is a "great bodhisattva," one who has practiced the bodhisattva path for countless kalpas.

13. Most of these numerical descriptors: "countless" (perhaps equals an "innumerable" [*agaṇeya* = 112th level]), "measureless" (*aparimāṇa* = 106th level), "boundless" (*aparyanta* = 108th level), "unequalable" (*asamanta* = 110th level), "innumerable" (*agaṇeya* = 112th level), "indescribable" (*atulya* = 114th level), "inconceivable" (*acintya* = 116th level) "immeasurable" (*ameya* = 118th level), and "ineffable" (*anabhilāpya* = 120th level) represent a specific nearly unimaginably large number described

in Chapter Thirty, "Asaṃkhyeyas," of the Flower Adornment Sutra wherein each of those numbers is defined as being the square of the immediately previous number the first of which is a *lakṣa* (100,000).

14. Although the Sanskrit refers here to this samādhi as "the bodhisattva samādhi known as 'the light of the Great Vehicle' (*mahāyānaprabhāsaṃ nāma bodhisattvasamādhiṃ*)," this may be a later textual modification of the text, for both SA and KB refer to it as "the great wisdom light samādhi."
15. A *koṭi* is a number that is defined in the Flower Adornment Sutra Chapter 30 as the product of multiplying a *lakṣa* (100,000) by a *lakṣa*. Hence it equals 10,000,000, i.e. ten million.
16. The text refers here to the first three of the ten standard names for a buddha.
17. "Contaminants" here translates the slightly ambiguous pre-Buddhist Jain term *āsrava*, translated into Chinese as "flows" (漏). The allusion is to the defiling influence (read "influents") of either three or four factors, as follows: 1) sensual desire (*kāma*); 2) [craving for] becoming (*bhāva*), i.e. the craving for continued existence; 3) ignorance (*avidyā*), i.e. delusion; 4) views (*dṛṣṭi*) This fourth type is not included in some listings. Often-encountered alternate translations include "taints," "outflows," "influxes," and "fluxes."
18. The Sanskrit references "*mahāprajñā*" here.
19. "*suviniścitamatikauśalyatāṃ.*"
20. "*tathāgatavaiśāradyānavalīnatāṃ.*"
21. The DSBC Sanskrit (*pratisaṃvid*) makes it clear that "knowledges" is intended to refer to the four types of unimpeded knowledge discussed at great length later in the text in the explanation of the ninth ground which SA renders as "Ground of Excellent Intelligence" (*sādhumatī-bhūmi*). Briefly, they are unimpeded knowledge of Dharma, meaning, language, and eloquence.
22. DSBC specifies: "*supariśodhitādhyāśayatayā ca,*" i.e. "has well purified his *higher* resolute intentions (or 'higher aspirations')."
23. "*svavadātajñānamaṇḍalatayā* ca."
24. "*susaṃbhṛtasaṃbhāratayā ca.*"
25. "*apramāṇasmṛtibhājanatayā.*"
26. "Resolute faith" (*adhimukti*) is a term that generally refers to confidently held, rationally based inclinations toward wholesome objective conditions or path-associated endeavors. That said, this term is *also* used to refer to sentient beings' strongly held habitual interests or predilections toward the whole range of wholesome, unwholesome,

or karmically neutral objective conditions or endeavors, hence it is incumbent on the teaching bodhisattva to be comprehensively cognizant of all of these different types of "resolute dispositions" along with the most skillful teaching stratagems to adopt in teaching the beings who possess them.

27. *Zongchi* (總持), "comprehensive retention," is the Chinese translation of the Sanskrit *dhāraṇī*. I sometimes redundantly translate the term as "comprehensive-retention *dhāraṇī*" to clarify what the Chinese text means by "comprehensive retention," especially when the term is not simply referring to mantras. "*Dhāraṇīs*" refers primarily to formulae that constitute a kind of pronunciation-dependent Sanskrit code language consisting of Sanskrit syllables which may or may not have a translatable meaning but which can never be translated into another language without destroying their primary functions which are of primarily two types: a) to facilitate the remembrance of teachings and their meanings even for many lifetimes; and b) when more-or-less equivalent to mantras, to protect the practitioner or other vulnerable beings from danger, the manifestation of karmic obstacles, or demonic influences.

    Dhāraṇīs may also facilitate the bodhisattva's unproduced-dharmas patience through which he can remain in *saṃsāra* for countless kalpas as he continues to work for the spiritual liberation of all other beings. They also may be used to invoke the manifestation of beneficial supernormal powers either in conjunction with or independent of *mudras* (hand postures) and/or visualizations.

28. "*dharmadhātujñānamudrāsumudritatayā ca.*"

29. Per DSBC, the names of the *bhūmis* are: *pramuditā; vimalā; prabhākarī; arciṣmatī; sudurjayā; abhimukhī; dūraṃgamā; acalā; sādhumatī; dharmameghā.*

30. SA,SD, and Prajñā all translate the name of this *bhūmi* as "the Ground of Blazing Intelligence" (焰慧地). This appears to be the result of an error arising from misinterpreting the Sanskrit name (*arciṣmatī*) by mistaking a suffix indicating possession (*-mat* modified to agree with the feminine noun *bhūmi* to become *-matī*) for a completely unrelated word that means "intelligence," "intellect," "mind" (*mati*). (BB, BR, KB, and the Tibetan all recognize *–matī* as a possessive suffix and hence accord with the Sanskrit meaning.) I have chosen to "bridge" the problem by translating the name of this ground as "the Ground of Blazing Brilliance" in order to allow both meanings the be reflected in the word "blazing" and thus more or less accurately translate both the (seemingly erroneous) SA translation and the correct meaning of the Sanskrit.

31. There seem to be two distinctly different understandings of the meaning of this ground:

DR, SA, BB, BR, SD, and Prajñā all translate the name of this *bhūmi* as "the Ground of Excellent Intelligence" (善慧地). DR translates that same meaning slightly differently: (善哉意). The Tibetan translation also corresponds to this with "the Ground of Excellent Insight" (*legs pa'i blo gros*). Strictly speaking, one could infer that these renderings all appear be the result of an error arising from misinterpreting the Sanskrit name (*sādhumatī*) by mistaking a suffix indicating possession (*-mat* modified to agree with the feminine noun *bhūmi* to become *-matī*) for a completely unrelated word that means "intelligence," "intellect," or "mind" (*mati*).

Of all of the Chinese and Tibetan translators, it appears that the Kumārajīva-Buddhayaśas translation team may have been the only one to render the name of this *bhūmi* more or less in accordance with the above-referenced "strictly correct" interpretation of the Sanskrit term as "the Ground of Sublime Goodness" (妙善地). The KB edition only employs the possibly erroneous Chinese and Tibetan default rendering once (in its initial listing of the ten bodhisattva grounds), but otherwise accords with the strictly grammatically correct interpretation of the term throughout its detailed discussion of the ninth *bhūmi* itself.

32. For the most part, throughout the text, in the introductory and reiterative verses for each of the chapters, SA's Chinese translation employs six or eight verse lines to translate the ideas contained in each four-line Sanskrit gatha when he is producing five-character Chinese verse lines. However, when he produces seven-character verse lines, he seems to more often follow the Sanskrit on a line by line basis. Even so, it is still not always possible to precisely map the Chinese onto the much later and somewhat "evolved" gathas found in the extant Sanskrit editions. Although the ideas are mostly all present in both editions, the exact content and sequencing often differ somewhat. To aid correlation with the Sanskrit edition, I have appended the verse number of the DSBC Sanskrit edition (in reduced font bold curly braces) to the last line of each equivalent SA verse.

33. Although the Chinese specifies "wisdom" here (*zhihui* / 智慧)," DSBC records the word more commonly rendered as "knowledge" (*jñāna*): "*guṇajñānasamanvitā*."

34. "Resolute intentions" translates the Chinese *shenxin* (深心), one of SA's translations of the Sanskrit *āśaya*.

35. The "provisions for the realization of the Path" (*bodhisaṃbhāra*) are the requisites for realization of buddhahood. These are often explained

as consisting of karmic merit on the one hand (*puṇya*) and "knowledge" (*jñāna*) or "wisdom" on the other.

36. "*mātṛkā*."

37. An *asaṃkhyeya* is an exceedingly large number the definition for which varies so widely in Buddhist texts that I have seen definitions ranging between 10 to the fifty-first power and 10 to a power the exponent for which is transcribed with 35 placeholders (i.e. exponent = 74,436,000,000,000,000,000,000,000,000,000,000).

38. Vasubandhu explains the comparison of the Buddha to empty space thus: "Again, as for 'like empty space,' [just as empty space cannot be stained by anything at all, so too, the Buddha] cannot be stained by worldly dharmas, this because all habitual karmic propensities associated with ignorance and afflictions have been extinguished." (復如虛空世間法不能染。無明煩惱習氣滅故。[131c05-06])

39. This is another reference to the provisions required for the realization of bodhi (*bodhisaṃbhāra*) usually explained as consistinig primarily of merit and knowledge or wisdom. "*susaṃbhṛtasaṃbhārāṇāṃ*."

40. DSBC: "*svayaṃbhūjñānānukūlaṃ*."

41. "*pramuditāyāṃ bodhisattvabhūmau sthito bodhisattvaḥ prāmodyabahulo bhavati prasādabahulaḥ prītibahula utplāvanābahula udagrībahula utsībahula utsāhabahulo 'saṃrambhabahulo 'vihiṃsābahulo 'krodhabahulo bhavati*."

42. Although the Chinese references "wisdom" here (*zhihui* / 智慧)," DSBC references the word more commonly rendered as "knowledge" (*jñāna*): "*jñānabhūmeḥ*."

43. Bhikkhu Bodhi points out that this same list appears in the Pali (albeit in slightly different order and with mild differences in the interpretation of two of the five points). See his translation of *Numerical Discourses* 9:5, p. 1255. The most exhaustive of all treatments of this list appears to be Nāgārjuna's discussion of it in his Ten Grounds Sutra commentary, for which see my complete translation of that entire text under separate cover.

44. "*prasādabahulatayā*." BHSD lists "faith" as the primary definition, although MW doesn't mention it at all and prefers definitions along the lines of "purity" and "tranquility" reflected here, hence the apparent discrepancy between KB and SA translations. BB follows KB precisely here, while SD similarly prefers "abundant realization of purity" (多證淨) and Bodhiruci falls somewhat farther afield with "abundant reverence" (多恭敬).

45. "*adhimuktiviśuddhyā*."

46. DSBC: "*ratnopamacittotpādātṛptābhinirhāratayā*."

47. In his Treatise on the Ten Grounds Sutra, (*Daśabhūmika-vibhāṣā* / 十住毘婆沙論 [T no. 1521]), Nāgārjuna devotes all of Chapter Five (T26n1521_p30b10-35a21) to an extensive explanation of the following ten vows. For an English translation of this, see my translation of this entire treatise.

48. DSBC = *"sarvajñajñānapratiṣṭhāpanāya."*

49. I opt for the first of Qingliang's two interpretations for the reading of this extremely ambiguous line not found at all in Bodhiruci, Śīladharma, Buddhabhadra, or the Sanskrit and only obliquely alluded to in Kumarajiva. (QL's other approved interpretation of " 若入若行若去" refers to these worlds subsuming or being subsumed by each other in an interpenetrating fashion wherein this bodhisattva freely travels to and returns from these many different sorts of worlds.)

50. DSBC doesn't specify "'wise' beings" so much as "beings possessed of knowledge": *"apramāṇajñānākarasattva."*

51. DSBC doesn't specify "wisdom," but rather "knowledge": *"tathāgatap rabhāvajñānānugamāya."*

52. DSBC does not specify "wisdom," but rather "knowledge": *"sahaghoṣ odāhārajñānānugamāya."*

53. Again, DSBC specifies "knowledge" rather than "wisdom": "mahābu ddhaviṣayaprabhāva**jñānā**nugamāya."

54. Again, DSBC specifies "knowledge" rather than "wisdom": *"mahājñānabhūmi."*

55. The following list of ten mental qualities is present with minor variations in BB, SA, and KB, but is missing seven of these mental qualities in SD and eight of these mental qualities in BR and the (very late) surviving Sanskrit editions of the Ten Grounds Sutra.

56. DSBC lists these expressions of faith as follows: *"tathāgatānām arhatāṃ samyaksaṃbuddhānāṃ pūrvāntacaryābhinirhārapraveśaṃ pāramitāsamudāgamaṃ bhūmipariniṣpattiṃ vaiśeṣikatāṃ balapariniṣpattiṃ vaiśāradyaparipūrim āveṇikabuddhadharmāsaṃhāryatām acintyāṃ buddhadharmatām anantamadhyaṃ tathāgataviṣayābhinirhāram aparimāṇajñānānugataṃ tathāgatagocarānupraveśaṃ phalapariniṣpattim abhiśraddadhāti."*

57. One could insert in brackets a tenth member of this list as "[and such insurmountability]" following both BB and KB (如是難壞), that is also found with mild permutations in most other editions. Bodhiruci (如是上。此諸佛法如是難得。) follows very closely the extant DSBC Sanskrit: *"evamudārāḥ evaṃ durāsadāśceme buddhadharmāḥ,"* i.e. "Such loftiness and so hard to approach."

58. This is a reference to the four inverted views (*viparyāsa*):
    1) Viewing as pleasurable what is in fact conducive to suffering;
    2) Viewing as permanent what is in fact impermanent;
    3) Viewing as lovely what is in fact unlovely by virtue of its impurity;
    4) Viewing as "self" what is in fact devoid of anything constituting an inherently and enduringly existent self.
59. These are collectively referred to as "the four floods" (*ogha*).
60. "Name-and-form" is a reference to the five aggregates of mentality and physicality that are generally falsely construed by unenlightened beings to constitute an inherently existent "self."
61. "The six sense bases" is a reference to the six sense faculties: eye, ear, nose, tongue, body, and intellectual mind faculty. They are commonly metaphorically referred to as a village wherein beings falsely impute the existence of an inherently existent self.
62. DSBC specifies "knowledge" (*jñāna*) rather than "wisdom."
63. For "Diligently cultivates irreversible renunciaton" (勤修出離。不退不轉。), the DSBC Sanskrit has "*naiṣkramyacārī avivartya*" for which BHSD foregrounds as definitions for "*naiṣkramya*": "departure from the world, renunciation of worldly things," and "renunciation as regards desires (lusts)" while Conze's MDPL has: "leaving home."
64. DSBC gives this entire list as: "*tadyathā - śraddhā karuṇā maitrī tyāgaḥ khedasahiṣṇutā śāstrajñatā lokajñatā hryapatrāpyaṃ dhṛtibalādhānaṃ tathāgatapūjopasthānamiti.*"
65. Although the phrasing of the Chinese text might lead one to think these are two separate dharmas, I follow QLSC in combining these two subcomponents as a single grounds-purifying dharma. The surviving Sanskrit for this tenth member of the list (per DSBC) is: "*tathāgatapūjopasthānamiti.*"
66. "The remaining two means of attraction" are "beneficial actions" and "joint endeavors."
67. "*yathābalaṃ yathābhajamānam.*"
68. DSBC specifies "knowledge" (*jñāna*) rather than "wisdom."
69. DSBC specifies "knowledge" (*jñāna*) rather than "wisdom."
70. DSBC specifies "knowledge" (*jñāna*) rather than "wisdom."
71. DSBC specifies "knowledge" (*jñāna*) rather than "wisdom."
72. DSBC specifies "knowledge" (*jñāna*) rather than "wisdom."
73. For "… should bring forth ten types of resolute intentions," DSBC has: "*tasya daśa cittāśayāḥ pravartante.*"

74. For these ten "resolute intentions" (*cittāśaya*), DSBC has: *ṛjvāśaya* (= *ārjava*?), *mṛdvāśaya, karmaṇyāśaya, damāśaya, śamāśaya, kalyāṇāśaya, asaṃsṛṣṭāśaya, anapekṣāśaya, udārāśaya, māhātmyāśaya.*

75. This refers to the avoidance of the ten courses of bad karmic action, namely: killing; taking what is not given; sexual misconduct; false speech; divisive speech; harsh speech; frivolous speech; covetousness; ill will; wrong views.

76. For these ten kinds of minds, DSBC gives: "...*hitacittatām utpādayati / sukhacittatāṃ maitracittatāṃ kṛpācittatāṃ dayācittatām anugrahacittatām ārakṣācittatāṃ samacittatām acāryacittatāṃ śāstṛcittatām utpādayati.*"

77. "The view imputing the existence of a true self in association with one's body" corresponds to the Sanskrit *satkāya-dṛṣṭi.*

78. The SA Chinese gives "礬石," the modern translation of which is "aluminite." This does not correspond to the DSBC Sanskrit which specifies "*kāsīsa*," a type of iron oxide. Hence I am compelled to prefer the Sanskrit antecedent term.

79. One may notice the seeming absence in this verse of two of the ten resolute intentions: "the unmixed resolute intention" (*asaṃsṛṣṭāśaya*) and "the unattached resolute intention" (*anapekṣāśaya*). It would appear then that they have somehow been replaced here by the phrase: "the swift exits from *saṃsāra*." (The BB and SD verses specify all ten mental dispositions and do not refer to anything corresponding to this phrase.) That neither BB, SD, DR, or the Sanskrit say anything at all about "*saṃsāra*" here suggests that perhaps this verse line was corrupted in the SA edition by a scribal error or translator misreading that ended up producing a substitution of "*saṃsāra*" for "*saṃsarga*," for the corresponding part of same line in the extant Sanskrit edition, per DSBC reads: "*saṃsargapekṣavigatāśca*," which clearly refers to the two missing list elements and does not refer to "swift exits from *saṃsāra*" at all.

80. As with the previous *bhūmi*, DSBC shows "*cittāśaya*" ("mental intentions") as the Sanskrit antecedent for "resolute intentions" (深心).

81. For these ten "resolute intentions" (*cittāśaya*), DSBC gives: *śuddha-cittāśaya, sthira-cittāśaya, nirvic-cittāśaya, avirāga-cittāśaya, avinivarta-cittāśaya, dṛḍha-cittāśaya, uttapta-cittāśaya, atṛpta-cittāśaya, udāra-cittāśaya*, and *māhātmya-cittāśaya*. (The last two correspond precisely to the last two listed for the second *bhūmi*.)

82. DSBC gives this tenfold list as: *acintya, atulya, aprameya, durāsada, asaṃspṛṣṭa, nirupadrava, nirupāyāsa, abhayapuragamanīya, apunarāvṛtti, bahujanaparitrāṇa.*

83. Again, DSBC has "*cittāśaya*" for these ten.

84. DSBC lists these as:
anāthātrāṇāpratiśaraṇacittāśaya;
nityadaridrapratiśaraṇacittāśaya;
rāgadveṣamohāgnisaṃpradīptapratiśaraṇacittāśaya;
bhavacārakāvaruddhapratiśaraṇacittāśaya;
satatasamitaklaśagahenāvṛtaprasuptapratiśaraṇacittāśaya;
vilokanasamarthapratiśaraṇacittāśaya;
kuśaladharmacchandarahitapratiśaraṇacittāśaya;
buddhadharmapramuṣitapratiśaraṇacittāśaya;
saṃsārasrotonuvāhipratiśaraṇacittāśaya;
mokṣopāyapraṇaṣṭapratiśaraṇacittāśaya.

85. DSBC seems to leave out part of this list, but it is complete in Rahder (herein bracketed): "*...paritrātavyāḥ parimocayitavyāḥ [pariśodhayitavyā uttārayitavyā niveśayitavyāḥ pratiṣṭhāpayitavyāḥ] paritoṣayitavyāḥ saṃropayitavyā vinetavyāḥ parinirvāpayitavyā....*"

86. Both the BB and KB editions appear to dispense with "non-production" here. (It is retained in SA, BR, SD, and the Sanskrit.) DSBC: "*sa ca sarvadharmayathāvadavabodho nānyatra apracārānutpādacāriṇyāḥ prajñāyāḥ.*"

87. DSBC lists these ten as: "*...dharmārāmo dharmarato dharmapratiśaraṇo dharmanimno dharmapravaṇo dharmaprāgbhāro dharmaparāyaṇo dharmalayano dharmatrāṇo dharmānudharmacārī.*"

88. The DSBC Sanskrit text clarifies that *xin* (心), otherwise legitimately translated as "minds," in fact refers more specifically to "dispositions," "mental intentions," or "inclinations" (*āśaya*).

89. The DSBC Sanskrit, SA, BR, and SD all speak here of only one means of attraction (beneficial action) and only one *pāramitā* (patience). However, BB and KB both speak here of two means of attraction (pleasing words and beneficial actions) and two *pāramitās* (patience and vigor).

90. The "non-harming mind" in this verse section corresponds to and is at variance with the initial prose section's "non-retreating mind."

91. This is a reference to the four immeasurable minds (*apramāṇa-citta*), all of which require identifying with all beings everywhere as equally deserving of kindness, compassion, sympathetic joy, and equanimity.

92. "*dharmālokapraveśa.*"

93. Just as he did in the previous ground's introductory section, SA used *xin* (心) here in these last two members of this list as an abbreviation for *shenxin* (深心), his usually rather standard rendering of "resolute

intentions" (*āśaya*). DSBC = "*udāra-āśaya-adhimukti-dhātu-vicaraṇāloka-praveśena.*")

94. "*māhātmya-āśaya-adhimukti-dhātu-vicaraṇāloka-praveśena.*"
95. "*jñānaparipācakairdharma.*"
96. "*tadātmakadharma.*"
97. "*saṃprajāna.*"
98. These contemplations are anchored to the four stations of mindfulness focusing on the body, feelings, thought / mind, and dharmas (*catuḥ-smṛty-upasthāna*).
99. This is a summation of the bodhisattva's exercise of the four right efforts (*samyak-pradhāna*).
100. "*vivekaniśritaṃ virāganiśritaṃ nirodhaniśritaṃ vyavasargapariṇataṃ.*"
101. This is a summation of the bodhisattva's practice of the four foundations of psychic power.
102. This is a summation of the bodhisattva's practice of the five root faculties.
103. This is a summation of the bodhisattva's practice of the five powers.
104. This is a summation of the bodhisattva's practice of the seven limbs of enlightenment.
105. This is a summation of the bodhisattva's practice of the eight-fold right path, hereby concluding the narration of the bodhisattva's practice of the thirty-seven enlightenment factors.
106. "In order to further his quest to acquire the most especially supreme path" (*uttarottara-vaiśeṣika-dharma-parimārgaṇatayā*) is found here in SA as well as in BR, SD, and the DSBC Sanskrit, but it is not found in the three earliest extant editions of this scripture: DR, KB, and BB.
107. This short section of the text regarding aligning practice with whatsoever the Tathāgata censures or praises is not found in KB and BB). The corresponding DSBC text is: "*sa yānīmāni karmāṇyakaraṇīyāni samyaksaṃbuddhavivarṇitāni saṃkleśopasaṃhitāni, tāni sarveṇa sarvaṃ prajahāti / yāni cemāni karmāṇi karaṇīyāni samyaksaṃbuddhapraśastāni bodhimārgasaṃbhārānukūlāni, tāni samādāya vartate /.*"
108. "*bodhimārgasaṃbhāra.*"
109. In this ten-fold list, SA, BR, SD, and the Sanskrit are very close, whereas KB and BB's lists are nine-fold and slightly variant. DSBC's tenfold list gives us: "*snigdhacittaśca bhavati, maducittaśca karmaṇyacittaśca hitasukhāvahacittaśca aparikliṣṭacittaśca uttarottaraviśeṣaparimārga ṇacittaśca jñānaviśeṣaṇābhilāṣacittaśca sarvajagatparitrāṇacittaśca gurugauravānukūlacittaśca yathāśrutadharmapratipatticittaśca.*"

110. SA, BR, SD, and the Sanskrit are all quite mutually consistent as reflected here in DSBC's tenfold list: "… *sa kṛtajñaśca bhavati, kṛtavedī ca sūrataśca sukhasaṃvāsaśca ṛjuśca mṛduśca agahanacārī ca nirmāyanirmāṇaśca suvacāśca pradakṣiṇagrāhī ca.*" KB and BB include "implementation of the practice of right concentration."

111. The lists of ten types of vigor are generally quite consistent in all six extant editions with the sole exception of BB's non-inclusion of the final member of all other lists: "The vigor that distinguishes what is and is not the Path." DSBC gives us: *"aprasrabdhavīryaśca bhavati aparikliṣṭaḥ / apratyudāvartyavīryaśca vipulavīryaśca anantavīryaśca uttaptavīryaśca asamavīryaśca asaṃhāryavīryaśca sarvasattvaparipācanavīryaśca nayānayavibhaktavīryaśca bhavati."*

112. It is clear from comparing all the editions and the Sanskrit that the first three elements referenced here, although differing somewhat in order from the Sanskrit, are higher aspirations (*adhyāśaya*), resolute intentions (*āśaya*), and resolute convictions (*adhimukti*).

113. *"apramāṇacittāśayatā ca samudāgacchāti."*

114. *"āśayādhyāśayādhimuktisamatā viśudhyati"* Most of the other editions (BB, KB, SD, DSBC) have not only SA's "resolute intentions" (*āśaya)* and "resolute faith" (*adhimukti*) but also include "higher aspirations" (*adhyāśaya*) and "impartiality" (*samatā*), thus producing a list of four elements. BR is slightly ambiguous and appears to include all but "higher aspirations."

115. DSBC: *"satkāyadṛṣṭi."*

116. This first quatrain condenses the first ten-fold list ("the ten gateways to Dharma illumination") that opens the initial discussion of this ground.

117. This quatrain along with the quatrain immediately preceding it are a condensation of the second ten-fold list set forth earlier in the discussion of this *bhūmi*, "the ten kinds of knowledge-maturing dharmas."

118. This quatrain together with the one immediately preceding it summarize the earlier discussion of the bodhisattva's cultivation of the thirty-seven enlightenment factors.

119. This quatrain together with the immediately preceding quatrain summarize the ten aims behind cultivation of the thirty-seven enlightenment factors that were brought up earlier in the discussion of this fourth ground.

120. Beginning here, these introductory verses to the fifth ground do not track well with the Sanskrit which itself is missing the ninth verse (that does survive in the Tibetan and in other Chinese editions). It appears from the Sanskrit that SA is missing the first line ("After

such a long time, the Great Muni is now met.") and the fourth line ("The Great Śrāmaṇa, worthy of reverence, is revered.") of the sixth verse, which according to DSBC is:

sucireṇa saṃgamu mahāmuninā
saṃprāpta sarvagūṇapāramitaḥ |
mada māna darpa prajahitva tamaṃ
pūjārhu pūjima mahāśramaṇam || 6 ||

What's more, SA seems to present verses seven and eight in reverse order.

121. *"āśayaviśuddhisamatā."*
122. HH explains this equally regarding pure mental disposition "toward the mind" as primarily meaning "toward the minds of beings."
123. Although DSBC gives us *"adhyāśaya"* here ("higher aspirations"), this is not supported by any other of the Chinese editions except the very latest one done by Śīladharma in 790 CE who renders this as "especially supreme dispositions / aspirations" (增上意樂). BB, KB, BR, and SA are all clearly translating simply *"āśaya,"* ("resolute intentions" or "intentions").
124. *"saṃvṛtisatya."*
125. *"paramārthasatya."*
126. *"lakṣaṇasatya."*
127. *"vibhāgasatya."*
128. *"nistīraṇasatya."*
129. *vastusatya.*
130. *prabhavasatya.*
131. *kṣayānutpādasatya.*
132. *mārgajñānāvatārasatya.*
133. *sarvabodhisattvabhūmikramānusaṃdhiniṣpādanatayā yāvat tathāgatajñānasamudayasatya.*
134. *"sa parasattvānāṃ yathāśayasaṃtoṣaṇātsaṃvṛtisatyaṃ prajānāti."*
135. *"ekanayasamavasaraṇātparamārthasatyaṃ prajānāti."*
136. *"svasāmanyalakṣaṇānubodhāllakṣaṇasatyaṃ prajānāti."*
137. *"dharmavibhāgavyavasthānānubodhādvibhāgasatyaṃ prajānāti."*
138. *"skandhadhātvāyatanavyavasthānānubodhānnistīraṇasatyaṃ prajānāti."*
139. *"cittaśarīraprapīḍanopanipātitatvādvastusatyam."*
140. *"gatisaṃdhisaṃbandhanatvātprabhavasatyam."*
141. *"sarvajvaraparidāhātyantopaśamātkṣayānutpādasatyam."*

142. For this passage, DSBC gives us the following: *"advayānutpādasatyam, advayābhinirhāranmārgajñānāvatārasatyam."*

143. DSBC:

"sarvākārābhisaṃbodhitsarvabodhisattvabhūmikramānusaṃdhiniṣpādanatayā yāvattathāgatajñānasamudayasatyaṃ prajānāti."

144. *"adhimukti."*

145. *"mārāśayagahana."*

146. Although the extant Sanskrit refers here only to a*kuśalavitarka* ("bad initial ideation"), the Chinese text of most editions (BB, KB, SA, and SD) uses the translation for both *vitarka* and *vicāra* ("ideation and mental discursion").

147. Most editions seem to vary somewhat, but only slightly. DSBC has:

tatsarvasattvaparitrāṇāyārabhate, sarvasattvahitāya, sarvasattvasukhāya, sarvasattvānukampāyai, sarvasattvānupadravāya, sarvasattvaparimocanāya, sarvasattvānukarṣāya, sarvasattvaprasādanāya, sarvasattvavinayāya, sarvasattvaparinirvāṇāy ārabhate.

148. *"buddhi."*

149. *"jñāna."*

150. *"prajñā."*

151. *"puṇyasaṃbhāra."*

152. *"jñānasaṃbhāra."*

153. *"mahāmaitrīkṛpāsaṃbhāra."*

154. MW defines *musāragalva* as "a kind of coral." Other definitions state that it is a kind of shell or mother-of-pearl.

155. As is often the case with these radically and tersely condensed verse lines, this one can only be made fully sensible by referring back to information solely available in the main text of this *bhūmi*. For comparison here, we have the following:

DSBC and KB are equally terse, both literally translated more or less as: "… on up to the truth associated with what is unimpeded," (*yāvantanāvaraṇasatya samosaranti* [Rahder footnotes a variant ending the line as *"samāsaranti"*]).

SD: "… on up to truth associated with the unimpeded knowledge of the Buddha," (乃至無礙佛智諦). SD is the only truly clear edition here, for only it can stand on its own without reference to information found in the main fifth ground text.

BB is a complete outlier barely relating in these verse lines to most of the other editions. And of course BR has no verses at all, only the main text of the Sutra itself.

156. As in the main text, the Sanskrit verse refers again to "*musāragalva.*"

157. "Knowing *dharmas as by nature transcendent*" (知法性離) corresponds to DSBC's "*sarvadharmāviviktāḥ*" which infers that all dharmas "are beyond distinctions or discriminations," hence my translation of the Chinese as "transcendent."

158. "*dharmasamatā.*"

159. Most extant editions are quite similar but slightly variant in a few list components. The DSBC Sanskrit gives us: *animitta; alakṣaṇa; anutpāda; ajāta; vivikta; adiviśuddhi; niṣprapañca; anāvyūhānirvyūha; māyāsvapnaprati-bhāsapratiśrutkodakacandrapratibimbanirmāṇa; bhāvābhāvādvaya.*

160. Nāgārjuna provides an extensive discussion of these similes in his Mppu (T25.1509.101c6-105c18 [fasc. 6]).

161. DSBC: "*tīkṣṇayā ānulomikyā kṣāntyā.*" (In MDPL, Conze suggests "adaptable patience" for *ānulomikī kṣānti.*)

162. The rather long (6 pages) ensuing discussion of causality more or less follows the listing of "the ten types of sequential and counter-sequential contemplation of the factors involved in conditioned arising" with which the discussion ends.

163. In the following discussion of origination through causes and conditions (*pratitya-samutpāda*), each of the characteristic features associated with the twelve links is italicized to enhance the reader's ease of understanding.

164. DSBC: "*puṇyāpuṇyāneñjyānabhisaṃskāra.*" Regarding the third of these three types of actions, QL interprets "actions leading to imperturbable states" as referring to the pure karma of the eight levels of *dhyāna* (which, of course would refer not only to abiding in those levels of meditative absorption, but also would refer to taking rebirth in the corresponding heavens). He also notes that this "pure karma of the eight *dhyānas* also qualifies as being a function of delusion," the rationale for that statement being that, rarified as these modes of existence are, as an end in themselves, they still do not constitute or conduce to liberation from cyclic existence and hence function as erroneous karmic paths.

165. The SA Chinese is mildly ambiguous here. Compare Buddhabhadra, Kumārajīva, and Bodhiruci, as below:

> BB: "Because of prior and subsequent continuity, these three paths are not severed. These three paths occur apart from a self or possessions of a self, and yet production and extinction [continue to] occur." (No mention in BB of the "reeds" analogy.)

KB: "On account of past and future continuity, these three paths are not cut off. These three paths exist apart from any self or possessions of a self and yet there exists this production and extinction. This is analogous to [the mutual dependence occurring in] two stalks of bamboo that, through leaning on each other, are thus able to stand up. Although they are not solidly established, it still appears as if they are solidly established."

BR: "On account of the ceaseless continuity of past and future, these three paths are not cut off. These three paths exist apart from any self or possessions of a self. Because they only occur as a process of production and extinction, their existence is analogous to a bundle of bamboo stalks."

166. *Shulu* (束蘆) here translates the Sanskrit *naḍa-kalāpa,* standing sheaves of reeds (as, for instance, *Phragmites karka india*), wherein, whether as they grow in naturally-occurring stands, or as they may be deliberately bundled together in the construction of shelters and such in order to remain upright, each reed serves to support the others while simultaneously relying entirely upon the support of the others to keep from collapsing. Hence we have in this phenomenon an analogy for the utter codependence of these three subsets of "links" comprising the twelve-fold chain of serially-unfolding conditioned coproduction. This is of course equally true of the mutually supporting and sustaining nature of all twelve of the links *individually* as well.

Bhikkhu Bodhi points out a scriptural citation for the "sheaves of reeds" causality analogy as *Saṃyutta Nikāya* 12-67: "The Sheaves of Reeds."

167. "Suffering associated with the karmic formative factors" = *xingku* (行苦) = *saṃskāraduḥkhatā.*

168. *Suffering of suffering* = *kuku* (苦苦) = *duḥkhaduḥkhatā.*

169. *Suffering associated with deterioration* = *huaiku* (壞苦) = *pariṇāmaduḥkhatā.*

170. "*sa evaṃ dvādaśākāraṃ pratītyasamutpādaṃ pratyavekṣate 'nulomapratilomaṃ.*"

171. All editions are fairly consistent throughout this list of ten contemplations with the exception of a possible textual corruption in the second contemplation in the KB edition wherein "body" is included as a fundamental basis for the twelve causal links.

DSBC gives the list as follows:

bhavāṅgānusaṃdhitaśca;
ekacittasamavasaraṇataśca;
svakarmāsaṃbhedataśca;
avinirbhāgataśca;

trivartmānuvartanataśca;
pūrvāntapratyutpannāparāntāvekṣaṇataśca;
triduḥkhatāsamudayataśca;
hetupratyayaprabhavataśca;
utpādavyayavinibandhanataśca;
abhāvākṣayatāpratyavekṣaṇataśca.

172. HH identifies these as the three paths discussed earlier in this passage on conditioned origination: the path of afflictions, the path of karmic actions, and the path of suffering.

173. "*śūnyatāvimokṣamukha.*"

174. "*ānimittavimokṣamukha.*"

175. "*apraṇihitavimokṣamukha.*"

176. These ten emptiness samādhis, per DSBC: *avatāraśūnyatā; svabhāvaśūnyatā; paramārthaśūnyatā; paramaśūnyatā; mahāśūnyatā; saṃprayogaśūnyatā; abhinirhāraśūnyatā; yathāvadavikalpaśūnyatā; sāpekṣaśūnyatā; vinirbhāgāvinirbhāgaśūnyatā.*

177. These ten types of resolute intentions per DSBC: *abhedyāśaya; niyatāśaya; kalyāṇāśaya; gambhīrāśaya; apratyudāvartyāśaya; apratiprasrabdhāśaya; vimalāśaya; anantāśaya; jñānābhilāṣāśaya; upāyaprajñāsaṃprayogāśaya.*

178. Context often requires a somewhat adaptive translation of *āśaya* that otherwise may mean "mental intention," "mental disposition," "intent," "resolution," or "mentality." Here I prefer Conze's (MDPL) "resolute intention."

179. "Acquiescent patience" = *ānulomikī kṣānti*. In his XHYJL, LTX points out that this "acquiescent patience" is the third of "the five types of patience" and the second of "the ten types of patience" and that in both cases, it is the level of patience acquired just before realizing "the unproduced-dharmas patience" (*anutpattika-dharma-kṣānti*). (T36n1739_p0899b7-12)

180. "King of the Fine Transformations Heaven" (善化天王) = *sunirmita-deva-rāja*. Bodhiruci translates this as "King of the Delight in Transformations Heaven" (化樂天王). This is a clear reference to the Nirmāṇa-rati Heaven, the heaven just above the Tuṣita Heaven within the six desire-realm heavens.

181. None of the Chinese editions (DR, BB, BR, KB, SA, SD) agree with the Sanskrit's inclusion of three instead of two factors here: skillful means, wisdom, and knowledge (*upāyaprajñājñāna*).

182. All other editions (BB, KB, BR, SD, and the Sanskrit) refer instead to the penetrating comprehension of dharmas' differences. DSBC: "*apramāṇaṃ ca dharmanānātvamavatarati.*"

183. *"apramāṇaṃ ca buddhānāṃ bhagavatāṃ jñānābhisaṃbodhimavatarati."*

184. SA, BR, and SD all specify "name-and-form bodies," whereas BB, KB, and the Sanskrit all refer only to "form bodies" (*rūpakāya*).

185. The four types of retention: dharmas, meanings, mantras, and patience.

186. *"bodhyaṅga."*

187. All other editions specify entry into both knowledge / wisdom and spiritual superknowledges (*jñānābhijñānacaryākramaṇī*).

188. All editions are fairly consistent here with the exception that BB and KB list eleven samādhis here, whereas most of the other editions collapse the final two list members in BB and KB into a single samādhi. DSBC provides the following list: *suvicitavicayaṃ; suvicintitārthaṃ; viśeṣamatiṃ; prabhedārthakośaṃ; sarvārthavicayaṃ; supratiṣṭhitadṛḍhamūlaṃ; jñānābhijñāmukhaṃ; dharmadhātu(pari) karmaṃ; tathāgatānuśaṃsaṃ; vicitrārthakośasaṃsāranirvāṇamukhaṃ.*

189. *"prajñājñānavicāraṇābhūmeḥ"* ("The ground of contemplating wisdom and knowledge.")

190. DSBC: *"na punaḥ svabuddhivicāreṇa."*

191. The Sanskrit text makes it clear that SA's "ultimate reality" (實際) apparently refers here not to its usual Sanskrit antecedent (*bhūtakoṭi*), but rather to *nirodha,* i.e. to a state of quiescent cessation synonymous with nirvāṇa.

192. DSBC: *"buddhajñānaviṣayakośa."*

193. There are four types of *māras* (*catur-māra*) that are often translated elsewhere as "demons" when not directly referencing the celestial *māras.* Those four types of *māras* are: affliction *māras* (*kleśa-māra*), the *māras* of the aggregates (*skandha-māra*), the *māras* of death (*mṛtyamāra*), celestial *māras* (*deva-putra-māra*).

194. HH clarifies that these "adorning phenomena" refer to the bodhisattva's cultivation and accumulation of many different sorts of roots of goodness and meritorious qualities with which he, figuratively speaking, "adorns" buddha lands: "菩薩以他修積的種種善 根功德，莊嚴佛的國土，無不超過天、龍，及八部神祇、帝釋、梵王、 四大天王等所有的莊嚴之事。"

195. Although *huo* (惑) is often legitimately translated as "delusion" in these sorts of texts, it is also very often a translation of "afflictions" (*kleśa*), for which the Chinese translation is more ordinarily *fannao* (煩惱). The preceding text (at the end of Section F) and the DSBC Sanskrit both make it clear that SA is actually translating *kleśa* ("afflictions") here even though he switches to the more standard Chinese

translation (煩惱) in the very next verse line. One obvious reason has to do with the need for economy in composing seven-character verse lines in sino-Buddhist Classical Chinese.

196. Vasubandhu correlates this with the bodhisattva's first ground practice.
197. Vasubandhu correlates this with the bodhisattva's second ground practice.
198. Vasubandhu correlates this with the bodhisattva's third ground practice.
199. Vasubandhu correlates this with the bodhisattva's fourth ground practice.
200. Vasubandhu correlates this with the bodhisattva's fifth ground practice. DSBC: *"supariśodhitādhyāśayasaṃkalpa."*
201. Vasubandhu correlates this with the bodhisattva's sixth ground practice.
202. Vasubandhu correlates this with the bodhisattva's seventh ground practice and also mentions that it is on account of his encounters with measurelessly many realms of beings that the bodhisattva "enters the path of measureless knowledge."
203. All editions' lists vary somewhat. DSBC has: *ajātatāṃ ca; alakṣaṇatāṃ ca; asaṃbhūtatāṃ ca; avināśitāṃ ca; aniṣṭhitatāṃ ca; apravṛttitāṃ ca; anabhinivṛttitāṃ ca; abhāvasvabhāvatāṃ ca; ādimadhyaparyavasānasamatāṃ ca; tathatāvikalpasarvajñajñānapraveśa tāṃ ca.*
204. Vasubandhu notes that this refers to "skillful abiding in the *ālayavijñāna*'s dharma of true suchness" (善住阿梨耶識真如法中).
205. *The four floods* (四流) refer to beings' submersion in the floods of: views (見流), desire (欲流), becoming (有流), ignorance (無明流).
206. *"sarvadharmāṇāṃ dharmatā."*
207. BB (圓光), BR (光輪), KB (圓光), SD (光輪), and the Sanskrit (*prabhāmaṇḍala*) all specify "aura."
208. *"dharmāloka."*
209. *"sarvadharmanirvikalpālokaḥ."*
210. It is apparent from the Sanskrit (*adhimukti*) as well as from DR, BB, KB, SD, and QLSC that SA's *jie* (解) is abbreviating *xinjie* (信解), "resolute faith."
211. *"āśayabala."*
212. *"kumārabhūmi."*

213. At this point in the text BB (566a10), KB (522b28), Bodhiruci (184c28), SD (561c08), and the Sanskrit all state that "He is able to receive measurelessly many predictions."

214. Neither the preceding prose text nor the Sanskrit support "meritorious qualities" here, but rather "merit and knowledge" (*punyajñāna*). Perhaps "meritorious qualities" here was the result of a scribal or SA translation error.

215. *"āśaya."*

216. KB and BB ((both have: 能得於十種 / 妙大自在智) as well as the Sanskrit (*vaśitā daśo vimala-jñāna-vicāra-prāptā*) clarify that this "ten *ārya* knowledges" refers to the ten types of "sovereign mastery" (*vaśitā*) listed earlier in the description of this eighth ground (sovereign mastery with regard to lifespan, mind, wealth, karmic deeds, rebirths, vows, understanding, utilization of psychic power, knowledge, and the Dharma).

217. *"praśamita."*

218. Although, due to the need for economy in composing 7-character lines, the Chinese does not specify "vehicle," the Sanskrit does specify *"yāna"*: *"yatra sattva tīkṣṇacitta pratyayānaniratā."*

219. "Effects of practicing" (lit. "actions") = Skt. *abhisaṃskāra*. (BHSD foregrounds "performance," "accomplishment," and "accumulation.") The intended reference here is to this bodhisattva's knowing in accordance with reality the karmic effects of implementing the various categories of dharmas arrayed in this list.

220. "Entangling thicket" = Skt. *gahana*. SA, BR, and SD all translate this as *choulin* (稠林) which means "thicket," whereas KB and BB translate it as "difficulty" (難).

221. Each of these "entangling thickets" (*gahana*) is explored in greater detail below in the subsections corresponding to the Sanskrit text's sections "E" through "K."

222. It is apparent from the Sanskrit (*adhimukti*) that SA's *jie* (解) is abbreviating *xinjie* (信解), "resolute beliefs."

223. "Sense realms" = Skt. *dhātu*. This refers to the eighteen sense realms: the six sense faculties, the six sense objects, and the six sense consciousnesses.

224. "Resolute intentions" = *"āśaya."*

225. "Latent tendencies" = *"anuśaya."*

226. *"upapatti."*

227. *"vāsana-anusaṃdhi."*

228. These "three groups" (三聚) refer to: 1) those fixed in their adherence to what is wrong; 2) those fixed in their adherence to what is right; 3) those who are "unfixed" as to their adherence to either what is wrong or what is right.

229. "Devoid of physical form" = Rahder Skt. *aśarīratāṁ*. (There is an error in DSBC which has *śarīratāṁ*.)

230. Bhikkhu Bodhi points out that this is a reference to the Buddha's statements on the boundlessness of consciousness found in DN 11 and MN 49 wherein "consciousness" there may be equated with "mind" as intended here. See *Long Discourses*, Walshe, p. 179 and *The Middle Length Discourses*, Bhikkhus Ñāṇamoli & Bodhi, p. 428.

231. Bhikkhu Bodhi points out that this is an allusion to a fourfold classification of karma at AN 4:232-233 for which see *The Numerical Discourses of the Buddha*, Bhikkhu Bodhi, p.601. KB, Bodhiruci, BB, and SD all break these out as four clearly stated items, for instance KB, as follows:

> "Their characteristic of rewarding black actions with black retributions; their characteristic of rewarding white actions with white retributions; their characteristic of rewarding a combination of black and white actions with a combination of black and white retributions; their characteristic of being amenable to ending through actions that are neither black nor white…."

232. SA is very close to the Sanskit (*karmakṣetrāpramāṇatāṃ ca*).

DR has "[The characteristic of having] farm fields of karmic offense and merit that are measureless" (罪福田地，則無有量).

Both KB and BB have: "He knows karmic actions' characteristic of involving countless causes and conditions in their arising" (知無量因緣起業相).

BR has "karmic actions' characteristic of involving measureless causes" (業因無量相).

SD has: "the field of karmic actions' nature of measurelessness" (業田無量性).

Hence we see that four editions (including the Sanskrit) involve a metaphor, whereas KB, BB, and BR all skip the metaphor entirely, preferring a brief explanation of the concept. For instance BR (very similar to KB and BB whose translations here are identical) has: "karmic actions' characteristic of involving measureless causes" (業因無量相).

233. "resolute beliefs" = "*adhimukti*."

234. "Sense realms" = "*dhātu*."

235. "Resolute intentions" = "*āśaya*."

236. "Latent tendencies" = "*anuśaya*

237. It is apparent from the Sanskrit that SA switched here to a different Chinese rendering for *āśaya* (深心 [*shenxin*]), a binome that literally means "resolute intentions."

238. "Habitual karmic propensities" = "*vāsanā*."

239. Again, this listing refers to the "three groups" of beings mentioned above as the last of the "entangling thickets" in Sanskrit section C above.

240. "Five heinous karmic offenses" refers to patricide, matricide, killing an arhat, spilling the blood of a buddha, and causing a sectarian schism in the monastic community.

241. As in the last of the "entangling thickets" in Sanskrit section C and as in the immediately preceding discussion that refers back to that particular "entangling thicket," "groups" here most likely refers to: 1) those fixed in their adherence to what is wrong; 2) those fixed in their adherence to what is right; 3) those who are "unfixed" as to their adherence to either what is wrong or what is right.

242. "*adhimukti*."

243. "Expounder" = "*dharmabhāṇaka*."

244. "Four unimpeded knowledges" = "*catuḥpratisaṃvid*." These are: *dharmapratisaṃvid*, *arthapratisaṃvid*, *niruktipratisaṃvid*, and pratibhānapratisaṃvid.

245. "*sarvadharmaprajñaptyacchedanadharmaṁ deśayati*." DSBC, BB, Bodhiruci, KB, and SD *all* specify what I insert in brackets here and hereafter: "conventional designations" (*prajñapti*). (SA only implies it obliquely.)

246. "*pratibhānapratisaṃvidā ekaikaṃ yānamaparyantadharmābhāsena deśayati*." BB, Bodhiruci, KB, and SD also corroborate this bracketed insertion of "light."

247. "*āśaya*."

248. "*adhimukti*."

249. "*adhimukti*."

250. "*āśaya*."

251. "The realm in which the Buddha courses" = Skt. *buddhagocara*.

252. "Mental dispositions" = "*āśaya*"

253. These three categorical types (三聚) refer to: 1) those fixed in their adherence to what is wrong; 2) those fixed in their adherence to what is right; 3) those who are "unfixed" as to their adherence to either what is wrong or what is right.

254. Neither BB nor KB include this first list component found in SA, BR, SD, and the Sanskrit (*suvicitavicayaḥ*).

255. This is clearly a reference to the ten types of "entangling thickets" (*gahana*) discussed at some length in relation to the ninth ground in a section beginning with their listing at 202a23–26.

256. Both BB and KB make the acquisition of the "stainless samādhi" a preliminary step before entering the ten samādhis listed immediately thereafter.

257. The Sanskrit samādhi designation per the DSBC text: "*sarvajñajñānav iśeṣābhiṣekavatannāma bodhisattvasamādhirāmukhībhavati.*"

258. In this case, "the beings residing in them" refers to the hungry ghosts (*pretas*).

259. I emend the reading of the Taisho text at 206a18 to correct a graphic-similarity scribal error that erroneously recorded *ge* (各) instead of *ming* (名). The emendation is supported by BB, QLSC, KB, BR, SD, the Sanskrit, one other edition of the SA text, and the requirements of sensibility.

260. Although the entire ensuing section of the Chinese text employs the Chinese character most commonly associated in Buddhist doctrinal discussions with the second of the four truths, i.e. "accumulation" or "origination" of suffering (集 [*ji*] = Skt. *samudaya*), as context demonstrates and the Sanskrit text corroborates, that is *not* the concept intended here. In this instance, the Sanskrit antecedent term is not *samudaya* but rather *samudāgama* which refers instead to "attainment." (MW = "Full or complete knowledge." BHSD = "*approach* [*to*], *arrival* [*of*], *attainment* [*of*], a religious goal, esp. enlightenment, which is to be understood when no goal is specifically named.") This being the case, I translate this character in this context as "attainment."

261. "Sustaining Bases" (持) = *adhiṣṭhāna*. Although this technical term is often translated as "empowerment," that would not be an appropriate rendering here as many of the members of this list may or may not be sustained through empowerments as they are for the most part causally sustained by past karmic actions.

262. Bhikkhu Bodhi points out that one example of this may be the bodhisattva's power to consciously pass away in the Tuṣita Heaven before taking his last birth in the human realm.

263. "Penetrating knowledge" = "*avatārajñāna.*"

264. "Ordinary common people," on the face of it, might appear to be a mistranslation of the Chinese term recorded here as 毛道, i.e. "hair path." But, as it turns out, this in fact *is* Śikṣānanda's very literal translation of the Sanskrit *vāla-patha*, lit. "hair path," apparently a

traditional Sanskrit corruption of *bāla* that is in turn an abbreviation for *bāla-pṛthagjana,* literally "foolish common person."

265. "*buddhakṣetrakāyābhisaṃbodhyavatārajñānaṃ.*"

266. "*mahāvijayo bhikṣu.*"

267. "*vajrapadmottarasya tathāgata.*"

268. An "ineffable" (*anabhilāpya*) is the name of one of a long series of extremely large numbers described in this scripture's "Asaṃkhyeya" chapter.

269. This samādhi per DSBC: "*sarvabuddhakṣetrakāyasvabhāvasaṃdarśanaṃ nāma bodhisattvasamādhiṃ.*"

270. "*sarvābhijñāmatirājaṃ nāma tathāgataṃ.*"

271. "*vaśavartino devarāja.*"

272. "*maheśvarasya devarājasya.*"

273. The DSBC edition of the surviving Sanskrit refers to this final section as the "*parīndanāparivartaḥ*" or "bequest."

274. Bhikkhu Bodhi points out that eight of these comparisons are found in Anguttara Nikāya 8:19 (The Simile of the Ocean).

275. From this point on, the verses in the very late Sanskrit edition diverge entirely from those found in any of the Chinese texts. Because their composition must be of relatively recent origin, there appears to be no clear way to correlate these Sanskrit verses with those of any of the Chinese texts, whether it be DR, BB, SA, KB, or SD, all of which date from a millennium or more earlier than the surviving Sanskrit edition.

Bibliography

Bodhi. (2000). *The Connected Discourses of the Buddha: A New Translation of the Saṃyutta Nikāya* ; translated from the Pāli ; original translation by Bhikkhu Bodhi. (Teachings of the Buddha). Somerville, MA: Wisdom Publications.

Bodhi. (2012). The Numerical Discourses of the Buddha: A Translation of the Aṅguttara Nikāya (Teachings of the Buddha). Boston: Wisdom Publications.

Bodhiruci (c. 508–511 CE). Shidi jing lun (十地經論). T26, no. 1522.

Buddhabhadra (c. 418–20 CE). Dafangguang fo huayan jing (大方廣佛華嚴經). T10, no. 278.

Cleary, T. (1984). The Flower Ornament Scripture: A Translation of the Avatamsaka Sutra. Boulder : [New York]: Shambhala Publications ; Distributed in the U.S. by Random House.

Conze, E., & Suzuki Gakujutsu Zaidan. (1967). Materials for a Dictionary of the Prajñāpāramitā Literature. Tokyo: Suzuki Research Foundation.

Dharmarakṣa (c. 297). Pusa shizhu xingdao pin (菩薩十住行道品). T10, no. 283).

Edgerton, F. (1953). Buddhist Hybrid Sanskrit grammar and dictionary. (William Dwight Whitney linguistic series). New Haven: Yale University Press.

Hirakawa, A. (1997). Buddhist Chinese-Sanskrit Dictionary / Bukkyō Kan-Bon daijiten. Tokyo]; [Tokyo] :: Reiyūkai : Hatsubaimoto Innātorippusha; 霊友会 : 発売元いんなあとりっぷ社.

Kumārajīva and Buddhayaśas (c. 408). Shizhu jing (十住經). T10, no. 286.

Ñāṇamoli, & Bodhi. (1995). The Middle Length Discourses of the Buddha: A New Translation of the Majjhima Nikāya (Teachings of the Buddha). Boston: Wisdom Publications in association with the Barre Center for Buddhist Studies.

Rahder, J. (1928). Glossary of the Sanskrit, Tibetan, Mongolian, and Chinese Versions of the Daśabhūmika-Sūtra. Compiled by J. Rahder. (Buddhica, Documents et Travaux pour l'Étude du Bouddhisme publiés sous la direction de J. Przyluski; Deuxième Série; Documents—Tome I). Paris: Librarie Orientaliste Paul Geuthner, 1928.

Rahder, J., & Vasubandhu. (1926). Daśabhumikasutra. Leuven: J.B. Istas.

Robinson, R. (1967). Early Mādhyamika in India and China. Madison: University of London.

Śīladharma (c. 790 CE) - T 287. Foshuo shidi jing (佛說十地經). T10, no. 287.

Sinor, D., Raghu Vira, Honda, Megumu, & Permanent International Altaistic Conference. (1968). Studies in South, East, and Central Asia: Presented as a memorial volume to the late Professor Raghu Vira (Śata-piṭaka series ; v. 74). New Delhi: International Academy of Indian Culture.

Rahder, J. (1928). Glossary of the Sanskrit, Tibetan, Mongolian, and Chinese Versions of the Daśabhūmika-Sūtra. Compiled by J. Rahder. (Buddhica, Documents et Travaux pour l'Étude du Bouddhisme publiés sous la direction de J. Przyluski; Deuxième Série; Documents—Tome I). Paris: Librarie Orientaliste Paul Geuthner, 1928.

Rahder, J., & Vasubandhu. (1926). Daśabhumikasutra. Leuven: J.B. Istas.

Śikṣānanda (c. 695–699 CE). Dafangguang fo huayan jing (大方廣佛華嚴經). T10, no. 279.

Takakusu, J., & Watanabe, Kaigyoku. (1924). Taishō shinshū Daizōkyō. Tōkyō; 東京 :: Taishō Issaikyō Kankōkai; 大正一切經刊行會.

Vaidya, P. L., ed. Daśabhūmikasūtram. Darbhanga: The Mithila Institute of Post-Graduate Studies and Research in Sanskrit Learning, 1969.

Walshe, M. (2012). The Long Discourses of the Buddha: A Translation of the Dīgha Nikāya (Teachings of the Buddha). Boston: Wisdom Publications.

Williams, M. Monier, Sir. (n.d.). A Sanskrit-English Dictionary. Delhi: Sri Satguru.

Zhonghua dian zi fo dian xie hui. (2004). CBETA dian zi fo dian ji cheng = CBETA Chinese electronic Tripitaka collection (Version 2004. ed.). Taibei; 台北 :: Zhonghua dian zi fo dian xie hui; 中華電子佛典協會.

Appendix: The P.L. Vaidya Sanskrit Text[1]

|| Daśabhūmikasūtram ||

1 pramuditā nāma prathamā bhūmiḥ |

A

evaṃ mayā śrutam | ekasmin samaye bhagavān paranirmitavaśavartiṣu devabhuvaneṣu viharati sma acirābhisaṃbuddho dvitīye saptāhe vaśavartino devarājasya vimāne maṇiratnagarbhe prabhāsvare prāsāde mahatā bodhisattvagaṇena sārdhaṃ sarvairavaivartikairekajātipratibaddhaiḥ | yaduta anuttarāyāṃ samyaksaṃbodhāvanyonyalokadhātusaṃnipatitaiḥ | sarvaiḥ sarvabodhisattvajñānaviṣayagocarapratilabdhavihāribhiḥ sarvatathāgatajñānaviṣayapraveśāvatārāpratiprasrabdhagocaraiḥ sarvajagatparipācanavinayayathākālakṣaṇādhiṣṭhānasarvakriyāsaṃdarśanakuśalaiḥ sarvabodhisattvapraṇidhānābhinirhārāpratiprasrabdhagocaraiḥ kalpārthakṣetracaryāsaṃvāsibhiḥ sarvabodhisattvapuṇyajñānarddhisaṃbhārasuparipūrṇākṣayasarvajagadupajīvyatāpratipannaiḥ sarvabodhisattvaprajñopāyaparamapāramitāprāptaiḥ saṃsāranirvāṇamukhasaṃdarśanakuśalaiḥ bodhisattvacaryopādānāvyavacchinnaiḥ sarvabodhisattvadhyānavimokṣasamādhisamāpatyabhijñājñānavikrīḍitābhijñāsarvakriyāsaṃdarśanakuśalaiḥ sarvabodhisattvarddhibalavaśitāprāptānabhisaṃskāracittakṣaṇasarvatathāgataparṣanmaṇḍalopasaṃkramaṇapūrvaṃgamakathāpuruṣaiḥ sarvatathāgatadharmacakrasaṃdhāraṇavipulabuddhapūjopasthānābhyutthitaiḥ sarvabodhisattvakarmasamādānasamatāprayogasarvalokadhātukāyapratibhāsaprāptaiḥ sarvadharmadhātvasaṅgasvararutaghoṣānuravitasarvatryadhvāsaṅgacittajñānaviṣayaspharaṇaiḥ sarvabodhisattvaguṇapratipattisuparipūrṇānabhilāpyakalpādhiṣṭhānasaṃprakāśanāparikṣīṇaguṇavarṇanirdeśakaiḥ | yadidamvajragarbheṇa ca bodhisattvena mahāsattvena | ratnagarbheṇa ca | padmagarbheṇa ca | śrīgarbheṇa ca | padmaśrīgarbheṇa ca | ādityagarbheṇa ca | sūryagarbheṇa ca | kṣitigarbheṇa ca | śaśivimalagarbheṇa ca | sarvavyūhālaṃkārapratibhāsasaṃdarśanagarbheṇa ca | jñānavairocanagarbheṇa ca | ruciraśrīgarbheṇa ca | candanaśrīgarbheṇa ca | puṣpaśrīgarbheṇa ca | kusumaśrīgarbheṇa ca | utpalaśrīgarbheṇa ca | devaśrīgarbheṇa ca | puṇyaśrīgarbheṇa ca | anāvaraṇajñānaviśuddhigarbheṇa ca | guṇaśrīgarbheṇa ca | nārāyaṇaśrīgarbheṇa ca |

amalagarbheṇa ca | vimalagarbheṇa ca | vicitrapratibhānālaṃkāragarbheṇa ca | mahāraśmijālāvabhāsagarbheṇa ca | vimalaprabhāsaśrītejorājagarbheṇa ca | sarvalakṣaṇapratimaṇḍitaviśuddhiśrīgarbheṇa ca | vajrārciḥśrīvatsālaṃkāragarbheṇa ca | jyotirjvalanārciḥśrīgarbheṇa ca | nakṣatrarājaprabhāvabhāsagarbheṇa ca | gaganakośānāvaraṇajñānagarbheṇa ca | anāvaraṇasvaramaṇḍalamadhuranirghoṣagarbheṇa ca | dhāraṇīmukhasarvajagatpraṇidhisaṃdhāraṇagarbheṇa ca | sāgaravyūhagarbheṇa ca | meruśrīgarbheṇa ca | sarvaguṇaviśuddhigarbheṇa ca | tathāgataśrīgarbheṇa ca | buddhaśrīgarbheṇa ca | vimukticandreṇa ca bodhisattvena mahāsattvena | evaṃpramukhairaparimāṇāprameyāsaṃkhyeyācintyātulyāmāpyānantāparyantāsīmāprāptānabhilāpyānabhilāpyair bodhisattvairmahāsattvaiḥ sārdhaṃ nānābuddhakṣetrasaṃnipatitairvajragarbhabodhisattvapūrvaṃgamaiḥ ||

B

atha khalu vajragarbho bodhisattvayāṃ velāyāṃ buddhānubhāvena mahāyānaprabhāsaṃ nāma bodhisattvasamādhiṃ samāpadyate sma |

C

samanantarasamāpannaśca vajragarbho bodhisattva imaṃ mahāyānaprabhāsaṃ nāma bodhisattvasamādhim,atha tāvadeva daśasu dikṣu daśabuddhakṣetrakoṭiparamāṇurajaḥsamānāṃ lokadhātūnāmapareṇa daśabuddhakṣetrakoṭiparamāṇurajaḥsamāstathāgatā mukhānyupardaṣayāmāsuṃ yadidaṃ vajragarbhasamanāmakā eva | te cainaṃ buddhā bhagavanta evamūcuḥ-sādhu sādhu bho jinaputra, yastvamimaṃ mahāyānaprabhāsaṃ bodhisattvasamādhiṃ samāpadyase | api tu khalu punastvaṃ kulaputra, amī daśasu dikṣu daśabuddhakṣetrakoṭiparamāṇurajaḥsamānāṃ lokadhātūnāmapareṇa daśabuddhakṣetrakoṭiparamāṇurajaḥsamāstathāgatā adhitiṣṭhanti sarve vajragarbhasamanāmānaḥ asyaiva bhagavato vairocanasya pūrvapraṇidhānādhiṣṭhānena tava ca puṇyajñānaviśeṣeṇa sarvabodhisattvānāṃ ca acintyabuddhadharmālokaprabhāvanājñānabhūmyavatāraṇāya |

D

sarvakuśalamūlasaṃgrahaṇāya | sarvabuddhadharmanirdeśāya | asaṃbhinnajñānavyavadānāya | sarvalokadharmānupalepāya | lokottarakuśalamūlapariśodhanāya | acintyajñānaviṣayādhigamāya

| yāvatsarvajñānaviṣayādhigamāya | yadidaṃ daśānāṃ bodhisattvabhūmīnāmārambhapratilambhāya | yathāvadbodhisattvabhūmivyavasthānanirdeśāya | sarvabuddhadharmādhyālambanāya | anāsravadharmapravibhāgavibhāvanāya | suvicitavicayamahāprajñālokakauśalyāya | sunistīritakauśalyajñānamukhāvatāraṇāya | yathārhasthānāntaraprabhāvanāmandapratibhānālokāya | mahāpratisaṃvidbhūministīraṇāya | bodhicittasmṛtyasaṃpramoṣāya | sarvasattvadhātuparipācanāya | sarvatrānugataviniścayakauśalyapratilambhāya |

E

api tu khalu punaḥ kulaputra pratibhātu te'yaṃ dharmālokamukhaprabhedakauśalyadharmaparyāyo buddhānubhāvena tathāgatajñānālokādhiṣṭhānena svakuśalamūlapariśodhanāya dharmadhātusuparyavadāpanāya sattvadhātvanugrahāya dharmakāyajñānaśārīrāya sarvabuddhābhiṣekasaṃpratīcchanāya sarvalokābhyudgatātmabhāvasaṃdarśanāya sarvalokagatisamatikramāya lokottadharmagatipariśodhanāya sarvajñajñānaparipūraṇāya | |

F

atha khalu te buddhā bhagavanto vajragarbhasya bodhisattvasya anabhibhūtātmabhāvatāṃ copasaṃharanti sma | asaṅgapratibhānanirdeśatāṃ ca suviśobhitajñānavibhaktipraveśatāṃ ca smṛtyasaṃprabhoṣādhiṣṭhānatāṃ ca suviniścitamatikauśalyatāṃ ca sarvatrānugatabuddhyanutsargatāṃ ca samyaksaṃbuddhabalānavamṛdyatāṃ ca tathāgatavaiśāradyānavalīnatāṃ ca sarvajñajñānapratisaṃvidvibhāgadharmanayanistīraṇatāṃ ca sarvatathāgatasuvibhaktakāyavākcittālaṃkārābhinirhāratāṃ copasaṃharanti sma |

G

tatkasmāddhetoḥ? yathāpi nāma asyaiva samādherdharmatāpratilambhena pūrvaṃ praṇidhānābhirhāreṇa ca supariśodhitādhyāśayatayā ca svavadātajñānamaṇḍalatayā ca susaṃbhṛtasaṃbhāratayā ca sukṛtaparikarmatayā ca apramāṇasmṛtibhājanatayā ca prabhāsvarādhimuktiviśodhanatayā ca supratividvadhāraṇīmukhāsaṃbhedanatayā ca dharmadhātujñānamudrāsumudritatayā ca | |

H

atha khalu te buddhā bhagavantastatrasthā eva ṛddhyanubhāvena dakṣiṇān pāṇīn prasārya vajragarbhasya bodhisattvasya śīrṣaṃ saṃpramārjayanti sma |

I

samanantaraspṛṣṭaśca vajragarbho bodhisattvastairbuddhairbhagavadbhiḥ, atha tāvadeva samādhestasmād vyutthāya tān bodhisattvānāmantrayate sma - suviniścitamidaṃ bhavanto jinaputrā bodhisattvapraṇidhānamasaṃbhinnamanavalokyaṃ dharmadhātuvipulaṃ ākāśadhātuparyavasānamaparāntakoṭiniṣṭhaṃ sarvasattvadhātuparitrāṇam | yatra hi nāma bhavanto jinaputrā bodhisattvā atītānāmapi buddhānāṃ bhagavatāṃ jñānabhūmimavataranti, anāgatānāmapi buddhānāṃ bhagavatāṃ jñānabhūmimavataranti pratyutpannānāmapi buddhānāṃ bhagavatāṃ jñānabhūmimavataranti, tatra bhavanto jinaputrā daśa bodhisattvabhūmayo buddhānāṃ bhagavatāṃ jñānabhūmimavataranti, tatra bhavanto jinaputrāśca daśa bodhisattvabhūmayo'tītānāgatapratyutpannairbuddhairbhagadbhirbhāṣitāśca bhāṣiṣyante ca bhāṣyante ca, yāḥ saṃdhāya ahaṃ evaṃ vadāmi | katamā daśa ? yaduta pramuditā ca nāma bodhisattvabhūmiḥ | vimalā ca nāma | prabhākarī ca nāma | arciṣmatī ca nāma | sudurjayā ca nāma | abhimukhī ca nāma | dūraṃgamā ca nāma | acalā ca nāma | sādhumatī ca nāma | dharmameghā ca nāma bodhisattvabhūmiḥ | imā bhavanto jinaputrā daśa bodhisattvānāṃ bodhisattvabhūmayaḥ, yā atītānāgatapratyutpannaīrbuddhairbhagavadbhirbhāṣitāśca bhāṣiṣyante ca bhāṣyante ca | nāhaṃ bhavanto jinaputrāstaṃ buddhakṣetraprasaraṃ samanupaśyāmi, yatra tathāgatā imā daśa bodhisattvabhūmīrna prakāśayanti | tatkasya hetoḥ ? sāmutkarṣiko›yaṃ bhavanto jinaputrā bodhisattvānāṃ mahāsattvānāṃ bodhi(sattva)mārgapariśodhanadharmamukhāloko yadidaṃ daśabhūmiprabhedavyavasthānam | acintyamidaṃ bhavanto jinaputrāḥ sthānaṃ yadidaṃ bhūmijñānamiti ||

K

atha khalu vajragarbho bodhisattva āsāṃ daśānāṃ bodhisattvabhūmīnāṃ nāmadheyamātraṃ parikīrtya tūṣṇīṃ babhūva, na bhūyaḥ prabhedaśo nirdiśati sma | atha khalu sā sarvāvatī bodhisattvaparṣat paritṛṣitā babhūva āsāṃ daśānāṃ bodhisattvabhūmīnāṃ nāmadheyamātraśravaṇena bhūmivibhāgānudīraṇena ca | tasyā etadabhavat-ko nu khalvatra hetuḥ kaśca pratyayaḥ, yadvajragarbho bodhisattva āsāṃ bodhisattvabhūmīnāṃ nāmadheya-mātraṃ parikīrtya tūṣṇīṃbhāvena atināmayati, na bhūyaḥ prabhedaśo nirdiśatīti ?

tena khalu punaḥ samayena tasminneva bodhisattvaparṣatsaṃnipāte vimukticandro nāma bodhisattvastasyā bodhisattvaparṣadaścittā-śayavicāramājñāya vajragarbhaṃ bodhisattvaṃ gāthābhigītena parigṛcchati sma -

kimarthaṃ śuddhasaṃkalpasmṛtijñānaguṇānvita |
samudīryottamā bhūmīrna prakāśayase vibho || 1 ||

viniścitā ime sarve bodhisattvā mahāyaśaḥ |
kasmādudīrya bhūmīśca(stvaṃ) pravibhāgaṃ na bhāṣase || 2 ||

śrotukāmā ime sarve jinaputrā viśāradāḥ |
vibhajyārthagatiṃ samyaragbhūmīnāṃ samudāhara || 3 ||

parṣadvi viprasanneyaṃ kausīdyāpagatā śubhā |
śuddhā pratiṣṭhitā sāre guṇajñānasamanvitā || 4 ||

nirīkṣamāṇā anyonyaṃ sthitāḥ sarve sagauravāḥ |
kṣaudraṃ hyaneḍakaṃ yadvatkāṅkṣanti tvamṛtopamam || 5 ||

tasya śrutvā mahāprajño vajragarbho viśāradaḥ |
parṣatsaṃtoṣaṇārthaṃ hi bhāṣate sma jinātmajaḥ || 6 ||

duṣkaraṃ paramametadadbhutaṃ
bodhisattvacaritapradarśanam |
bhūmikāraṇavibhāga uttamo
buddhabhāvasamudāgamo yataḥ || 7 ||

sūkṣma durdṛśa vikalpavarjita-
ścittabhūmivigato durāsadaḥ |
gocaro hi viduṣāmanāsravo
yatra muhyati jagacchave sati || 8 ||

vajropamaṃ hṛdayaṃ sthāpayitvā
buddhajñānaṃ paramaṃ cādhimucya |
anātmānaṃ cittabhūmiṃ viditvā
śakyaṃ śrotuṃ jñānametatsusūkṣmam || 9 ||

antarīkṣa iva raṅgacitraṇā
mārutaḥ khagapathāśrito yathā |
jñānamevamiha bhāgaśaḥ kṛtaṃ
durdṛśaṃ bhagavatāmanāsravam || 10 ||

tasya me bhavati buddhirīdṛśī
durlabho jagati yo'sya vedakaḥ |
śraddhadhīta ca ya etaduttamaṃ
na prakāśayitumutsahe yataḥ || 11 ||

L

evamukte vimukticandro bodhisattvo vajragarbhaṃ bodhisattvam-etadavocat - supariśuddho batāyaṃ bho jinaputra parṣatsaṃnipātaḥ supariśodhitādhyāśayānāṃ bodhisattvānāṃ supariśodhita-saṃkalpānāṃ sucaritacaraṇānāṃ suparyupāsitabahubuddhakoṭi-śatasahasrāṇāṃ susaṃbhṛtasaṃbhārāṇāmaparimitaguṇajñāna-samanvāgatānāmapagatavimatisaṃdehānāmanaṅgaṇānāṃ supra-tiṣṭhitādhyāśayādhimuktīnāmaparapratyayānāmeṣu buddha-dharmeṣu | tatsādhu bho jinaputra, prabhāṣasva | pratyakṣavihāriṇo hyate bodhisattvā atra sthāne ||

M

vajragarbha āha - kiṃcāpi bho jinaputra ayaṃ bodhisattvaparṣat-saṃnipātaḥ supariśuddhaḥ | peyālaṃ | atha ca punarye'nye imānyevaṃrūpāṇyacintyāni sthānāni śṛṇuyuḥ, śrutvā ca vimatisaṃdehamutpādayeyuḥ, teṣāṃ tatsyāddīrgharātramanarthāya ahitāya duḥkhāya | iyaṃ me kāruṇyacittatā, yena tūṣṇīṃbhāvamevābhirocayāmi ||

N

atha khalu vimukticandro bodhisattvaḥ punareva vajragarbhaṃ bodhisattvametamevārthamadhyeṣate sma - tatsādhu bho jinaputra, prabhāṣasva | tathāgatasyaivānubhāvena imānyevaṃrūpāṇy-acintyāni sthānāni svārakṣitāni śraddheyāni bhaviṣyanti | taskasya hetoḥ? tathā hi bho jinaputra asmin bhūminirdeśe bhāṣyamāṇe dharmatāpratilambha eṣa yatsarvabuddhasamanvāhāro bhavati I sarve bodhisattvāśca asyā eva jñānabhūmerārakṣārthamautsukyam-āpadyante I tatkasya hetoḥ? eṣā hyādicaryā I eṣa samudāgamo buddhadharmāṇām I tadyathāpi nāma bho jinaputra sarva-lipyakṣarasaṃkhyānirdeśo mātṛkāpūrvaṃgamo mātṛkāpary-avasānaḥ nāsti sa lipyakṣarasaṃkhyānirdeśo yo vinā mātṛkānir-deśam, evameva bho jinaputra sarve buddhadharmā bhūmipūrva-ṃgamāśca caryāpariniṣpattito bhūmiparyavasānāḥ svayaṃbhūjñān-ādhigamatayā I tasmāttarhi bho jinaputra, prabhāṣasva I tathāgatā eva arhantaḥ samyaksaṃbuddhā ārakṣāmadhiṣṭhāsyanti I I

O

atha khalu te sarve bodhisattvā ekasvarasaṃgītena tasyāṃ velāyāṃ vajragarbhaṃ bodhisattvaṃ gāthābhigītenaiva tamartham-adhyeṣante sma -

pravaravaravimalabuddhe svabhidhānānantaghaṭitapratibha I
pravyāhara madhuravarāṃ vācaṃ paramārthasaṃyuktām I I 12 I I

smṛtidhṛtiviśuddhabuddhe daśabalabalalābhamāśayaviśuddhim I
pratisaṃviddaśavicayaṃ bhāṣasva daśottamā bhūmīḥ I I 13 I I

śamaniyamanibhṛtasumanāḥ prahīṇamadamānadṛṣṭisaṃkleśā I
niṣkāṅkṣā parṣadiyaṃ prārthayate bhāṣitāni tava I I 14 I I

tṛṣita iva śītamudakaṃ bubhukṣito'nnaṃ subheṣajamivārtaḥ I
kṣaudramiva sa madhukaragaṇastava vācamudīkṣate parṣat I I 15 I I

tatsādhu vimalabuddhe bhūmiviśeṣān vadasva virajaskān I
daśabalayuktāsaṅgāṃ sugatagatimudīrayannikhilām I I 16 I I

P

atha khalu tasyāṃ velāyāṃ bhagavataḥ śākyamunerūrṇākośād bodhisattvabalāloko nāma raśmirniścacāra asaṃkhyeyāsaṃkhyeya-raśmiparivārā I sā sarvāsu daśasu dikṣu sarvalokadhātupra-sarānavabhāsya sarvāpāyaduḥkhāni pratiprasrabhya sarvamāra-bhavanāni dhyāmīkṛtya aparimitāni buddhaparṣanmaṇḍalāny-avabhāsya acintyaṃ buddhaviṣayākāraprabhāvaṃ nidarśya sarvāsu daśasu dikṣu sarvalokadhātuprasareṣu sarvatathāgataparṣanmaṇḍaleṣu dharmadeśanādhiṣṭhānādhiṣṭhitān bodhisattvān-avabhāsya acintyaṃ buddhavikurvaṇaṃ saṃdarśya uparyantarīkṣe mahāraśmighanābhrajālakūṭāgāraṃ kṛtvā tasthau । teṣāmapi buddhānāṃ bhagavatāmūrṇākośebhya evameva bodhisattvabalālokā nāma raśmayo niśceruḥ । niścarya asaṃkhyeyāsaṃkhyeyaraśmi-parivārāstāḥ sarvāsu....pe...buddhavikurvaṇamādarśya idaṃ bhagavataḥ śākyamuneḥ parṣanmaṇḍalaṃ vajragarbhasya bodhi-sattvasyātmabhāvamavabhāsya uparyantarīkṣe evameva mahāraśmi-ghanābhrajālakūṭāgāraṃ kṛtvā tasthuḥ । iti hi ābhiśca bhagavataḥ śākyamunerūrṇākośaprasṛtābhī raśmibhiste lokadhātavastāni ca buddhaparṣanmaṇḍalāni teṣāṃ ca bodhisattvānāṃ kāyā āsanāni ca sphuṭānyavabhāsitāni saṃdṛśyante sma । teṣāṃ ca aparimāṇeṣu lokadhātuṣu buddhānāṃ bhagavatāmūrṇākośaprasṛtābhī raśmi-bhirayaṃ trisāhasramahāsāhasralokadhāturidaṃ ca bhagavataḥ śākyamuneḥ parṣanmaṇḍalaṃ vajragarbhasya ca bodhisattvasya kāya āsanaṃ sphuṭamavabhāsitaṃ saṃdṛśyante sma । atha khalu tato mahāraśmighanābhrajālakūṭāgārādvuddhānubhāvena ayam-evaṃrūpaḥ śabdo niścarati sma –

asamasamākāśamairdaśabalavṛṣabhairanantamukhyaguṇaiḥ ।
śākyakulajasya dharmairdevamanuṣyottamaiḥ kṛtamadhiṣṭhānam ।।
17 ।।

anubhāvātsugatānāṃ kośaṃ vivṛṇuṣva dharmarājānām ।
caryāvarāmudārāṃ prabhedaśo jñānabhūmiṃ ca ।। 18 ।।

adhiṣṭhitāste sugatairdhāritā bodhisattvaiśca ।
yeṣāṃ śrotrapathāgataḥ śreṣṭho yo dharmaparyāyaḥ ।। 19 ।।

daśa bhūmīrvirajasaḥ pūrayitvānupūrveṇa ।
balāni daśa ca prāpya jinatāmarpayiṣyanti ।। 20 ।।

sāgarajale nimagnāḥ kalpoddāheṣu prakṣiptāḥ ।
bhavyāste dharmaparyāyamimaṃ śrotumasaṃdigdhāḥ ।। 21 ।।

ye tu vimatisaktāḥ saṃśayaiścābhyupetāḥ ।
sarvaśo na hi teṣāṃ prāpsyate śrotrametat ।। 22 ।।

bhūmijñānapathaṃ śreṣṭhaṃ praveśasthānasaṃkramam |
anupūrveṇa bhāṣasva caryāviṣayameva ca || 23 ||

Q

atha khalu vajragarbho bodhisattvo daśa diśo vyavalokya bhūyasyā mātrayā tasyāḥ parṣadaḥ saṃprasādarnārthaṃ tasyāṃ velāyāmimā gāthā abhāṣata -

sūkṣmaṃ durājñeyapadaṃ maharṣiṇā-
makalpakalpāpagataṃ suduḥspṛśam |
anāvilaṃ paṇḍitavijñaveditaṃ
svabhāvaśāntaṃ hyanirodhasaṃbhavam || 24 ||

svabhāvaśūnyaṃ praśamādvayakṣayaṃ
gatyā vimuktaṃ samatāptinirvṛtam |
anantamadhyaṃ vacasānudīritaṃ
triyaghvavimuktaṃ nabhasā samānakam || 25 ||

śāntaṃ praśāntaṃ sugatapraveditaṃ
sarvairudāhārapadaiḥ sudurvacam |
bhūmiśca caryāpi ca tasya tādṛśī
vaktuṃ suduḥkhaḥ kuta eva śrotum || 26 ||

taccintayā cittapathaiśca varjitaṃ
jñānābhinirhāramunīndraveditam |
na skandhadhātvāyatanaprabhāvitaṃ
na cittagamyaṃ na manovicintitam || 27 ||

yathāntarīkṣe śakuneḥ padaṃ budhai-
rvaktuṃ na śakyaṃ na ca darśanopagam |
tathaiva sarvā jinaputra bhūmayo
vaktuṃ na śakyāḥ kuta eva śrotum || 28 ||

pradeśamātraṃ tu tato'bhidhāsye
maitrīkṛpābhyāṃ praṇidhānataśca |
yathānupūrvaṃ na ca cittagocaraṃ
zñānena tāḥ pūrayatāṃ yathāśayam || 29 ||

etādṛśo gocara durdṛśo'sya
vaktuṃ na śakyaḥ sa hi svāśayasthaḥ |
kiṃ tu pravakṣyāmi jinānubhāvataḥ
śṛṇvantu sarve sahitāḥ sagauravāḥ || 30 ||

jñānapraveśaḥ sa hi tādṛśo'sya
vaktuṃ na kalpairapi śakyate yat |
samāsatastacchṛṇuta bravīmyahaṃ
dharmārthatattvaṃ nikhilaṃ yathāsthitam || 31 ||

sagauravāḥ santa(ḥ) sajjā bhavanto
vakṣyāmyahaṃ sādhu jinānubhāvataḥ |
udīrayiṣye varadharmaghoṣaṃ
dṛṣṭāntayuktaṃ sahitaṃ samākṣaram || 32 ||

suduṣkaraṃ tadvacasāpi vaktuṃ
yaścāprameyaḥ sugatānubhāvaḥ |
mayi praviṣṭaḥ sa ca raśmimūrti-
ryasyānubhāvena mamāsti śaktiḥ || 33 ||

R

tatra bhavanto jinaputrāḥ sūpacitakuśalamūlānāṃ sucarita-caraṇānāṃ susaṃbhṛtasaṃbhārāṇāṃ suparyupāsitabuddh-otpādānāṃ suparipiṇḍitaśukladharmāṇāṃ suparigṛhītakalyāṇa-mitrāṇāṃ suviśuddhāśayānāṃ vipulāghyāśayopagatānāṃ udārādhi-muktisamanvāgatānāṃ kṛpākaruṇābhimukhānāṃ (bodhi)sattvānāṃ bodhāya cittamutpādyate |

S

buddhajñānābhilāṣāya daśabalabalādhigamāya mahāvaiśārady-ādhigamāya samatābuddhadharmapratilambhāya sarvajagatpari-trāṇāya mahākṛpākaruṇāviśodhanāya daśadigaśeṣajñānādhigamāya sarvabuddhakṣetrāsaṅgapariśodhanāya tryadhvaikakṣaṇavibodhāya mahādharmacakrapravartanavaiśāradyāya ca taccittamutpadyate bodhisattvānāṃ

T

mahākaruṇāpūrvaṃgamaṃ prajñājñānādhipateyamupāyakauśalya-parigṛhītamāśayādhyāśayopastabdhaṃ tathāgatabalāprameyaṃ sattvabalabuddhibalasuvicitavicayamasaṃbhinnajñānābhimukhaṃ svayaṃbhūjñānānukūlaṃ sarvabuddhadharmaprajñājñānāvavādasaṃpratyeṣakaṃ dharmadhātuparamamākāśadhātusthitakamaparāntakoṭiniṣṭham ।

U

yena cittotpādena sahotpannena bodhisattvo'tikrānto bhavati, pṛthagjñānabhūmīmavakrānto bhavati, bodhisattvaniyāmaṃ jāto bhavati, tathāgatakule'navadyo bhavati, sarvajātivādena vyāvṛtto bhavati, sarvalokagatibhyo'vakrānto bhavati, lokottarāṃ gatiṃ sthito bhavati, bodhisattvadharmatāyāṃ suvyavasthito bhavati, bodhisattvāvasthānena samatānugato bhavati, tryaghvatathāgatavaṃśaniyato bhavati saṃbodhiparāyaṇaḥ । evaṃrūpadharmavyavasthito bhavanto jinaputrā bodhisattvaḥ pramuditāyāṃ bodhisattvabhūmau vyavasthito bhavatyacalanayogena ।।

V

atra bhavanto jinaputrāḥ pramuditāyāṃ bodhisattvabhūmau sthito bodhisattvaḥ prāmodyabahulo bhavati prasādabahulaḥ prītibahula utplāvanābahula udagrībahula utsībahula utsāhabahulo'saṃrambhabahulo'vihiṃsābahulo'krodhabahulo bhavati ।

W

iti hi bhavanto jinaputrāḥ pramuditāyāṃ bodhisattvabhūmau sthito bodhisattvan pramudito bhavati, buddhān bhagavato›nusmaran buddhadharmān bodhisattvān bodhisattvacaryāḥ pāramitāviśuddhiṃ bodhisattvabhūmiviśeṣān bodhisattvāsaṃhāryatāṃ tathāgatāvavādānuśāsanīṃ sattvārthasaṃprāpaṇam । pramudito bhavati sarvatathāgatajñānapraveśaprayogamanusmaran । bhūyaḥ prāmodyavān bhavati –

X

vyāvṛtto'smi sarvajagadviṣayāt, avatīrṇo'smi buddhabhūmisamīpam, dūrībhūto'smi bālapṛthagjanabhūmeḥ, āsanno'smi jñānabhūmeḥ, vyavacchinno'smi sarvāpāyadurgativinipātāt, pratiśaraṇabhūto'smi sarvasattvānām, āsannadarśano'smi sarvatathāgatānām, saṃbhūto'smi sarvabuddhaviṣaye, sarvabodhisattvasamatāmupagato'smi । vigatāni me sarvabhayatrāsacchambhitatvānīti prāmodyamutpādayati ।

Y

tatkasya hetoḥ ? tathā hi bhavanto jinaputrā bodhisattvasya asyāḥ pramuditāyā bodhisattvabhūmeḥ sahapratilambhena yānīmāni bhayāni bhavanti - yadidamājīvikābhayaṃ vā aślokabhayaṃ vā maraṇabhayaṃ vā durgatibhayaṃ vā parṣacchāradyabhayaṃ vā, tāni sarvāṇi vyapagatāni bhavanti । tatkasya hetoḥ ? yathāpi idamātmasaṃjñāpagamādātmasneho›sya na bhavati, kutaḥ punaḥ sarvopakaraṇasnehaḥ ? ato'sya ājīvikābhayaṃ na bhavati । na ca kaṃcitsatkāraṃ kasyacitsakāśātpratikāṅkṣati, anyatra mayaiva teṣāṃ sattvānāṃ sarvopakaraṇabāhulyamupanāmayitavyamiti, ato'sya aślokabhayaṃ na bhavati । ātmadṛṣṭivigamācca asyātmasaṃjñā na bhavati, ato'sya maraṇabhayaṃ na bhavati । mṛtasyaiva me niyataṃ buddhabodhisattvairna virahito bhaviṣyāmīti, ato'sya durgatibhayaṃ na bhavati । nāsti me kaścidāśayena sarvaloke samasamaḥ, kutaḥ punaruttara ityato'sya parṣacchāradyabhayaṃ na bhavati । evaṃ sarvabhayatrāsacchambhitatvaromaharṣāpagataḥ ।।

Z

atha khalu punarbhavanto jinaputrā bodhisattvo mahākaruṇāpuraskṛtatvādanupahatena aprākṛtenādhyāśayena bhūyasyā mātrayā prayujyate sarvakuśalamūlamudāgamāya ।

AA

sa śraddhādhipateyatayā prasādabahulatayā adhimuktiviśuddhyā avakalpanābahulatayā kṛpākaruṇābhinirhāratayā mahāmaitryupetatayā aparikhinnamānasatayā hryapatrāpyālaṃkāratayā kṣāntisauratyopetatayā tathāgatārhatsamyaksaṃbuddhaśāsanagauravacitrīkaraṇatayā

BB

rātriṃdivātṛptakuśalamūlopacayatayā kalyāṇamitraniṣevaṇatayā dharmārāmābhiratatayā atṛptabāhuśrutyaparyeṣaṇatayā yathāśrutadharmayoniśaḥpratyavekṣaṇatayā aniketamānasatayā anadhyavasitalābhasatkāraślokatayā anabhinanditopakaraṇasnehatayā ratnopamacittotpādātṛptābhinirhāratayā

CC

sarvajñabhūmyabhilāṣaṇatayā tathāgatabalavaiśāradyāveṇikabuddhadharmādhyālambanatayā pāramitāsaṅgaparyeṣaṇatayā māyāśāṭhyaparivarjanatayā yathāvāditathākāritayā satatasamitaṃ satyavacanānurakṣaṇatayā tathāgatakulabhūṣaṇatayā bodhisattvaśikṣānutsarjanatayā mahāśailendrarājopamasarvajñatācittāprakampanatayā sarvalokakriyānabhilakṣaṇatayā utsargalokottarapathopetatayā atṛptabodhyaṅgasaṃbhāropacayatayā satatasamitamuttarottaraviśeṣaparimārgaṇatayā I evaṃrūpairbhavanto jinaputrā bhūmipariśodhakairdharmaiḥ samanvāgato bodhisattvaḥ supratiṣṭhito bhavati pramuditāyāṃ bodhisattvabhūmau I I

DD

so'syāṃ pramuditāyāṃ bodhisattvabhūmau sthitaḥ san imānyevaṃrūpāṇi mahāpraṇidhānāni mahāvyavasāyān mahābhinirhārānabhinirharati - yaduta aśeṣaniḥśeṣānavaśeṣasarvabuddhapūjopasthāpanāya sarvākāravaropetamudārādhimuktiviśuddhaṃ dharmadhātuvipulamākāśadhātuparyavasānamaparāntakoṭiniṣṭhaṃ sarvakalpasaṃkhyābuddhotpādaṃsaṃkhyāpratiprasrabdhaṃ mahāpūjopasthānāya prathamaṃ mahāpraṇidhānamabhinirharati I

EE

yaduta sarvatathāgatabhāṣitadharmanetrīsaṃdhāraṇāya sarvabuddhabodhisattvasuparigrahāya sarvasamyaksaṃbuddhaśāsanaparirakṣaṇāya....buddhotpādasaddharmaparigrahāya dvitīyam I

FF

yaduta sarvabuddhotpādaniravaśeṣasarvalokadhātuprasareṣu tuṣitabhavanavāsamādiṃ kṛtvā cyavanāsaṃkramaṇagarbhasthitijanmakumārakrīḍāntaḥpuravāsābhiniṣkramaṇaduṣkaracaryābo dhimaṇḍopa-saṃkramaṇamāragharṣaṇābhisaṃbodhyadhyeṣaṇamahādharmacakrapravartanamahāparinirvāṇopasaṃkramaṇāya pūjādharmasaṃgrahaprayogapūrvaṃgamaṃ kṛtvā sarvatraikakālavivartanāya...buddhotpāda....yāvanmahāparinirvāṇopasaṃkramaṇā ya tṛtīyam I

GG

yaduta sarvabodhisattvacaryāvipulamahadgatāpramāṇāsaṃbhinnasarvapāramitāsaṃgṛhītasarvabhūmipariśodhanaṃ sāṅgopāṅganirhārasalakṣaṇasaṃvartavivartasarvabodhisattvacaryābhūtayathāva dbhūmipathopadeśapāramitāparikarmāvavādānuśāsanyanupradāno pastabdhacittotpādābhinirhārāya...caryā...cittotpādābhinirhārāya caturtham I

HH

yaduta niravaśeṣasarvasattvadhāturūpyarūpisaṃjñāsaṃjñinaivasaṃjñināsaṃjñāṇḍajajarāyujasaṃsvedajaupapāduka-... traidhātukaparyāpannaṣaḍgatisamavasṛtasarvopapattiparyāpannanāmarūpasaṃ gṛhītāśeṣasarvasattvadhātuparipācanāya sarvabuddhadharm-āvatāraṇāya sarvagatisaṃkhyāvyavacchedanāya sarvajñajñānaprati-ṣṭhāpanāya...sattvadhātu...sarvasattvadhātuparipācanāya pañcamam ।

II

yaduta niravaśeṣasarvalokadhātuvipulasaṃkṣiptamahadgatāpramā ṇa-

sūkṣmaudārikavyatyastāvamūrdhasamatalapraveśasamavarasaraṇā nugatendrajālavibhāgadaśadigaśeṣavimātratāvibhāgapraveśajñānān ugamapratyakṣatāyai...lokadhātu...lokadhātuvaimātryāvatāraṇāya ṣaṣṭham ।

JJ

yaduta sarvakṣetraikakṣetraikakṣetrasarvakṣetrasamavasaraṇapariśod hana

mapramāṇabuddhakṣetraprabhāvyūhālaṃkārapratimaṇḍitaṃ sarva-kleśāpanayanapariśuddhapathopetamapramāṇajñānākarasattvapari pūrṇamudārabuddhaviṣayasamavasaraṇaṃ yathāśayasarvasattva-saṃdarśanasaṃtoṣaṇāya...buddhakṣetra...sarvabuddhakṣetrapariśod hanāya saptamam ।

KK

yaduta sarvabodhisattvaikāśayaprayogatāyai niḥsapatnakuśalamūl-opacayāya ekālambanasarvabodhisattvasamatāyai avirahitasatatasa-mitabuddhabodhisattvasamavadhānāya yatheṣṭabuddhotpādasaṃ-darśanāya svacittotpādatathāgataprabhāvajñānānugamāya acyut-ānugāminyabhijñāpratilambhāya sarvalokadhātvanuvicaraṇāya sarvabuddhaparṣanmaṇḍalapratibhāsaprāptaye sarvopapattisva-śarīrānugamāya acintyamahāyānopetatāyai bodhisattvacaryā-caraṇāvyavacchedāya...caryā...mahāyānāvatāraṇāya aṣṭamam ।

LL

yaduta avivartyacakrasamārūḍhabodhisattvacaryācaraṇāya amogha-kāyavāṅmanaskarmaṇe sahadarśananiyatabuddhadharmatvāya sahaghoṣodāhārajñānānugamāya sahaprasādakleśavinivartanāya mahābhaiṣajyarājopamāśrayapratilambhāya cintāmaṇivat-kāyapratilambhāya sarvabodhisattvacaryā-

caraṇāya...caryā...amoghasarvaceṣṭatāyai navamam ।

MM

yaduta sarvalokadhātuṣvanuttarasamyaksaṃbodhyabhisaṃbodhāya

ekavālapathāvyativṛttasarvabālapṛthagjanajanmopapatyabhiniṣkram aṇavikurvaṇabodhimaṇḍadharmacakrapravartanamahāparinirvāṇop adarśanāya mahābuddhaviṣayaprabhāvajñānānugamāya sarva-sattvadhātuyathāśayabuddhotpādakṣaṇakṣaṇavibhaṅgavibodhapraś amaprāpaṇasaṃdarśanāya ekābhisaṃbodhisarvadharmanirmāṇa-spharaṇāya ekaghoṣodāhārasarvasattvacittāśayasaṃtoṣaṇāya mahā-parinirvāṇopadarśanacaryābalāvyavacchedāya mahājñānabhūmi-sarvadharmavyavasthāpanasaṃdarśanāya dharmajñānarddhim-āyābhijñāsarvalokadhātuspharaṇāya abhisaṃbodhimahājñānābhijñ-ābhinirhārāya daśamam । iti hi bhavanto jinaputrā imānyevaṃ-rūpāṇi mahāpraṇidhānāni mahāvyavasāyān mahābhinirhārān daśa praṇidhānamukhāni pramukhaṃ kṛtvā paripūrṇāni daśapraṇidhān-āsaṃkhyeyaśatasahasrāṇi yāni bodhisattvaḥ pramuditāyāṃ bodhi-sattvabhūmau sthito'bhinirharati pratilabhate ca । ।

NN

tāni ca mahāpraṇidhānāni daśabhirniṣṭhāpadairabhinirharati । katamairdaśabhiḥ? yaduta sattvadhātuniṣṭhayā ca lokadhātuniṣṭhayā ca ākāśadhātuniṣṭhayā ca dharmadhātuniṣṭhayā ca nirvāṇadhātu-niṣṭhayā ca buddhotpādadhātuniṣṭhayā ca tathāgatajñānadhātu-niṣṭhayā ca cittālambanadhātuniṣṭhayā ca buddhaviṣayajñāna-praveśadhātuniṣṭhayāḥ ca lokavartanīdharmavartanījñāna-vartanīdhātuniṣṭhayā ca । iti hi yā niṣṭhā sattvadhātuniṣṭhāyāḥ, sā me niṣṭhā eṣāṃ mahāpraṇidhānānāṃ bhavatu । yā niṣṭhā yāvajjñānavartanīdhātuniṣṭhāyāḥ, sā me niṣṭhā eṣāṃ mahāpraṇi-dhānānāṃ bhavatu । iti hyaniṣṭhā sattvadhātuniṣṭhā । aniṣṭhānīmāni me kuśalamūlāni bhavantu । aniṣṭhā yāvajjñānavartanīdhātuniṣṭhā । aniṣṭhānīmāni me kuśalamūlāni bhavantviti । ।

OO

sa evaṃ svabhinihṛrtapraṇidhānaḥ karmaṇyacitto mṛducitto'saṃ-hāryaśraddho bhavati । so'bhiśraddadhāti tathāgatānāmarhatāṃ samyaksaṃbuddhānāṃ pūrvāntacaryābhinirhārapraveśaṃ pāramit-āsamudāgamaṃ bhūmipariniṣpattiṃ vaiśeṣikatāṃ balapariniṣpattiṃ vaiśāradyaparipūrimāveṇikabuddhadharmāsaṃhāryatāmacintyāṃ buddhadharmatāmanantamadhyaṃ tathāgataviṣayābhinirhārama-parimāṇajñānānugataṃ tathāgatagocarānupraveśaṃ phalapari-niṣpattimabhiśraddadhāti । samāsataḥ sarvabodhisattvacaryāṃ yāvattathāgatabhūmijñānanirdeśādhiṣṭhānamabhiśraddadhāti । ।

PP

tasyaivaṃ bhavati - evaṃ gambhīrāḥ khalu punarime buddhadharmāḥ evaṃ viviktāḥ evaṃ śāntāḥ evaṃ śūnyāḥ evamānimittāḥ evamapraṇihitāḥ evaṃ nirupalepāḥ evaṃ vipulāḥ evamaparimāṇāḥ evamudārāḥ evaṃ durāsadāśceme buddhadharmāḥ ।

QQ

atha ca punarime bālapṛthagjanāḥ kudṛṣṭipatitayā saṃtatyā avidyāndhakārapayarvanaddhamānasena mānadhvajasamucchrittaiḥ saṃkalpaistṛṣṇājālābhilaṣitairmanasikārairmāyāśāṭhyagahanānucarit aiścittāśayairīrṣyāmātsaryasaṃprayuktairgatyupapattiprayogai rāgadveṣamohaparicittaiḥ karmopacayaiḥ krodhopanāhasaṃdhukṣitābhiścittajvālābhirviparyāsasaṃprayuktaiḥ karmakriyābhinirhāraiḥ kāmabhavāvidyāsravānubaddhaiścittamanovijñānabījais

RR

traidhātuke punarbhavāṅkuramabhinirvartayanti yadidaṃ nāmarūpasahajāvinirbhāgagatam । tenaiva ca nāmarūpeṇa vivardhitena eṣāṃ ṣaḍāyatanagrāmaḥ saṃbhavati । saṃbhūteṣvāyataneṣvanyonyasparśanipātato vedanā saṃbhavati । tāmeva vedanāṃ bhūyo bhūyo'bhinandatāṃ tṛṣṇopādānaṃ vivardhate । vivṛddhe tṛṣṇopādāne bhavaḥ saṃbhavati । saṃbhūte ca bhave jātijarāmaraṇaśokaparidevaduḥkhadaurmanasyopāyāsāḥ prādurbhavanti । evameteṣāṃ sattvānāṃ duḥkhaskandho'bhinirvartate ātmātmīyavigato riktastucchaḥ śūnyo nirīho niśceṣṭo jaḍastṛṇakāṣṭhakuḍyavartmapratibhāsopamaḥ । na caivamavabudhyanta iti ।

SS

teṣāmevaṃrūpeṇa sattvānāṃ duḥkhaskandhāvipramokṣaṃ dṛṣṭvā sattveṣu mahākaruṇonmiñjaḥ saṃbhavati - ete'smābhiḥ sattvāḥ paritrātavyāḥ parimocayitavyā ato mahāsaṃmohāt, atyantasukhe ca nirvāṇe pratiṣṭhāpayitavyāḥ iti । ato'sya mahāmaitryunmiñjaḥ saṃbhavati ।।

TT

evaṃ kṛpāmaitryanugatena khalu punarbhavanto jinaputrā bodhisattvo'dhyāśayena prathamāyāṃ bodhisattvabhūmau vartamānaḥ sarvavastuṣu sāpekṣacittaṃ parivarjya buddhajñāne ca udāraspṛhābhilāṣabuddhirmahātyāgeṣu prayuñjate । sa ya ime tyāgāḥ - yaduta dhanadhānyakośakoṣṭhāgāraparityāgo vā hiraṇyasuvarṇamaṇimuktāvaiḍūryaśaṅkhaśilāpravālajātarūparajataparityāgo vā ratnābharaṇavibhūṣaṇaparityāgo vā hayarathagajapativāhanaparityāgo vā udyānatapovanavihāraparityāgo vā dāsīdāsakarmakarapauruṣeya-parityāgo vā grāmanagaranigamajanapadarāṣṭrarājadhānīparityāgo vā bhāryāputraduhitṛparityāgo vā sarvapriyamanāpavastuparityāgo vā śiraḥkarṇanāsākaracaraṇanayanasvamāṃsaśoṇitāsthimajjā-medaśchavicarmahṛdayasarvātmabhāvaparityāgo vā, teṣvanapekṣo bhūtvā sarvavastuṣu buddhajñāne ca udāraspṛhābhilāṣabuddhiḥ parityajati | evaṃ hyasya prathamāyāṃ bodhisattvabhūmau sthitasya mahātyāgaḥ saṃbhavati ||

UU

sa evaṃ karuṇāmaitrītyāgāśayo bhūtvā sarvasattvaparitrāṇārthaṃ bhūyo bhūyo laukikalokottarānarthān parimārgate parigaveṣate | parimārgamāṇaḥ parigaveṣamāṇaśca aparikhedacittamutpādayati | evamasyāparikhedaḥ saṃbhavati | aparikhinnaśca sarvaśāstra-viśārado bhavati | ato'sya śāstrajñatā saṃbhavati | sa evaṃ śāstr-opetaḥ kriyākriyāvicāritayā buddhyā hīnamadhyapraṇīteṣu sattveṣu tathatvāya pratipadyate yathābalaṃ yathābhajamānam | ato'sya lokajñatā saṃbhavati | lokajñaśca kālavelāmātracārī hryapatrāpyavi-bhūṣitayā saṃtatyā ātmārthaparārtheṣu prayujyate | ato'sya hryapatrāpyaṃ saṃbhavati | teṣu ca prayogeṣu naiṣkramyacārī avivartyāpratyudāvartyabalādhānaprāpto bhavati | evamasya dhṛtibalādhānamājataṃ bhavati | dhṛtibalādhānaprāptaśca tathāgatapūjopasthāneṣu prayujyate, śāsane ca pratipadyate | evaṃ hyasyeme daśa bhūmipariśodhakā dharmā ājātā bhavanti | tadyathā - śraddhā karuṇā maitrī tyāgaḥ khedasahiṣṇutā śāstrajñatā lokajñatā hryapatrāpyaṃ dhṛtibalādhānaṃ tathāgatapūjopasthānamiti ||

VV

tasya asyāṃ pramuditāyāṃ bodhisattvabhūmau sthitasya bodhi-sattvasya bahavo buddhā ābhāsamāgacchanti audārikadarśanena praṇidhānabalena ca | bahūni buddhaśatāni bahūni buddha-sahasrāṇi bahūni buddhaśatasahasrāṇi bahūni buddhanayuta-śatasahasrāṇi bahavo buddhakoṭyo bahūni buddhakoṭīśatāni bahūni buddhakoṭīsahasrāṇi bahūni buddhakoṭīśatasahasrāṇi bahūni buddhakoṭīnayutaśatasahasrāṇyābhāsamāgacchanti audārika-darśanena praṇidhānabalena ca | sa tāṃstathāgatānarhataḥ samyak-saṃbuddhān dṛṣṭvā udārādhyāśayena satkaroti gurukaroti mānayati pūjayati, cīvarapiṇḍapātraśayanāsanaglānapratyayabhaiṣajya-

pariṣkāraiśca pratipādayati | bodhisattvasukhopadhānaṃ copasaṃharati | saṃghagaṇasaṃmānatāṃ ca karoti | tāni ca kuśalamūlānyanuttarāyāṃ samyaksaṃbodhau pariṇāmayati | tāṃśca asya buddhān bhagavataḥ pūjayataḥ sattvaparipāka ājāto bhavati | sa sattvāṃśca paripācayati dānena priyavadyena ca adhimuktibalena ca | asyopari dve arthasaṃgrahavastūnyājāyete na tu khalvaśeṣajñānaprativedhapratilambhena | tasya daśabhyaḥ pāramitābhyo dānapāramitā atiriktatamā bhavati, na ca pariśeṣāsu na samudāgacchati yathābalaṃ yathābhajamānam | sa yathā yathā buddhāṃśca bhagavataḥ pūjayati, sattvaparipākāya ca prayujya tānimān daśa bhūmipariśodhakān dharmān samādāya vartate, tathā tathāsya tāni kuśalamūlāni sarvajñatāpariṇāmitāni bhūyasyā mātrayottapyante, pariśuddhyanti, karmaṇyāni ca bhavanti yathākāmatayā | tadyathāpi nāma bhavanto jinaputrā jātarūpaṃ kuśalena karmāreṇa yathā yathāgnau prakṣipyate, tathā tathā pariśuddhyati karmaṇyaṃ ca bhavati vibhūṣaṇālaṃkāravidhiṣu yathākāmatayā, evameva bhavanto jinaputrā yathā yathā bodhisattvo-
...peyālaṃ...yathākāmatayā | |

WW

punaraparaṃ bhavanto jinaputra bodhisattvena asyāṃ prathamāyāṃ bodhisattvabhūmau sthitena asyā eva prathamāyā bodhisattvabhūmerākārapratilambhaniṣyandāḥ parimārgitavyāḥ parigaveṣitavyāḥ paripraṣṭavyāḥ | buddhabodhisattvānāṃ kalyāṇamitrāṇāṃ ca sakāśādatṛptena ca bhavitavyaṃ bhūmyaṅgapariniṣpādanāya | evaṃ yāvaddaśamyā bodhisattvabhūmeraṅgapariniṣpādanāya | tena bhūmipakṣapratipakṣakuśalena ca bhavitavyaṃ bhūmisaṃvartavivartakuśalena ca bhūmyākāraniṣyandakuśalena ca bhūmipratilambhavibhāvanākuśalena ca bhūmyaṅgapariśodhanakuśalena ca bhūmerbhūmisaṃkramaṇakuśalena ca bhūmibhūmivyavasthānakuśalena ca bhūmibhūmiviśeṣajñānakuśalena ca bhūmibhūmipratilambhāpratyudāvartyakuśalena ca sarvabodhisattvabhūmipariśodhanatayā tathāgatajñānabhūmyākramaṇakuśalena ca bhavitavyam | evaṃ bhūmyākārābhinirhārakuśalasya hi bhavanto jinaputrā bodhisattvasya prathamāyā bodhisattvabhūmerucchalitasya niṣṭhānaṃ na saṃbhavati yāvaddaśabhūmibhūmyākramaṇamiti | mārgādhiṣṭhānāgamena ca bhūmejñānālokena ca buddhajñānālokaṃ prāpnoti | tadyathāpi nāma bhavanto jinaputrāḥ

kuśalaḥ sārthavāho mahāsārthaparikarṣaṇābhiprāyo mahānagara-
manuprāpayitukāmaḥ ādāveva mārgaguṇāṃśca mārgavivarta-
doṣāṃśca mārgasthānāntaraviśeṣāṃśca mārgasthānāntaravivarta-
doṣāṃśca mārgakriyāpathyodanakāryatāṃ ca parimārgayati pari-
gaveṣayate | sa yāvanmahānagarānuprāptaye kuśalo bhavaty-
anuccalita eva prathamānmārgāntarasthānāt | sa evaṃ jñāna-
vicāritayā buddhyā mahāpathyodanasamṛddhyā anupūrveṇa mahā-
sārthena sārdhaṃ yāvanmahānagaramanuprāpnoti, na cāṭavīkānt-
āradoṣaiḥ sārthasya vā ātmano vāsyopaghātaḥ saṃpadyate | evam-
eva bhavanto jinaputrā bodhisattvaḥ kuśalo mahāsārthavāho yadā
prathamāyāṃ bodhisattvabhūmau sthito bhavati, tadā bhūmipakṣa-
pratipakṣakuśalo bhavati, bhūmisaṃvartavivartakuśalo bhavati,
bhūmyākāraniṣyandakuśalo bhavati, bhūmipratilambhavibhāvan-
ākuśalo bhavati, bhūmyaṅgapariśodhanakuśalo bhavati, bhūmer-
bhūmisaṃkramaṇakuśalo bhavati, bhūmibhūmivyavasthānakuśalo
bhavati, bhūmibhūmiviśeṣajñānakuśalo bhavati, bhūmibhūmiprati-
lambhāpratyudāvartyakuśalo bhavati, sarvabodhisattvabhūmi-
pariśodhanatayā tathāgatajñānabhūmyākramaṇakuśalaśca bhavati |
tadā bodhisattvo mahāpuṇyasaṃbhārapathyodanasusaṃgṛhito
jñānasaṃbhārasukṛtavicayo mahāsattvasārthaparikarṣaṇābhiprāyaḥ
sarvajñatāmahānagaramanuprāpayitukāmaḥ ādāveva bhūmimārga-
guṇāṃśca bhūmimārgavivartadoṣāṃśca bhūmimārgasthānāntara-
viśeṣāṃśca bhūmimārgasthānāntaravivartadoṣāṃśca mahāpuṇya-
jñānasaṃbhārapathyadanakriyākāryatāṃ ca parimārgate pari-
gaveṣate buddhānāṃ bhagavatāṃ bodhisattvānāṃ kalyāṇamitrāṇāṃ
ca sakāśāt | sa yāvatsarvajñatāmahānagarānuprāptikuśalo bhavaty-
anuccalita eva prathamānmārgāntarasthānāt | sa evaṃ jñāna-
vicāritayā buddhyā mahāpuṇyajñānasaṃbhārapathyadanasaṃ-
ruddhayā mahāntaṃ sattvasārthaṃ yathāparipācitaṃ saṃsārāṭavīk-
āntāradurgādatikramya yāvatsarvajñatāmahānagaramanuprāpayati
| na saṃsāraṭavīkāntāradoṣaiḥ sattvasārthasya vā ātmano vā asy-
opaghātaḥ saṃpadyate | tasmāttarhi bhavanto jinaputrā bodhi-
sattvena aparikhinnena bhūmiparikarmaparikarmaviśeṣābhiyuktena
bhavitavyam | ayaṃ bhavanto jinaputrā bodhisattvasya
prathamāyāḥ pramuditāyā bodhisattvabhūmermukhapraveśaḥ
samāsato nirdiśyate | |

XX

yo'syāṃ pratiṣṭhito bodhisattvo bhūyastvena jambūdvīpeśvaro bhavati mahaiśvaryādhipatyapratilabdho dharmānurakṣī kṛtī prabhuḥ sattvān mahātyāgena saṃgrahītukuśalaḥ sattvānāṃ mātsaryamalavinivṛttaye'paryanto mahātyāgārambhaiḥ | yacca kiṃcitkarmārabhate dānena vā priyavadyatayā vā arthakriyayā vā samānārthatayā vā, tatsarvamavirahitaṃ buddhamanasikārairdharmamanasikāraiḥ saṃghamanasikārairbodhisattvamanasikārairbodhisattvacaryāmanasikāraiḥ pāramitāmanasikārairbhūmimanasikārairbalamanasikārairvaiśāradyamanasikārairāveṇikabuddhadharmamanasikārairyāvatsarvākāravaropetasarvajñajñānamanasikaraiḥ | kimiti ? sarvasattvānāmagryo bhaveyaṃ śreṣṭho jyeṣṭho varaḥ pravara uttamo'nuttamo nāyako vināyakaḥ pariṇāyako yāvatsarvajñajñānapratiśaraṇo bhaveyam iti | ākāṅkṣaṃśca tathārūpaṃ vīryamārabhate yathārūpeṇa vīryārambheṇa sarvagṛhakalatrabhogānutsṛjya tathāgataśāsane pravrajati | pravrajitaśca san ekakṣaṇalavamuhūrtena samādhiśataṃ ca pratilabhate samāpadyate ca | buddhaśataṃ ca paśyati, teṣāṃ cādhiṣṭhānaṃ saṃjānīte | lokadhātuśataṃ ca kampayati | kṣetraśataṃ cākramati | lokadhātuśataṃ cāvabhāsayati | sattvaśataṃ ca paripācayati | kalpaśataṃ ca tiṣṭhati | kalpaśataṃ ca pūrvāntāparāntataḥ praviśati | dharmamukhaśataṃ ca pravicinoti | kāyaśataṃ cādarśayati | kāyaṃ kāyaṃ ca bodhisattvaśataparivāramādarśayati |

YY

tathā uttare praṇidhānabalikā bodhisattvāḥ praṇidhānaviśeṣikatayā vikurvanti yeṣāṃ na sukarā saṃkhyā kurtuṃ kāyasya vā prabhāyā vā ṛdvervā cakṣuṣo vā gocarasya vā svarasya vā caryāyā vā vyūhasya vā adhiṣṭhānasya vā adhimuktervā abhisaṃskārāṇāṃ vā yāvadevatāvadbhirapi kalpakoṭiniyutaśatasahasrairiti ||

pramuditā nāma prathamā bhūmiḥ ||

[Beginning of first bhūmi's final gathas]

1 pramuditā nāma prathamā bhūmiḥ ।

upakramaḥ ।

te śukladharmupacitāḥ kuśalopapetāḥ
paryupāsitāḥ sugatamaitrakṛpānukūlāḥ ।
adhimuktyudāra kuśalāśaya śuddhabhāvā-
ścittaṃ janenti atulaṃ jinajñānahetoḥ ।। 1 ।।

sarvajñabuddhabalaśodhanavīryasthāmā
jinadharmaniṣpattijagatparitrāyaṇārthāḥ ।
mahākṛpocayavartanadharmacakraṃ
jinakṣetraśodhamupapadyati cittaśreṣṭham ।। 2 ।।

tryadhvaikavīkṣaṇavibuddhananirvikalpā
nānāvidhe jagati kālaviśodhanārtham ।
saṃkṣepasarvaguṇa eṣitu nāyakānām
ākāśatulya samudeti udāracittam ।। 3 ।।

prajñādhipatya kṛpapūrvamupāyayuktam
adhimukti - āśaya - viśuddha - balāpramāṇam ।
āsaṅgatābhimukhatā - aparapraṇeyaṃ
samatopapeta - sugataṃ varacittajātam ।। 4 ।।

sahajāticittaratanaṃ sugatātmajānām
atikrānta bālacari buddhacari hyupetaḥ ।
jātaḥ kule daśabalāna anodyapadyaḥ
samatāṃ jine anugato niyatāgrabodhiḥ ।। 5 ।।

ekasmi citta upapadyati bhūmilābho
bhavate acalyu girirājasamāśayaśca ।
prāmodyaprītibahulaśca prasādavāṃśca
utsāhavegavipulaḥ sadudagracittaḥ ।। 6 ।।

saṃrambhahiṃsavigataśca akrodhanaśca
hrīgauravārjavataraśca susaṃvṛtaśca |
jagatāyanaṃ smarati apratimānajñānaṃ
prītiṃ janetyupagataspṛhameta sthānam || 7||

pañcā bhayā apagatāḥ sahabhūmilābho
ājīvikā maraṇa kīrtyatha durgatiśca |
parṣadbhayaṃ ca vigataṃ tatha chambhitatvaṃ
kiṃ kāraṇaṃ tatha hi ātmaniketu nāsti || 8 ||

te chambhitatvavigatāḥ kṛpamaitrayuktāḥ
śraddhāsagauravahriyopagatā guṇāḍhyāḥ |
rātriṃdivaṃ kuśalapakṣa niṣevamāṇāḥ
satyārtha dharmaniratā na tu kāmabhogaiḥ || 9 ||

śrutadharmacintakuśalā aniketacittā
lābhādaśīcittagatā uta bodhicittāḥ |
jñānābhilāṣi balaśodhanabuddhadharmā
eṣanti pāramita varjitamāyaśāṭhyāḥ || 10 ||

yathāvādinastathakriyāḥ sthitasatyavākyā
na tu dūṣaṇā jinakule cari bodhiśikṣām |
lokakriyāya vigatā niratā jagārthaṃ
śuklairatṛpta bhumayottarimārabhante || 11 ||

te eva dharmaniratā guṇārthayuktā
abhinirharanti praṇidhiṃ jinadarśanāya |
saddharmadhāraṇa upasaṃkramaṇā ṛṣiṇām
abhinirharanti praṇīdhiṃ varacārikāyām || 12 ||

paripākasattvapariśodhanabuddhakṣetraṃ
te cāsya kṣetra sphuṭikā jinaaurasehi |
ekāśayā jinasutehi amoghatāyāḥ
sarvatra bālapathi buddhiya hetumarthe || 13 ||

etāṃśca naikapraṇidhīnabhinirharanti
te co anantavipulāya anantatāyai |

ākāśadhātusattvadharmatanirvṛtaṃ ca
loko hyaniṣṭha jinamutpadi jñānabhūmī || 14 ||

cittasya no viṣayajñānapraveśaniṣṭhā
yā vartani trividhaniṣṭha jagatyanantā |
praṇidhānaniṣṭhitu bhavenna mamaivarūpā
yatha eta niṣṭha tatha carya samā labheyam || 15 ||

evaṃ sunirhṛtasumārdavasnigdhacittāḥ
śraddheta buddhaguṇa sattva vilokayantaḥ |
prītyāntulambhupagataḥ kṛpamaitratāṃ ca
paritāyitavya maya sattva dukhārditāni || 16 ||

teṣārthi tyāga vividhaṃ puna ārabhante
rājyaṃ varaṃ vividharatnahayān gajāṃśca |
śirahastapādanayanā svakamātmamāṃsaṃ
sarvaṃ tyajanti na ca dīnamanā bhavanti || 17 ||

eṣanti śāstra vividhānna ca khedamenti |
śāstrajña lokacaritānyanuvartayanti |
lokajñatāmupagatā hriyatā dhṛtiṃ ca
pūjyanti cāpratisamān gurugauraveṇa || 18 ||

eṣābhiyuktavidunā divarātri nityam
uttapyate kuśala svarṇa yathaiva agnau |
so cāpi eva parikarma daśāna bhūmī
kṛtvā asaṅgatamupeti aviṣṭhihantā || 19 ||

yatha sārthavāha mahasārthahitāya yukto
pucchitva mārgaguṇa kṣematamabhyupeti |
emeva bhūmi prathamā sthita bodhisattvaḥ
kṛtaniṣkramo daśabhibodhimupetyasaṅgaḥ || 20 ||

atra sthitā guṇadharā nṛpatī bhavanti
dharmānuśāsaka ahiṃsaka maitrayuktāḥ |
jambudhvajaṃ sakalarājya praśāsayantaḥ
sthāpenti tyāgi janatāṃ varabuddhajñāne || 21 ||

ākāṅkṣamāṇa vṛṣabhā vijahitva rājyaṃ
jinaśāsane upagatāścari ārabhantaḥ ।
labdhvā samādhiśata buddhaśataṃ ca paśyi
kampenti kṣetraśatu bhāsi atikramanti ।। 22 ।।

śodhyanti sattvaśata dharmamukhān viśanti
praviśanti kalpaśatakāyaśataṃ nidarśi ।
pūrṇaṃ śataṃ jinasutāna nidarśayanti
bhūyottari praṇidhiśreṣṭhabalāpramāṇāḥ ।। 23 ।।

ityeṣā prathamā bhūmirnidiṣṭā sugatātmajāḥ ।
sarvalokahitaiṣīṇāṃ bodhisattvānanutamā ।। 24 ।।

[End of first bhūmi's final gathas]

[Beginning of second bhūmi's initial gathas]

2 vimalā nāma dvitīyā bhūmiḥ ।

upakramagāthāḥ ।

śrutvaitaduttamaṃ sthānaṃ bhūmyāḥ śreṣṭhaṃ manoramam ।
prasannamanasaṃkalpaharṣitāḥ sugatātmajāḥ ।। 1 ।।

abhyutthitā āsanebhya abhyudgamya khagapathe ।
abhyokiranti kusumaiḥ sādhviti vyāharī girā ।। 2 ।।

sādhu sādhu mahāprājña vajragarbha viśārada ।
yannirdiṣṭā tvayā bhūmi bodhisattvāna yā carī ।। 3 ।।

parṣaddhi viprasannā tu vimukticandraḥ pṛcchati ।
uttariṃ kīrtiyā bhūmiṃ dvitīyāṃ sugatātmajāḥ ।। 4 ।।

kīdṛśā manasaṃkalpā dvitīyāmabhilakṣataḥ ।
pravyāhara mahāprājña śrotukāmā jinātmajāḥ ।। 5 ।।

[End of second bhūmi's initial gathas]

2 vimalā nāma dvitīyā bhūmiḥ ।

A

vajragarbho bodhisattva āha–yo'yaṃ bhavanto jinaputrā bodhisattvaḥ prathamāyāṃ bodhisattvabhūmau suparikarmakṛto dvitīyāṃ bodhisattvabhūmimabhilaṣati, tasya daśa cittāśayāḥ pravartante । katame daśa? yaduta ṛjvāśayatā ca mṛdvāśayatā ca karmaṇyāśayatā ca damāśayatā ca śamāśayatā ca kalyāṇāśayatā ca asaṃsṛṣṭāśayatā ca anapekṣāśayatā ca udārāśayatā ca māhātmyāśayatā ca । ime daśa cittāśayāḥ pravartante । tato dvitīyāyāṃ bodhisattvabhūmau vimalāyāṃ pratiṣṭhito bhavati ।।

B

tatra bhavanto jinaputrā vimalāyāṃ bodhisattvabhūmau sthito bodhisattvaḥ prakṛtyaiva daśabhiḥ kuśalaiḥ karmapathaiḥ samanvāgato bhavati । katamairdaśabhiḥ? yaduta prāṇātipātātprativirato bhavati। nihatadaṇḍo nihataśastro nihatavairo lajjāvān dayāpannaḥ sarvaprāṇibhūteṣu hitasukhānukampī maitracittaḥ । sa saṃkalpairapi prāṇivihiṃsāṃ na karoti, kaḥ punarvādaḥ parasattveṣu sattvasaṃjñinaḥ saṃcintyaudārikakāyaviheṭhanayā ।।

C

adattādānātprativirataḥ khalu punarbhavati svabhogasaṃtuṣṭaḥ parabhogānabhilāṣī anukampakaḥ । sa paraparigṛhītebhyo vastubhyaḥ paraparigṛhītasaṃjñī steyacittamupasthāpya antaśastṛṇaparṇamapi nādattamādātā bhavati, kaḥ punarvādo'nyebhyo jīvitopakaraṇebhyaḥ ।।

D

kāmamithyācārātprativirataḥ khalu punarbhavati svadārasaṃtuṣṭaḥ paradārānabhilāṣī । sa paraparigṛhītāsu strīṣu parabhāryāsu gotradhvajadharmarakṣitāsu abhidhyāmapi notpādayati, kaḥ punarvādo dvīndriyasamāpatyā vā anaṅgavijñaptyā vā ।।

E

anṛtavacanātprativirataḥ khalu punarbhavati satyavādī bhūtavādī kālavādī, yathāvādī tathākārī । so'ntaśaḥ svapnāntaragato'pi vinidhāya dṛṣṭiṃ kṣāntiṃ ruciṃ matiṃ prekṣāṃ visaṃvādanābhiprāyo nānṛtāṃ vācaṃ niścārayati, kaḥ punarvādaḥ samanvāhṛtya ।

F

piśunavacanātprativirataḥ khalu punarbhavati abhedāviheṭhāpratipannaḥ sattvānām | sa netaḥ śrutvā amutrākhyātā bhavatyamīṣāṃ bhedāya | na amutaḥ śrutvā ihākhyātā bhavatyeṣāṃ bhedāya | na saṃhitān bhinatti, na bhinnānāmanupradānaṃ karoti | na vyagrārāmo bhavati na vyagrarato na vyagrakaraṇīṃ vācaṃ bhāṣate sadbhūtāmasadbhūtāṃ vā ||

G

paruṣavacanātprativirataḥ khalu punarbhavati | sa yeyaṃ vāgadeśā karkaśā parakaṭukā parābhisaṃjananī anvakṣānvakṣaprāgbhārā grāmyā pārthagjanakī anelā akarṇasukhā krodharoṣaniścāritā hṛdayaparidahanī manaḥsaṃtāpakarī apriyā amanaāpā amanojñā svasaṃtānaparasaṃtānavināśinī | tathārūpāṃ vācaṃ prahāya yeyaṃ vāk snigdhā mṛdvī manojñā madhurā priyakaraṇī manaāpakaraṇī hitakaraṇī nelā karṇasukhā hṛdayaṃgamā premaṇīyā paurī varṇavispaṣṭā vijñeyā śravaṇīyā niśritā bahujaneṣṭā bahujanakāntā bahujanapriyā bahujanamanaāpā vijñāpannā sarvasattvahitasukhāvahā samāhitā manautplāvanakarī manaḥprahlādanakarī svasaṃtānaparasaṃtānaprasādanakarī tathārūpāṃ vācaṃ niścārayati ||

H

saṃbhinnapralāpātprativirataḥ khalu punarbhavati suparihāryavacanaḥ kālavādī bhūtavādī arthavādī dharmavādī nyāyavādī vinayavādī | sa nidānavatīṃ vācaṃ bhāṣate kālena sāvadānam | sa cāntaśa itihāsapūrvakamapi vacanaṃ parihārya pariharati, kaḥ punarvādo vāgvikṣepeṇa ||

I

anabhidhyāluḥ khalu punarbhavati parasveṣu parakāmeṣu parabhogeṣu paravittopakaraṇeṣu | paraparigṛhīteṣu spṛhāmapi notpādayati, kimiti yatpareṣāṃ tannāma syāditi nābhidhyāmutpādayati, na prārthayate na praṇidadhāti, na lobhacittamutpādayati ||

J

avyāpannacittaḥ khalu punarbhavati | sarvasattveṣu maitracitto hitacitto dayācittaḥ sukhacittaḥ snigdhacittaḥ sarvajagadanugrahacittaḥ sarvabhūtahitānukampācittaḥ | sa yānīmāni krodhopanāhakhilamalavyāpādaparidāhasaṃdhukṣitapratighādyāni tāni prahāya yānīmāni hitopasaṃhitāni maitryupasaṃhitāni sarvasattvahitasukhāya vitarkitavicāritāni, tānyanuvitarkayitā bhavati ||

K

samyagdṛṣṭiḥ khalu punarbhavati samyakpathagataḥ kautuka-maṅgalanānāprakārakuśīladṛṣṭivigatarjudṛṣṭiraśaṭho'māyāvī buddhadharmasaṃghaniyatāśayaḥ । sa imān daśa kuśalān karmapathān satatasamitamanurakṣan

L

evaṃ cittāśayamabhinirharati - yā kācitsattvānāmapāyadurgati-vinipātaprajñaptiḥ sarvā sā eṣāṃ daśānāmakuśalānāṃ karma-pathānāṃ samādānahetoḥ । hanta ahamātmanaiva samyakprati-pattisthitaḥ parān samyakpratipattau sthāpayiṣyāmi । tatkasya hetoḥ? asthānametadanavakāśo yadātmā vipratipattisthitaḥ parān samyakpratipattau sthāpayet, naitasthānaṃ vidyata iti ।

M

sa evaṃ pravicinoti - eṣāṃ daśānāṃ akuśalānāṃ karmapathānāṃ samādānahetornirayatiryagyoniyamalokagatayaḥ prajñāyante। punaḥ kuśalānāṃ karmapathānāṃ samādānahetormanuṣy-opapattimādiṃ kṛtvā yāvadbhavāgramityupapattayaḥ prajñāyante । tata uttaṃra ta eva daśa kuśalāḥ karmapathāṃ prajñākāreṇa pari-bhāvyamānāḥ prādeśikacittatayā traidhātukottrastamānasatayā mahākaruṇāvikalatayā parataḥ śravaṇānugamena ghoṣānugamena ca śrāvakayānaṃ saṃvartayanti ।

N

tata uttarataraṃ pariśodhitā aparapraṇeyatayā svayaṃbhūtv-ānukūlatayā svayamabhisaṃbodhanatayā parato'parimārgaṇatayā mahākaruṇopāyavikalatayā gambhīredaṃpratyayānubodhanena pratyekabuddhayānaṃ saṃvartayati ।

O

tata uttarataraṃ pariśodhitāvipulāpramāṇatayā mahākaruṇopetatayā upāyakauśalasaṃgṛhītatayā saṃbaddhamahāpraṇidhānatayā sarva-sattvāparityāgatayā buddhajñānavipuladhyālambanatayā bodhi-sattvabhūmipariśuddhyai pāramitāpariśuddhyai caryāvipulatvāya saṃvartante ।

P

tata uttarataraṃ pariśodhitāḥ sarvākārapariśodhitatvādyāvaddaśa-balabalatvāya sarvabuddhadharmāḥ samudāgamāya saṃvartante । tasmāt tarhyasmābhiḥ samābhinirhāre sarvākārapariśodhanābhi-nirhāra eva yogaḥ karaṇīyaḥ ।।

Q

sa bhūyasyā mātrayā evaṃ pratisaṃśikṣate - ime khalu punardaśākuśalāḥ karmapathā adhimātratvādāsevitā bhāvitā bahulīkṛtā nirayaheturmadhyatvāt tiryagyoniheturmṛdutvādyamalokahetuḥ | tatra prāṇātipāto nirayamupanayati tiryagyonimupanayati, yamalokamupanayati | atha cetpunarmanuṣyeṣu upapadyate, dvau vipākāvabhinirvartayati alpāyuṣkatāṃ ca bahuglānyatāṃ ca | adattādanaṃ...peyālaṃ...parīttabhogatāṃ ca sādhāraṇabhogatāṃ ca | kāmamithyācāro...anājāneyaparivāratāṃ ca sasapatnadāratāṃ ca | mṛṣāvādo...abhyākhyānabahulatāṃ ca parairvisaṃvādanatāṃ ca | paiśunyaṃ...bhinnaparivāratāṃ ca hīnaparivāratāṃ ca | pāruṣyaṃ...amanāpaśravaṇatāṃ ca kalahavacanatāṃ ca | saṃbhinnapralāpo...anādeyavacanatāṃ ca aniścitapratibhānatāṃ ca | abhidhyā...asaṃtuṣṭitāṃ ca mahecchatāṃ ca | vyāpādo...ahitaiṣitāṃ ca parotpīḍanatāṃ ca | mityādṛṣṭiḥ...kudṛṣṭipatitaśca bhavati śaṭhaśca māyāvī | evaṃ khalu mahato'parimāṇasya duḥkhaskandhasya ime daśākuśalāḥ karmapathāḥ samudāgamāya saṃvartante |

R

hanta vayaṃ imān daśākuśalān karmapathān vivarjya dharmārāmaratiratā viharāma |

S

sa imān daśākuśalān karmapathān prahāya daśakuśalakarmapathapratiṣṭhitaḥ parāṃsteṣveva pratiṣṭhāpayati |

T

sa bhūyasyā mātrayā sarvasattvānāmantike hitacittatāmutpādayati | sukhacittatāṃ maitracittatāṃ kṛpācittatāṃ dayācittatāmanugrahacittatāmārakṣācittatāṃ samacittatāmacāryacittatāṃ śāstṛcittatāmutpādayati |

U

tasyaivaṃ bhavati - kudṛṣṭipatitā bateme sattvā viṣamamatayo viṣamāśayā utpathagahanacāriṇaḥ | te'smābhirbhūtapathasamyagdṛṣṭimārgayāthātathye pratiṣṭhāpayitavyāḥ |

V

bhinnavigṛhītacittavivādopapannā bateme sattvāḥ satatasamitaṃ krodhopanāhasaṃdhukṣitāḥ | te'smābhiranuttare mahāmaitryupasaṃhāre pratiṣṭhāpayitavyāḥ |

W

atṛptā bateme sattvāḥ paravittābhilāṣiṇo viṣamājīvānucaritāḥ | te'smābhiḥ pariśuddhakāyavāṅmanaskarmāntājīvikāyāṃ pratiṣṭhāpayitavyāḥ |

X

rāgadveṣamohatrinidānānugatā bateme sattvā vividhakleśāgnijvālābhiḥsatatasamitaṃ pradīptāḥ | na ca tato'tyantaniḥsaraṇopāyaṃ parimārgayanti | te'smābhiḥ sarvakleśapraśame nirupadrave nirvāṇe pratiṣṭhāpayitavyāḥ |

Y

mahāmohatamastimirapaṭalāvidyāndhakārāvṛtā bateme sattvā mahāndhakāragahanānupraviṣṭāḥ prajñālokasudūrībhūtā mahāndhakārapraskannāḥ kudṛṣṭikāntārasamavasṛtāḥ | teṣāmasmābhiranāvaraṇaṃ prajñācakṣurviśodhayitavyaṃ yathā sarvadharmayāthātathyāparapraṇayatāṃ pratilapsyante |

Z

mahāsaṃsārāṭavīkāntāramārgaprapannā bateme sattvā ayogakṣemiṇo'nāśvāsaprāptā mahāprapātapatitā nirayatiryagyoniyamalokagatiprapātābhimukhāḥ kudṛṣṭiviṣamajālānuparyavanaddhā mohagahanasaṃchannā mithyāmārgavipathaprayātā jātyandhībhūtāḥ pariṇāyakavikalā aniḥsaraṇe niḥsaraṇasaṃjñino namucipāśabaddhā viṣayataskaropagṛhītāḥ kuśalapariṇāyakavirahitā mārāśayagahanānupraviṣṭā buddhāśayadūrībhūtāḥ | te'smābhirevaṃvidhāt saṃsārāṭavīkāntāradurgāduttārayitavyā abhayapure ca sarvajñatānagare nirupadrave nirupatāpe pratiṣṭhāpayitavyāḥ |

AA

mahaughormyāmathairnimagnā bateme sattvāḥ kāmabhavāvidyādṛṣṭyoghasamavasṛṣṭāḥ saṃsārasrotonuvāhinastṛṣṇānadīprapannā mahāvegagrastā avilokanasamarthāḥ kāmavyāpādavihiṃsāvitarkapratānānucaritāḥ satkāyadṛṣṭyudakarākṣasagṛhītāḥ kāmagahanāvartānupraviṣṭā nandīrāgamadhyasaṃchannā asmimānasthalotsannā dauḥśīlyaviṣamācārāntaḥpuṭībhūtāḥ ṣaḍāyatanagrāmabhayatīramanuccalitāḥ kuśalasaṃtārakavirahitā anāthā aparāyaṇā aśaraṇāḥ | te'smābhirmahākaruṇākuśalamūlabalenoddhṛtya nirupadrave'rajasi kṣeme śive'bhaye sarvabhayatrāsāpagate sarvajñatāratnadvīpe pratiṣṭhāpayitavyāḥ |

BB

ruddhā bateme sattvā bahuduḥkhadaurmanasyopāyāsabahule-

'nunayapratighapriyāpriyavinibandhane saśokaparidevānucarite tṛṣṇānigaḍabandhane māyāśāṭhyāvidyāgahanasaṃchanne traidhātukacārake | te'smābhiḥ sarvatraidhātukaviveke sarvaduḥkhopaśame'nāvaraṇanirvāṇe pratiṣṭhāpayitavyāḥ |

CC

ātmātmīyābhiniviṣṭā bateme sattvāḥ skandhālayānuccalitāścaturviparyāsānuprayātāḥ ṣaḍāyatanaśūnyagrāmasaṃniśritāścaturmahābhūtoragābhidrutāḥ skandhavadhakataskarābhighātitā aparimāṇaduḥkhapratisaṃvedinaḥ | te'smābhiḥ paramasukhe sarvaniketavigame pratiṣṭhāpayitavyā yaduta sarvāvaraṇaprahāṇanirvāṇe |

DD

hīnalīnadīnādhimuktā bateme sattvā agryasarvajñajñānacittavikalāḥ sati niḥsaraṇe mahāyāne śrāvakapratyekabuddhayānāvatīrṇamatayaḥ | te'smābhirudārabuddhadharmamativipulādhyālambena sarvajñajñānalocanatayā anuttare mahāyāne pratiṣṭhāpayitavyāḥ ||

iti hi bhavanto jinaputrā evaṃ śīlabalādhānānugatasya bodhisattvasya kṛpākaruṇāmaitryabhinirhārakuśalasya sarvasattvānavadhīṣṭakalyāṇamitrasyāparityaktasarvasattvasya kriyākriyābhinirhārakuśalasya

EE

vimalāyāṃ bodhisattvabhūmau pratiṣṭhitasya bahavo buddhā ābhāsabhāgacchānti...audārika...peyālaṃ...pariṇāmayati | tāṃśca tathāgatānarhataḥ samyaksaṃbuddhān paryupāsate, teṣāṃ ca sakāśebhyo gauraveṇemāneva daśa kuśalān karmapathān pratigṛhṇāti, yathāpratigṛhītāṃśca nāntarā praṇāśayati | so'nekān kalpānanekāni kalpaśatāni anekāni kalpasahasrāṇi anekāni kalpaśatasahasrāṇi anekāni kalpaniyutaśatasahasrāni anekakalpakoṭīranekāni kalpakoṭiśatāni anekāni kalpakoṭiśatasahasrāni anekāni kalpakoṭiniyutaśatasahasrāṇi mātsaryadauḥśīlyamalāpanītatayā tyāgaśīlaviśuddhau samudāgacchati | tadyathāpi nāma bhavanto jinaputrāstadeva jātarūpaṃ kāsīsaprakṣiptaṃ bhūyasyā mātrayā sarvamalāpagataṃ bhavati, evameva bhavanto jinaputrāstadeva jātarūpaṃ kāsīsaprakṣiptaṃ bhūyasyā mātrayā sarvamalāpagataṃ bhavati, evameva bhavanto jinaputrā bodhisattvo'syāṃ vimalāyāṃ bodhisattvabhūmau sthito'nekān kalpān yāvadanekāni kalpakoṭiniyutaśatasahasrāṇi mātsaryadauḥśīlyamalāpanītatayā tyāgaśīlaviśudvau samudāgacchati | tasya caturbhyaḥ saṃgrahavastubhyaḥ priyavadyatā atiriktatamā bhavati | daśabhyaḥ pāramitābhyaḥ śīlapāramitā atiriktatamā bhavati | na ca pariśeṣāsu na samudāgacchati yathābalaṃ yathābhajamānam ||

iyaṃ bhavanto jinaputrā bodhisattvasya vimalā nāma dvitīyā bodhisattvabhūmiḥ samāsanirdeśataḥ, yasyāṃ pratiṣṭhito bodhisattvo bhūyastvena rājā bhavati cakravartī caturdvīpādhipatidharmādhipatyapratilabdhaḥ saptaratnasamanvāgataḥ kṛtī prabhuḥ sattvānāṃ dauḥśīlyamalavinivartanāya kuśalaḥ sattvān daśasu kuśaleṣu karmapatheṣu pratiṣṭhāpayitum | yacca kiṃcit karmārabhate...peyālam ||

vimalā nāma dvitīyā bhūmiḥ ||

[Beginning of 2nd bhūmi's final gathas]

upasaṃhāragāthāḥ |

te mārdavārjavamṛdūkarmaṇīyacittāḥ
kalyāṇaāśaya damāśayatābhyupetāḥ |
saṃsargapekṣavigatāśca udārabuddhi
māhātmya āśayavid dvitīyākramanti || 6 ||

atra sthitā guṇadharāḥ kuśalopapetāḥ
prāṇātipātavigatā avihiṃsacittāḥ |
adattadānapagatāḥ paradāratāṃ ca
satyānvitā apiśunaḥ puruṣapradhānāḥ || 7 ||

parabhogabhidyavigatā vidu maitracittāḥ
samyakpathe upagatā aśaṭhajñakāśca |
nirmāṇakāyagrahaṇāśca supeśalāśca
rakṣanti śāstuśaraṇaṃ sada apramattāḥ || 8 ||

duḥkhāni yāni niraye tatha tiryagyonau
yamaśāsane jvalitaāśrayanityupetāḥ |
sarve ti pāpapatitākṣalāḥ prabhonti
hantā vivarjiya upemahi satyadharmam || 9 ||

ādau ca kṛtva manujānupapattimiṣṭāṃ
yāvadbhavāgramaraṇāśayadhyānu śikṣām |
pratyekayānamatha śrāvakabuddhayānaṃ
sarve ito daśabhi śuklapathaiḥ prabhūtam || 10 ||

evaṃ viditva satataṃ vidu apramattāḥ
śīleṣu saṃsthita parānapi sthāpayanti |
bhūyottare karuṇaāśayatābhyupetāḥ
sattvān viditva dukhitān kṛpa saṃjanenti || 11 ||

hanto vidṛṣṭipatitā imi bālabuddhī
krodhopanāhadrutacitta vivādaprāptāḥ |

satataṃ atṛpta viṣaye bhuyu prārthayanti
trinidāna sattva parimocayitavya ete || 12 ||

mahaandhakāratamasāvṛta mohachannāḥ
kāntāramārgapatitā mahadṛṣṭijāle |
saṃsārapañjaragatā ripu dharṣayanti
mokṣāmyahaṃ namucipañjaramadhyaprāptān || 13 ||

kleśormibhihriyata oghacaturnimagnā
traidhātuke dukhaśataiḥ paripīḍyamānāḥ |
skandhālayābhyupagatā vṛtaātmasaṃjñā
teṣārthi yujyami ahaṃ dukhamocanārtham || 14 ||

avasṛjya śreṣṭhapravaraṃ ima buddhajñānaṃ
sati eva niḥsaraṇi hīnamatiṃ janenti |
sthāpemi tān vimalajñāni tathāgatānāṃ
vīryārabhanti atulaṃ vidu bodhihetoḥ || 15 ||

atra sthitā guṇaśatopacitā maharṣi
paśyanti naikasugatānapi pūjayanti |
teṣāṃ śubhaṃ bhuyu uttapyati kalpakoṭyāṃ
kāsīsakāñcanavaraṃ ca yathā nikṣiptam || 16 ||

atra sthitā jinasutā nṛpacakravarti
bhūtvā praṇenti daśabhiḥ kuśalebhi sattvān |
yaccaiva saṃci śubhasaṃcaya saṃcinanti
trātā bhavema jagato daśabhirbalāḍhyaiḥ || 17 ||

ākāṅkṣamāṇa vijahitva ca rajabhogān
pravrajya śāsanavare upagamya dhīrāḥ |
vīryānvitā labhiya śreṣṭhavaraṃ samādhiṃ
buddhā sahasra paripūrṇa kṣeṇe dṛśanti || 18 ||

evaṃvidhā gaṇanayā bhuyu anya nekā
ādarśayanti vṛṣabhī sthita atra bhūmau |
ata uttari praṇidhijñānavarābhyupetā
naikā vikurvitavidhau vinayanti sattvān || 19 ||

ityeṣā dvitiyā bhūmirnirdiṣṭā sugatātmajāḥ |
sarvalokahitaiṣīṇāṃ bodhisattvānanuttamā || 20 ||

[End of 2nd bhūmi's final gathas]

[Beginning of third bhūmi's initial gathas]

3 prabhākarī nāma tṛtīyā bhūmiḥ |

upakramagāthāḥ |

evaṃ śruṇitva caribhūmimuttamāṃ
bodhisattvaviṣaye acintiyām |
harṣita jinasutāḥ sagauravāḥ
puṣpamegha nabhataḥ pramuñciṣuḥ || 1 ||

sādhu sādhu girisārasākaya (?)
deśito viduna śīlasaṃvaraḥ |
sarvasattvakaruṇāya āśayo
bhūmiśreṣṭha dvitiyāya gocaraḥ || 2 ||

bhūtatattva vitathāmananyathā
bodhisasattvacaraṇaṃ manoramam |
sarvalokahitaśaukhyacintanā
deśitaṃ tu paramaprabhāsvaram || 3 ||

bhūyu bhūyu naradevapūjitāṃ
bhūmiśreṣṭha tṛtiyāmudāhara |
dharmajñānakriyamukti sūcaya
yādṛśo'nubhava tādṛ(śo) gocaraḥ || 4 ||

dānaśīlacaraṇaṃ maharṣiṇāṃ
kṣāntivīryaśamaprajñupāyatām |
maitraśreṣṭha karuṇāya mārgaṇaṃ
bhāṣadhvaṃ jinacarīviśodhanam || 5 ||

vimukticandra uvāca vajragarbhaviśāradam |
tṛtīyā saṃkramantānāmāśayaṃ bhaṇa sūraṇa || 6 ||

[End of third bhūmi's initial gathas]

3 prabhākarī nāma tṛtīyā bhūmiḥ ǀ

A

vajragarbho bodhisattva āha - yo'yaṃ bhavanto jinaputrā bodhisattvo dvitīyāyāṃ bodhisattvabhūmau supariśodhitādhyāśayastṛtīyāṃ bodhisattvabhūmimākramati, sa daśabhiścittāśayamanaskārairākramati ǀ katamairdaśabhiḥ ? yaduta śuddhacittāśayamanaskāreṇa ca sthiracittāśayamanaskāreṇa ca nirviccittāśayamanaskāreṇa ca avirāgacittāśayamanaskāreṇa ca avinivartacittāśayamanaskāreṇa ca dṛḍhacittāśayamanaskāreṇa ca uttaptacittāśayamanaskāreṇa ca atṛptacittāśayamanaskāreṇa ca udāracittāśayamanaskāreṇa ca māhātmyacittāśayamanaskāreṇa ca ǀ ebhirdaśabhiścittāśayamanaskārairākramati ǀ

B

sa khalu punarbhavanto jinaputrā bodhisattvastṛtīyāyāṃ bodhisattvabhūmau sthito'nityatāṃ ca sarvasaṃskāragatasya yathābhūtaṃ pratyavekṣate, duḥkhatāṃ ca aśubhatāṃ ca anāśvāsikatāṃ ca vipralopatāṃ ca acirasthitikatāṃ ca kṣaṇikotpādanirodhatāṃ ca pūrvantāsaṃbhavatāṃ ca aparāntāsaṃkrāntitāṃ ca pratyutpannāvyavasthitatāṃ ca sarvasaṃskāragatasya pratyavekṣate ǀ

C

sa evaṃbhūtaṃ sarvasaṃskāragataṃ saṃpaśyannanabhisaraṃ nirākrandaṃ saśokaṃ saparidevaṃ sopāyāsaṃ priyāpriyavinibaddha duḥkhadaurmanasyopāyāsābahulamasaṃnicayabhūtaṃ rāgadveṣamohāgnisaṃpradīptamanekavyādhivivardhitaṃ ca ātmabhāvaṃ saṃpaśyan

D

bhūyasyā mātrayā sarvasaṃskārebhyaścittamuccālayati, tathāgatajñāne ca saṃpreṣayati ǀ sa tathāgatajñānasyācintyatāṃ ca samanupaśyati, atulyatāṃ ca aprameyatāṃ ca durāsadatāṃ ca asaṃspṛṣṭatāṃ ca nirupadravatāṃ ca nirupāyāsatāṃ ca abhayapuragamanīyatāṃ ca apunarāvṛttitāṃ ca bahujanaparitrāṇatāṃ ca samanupaśyati ǀ

E

sa evamapramāṇatāṃ ca tathāgatajñānasya samanupaśyan evaṃ bahūpadravatāṃ ca sarvasaṃskāragatasya vyupaparīkṣamāṇo bhūyasyā mātrayā sattvānāmantike daśa cittāśayānupasthāpayati ǀ

katamān daśa? yaduta anāthātrāṇāpratiśaraṇacittāśayatāṃ ca nityadaridrapratiśaraṇacittāśayatāṃ ca rāgadveṣamohāgnisaṃpradīptapratiśaraṇacittāśayatāṃ ca bhavacārakāvaruddhapratiśaraṇacittāśayatāṃ ca satatasamitaklaśagahenāvṛtaprasuptapratiśaraṇacittāśayatāṃ ca vilokanasamarthapratiśaraṇacittāśayatāṃ ca kuśaladharmacchandarahitapratiśaraṇacittāśayatāṃ ca buddhadharmapramuṣitapratiśaraṇacittāśayatāṃ ca saṃsārasrotonuvāhipratiśaraṇacittāśayatāṃ ca mokṣopāyapraṇaṣṭapratiśaraṇacittāśayatāṃ ca । imān daśa cittāśayanupasthāpayati ।।

F

sa evaṃ bahūpadravaṃ sattvadhātuṃ samanupaśyan evaṃ vīryamārabhate - mayaivaite sattvāḥ paritrātavyāḥ parimocayitavyāḥ paritoṣayitavyāḥ saṃropayitavyā vinetavyāḥ parinirvāpayitavyā iti ।

G

sa evaṃ nirvidanugataśca sarvasaṃskāragatyā upekṣānugataśca sarvasattveṣu anuśaṃsānugataśca sarvajñajñāne tathāgatajñānapratiśaraṇaḥ sarvasattvaparitrāṇāyābhiyuktaḥ evaṃ vyupaparīkṣate - katamena khalu upāyamārgeṇa śakyā ime sattvā evaṃ bahuduḥkhopakleśaprapatitā abhyuddhartum, atyantasukhe ca nirvāṇe pratiṣṭhāpayitum, sarvadharmaniḥsaṃśayatāṃ cānuprāpayitumiti?

H

tasya bodhisattvasyaivaṃ bhavati - nānyatra anāvaraṇavimokṣajñānasthānāt । tacca anāvaraṇajñānavimokṣasthānam nānyatra sarvadharmayathāvadavabodhāt । sa ca sarvadharmayathāvadavabodho nānyatra apracārānutpādacāriṇyāḥ prajñāyāḥ । sa ca prajñāloko nānyatra dhyānakauśalyaviniścayabuddhipratyavekṣaṇāt । tacca dhyānakauśalyaviniścayabuddhipratyavekṣaṇaṃ nānyatra śrutakauśalyāditi ।।

I

sa evaṃ pratyavekṣitajñāno bhūyasyā mātrayā saddharmaparyeṣaṇābhiyukto viharati । rātridivaṃ dharmaśravaṇārthiko dharmakāmātṛptāpratiprasrabdho buddhardharmaparyeṣṭihetoḥ । dharmārāmo dharmarato dharmapratiśaraṇo dharmanimno dharmapravaṇo dharmaprāgbhāro dharmaparāyaṇo dharmalayano dharmatrāṇo dharmānudharmacārī ।

J

sa evaṃ buddhadharmaparyeṣaṇābhiyukto nāsti tatkiṃcid dravya-

vittajātaṃ vā dhanadhānyakośakoṣṭhāgārajātaṃ vā hiraṇyasuvarṇa-
maṇimuktāvajravaiḍūryaśaṅkhaśilāpravālajātarūparajatajātaṃ vā
yāvatsarvāṅgapratyaṅgaparityāgo vā yanna parityajati tayā dharma-
kāmatayā | na ca tasmādduṣkarasaṃjñī bhavati anyatra tasminneva
dharmabhāṇakapudgale duṣkarasaṃjñī bhavati yo'syaikadharma-
padamapi deśayati | sa dharmahetornāsti tatkiṃcidupātaṃ bāhyaṃ
vastu yanna parityajati | nāsti tatkiciṃdādhyātmikaṃ vastu yanna
parityajati | nāsti tatkiṃcidguruparicaryopasthānaṃ yannopādatte |
nāsti sā kācid mānābhimānotsarganirmāṇopacāratā yāṃ nopādatte |
nāsti sā kācitkāyikī pīḍā yāṃ nopādatte | sa citro bhavatyaśruta-
dharmapada śravaṇena, na tveva trisāhasramahāsāhasralokadhātu-
pratimena ratnarāśipratilambhena | sa citro bhavatyekasubhāṣita-
gāthāśravaṇena na tveva cakravartirājyapratilambhena | sa citro
bhavatyaśrutadharmapadaśravaṇena bodhisattvacaryāpari-
śodhanena na tveva śakratvabrahmatvapratilambhena bahukalpa-
śatasahasraparyavasānena | sacedidaṃ kaścidevaṃ brūyāt – evam-
ahaṃ tulyamidaṃ dharmapadaṃ samyaksaṃbuddhopanītaṃ bodhi-
sattvacaryāpariśodhanaṃ saṃśrāvayeyam, sacettvaṃ mahatyām-
agnikhadāyāṃ saṃprajvalitāyāmekajvālībhūtāyāmātmānaṃ pra-
pātayeḥ, mahāntaṃ ca duḥkhavedanopakramaṃ svaśarīreṇ-
opādadyā iti | tasyaivaṃ bhavati - utsahe'hamekasyāpi dharma-
padasya samyaksaṃbuddhopanītasya bodhisattvacaryāpari-
śodhanasyārthāya trisāhasramahāsāhasralokadhātāvagniparipūrṇe
brahmalokādātmānamutsraṣṭum, kiṃ punaḥ prākṛtāyāṃ agni-
khadāyām | api tu khalu punaḥ sarvairnirayāpāyaduḥkhasaṃvāsair-
apyasmābhirbuddhadharmāḥ paryeṣitavyāḥ, kiṃ punarmanuṣya-
duḥkhasaṃvāsairiti | sa evaṃrūpeṇa vīryārambheṇa dharmān
paryeṣate | yathāśruteṣu dharmeṣu ca yoniśaḥ pratyavakṣeṇajātīyo
bhavati |
K
tāṃśca dharmān śrutvā svacittanidhyaptyā eko rahogata evaṃ
mīmāṃsate - dharmānudharmapratipattyā ime buddhadharmā anu-
gantavyā na kevalaṃ vākkarmapariśuddhyeti | so'syāṃ prabhā-
karyāṃ bodhisattvabhūmau sthito bodhisattvo dharmānudharma-
pratipattihetorviviktaṃ kāmairviviktaṃ pāpakairakuśaladharmaiḥ
savitarkaṃ savicāraṃ vivekajaṃ prītisukhaṃ prathamaṃ dhyānam-
upasaṃpadya viharati | sa vitarkavicārāṇāṃ vyupaśamādadhyātma-

saṃprasādāccetasa ekotībhāvādavitarkamavicāraṃ samādhijaṃ prītisukhaṃ dvitīyaṃ dhyānamupasaṃpadya viharati | sa prīter-virāgādupekṣako viharati smṛtimān saṃprajānan | sukhaṃ ca kāyena pratisaṃvedayati yattadāryā ācakṣante - upekṣakaḥ smṛtimān | sukhavihārī niṣprītikaṃ tṛtīyaṃ dhyānamupasaṃpadya viharati | sa sukhasya ca prahāṇādduḥkhasya ca prahāṇātpūrvam-eva ca saumanasyadaurmanasyayorastaṃgamādaduḥkhāsukham-upekṣāsmṛtipariśuddhaṃ caturthaṃ dhyānamupasaṃpadya viharati | sa sarvaśo rūpasaṃjñānāṃ samatikramāt pratighasaṃjñānām-astaṃgamānnānātvasaṃjñānāmamanasikārādanantakamākāśamityā kāśānantyāyatanamupasaṃpadya viharati | sa sarvaśa ākāśānanty-āyatanasamatikramādanantaṃ vijñānamiti vijñānānantyāyatanam-upasaṃpadya viharati | sa sarvaśo vijñānānantyāyatanasamati-kramānnāsti kiṃcidityākiṃcanyāyatanamupasaṃpadya viharati | sa sarvaśa ākiṃcanyāyatanasamatikramānnaivasaṃjñānāsaṃjñ-āyatanamupasaṃpadya viharati tenānabhiratipadasthānena n-ānyatra dharmānudharmapratipattimupādāya |

L

sa maitrīsahagatena cittena vipulena mahadgatenādvayenāpra-māṇenāvaireṇāsapatnenānāvaraṇenāvyābādhena sarvatrānugatena dharmadhātuparame loke ākāśadhātuparyavasāne sarvāvantaṃ lokaṃ spharitvopasaṃpadya viharati | evaṃ karuṇāsahagatena cittena | muditāsahagatena cittena | upekṣāsahagatena cittena viharati ||

M

so'nekavidhāṃ ṛddhividhiṃ pratyanubhavati | pṛthivīmapi kampayati | eko'pi bhūtvā bahudhā bhavati | bahudhāpi bhūtvaiko bhavati | āvirbhāvaṃ tirobhāvamapi pratyanubhavati | tiraḥ-kuḍyaṃ tiraḥprākāraṃ parvatamapyasajjan gacchati tadyathāpi nāma ākāśe | ākāśe'pi paryaṅkena krāmati tadyathāpi nāma pakṣi-śakuniḥ | pṛthivyāmapyunmajjananimajjanaṃ karoti tadyathāpi nāma udake | udake'pyamañjan gacchati tadyathāpi pṛthivyām | dhūmayati prajvalati, tadyathāpi nāma mahānagniskandhaḥ | sva-kāyādapi mahāvāridhārā utsṛjati tadyathāpi nāma mahāmeghaḥ | yābhirvāridhārābhirayaṃ trisāhasramahāsāhasro lokadhāturādīptaḥ pradīptaḥ saṃprajvalito'gninā ekajvālībhūto nirvāpyate | imāvapi candrasūryāvevaṃmaharddhikau evaṃmahānubhāvau pāṇinā parāmṛśati parimārṣṭi yāvadbrahmalokamapi kāyena vaśaṃ vartayati । ।

sa divyena śrotradhātunā [viśuddhenā]tikrāntamānuṣyakena ubhayān śabdān śṛṇoti divyān mānuṣyākān, sūkṣmānaudārikāṃśca । ye dūre'ntike vā antaśo daṃśamaśakakīṭamakṣikāṇāmapi śabdān śṛṇoti । [eṣā divyaśrotrābhijñā] । ।

sa parasattvānāṃ parapudgalānāṃ cetasaiva cittaṃ yathābhūtaṃ prajānāti । sarāgaṃ cittaṃ sarāgacittamiti yathābhūtaṃ prajānāti । virāgaṃ cittaṃ virāgacittamiti prajānāti । sadoṣaṃ...vigatadoṣaṃ... samohaṃ...vigatamohaṃ...sakleśaṃ...niḥkleśaṃ...parīttaṃ... vipulaṃ...mahadgataṃ...apramāṇaṃ...saṃkṣiptaṃ...[vistīrṇaṃ]... samāhitaṃ...asamāhitaṃ...vimuktaṃ...avimuktaṃ...sāṅganam... anaṅganam...audārikaṃ cittamaudārikacittamiti yathābhūtaṃ prajānāti । anaudārikaṃ cittamanaudārikaṃ cittamiti yathābhūtaṃ prajānāti । iti parasattvānāṃ parapudgalānāṃ cetasaiva cittaṃ yathābhūtaṃ prajānāti । [ityeṣā paracittajñānāmijñā] । ।

so'nekavidhaṃ pūrvanivāsamanusmarati । ekāmapi jātimanusmarati । dve tisraścatasraḥ pañca daśa viṃśatiḥ triṃśataṃ catvāriṃśataṃ pañcāśataṃ jātiśatamanusmarati । anekānyapi jātiśatāni । anekānyapi jātiśatasahasrāṇi । saṃvartakalpamapi vivartakalpamapi । anekānapi saṃvartavivartakalpānapyanusmarati । kalpaśatamapi kalpasahasramapi kalpakoṭīmapi kalpakoṭīśatamapi kalpakoṭīsahasramapi kalpakoṭīśatasahasramapi yāvadanekānyapi kalpakoṭīniyutaśatasahasrāṇyanusmarati - amutrāhamāsaṃ evaṃnāmā । evaṃgotraḥ evaṃjātiḥ evamāhāra evamāyuḥpramāṇaḥ evaṃ cirasthitikaḥ evaṃ sukhaduḥkhapratisaṃvedī । so'haṃ tataścyuto'tropapannaḥ । tataścyuta ihopapannaḥ । iti sākāraṃ soddeśaṃ sanimittamanekavidhaṃ pūrvanivāsamanusmarati । [eṣā pūrvanivāsānusmṛtyabhijñā] । ।

sa divyena cakṣuṣā viśuddhenātikrāntamānuṣyakeṇa sattvān paśyati cyavamānānupapadyamānān suvarṇān durvarṇān sugatān durgatān praṇītān hīnān । yathākarmopagān sattvān yathābhūtaṃ prajānāti - ime bhavantaḥ sattvāḥ kāyaduścaritena samanvāgatā vāgduścaritena samanvāgatā [manoduścaritena samanvāgatāḥ] । āryāṇāmapavādakā mithyādṛṣṭayaḥ mithyādṛṣṭikarmasamādānahetostaddhetuṃ tatpratyayaṃ kāyasya bhadātparaṃ maraṇādapāyadurgativinipātanirayeṣūpapadyante | ime punarbhavantaḥ sattvāḥ kāyasucaritena samanvāgatā [vāksucaritena samanvāgatā manaḥsucaritena samanvāgatā] āryāṇāmanapavādakāḥ | samyagdṛṣṭikarmasamādānahetostaddhetuṃ tatpratyayaṃ kāyasya bhedāt paraṃ maraṇātsugatau svarge devalokeṣūpapadyanta iti |[prajānāti | evaṃ] divyena cakṣuṣā viśuddhenātikrāntamanuṣyeṇa sākāraṃ soddeśaṃ sanimittaṃ sattvān paśyati | cyavamānānupapadyamānān...yathābhūtaṃ paśyati ||

sa imāni dhyānāni vimokṣān samādhīn samāpattīśca samāpadyate, vyuttiṣṭhete | na ca teṣāṃ vaśenopapadyate'nyatra yatra bodhyaṅgaparipūriṃ paśyati tatra saṃcintya praṇidhānavaśenopapadyate | tatkasya hetoḥ? tathā hi tasya bodhisattvasyopāyakauśalyābhinirhatā cittasaṃtatiḥ ||

N

tasya asyāṃ prabhākaryāṃ bodhisattvabhūmau sthitasya bodhisattvasya bahavo buddhā ābhāsamāgacchanti | peyālaṃ | pariṇāmayati | tāṃśca tathāgatānarhataḥ samyaksaṃbuddhān paryupāste | teṣāṃ ca dharmadeśanāṃ satkṛtya śṛṇoti udgṛhṇāti dhārayati | śrutvā ca yathābhajamānaṃ pratipattyā samādayati | sa sarvadharmāṇāmasaṃkrāntitāṃ ca avināśitāṃ ca pratītya pratyayatayā vyavalokayati ||

O

tasya bhūyasyā mātrayā sarvāṇi kāmabandhanāni tanūni bhavanti | sarvāṇi rūpabandhanāni sarvāṇi bhavabandhanāni sarvāṇyavidyābandhanāni tanūni bhavanti | dṛṣṭikṛtabandhanāni ca pūrvameva prahīṇāni bhavanti | tasya asyāṃ prabhākaryāṃ bodhisattvabhūmau sthitasya bodhisattvasya...peyālaṃ...anupacayaṃ mithyārāgaḥ prahāṇaṃ gacchati anupacayaṃ mithyādoṣaḥ prahāṇaṃ gacchati, anupacayaṃ mithyāmohaḥ prahāṇaṃ gacchati | tāni cāsya kuśalamūlānyuttapyante pariśuddhyanti karmaṇyāni ca bhavanti | tadyathāpi nāma bhavanto jinaputrāstadeva jātarūpaṃ kuśalasya karmārasya hastagataṃ tulyadharaṇameva pramāṇenāvatiṣṭhate, evameva bhavanto jinaputrā bodhisattvasya asyāṃ prabhākaryāṃ bodhisattvabhūmau sthitasya anekān kalpān yāvadanekāni kalpakoṭiniyutaśatasahasrāṇi....prahāṇaṃ gacchanti | tasya bhūyasyā mātrayā kṣāntisauratyāśayatā ca pariśuddhyati, sākhilyamādhuryāśayatā ca akopyāśayatā ca akṣubhitāśayatā ca alubhitāśayatā ca anunnāmavanāmāśayatā ca sarvakṛtapratikṛtānāṃ niḥkāṅkṣāśayatā ca sattvakṛtapratikṛtānāṃ kāṅkṣāśayatā ca aśāṭhyamāyāvitāśayatā ca agahanāśayatā ca pariśuddhyati | tasya caturbhyaḥ saṃgrahavastubhyo'rthacaryā atiriktatamā bhavati | daśabhyaḥ pāramitābhyaḥ kṣāntipāramitā atiriktatamā bhavati | na ca pariśeṣāsu na samudāgacchati yathābalaṃ yathābhajamānam | iyaṃ bhavanto jinaputrā bodhisattvasya prabhākarī nāma tṛtīyā bodhisattvabhūmiḥ samāsanirdeśataḥ,

P

yasyāṃ pratiṣṭhito bodhisattvo bhūyastvena indro bhavati devarājastridaśādhipatiḥ kṛtī prabhuḥ sattvānāṃ kāmarāgavinivartanopāyopasaṃhārāya kuśalaḥ sattvān kāmapaṅkādabhyuddhartum, yacca kiṃcit...peyālaṃ...yathārūpeṇa vīryārambheṇa ekakṣaṇalavamuhūrtena samādhiśatasahasraṃ ca pratilabhate... | |

prabhākarī nāma tṛtiyā bhūmiḥ | |

[Beginning of third bhūmi's final gathas]

upasaṃhāragāthāḥ |

te śuddhaāśaya guṇākara tīkṣṇacittā
nirviṇṇa rāgavigatā anivartiyāśca |
dṛḍhacitta taptadhṛtiyukti udāravegā
māhātmyatāśayavidū tṛtiyākramanti || 7 ||

atra sthitā vidu prabhākaribhūmideśe
duḥkhaṃ anityamaśuciṃ ca pralopadharmam |
acirasthitāka kṣaṇikaṃ ca nirodhakaṃ ca
vicinanti saṃskṛtagatīkamanāgatīkam || 8 ||

te rogabhūtasahaśokaparadevanaṃ ca
sopāyasaṃ ca priya apriyatānubaddham |
duḥkhadaurmanasyanilayaṃ jvalitāgnikalpaṃ
paśyanti saṃskṛtamananta samujjvalanti || 9 ||

udvigna sarva tribhave anapekṣacittā
jñānābhilāṣa sugatānamananyabuddhiḥ |
avicintiyaṃ atuliyaṃ asamantapāraṃ
saṃpaśyate nirupatāpa jināna jñānam || 10 ||

te buddhajñāna nirupadravamīkṣamāṇā
atrāṇa nātharahitā vrajate caranti |
nityaṃ daridra tribhiragnibhi saṃpradīptā
bhavacārake dukhaśatairvinibaddhacittāḥ || 11 ||

kleśāvṛtāśca avilokana chandahīnāḥ
sugatāna dharmaratanānupranaṣṭa bālāḥ |
saṃsārasrotaanuvāhina mokṣatrastā
me trāyitavya dṛḍha vīrya samārabhante || 12 ||

jñānābhilāṣa anapekṣa jagārthacārī
vyuparīkṣate katama hetu jagasya mokṣe |

nānyatra nāvaraṇajñāna tathāgatānāṃ
jñānaṃ ca prajñaprabhavaṃ sugatānanantam | | 13 | |

prajñā śrutāttu iti cintayi bodhisattvo
jñātvā tamārabhati vīrya śrutārthacārī |
rātriṃdivaṃ śravaṇahetu ananyakarmā
arthārthiko bhavati dharmaparāyaṇaśca | | 14 | |

maṇimuktiratnanilayān priyabāndhavāṃśca
rājyaṃ ananta vividhān pura sthānaśreṣṭhān |
bhāryāsutāṃśca parivāra manonukūlān
anapekṣacittu tyajate vidu dharmahetoḥ | | 15 | |

śira hastapāda nayana svakamātmamāṃsaṃ
jihvā ca daṃṣṭra śrava nāsika śoṇitaṃ ca |
hṛdayaṃ tupādya priya majja parityajanti
nā duṣkaretamatha duṣkara yacchṛṇoti | | 16 | |

yadi kaścidenamupagamya vadeyya evaṃ
yadi agnigarbha prapate jvalitāpi ghoram |
prāpiṣya dharmaratanaṃ sugatopanītaṃ
śrutvā adīnamanasaḥ prapate guṇārthī | | 17 | |

ekasya dharmapada artha sumerumūrdhnā
trisahasra agnirucitaṃ api brahmalokāt |
sūdūrlabhā imi jinasya udārabodhiḥ
ye mānuṣyeṇa sukha labhyati evarūpam | | 18 | |

yāvattareṇa pavararṣiṇa jñānalābha-
stāvattaraṃ dukhamavīcikamutsahyami |
kiṃ vā punarvividhamānuṣaduḥkhaskandhaṃ
hantābhyupemi varadharmipadārthiduḥkham | | 19 | |

dharmaṃ ca śrutva puna yoniṣu cintayāti
dhyānāpramāṇa caturaśca tathā arūpyā |
pañcāpyabhijña pravarā abhinirharanti
nā cāpi teṣu vaśitā upapadya yāti | | 20 | |

atra sthitā guṇadharā bahubuddhakoṭyaḥ
pūjyanti niścitamanā śṛṇuvanti dharmam |
tanubhūtva mithyapagatāḥ pariśuddhayanti
svarṇe yathā vigatadoṣa pramāṇatulyam || 21 ||

atra sthitā guṇadharāstridaśādhipatyaṃ
kārenti īśvara nivartitu kāmarāgāḥ |
marusaṃgha nekavividhān kuśalāna mārge
sthāpentyananyamana buddhaguṇābhilāṣe || 22 ||

atra sthitā jinasutā viriyārabhante
labdhvā samādhina sahasraśataṃ anūnam |
paśyanti buddhavara lakṣaṇacitrigātrāṃ
bhūyo ataḥ praṇidhiśreṣṭha guṇāpramāṇāḥ || 23 ||

ityeṣā tṛtiyā bhūminirdiṣṭā sugatātmajāḥ |
sarvalokahitaiṣiṇāṃ bodhisattvānanuttamā || 24 ||

[End of third bhūmi's final gathas]

[Beginning of fourth bhūmi's initial gathas]

4 arciṣmatī nāma caturthī bhūmiḥ ।

upakramagāthāḥ ।

evaṃ śrūṇitva caraṇaṃ vipulaṃ
bhūmyuttamaṃ manuramaṃ pravaram ।
saṃharṣitā jinasutāttamanā
abhyokiranti kusumebhi jinam ।। 1 ।।

saṃkampitā lavaṇatoyadharā
iha dharmadeśanamudīrayatām ।
marukanyakā abhimanorucirāḥ
saṃgītiyukta varadharmaratāḥ ।। 2 ।।

vaśavarti devapatirāttamanā
maṇiratna divya sugatasya kṣipī ।
vācaṃ abhāṣi atha eva jino
utpanna artha guṇapāragato ।। 3 ।।

kiṃ kāraṇaṃ tatha hi dharmavaraṃ
saṃbodhisattvacaraṇaṃ paramam ।
bhūmirvidū na iyamadya śrutā
yasyāśravo durlabha kalpaśataiḥ ।। 4 ।।

bhūyaḥ prabhāṣa naradevahitā
caryāvarāṃ jinasutān vidū ।
śroṣyanti te marutasaṃghagaṇā
bhūtaṃ viniścayamananyapadam ।। 5 ।।

vimukticandraḥ punarvīro ālapī sugatātmajam ।
caturthī saṃkramantānāṃ gocaraṃ bhaṇa uttamam ।। 6 ।।

[End of fourth bhūmi's initial gathas]

4 arciṣmatī nāma caturthī bhūmiḥ |

A

vajragarbha āha - yo'yaṃ bhavanto jinaputrā bodhisattvastṛtīyāyāṃ bodhisattvabhūmau supariśuddhālokaścaturthī bodhisattvabhūmimākramati, sa daśabhirdharmālokapraveśairākramati | katamairdaśabhiḥ? yaduta sattvadhātuvicāraṇālokapraveśena ca lokadhātuvicaraṇālokapraveśena ca dharmadhātuvicāraṇālokapraveśena ākāśadhātuvicāraṇālokapraveśena ca vijñānadhātuvicāraṇā lokapraveśena ca kāmadhātuvicaraṇālokapraveśena ca rūpadhātuvicaraṇālokapraveśena ca ārūpyadhātuvicaraṇālokapraveśena udārāśayādhimuktidhātuvicaraṇālokapraveśena ca māhātmyāśayādhimuktidhātuvicaraṇālokapraveśena | ebhirdaśabhirdharmālokapraveśairākramati | |

B

tatra bhavanto jinaputrā arciṣmatyā bodhisattvabhūmeḥ sahapratilambhena bodhisattvaḥ saṃvṛtto bhavati tathāgatakule tadātmakadharmapratilambhāya daśabhirjñānaparipācakairdharmaiḥ | katamairdaśabhiḥ? yaduta apratyudāvartyāśayatayā ca triratnābhedyaprasādaniṣṭhāgamanatayā ca saṃskārodayavyayavibhāvanatayā ca svabhāvānutpattyāśayatayā ca lokapravṛttinivṛttyāśayatayā ca karmabhavopapattyāśayatayā ca saṃsāranirvāṇāśayatayā ca sattvakṣetrakarmāśayatayā ca pūrvāntāparāntāśayatayā abhāvakṣayāśayatayā ca | ebhirbhavanto jinaputrā daśabhirjñānaparipācakairdharmaiḥ samanvāgato bodhisattvaḥ saṃvṛtto bhavati tathāgatakule tadātmakadharmapratilambhāya |

C

sa khalu punarbhavanto jinaputrā bodhisattvo'syāmarciṣmatyāṃ bodhisattvabhūmau pratiṣṭhito'dhyātmaṃ kāye kāyānudarśī viharati ātāpī saṃprajānan smṛtimān vinīya loke'bhidhyādaurmanasye bahirdhā kāye...adhyātmaṃ bahirdhā kāye | evamevādhyātmaṃ vedanāsu bahirdhā vedanāsu adhyātmaṃ bahirdhā vedanāsu | evamadhyātmaṃ citte bahirdhā citte'dhyātmaṃ citte | adhyātmaṃ dharmeṣu dharmānudarśī...bahirdhā dharmeṣu dharmānudarśī...evamadhyātmaṃ bahirdhā dharmeṣu... | so'nutpannānāṃ pāpakānāmakuśalānāṃ dharmāṇāmanutpādāya cchandaṃ janayati vyāyacchate vīryamārabhate cittaṃ pragṛhṇāti samyakpraṇidadhāti

| utpannānāṃ pāpakānāmakuśalānāṃ dharmāṇāṃ prahāṇāya... | anutpannānāṃ kuśalānāṃ dharmāṇāmutpādāya... | utpannānāṃ kuśalānāṃ dharmāṇāṃ sthitaye'saṃpramoṣāya vaipulyāya bhūyobhāvāya bhāvanāya paripūraye... | chandasamādhiprahāṇa-saṃskārasamanvāgataṃ ṛddhipādaṃ bhāvayati vivekaniśritaṃ virāganiśritaṃ nirodhaniśritaṃ vyavasargapariṇataṃ vīrya-pariṇataṃ cittapariṇataṃ mīmāṃsāpariṇatam | sa śraddhendriyaṃ bhāvayati vivekaniśritaṃ...vīryendriyaṃ...smṛtīndriyaṃ...-samādhīndriyaṃ...prajñendriyaṃ...sa | śraddhābalaṃ bhāvayati...vīryabalaṃ...smṛtibalaṃ...samādhibalaṃ...prajñābalaṃ... | smṛtisaṃbodhyaṅgaṃ bhāvayati dharmapravicaya...vīrya...prīti-...prasrabdhi...samādhi...upekṣā... | samyakdṛṣṭiṃ bhāvayati-...samyaksaṃkalpaṃ...samyagvācaṃ...samyakkarmāntaṃ...samyagājī vaṃ...samyagvyāyāmaṃ...samyaksmṛtiṃ...samyaksamādhiṃ... | |

D

tacca sarvasattvasāpekṣatayā ca pūrvapraṇidhānābhinirhār-opastabdhatayā ca mahākaruṇāpūrvaṃgamatayā ca mahāmaitry-upetatayā ca sarvajñajñānādhyālambanatayā ca buddhakṣetraviṭha-panālaṃkārābhinirhāratayā ca tathāgatabalavaiśāradyāveṇika-buddhadharmalakṣaṇānuvyañjanasvaraghoṣasaṃpadabhinirhāratay ā ca uttarottaravaiśeṣikadharmaparimārgaṇatayā ca gambhīra-buddhadharmavimokṣaśravaṇānugamanatayā ca mahopāya-kauśalyabalavicāraṇatayā ca |

E

tasya khalu punarbhavanto jinaputrā bodhisattvasya asyām-arciṣmatyāṃ bodhisattvabhūmau sthitasya yānīmāni satkāyadṛṣṭipūrvaṃgamāni ātmasattvajīvapoṣapudgalaskandha-dhātvāyatanābhiniveśasamucchritāni unmiñjitāni nimiñjitāni vicintitāni vitarkitāni kelāyitāni mamāyitāni dhanāyitāni niketa-sthānāni, tāni sarvāṇi vigatāni bhavanti sma |

F

sa yānīmāni karmāṇyakaraṇīyāni samyaksaṃbuddhavivarṇitāni saṃkleśopasaṃhitāni, tāni sarveṇa sarvaṃ prajahāti | yāni cemāni karmāṇi karaṇīyāni samyaksaṃbuddhapraśastāni bodhimārga-saṃbhārānukūlāni, tāni samādāya vartate |

G

sa bhūyasyā mātrayā yathā yathopāyaprajñābhinirhṛtāni mārgasamudāgamāya mārgāṅgāni bhāvayati, tathā tathā snigdhacittaśca bhavati, maducittaśca karmaṇyacittaśca hitasukhāvahacittaśca apariklişṭacittaśca uttarottaraviśeṣaparimārgaṇacittaśca jñāna-viśeṣaṇābhilāṣacittaśca sarvajagatparitrāṇacittaśca gurugauravānukūlacittaśca yathāśrutadharmapratipatticittaśca bhavati |

H

sa kṛtajñaśca bhavati, kṛtavedī ca sūrataśca sukhasaṃvāsaśca ṛjuśca mṛduśca agahanacārī ca nirmāyanirmāṇaśca suvacāśca pradakṣiṇagrāhī ca bhavati | sa evaṃ kṣamopeta evaṃ damopeta evaṃ śamopeta evaṃ kṣamadamaśamopeta uttarāṇi bhūmipariśodhakāni mārgāṅgāni manasi kurvāṇaḥ samudācaran

I

aprasrabdhavīryaśca bhavati apariklişṭaḥ | apratyudāvartyavīryaśca vipulavīryaśca anantavīryaśca uttaptavīryaśca asamavīryaśca asaṃhāryavīryaśca sarvasattvaparipācanavīryaśca nayānayavibhaktavīryaśca bhavati |

J

tasya bhūyasyā mātrayā āśayadhātuśca viśuddhyati, adhyāśayadhātuśca na vipravasati, adhimuktidhātuścottapyate, kuśalamūlavivṛddhiścopajāyate, lokamalakaṣāyatā cāpagacchati, sarv asaṃśayavimatisaṃdehāścāsyocchidyante, niṣkāṅkṣābhimukhatā ca paripūryate, prītiprasabdhī ca samudāgacchati, tathāgatādhiṣṭhānaṃ cābhimukhībhavati, apramāṇacittāśayatā ca samudāgacchāti | |

K

tasya asyāmarciṣmatyāṃ bodhisattvabhūmau sthitasya bodhisattvasya...peyālaṃ... | bhūyastvena ca teṣāṃ tathāgatānāṃ śāsane pravrajati | tasya bhūyasyā mātrayā āśayādhyāśayādhimuktisamatā viśudhyati | tasya asyāmarciṣmatyāṃ bodhisattvabhūmau sthitasya bodhisattvasya...āśayādhyāśayādhimuktisamatāviśuddhi stiṣṭhati, tāni cāsya kuśalamūlāni sūttaptāni prabhāsvaratarāṇi ca bhavanti | tadyathāpi nāma bhavanto jinaputrāstadeva jātarūpaṃ kuśalena karmāreṇābharaṇīkṛtamasaṃhāryaṃ bhavati tadanyairakṛtābharaṇairjātarūpaiḥ, evameva bhavanto jinaputrā bodhisattvasya asyāmarciṣmatyāṃ bodhisattvabhūmau sthitasya tāni kuśalamūlānyasaṃhāryāṇi bhavanti tadanyeṣāmadharabhūmisthitānāṃ bodhisattvānāṃ kuśalamūlaiḥ |

tadyathāpi nāma bhavanto jinaputrā maṇiratnaṃ jātaprabhaṃ pariśu ddharaśmimaṇḍalamālokapramuktamasaṃhāryaṃ bhavati tadanyai-rapi śuddhaprabhai ratnajātaiḥ, anācchedyaprabhaṃ ca bhavati sarvamārutodakapravarṣaiḥ, evameva bhavanto jinaputrā bodhisattvo'syāmarciṣmatyāṃ bodhisattvabhūmau sthitaḥ sanna-saṃhāryo bhavati tadanyairadharabhūmisthitairbodhisattvaiḥ, anācchedyajñānaśca bhavati sarvamārakleśasamudācāraiḥ । tasya caturbhyaḥ saṃgrahavastubhyaḥ samānārthatā atiriktatamā bhavati । daśabhyaḥ pāramitābhyo vīryapāramitā atiriktatamā bhavati, na ca pariśeṣāsu na samudāgacchati yathābalaṃ yathābhajamānam । iyaṃ bhavanto jinaputrā bodhisattvasyārciṣmatī nāma caturthī bhūmiḥ samāsanirdeśataḥ, yasyāṃ pratiṣṭhito bodhisattvo bhūyastvena suyāmo bhavati devarājaḥ kṛtī prabhuḥ sattvānāṃ satkāyadṛṣṭi-samuddhātāya kuśalaḥ sattvān samyagdarśane pratiṣṭhāpayitum । yacca kiṃcit........॥

arciṣmatī nāma caturthī bhūmiḥ ॥

[Beginning of fourth bhūmi's final gathas]

upasaṃhāragāthāḥ |

parikarmitā tṛtīyabhūmiprabhaṃkarāya
sattvacaryaloka tatha dharma vicāryamāṇaḥ |
ākāśadhātu manadhātu trayaśca dhātu
adhimukti āśaya viśuddhi samākramanti | | 7 | |

sahaprāptu arciṣmati bhūmi mahānubhāvaḥ
saṃvṛttu śāstu kulu bhūyu vivartiyatve |
abhedya buddharatane tatha dharmasaṃghe
udayavyayasthiti nirīhaka prekṣamāṇaḥ | | 8 | |

lokapravṛtti kriyakarma bhavopapattiṃ
saṃsāranirvṛtivibhāvana kṣetrasattvān |
dharmāñca pūrvamaparānta kṣayānutpādaṃ
saṃvṛttu bhāvayati śāstu kulānuvartī | | 9 | |

so eṣu dharmu samupetu hitānukampī
bhāveti kāyamapi vedana cittadharmān |
adhyātmabāhyubhayathā vidu bhāvayāti
smṛtyopasthānabhāvana niketavarjitā | | 10 | |

pāpakṣayātkuśaladharmavivardhitā ca
samyakprahāṇa caturo vidu bhāvayanti |
caturddhipāda bala indriya bhāvayanti
bodhyaṅgaratna ruciraṃ tatha mārga śreṣṭham | | 11 | |

bhāventi tān janayatāṃ samavekṣya buddhim
upastambhayanti praṇidhiṃ kṛtapūrvamaitrāḥ |
sarvajñajñānamabhiprārthana buddhakṣetraṃ
balaśreṣṭhamuttamapathaṃ anucintayantaḥ | | 12 | |

vaiśāradaṃ api ca dharma ahārya śāstuḥ
varavuddhaghoṣamabhiprārthayamāna dhīrāḥ |
gambhīramārgaratanaṃ ca vimokṣasthānaṃ

mahatāmupāya samudāgama bhāvayanti | | 13 | |

satkāyadṛṣṭivigatāśca dviṣaṣṭidṛṣṭī
attāttamīyavigatāstatha jīvalābham |
skandhāstu dvāra tatha dhātuniketasthānaṃ
sarvaprahāṇa viduṣaṃ catuthāya bhūmyām | | 14 | |

so yānimāni sugatena vivarṇitāni
karmāṇi kleśasahajāni anarthakāni |
tāni prahāya vidu āśayato viśuddhā
dharmārabhanti kuśalaṃ jaga–tāyaṇārtham | | 15 | |

susnigdhacitta bhavatī vidu apramatto
mṛducittu sārjava hitāsukhaāvahaśca |
aparikliṣṭaśca parimārgati uttamārthaṃ
jñānābhiṣekamabhilāṣi jagārthacārī | | 16 | |

gurugauraveṣupagataḥ pratipattikāmo
bhavate kṛtajña sumanāśca akūhakāśca |
nirmāyatāgahana āśayasūrataśca
avivartyavīryu bhavate samudānayantaḥ | | 17 | |

tasyātra bhūmi rucirāya pratiṣṭhitasya
adhyāśayaṃ api ca śuddhamupeti dharmam |
adhimukti tapyati vivardhati śukladharmo
malakalmaṣaṃ vimati śaṃśaya sarva yānti | | 18 | |

atra sthitā naravararṣabha bodhisattvāḥ
sugatānanekanayutānabhipūjayanti |
śṛṇvanti dharma yatha śāsani pravrajanti
asaṃhārya śakya kṛtakāñcanabhūṣaṇaṃ vā | | 19 | |

atra sthitāna vidunā guṇamāśayaṃ ca
jñānaṃ upāya caraṇaṃ ca viśuddhimārgaḥ |
no śakyu māranayutebhi nivartanāya
ratnaprabheva yatha varṣajalairahāryā | | 20 | |

atra sthitā naramarudgaṇapūjanārhā
bhontī suyāmapatirīśvara dharmacārī |
sattvāni dṛṣṭigahanādvinivartayanti
saṃbhārayanti kuśalā jinajñānahetoḥ || 21 ||

viryopapeta śatakoṭi mararṣabhāṇāṃ
paśyantyananyamanasaḥ susamāhitatvāt |
tata uttariṃ bahukalpamabhinirharanti
jñānākarā praṇidhiśreṣṭha guṇārthacārī || 22 ||

caturthī itiyaṃ bhūmirviśuddhā śubhacāriṇī |
guṇārthajñānayuktānāṃ nirdiṣṭā sugatātmajāḥ || 23 ||

[End of fourth bhūmi's final gathas]

[Beginning of fifth bhūmi's initial gathas]

5 sudurjayā nāma pañcamī bhūmiḥ ।

upakramagāthāḥ ।

caraṇamatha śruṇitvā bhūmiśreṣṭhāṃ vidūnāṃ
jinasuta parituṣṭā harṣitā dharmahetoḥ ।
gagani kusumavarṣaṃ utsṛjantī udagrāḥ
sādhu sugataputra vyāhṛtaṃ te mahātmā ।। 1 ।।

marupati vaśavartī sārdha devāgaṇena
svagagata sugatasya pūjānārthaṃ udagrā ।
vividharucirameghāḥ snigdhaābhā manojñāḥ
abhikira sugatasya harṣitāḥ prīṇitāśca ।। 2 ।।

gītaruta manojñā vādyatūryābhinādā
devavadhuprayuktāḥ śāstu saṃpūjanārtham ।
jina puna tatharūpaṃ darśayanti sma sthānaṃ
sarvarutasvarebhī eva śabdaḥ prayuktaḥ ।। 3 ।।

sucireṇa āśayu prapūrṇa muneḥ
sucireṇa bodhi śiva prāpta jinaḥ ।
sucireṇa dṛṣṭa naradevahitaḥ
saṃprāpta devapuri śākyamuniḥ ।। 4 ।।

sucireṇa sāgarajalāḥ kṣubhitāḥ
sucireṇa ābha śubha munni jane ।
sucireṇa sattva sukhitāḥ -
sucireṇa śāsu śruta kāruṇikaḥ ।। 5 ।।

sucireṇa saṃgamu mahāmuninā
saṃprāpta sarvagūṇapāramitaḥ ।
mada māna darpa prajahitva tamaṃ
pūjārhu pūjima mahāśramaṇam ।। 6 ।।

(iha pūji kṛtva khagamārgagatā)
iha pūji kṛtva sukha nekavidham |
iha pūji kṛtva dukhasarvakṣaye
iha pūji kṛtva jina jñānavaram || 7 ||

gaganopamaḥ paramuśuddhu jinu
jagatī aliptu yatha padmu jale |
abhyudgato udadhi meruriva
harṣitva cittu jina pūjayathā || 8 ||

athābravīdvajragarbhaṃ vimukticandro viśāradaḥ |
pañcamyā bhūmya ākarān nirdiśasva viśārada || 10 ||

[End of fifth bhūmi's initial gathas]

5 sudurjayā nāma pañcamī bhūmiḥ ।

A

vajragarbha āha - yo'yaṃ bhavanto jinaputrā bodhisattvaścaturthyāṃ bodhisattvabhūmau suparipūrṇamārgaḥ pañcamīṃ bodhisattvabhūmimavatarati, sa daśabhiścittāśayaviśuddhisamatābhiravatarati । katamābhirdaśabhiḥ? yaduta atītabuddhadharmaviśuddhyāśayasamatayā ca anāgatabuddhadharmaviśuddhyāśayasamatayā ca pratyutpannabuddhadharmaviśuddhyāśayasamatayā ca śīlaviśuddhyāśayasamatayā ca cittaviśuddhyāśayasamatayā ca dṛṣṭikāṅkṣāvimativilekhāpanayanaviśuddhyāśayasamatayā ca mārgāmārgajñānaviśuddhyāśayasamatayā ca pratipatprahāṇājñānaviśuddhyāśayasamatayā ca sarvabodhipakṣyadharmottarottaravibhāvanaviśuddhyāśayasamatayā ca sarvasattvaparipācanaviśuddhyāśayasamatayā ca । ābhirdaśabhiścittāśayaviśuddhisamatābhiravatarati ।

B

sa khalu punarbhavanto jinaputrā bodhisattvaḥ pañcamīṃ bodhisattvabhūmimanuprāptaḥ eṣāmeva bodhipakṣyāṇāṃ mārgāṅgānāṃ suparikarmakṛtatvātsupariśodhitādhyāśayatvācca bhūya uttarakālamārgaviśeṣamabhiprārthayamānastathatvānupratipannaśca praṇidhānabalādhānataśca kṛpāmaitrībhyāṃ sarvasattvāparityāgataśca puṇyavijñānasaṃbhāropacayataśca apratiprasrabdhitaśca upāyakauśalyābhinirhārataśca uttarottarabhūmyavabhāsālocanataśca tathāgatādhiṣṭhānasaṃpratyeṣaṇataśca smṛtimatigatibuddhibalādhānataśca apratyudāvartanīyamanasikāro bhūtvā

C

idaṃ duḥkhamāryasatyamiti yathābhūtaṃ prajānāti । ayaṃ duḥkhasamudayaḥ āryasatyamiti yathābhūtaṃ prajānāti । ayaṃ duḥkhanirodhaḥ āryasatyamiti yathābhūtaṃ prajānāti । iyaṃ duḥkhanirodhagāminī pratipadāryasatyamiti yathābhūtaṃ prajānāti । sa saṃvṛtisatyakuśalaśca bhavati । paramārthasatyakuśalaśca bhavati । lakṣaṇasatyakuśalaśca bhavati । vibhāgasatyakuśalaśca bhavati । nistīraṇasatyakuśalaśca bhavati । vastusatyakuśalaśca bhavati । prabhavasatyakuśalaśca bhavati । kṣayānutpādasatyakuśalaśca bhavati । mārgajñānāvatārasatyakuśalaśca bhavati । sarvabodhisattvabhūmikramānusaṃdhiniṣpādanatayā yāvattathāgatajñānasamudayasatyakuśalaśca bhavati I sa parasattvānāṃ yathāśayasaṃtoṣaṇātsaṃvṛti-satyaṃ prajānāti I ekanayasamavasaraṇātparamārthasatyaṃ prajānāti I svasāmanyalakṣaṇānubodhāllakṣaṇasatyaṃ prajānāti I dharmavibhāgavyavasthānānubodhādvibhāgasatyaṃ prajānāti I skandhadhātvāyatanavyavasthānānubodhānnistīraṇasatyaṃ prajānāti I cittaśarīraprapīḍanopanipātitatvādvastusatyam, gati-saṃdhisaṃbandhanatvātprabhavasatyam, sarvajvaraparidāhātyantopaśamātkṣayānutpādasatyam, advayānutpādasatyam, advayābhinirhāranmārgajñānāvatārasatyam, sarvākārābhisaṃbodhitsarvabodhisattvabhūmikramānusaṃdhiniṣpādanatayā yāvattathāgatajñānasamudayasatyaṃ prajānāti adhimuktijñānabalādhānānna khalu punarniravaśeṣajñānāt I I

D

sa evaṃ satyakauśalyajñānābhinirhṛtayā buddhyā sarvasaṃskṛtaṃ riktaṃ tucchaṃ mṛṣā moṣadharma avisaṃvādakaṃ bālālāpanamiti yathābhūtaṃ prajānāti I tasya bhūyasyā mātrayā sattveṣu mahākaruṇā abhimukhībhavati, mahāmaitryālokaśca prādurbhavati I I

E

sa evaṃ jñānabalādhanaprāptaḥ sarvasattvasāpekṣo buddhajñānābhilāṣī pūrvāntāparāntaṃ sarvasaṃskāragatasya pratyavekṣate yathā pūrvāntato'vidyābhavatṛṣṇāprasṛtānāṃ sattvānāṃ saṃsārasroto'nuvāhināṃ skandhālayānucchalitānāṃ duḥkhaskandho vivardhate, nirātmā niḥsattvo nirjīvo niṣpoṣo niṣpudgala ātmātmīyavigataḥ, taṃ yathābhūtaṃ prajānāti I yathā ca anāgatasyaiva asatsaṃmohābhilāṣasya vyavacchedaḥ paryanto niḥsaraṇaṃ nāstyasti ca, tacca yathābhūtaṃ prajānāti I I

F

tasyaivaṃ bhavati - āścaryaṃ yāvadajñānasamūḍhā bateme bālapṛthagjanāḥ, yeṣāmasaṃkhyeyā ātmabhāvā niruddhāḥ, nirudhyante nirotsyante ca I evaṃ ca kṣīyamāṇāḥ kāye na nirvidamutpādayanti I bhūyasyā mātrayā duḥkhayantraṃ vivardhayanti I saṃsārasrotasaśca mahābhayānna nivartante I skandhālayaṃ ca notsṛjanti I dhātūragebhyaśca ga nirvidyante I nandīrāgataścārakaṃ ca nāvabudhyante I ṣaḍāyatanaśūnyagrāmaṃ ca na vyavalokayanti I ahaṃkāramamakārābhiniveśānuśayaṃ ca na prajahanti I mānadṛṣṭiśalyaṃ ca noddharanti I rāgadveṣamohajvalanaṃ ca na praśamayanti I avidyāmohāndhakāraṃ ca na vidhamayanti I tṛṣṇārṇavaṃ ca nocchoṣayanti । daśabalasārthavāhaṃ ca na paryeṣante । mārāśaya-gahanānugataśca saṃsārasāgare vividhākuśalavitarkagrāhākule pariplavante ।

G

apratiśaraṇāstathā saṃvegamāpadyante, bahūni duḥkhāni pratyanubhavanti yaduta jātijarāvyādhimaraṇaśokaparidevaduḥkha-daurmanasyopāyāsān । hanta ahameṣāṃ sattvānāṃ duḥkhārt-ānāmanāthānāmatrāṇānāmaśaraṇānāmalayanānāmaparāyaṇānāman dhānāmavidyāṇḍakośapaṭalaparyavanaddhānāṃ tamobhi-bhūtānāmarthāya eko'dvitīyo bhūtvā tathārūpaṃ puṇyajñānasaṃ-bhāropacayaṃ bibharmi, yathārūpeṇa puṇyajñānasaṃbhār-opacayena saṃbhṛtena ime sarvasattvā atyantaviśuddhim-anuprāpnuyuḥ, yāvaddaśabalabalatāmasaṅgajñānaniṣṭhām-anuprāpnuyuriti ॥

H

sa evaṃ suvilokitajñānābhinirhṛtayā buddhyā yatkiṃcit kuśalamūla-bhārabhate, tatsarvasattvaparitrāṇāyārabhate । sarvasattvahitāya sarvasattvasukhāya sarvasattvānukampāyai sarvasattvānupadravāya sarvasattvaparimocanāya sarvasattvānukarṣāya sarvasattvaprasād-anāya sarvasattvavinayāya sarvasattvaparinirvāṇāyārabhate ॥

I

sa bhūyasyā mātrayā asyāṃ pañcamyāṃ sudurjayāyāṃ bodhisattva-bhūmau sthito bodhisattvaḥ smṛtimāṃśca bhavati, asaṃpramoṣa-dharmatayā matimāṃśca bhavati, suviniścitajñānatayā gatimāṃśca bhavati, sūtrārthagatisaṃdhāyabhāṣitāvabodhatayā hrīmāṃśca bhavati, ātmaparānurakṣaṇatayā dhṛtimāṃśca bhavati, saṃvara-cāritrānutsargatayā buddhimāṃśca bhavati, sthānāsthānakauśalya-suvicāritatayā jñānānugataśca bhavati, aparapraṇeyatayā prajñānu-gataśca bhavati, arthānarthasaṃbhedapadakuśalatayā abhijñānir-hāraprāptaśca bhavati, bhāvanābhinirhārakuśalatayā upāyakuśalaśca bhavati lokānuvartanatayā ।

J

atṛptaśca bhavati puṇyasaṃbhāropacayatayā । apratiprasrabdha-vīryaśca bhavati jñānasaṃbhāraparyeṣaṇatayā । aparikhinnāśayaśca bhavati mahāmaitrīkṛpāsaṃbhārasaṃbhṛtatayā । aśithilaparyeṣaṇ-ābhiyuktaśca bhavati tathāgatabalavaiśāradyāveṇikabuddhadharma-paryeṣaṇatayā । svabhinirhṛtamanasikārānugataśca bhavati buddhakṣetraviṭhapanālaṃkārābhinirhṛtatayā I vicitrakuśalakriyābhiyuktaś-ca bhavati lakṣaṇānuvyañjanasamudānayanatayā I satatasamitaṃ svabhiyuktaśca bhavati tathāgatakāyavākcittālaṃkāraparyeṣaṇatayā I mahāgauravopasthānaśīlaśca bhavati sarvabodhisattvadharma-bhaṇākaśuśrūṣaṇatayā I apratihatacittaśca bhavati bodhicittamah-opāyakauśalyasaṃdhyupasaṃhitalokapracāratayā I rātriṃdiva-manyacittaparivarjitaśca bhavati sarvasattvaparipācanābhiyogatayā I I

K

sa evamabhiyukto dānenāpi sattvān paripācayati, priyavadyatayāpi, arthakriyayāpi, samānārthatayāpi, rūpakāyasaṃdarśanenāpi, dharmadeśanayāpi, bodhisattvacaryāprabhāvanayāpi, tathāgata-māhātmyaprakāśanatayāpi, saṃsāradoṣasaṃdarśanenāpi, buddha-jñānānuśaṃsāparikīrtanenāpi, maharddhivikurvaṇābhinirhāraṇ-ānopacārakriyāprayogairapi sattvān paripācayati I sa evaṃ sattva-paripācanābhiyukto buddhajñānānugatacittasaṃtāno'pratyud-āvartanīyakuśalamūlaprayogo vaiśeṣikadharmaparimārgaṇābhi-yuktaḥ

L

yānīmāni sattvahitāni loke pracaranti, tadyathā – lipiśāstramudrāsaṃkhyāgaṇanānikṣepādīni nānādhātutantracikitsā-tantrāṇi śoṣāpasmārabhūtagrahapratiṣedhakāni viṣavetālaprayoga-pratighātakāni kāvyanāṭakākhyānagāndharvetihāsasaṃpraharṣaṇāni grāmanagarodyānanadīsarastaḍāgapuṣkariṇīpuṣpaphalauṣadhivana ṣaṇḍābhinirhārāṇi suvarṇarūpyamaṇimuktāvaiḍūryaśaṅkhaśilā-pravālaratnākaranidarśanāni candrasūryagrahajyotirnakṣatrabhūmi-cālamṛgaśakunisvapnanimittāni pradeśapraveśāni sarvāṅgapraty-aṅgalakṣaṇāni cārānucāraprayoganimittāni saṃvaracāritrasthāna-dhyānābhijñāpramāṇārūpyasthānāni, yāni cānyānyapi aviheṭhan-āvihiṃsāsaṃprayuktāni sarvasattvahitasukhāvahāni, tānyapyabhi-nirharati kāruṇikatayā anupūrvabuddhadharmapratiṣṭhāpanāya I I

M

tasya asyāṃ sudurjayāyāṃ bodhisattvabhūmau sthitasya bodhi-sattvasya....peyālaṃ...pariṇāmayati I tāṃśca tathāgatānarhataḥ samyaksaṃbuddhān paryupāsate, teṣāṃ ca sakāśād gaurava-citrīkāreṇa satkṛtya dharmadeśanāṃ śṛṇoti udgṛhṇāti dhārayati I śrutvā ca yathābalaṃ yathābhajamānaṃ pratipatyā saṃpādayati I bhūyastvena ca teṣāṃ tathāgatānāṃ śāsane pravrajati । pravrajitaśca śrutadhārī dharmabhāṇako bhavati । sa bhūyasyā mātrayā śrutācāra-dhāraṇīpratilabdho dharmabhāṇako bhavati anekeṣāṃ ca buddha-koṭiniyutaśatasahasrāṇāmantike anekakalpakoṭiniyutaśatasahasrāṇy-asaṃpramoṣatayā । tasya asyāṃ sudurjayāyāṃ bodhisattvabhūmau sthitasya anekān kalpāṃstāni kuśalamūlānyuttapyante pari-śudhyanti prabhāsvaratarāṇi ca bhavanti, anekāni kalpaśatāni... । tasya tāni kuśalamūlānyuttapyante pariśuddhyanti prabhāsva-ratarāṇi ca bhavanti । tadyathāpi nāma bhavanto jinaputrāstadeva jātarūpaṃ musārgalvasṛṣṭaṃ bhūyasyā mātrayottapyate pari-śudhyati prabhāsvarataraṃ bhavati, evameva bhavanto jinaputrā bodhisattvasya asyāṃ sudurjayāyāṃ bodhisattvabhūmau sthitasya tāni kuśalamūlānyupāyaprajñāvicāritāni bhūyasyā mātrayottapyante pariśuddhyanti, prabhāsvaratarāṇi ca bhavanti, jñānaprayogaguṇ-ābhinirhārādasaṃhāryavicāritatamāni ca bhavanti । tadyathāpi nāma bhavanto jinaputrāścandrasūryagrahajyotirnakṣatrāṇāṃ vimānāloka-prabhavātamaṇḍalībhirasaṃhāryā bhavati mārutāsādhāraṇā ca, evameva bhavanto jinaputrā bodhisattvasya asyāṃ sudurjayāyāṃ bodhisattvabhūmau sthitasya tāni kuśalamūlānyupāyaprajñājñāna-cittavicāraṇānugatānyasaṃhāryāṇi bhavanti, sarvaśrāvakapratyeka-buddhairlaukikāsādhāraṇāni ca bhavanti । tasya daśabhyaḥ pāra-mitābhyo dhyānapāramitā atiriktatamā bhavati, na ca pariśeṣāsu na samudāgacchati yathābalaṃ yathābhajamānam । iyaṃ bhavanto jinaputrā bodhisattvasya sudurjayā nāma pañcamī bodhisattva-bhūmiḥ samāsanirdeśataḥ, yasyāṃ pratiṣṭhito bodhisattvo bhūyastvena saṃtuṣito bhavati, devarājaḥ kṛtī prabhuḥ sattvānāṃ sarvatīrthyāyatanavinivartanāya kuśalaḥ sattvān satyeṣu prati-ṣṭhāpayitum । yatkiṃcit..... ॥

sudurjayā nām pañcamī bhūmiḥ ॥

[Beginning of fifth bhūmi's final gathas]

upasaṃhāragāthāḥ |

evaṃ viśodhita caturṣu jinacarīṣu
buddhayā triyādhvasamatā anucintayanti |
śīlaṃ ca cittapratipattitu mārgaśuddhiḥ
kāṅkṣāvinīta vidu pañcami ākramanti || 11 ||

smṛti cāpa indriya iṣu anivartitāśca
samyakprahāṇa haya vāhana ṛddhipādāḥ |
pañca balāḥ kavaca sarvapipūabhebyāḥ
śūrāṇivarti vidu pañcami ākramanti || 12 ||

hyapatrāpyavastravidunāṃ śuciśīlagandho
bodhyaṅgamālyavaradhyānavilepanaṃ ca |
prajñāvicāraṇavibhūṣaṇupāyaśreṣṭham
udyānadhāraṇita pañcamimākramanti || 13 ||

caturddhipādacaraṇāḥ smṛtiśuddhigrīvāḥ
kṛpamaitraśreṣṭhanayanā varaprajñadaṃṣṭrā |
nairātmyanāda ripukleśa pradharṣamāṇā
narasiṃha samya vidu pañcamimākramanti || 14 ||

te pañcamīmupagatā varabhūmiśreṣṭhāṃ
pariśuddhamārga śubhamuttari bhāvayanti |
śuddhāśayā vidu jinatvanuprāpaṇārthī
kṛpamaitrakhedavigatā anucintayanti || 15 ||

saṃbhārapuṇyupacayā tatha jñāna śreṣṭhaṃ
naikā upāya abhirocanabhūmya bhāsān |
buddhadhiṣṭhāna smṛtimāṃ matibuddhiprāptā
cattvāri satya nikhilānanucintayanti || 16 ||

paramārthasatyamapi saṃvṛtilakṣaṇaṃ ca
satyavibhāgamatha satyanitīraṇaṃ ca |

tatha vastu sāsrava kṣayaṃ api mārgasatyaṃ
yāvantanāvaraṇasatya samosaranti || 17 ||

evaṃ ca satya parimārgati sūkṣmabuddhiḥ
na ca tāvadanāvaraṇaprāptu vimokṣaṃ śreṣṭham |
jñānādhimuktivipulāttu guṇākarāṇām
atibhonti sarvajagato arhapratyayānām || 18 ||

so eva satyaabhinirhṛta tattvabuddhiḥ
jānāti saṃskṛta mṛṣāprakṛtī asāram |
kṛpamaitraābha labhate sugatāna bhūyaḥ
sattvārthikaḥ sugatajñāna gaveṣamāṇaḥ || 19 ||

pūrvāpare vidu nirīkṣatu saṃskṛtasya
mohāndhakāratamasāvṛta duḥkhalagnā |
abhyuddharoti jagato dukhaskandhavṛddhān
nairātmyajīvarahitāṃstṛṇakāṣṭhatulyān || 20 ||

kleśādvayena yugapatpunarbhāsi tryadhvaṃ
chedo dukhasya na ca anta samosarantaḥ |
hanto praṇaṣṭa jana te'tidayābhijātā
saṃsārasrota na nivartati niḥsvabhāvam || 21 ||

skandhālayā uragadhātu kudṛṣṭiśalyāḥ
saṃtapta agnihṛdayāvṛta andhakāre |
tṛṣṇārṇavaprapatitā avalokanatvāt
jinasārthavāhavirahā dukhaarṇavasthāḥ || 22 ||

evaṃ viditva punarārabhate'pramatto
taccaiva ārabhati sarvajagadvimokṣī |
smṛtimantu bhonti matimān gatimān dhṛtīṃ ca
hrīmāṃśca bhonti tatha buddhina prajñavāṃśca || 23 ||

avitṛptu puṇyupacaye tatha jñāna śreṣṭhaṃ
no khedavānna śithilo balameṣamāṇaḥ |
kṣetraṃ vidhāya jinalakṣaṇabuddhaghoṣam
avitṛptasarvakriya sattvahitārthayuktaḥ || 24 ||

paripācanāya jagato vidu śilpasthānān
lipimudrasaṃkhyagaṇadhātucikitsatantrān |
bhūtagrahāviṣamaroganivartanārthaṃ
sthāpenti śastra rucirān kṛpamaitrabuddhī || 25 ||

varakāvyanāṭakamatiṃ vividhapraharṣān
nadyodiyānaphalapuṣpanipadyasthānān |
sthāpenti nekakriya sattvasukhāpanārthaṃ
ratnākarāṃśca upadarśayi naikarūpān || 26 ||

bhūmīcalaṃ ca graha jyotiṣa candrasūryau
sarvāṅgalakṣaṇavicāraṇarājyasthānam |
ārūpyadhyāna tathabhijña athāpramāṇā
abhinirharanti hitasaukhyajagārthakāmāḥ || 27 ||

iha durjayāmupajatā varaprajñacārī
pūjenti buddha nayutā śṛṇuvanti dharmam |
teṣāṃ śubhaṃ punaruttapyati āśayaśca
svarṇaṃ yathā musaragalvayasaṃvimṛṣṭam || 28 ||

ratnāmayā grahavimān vahanti vātā
te yehi tehi tu vahanti asaṃhṛtāśca |
tatha lokadharmi caramāna jagārthacārī
asaṃhārya bhonti yatha padma jale aliptam || 29 ||

atra sthitā tuṣita īśvara te kṛtāvī
nāśenti tīrthyacaraṇān pṛthudṛṣṭisthānān |
yaccācaranti kuśalaṃ jinajñānahetoḥ
sattvāna trāta bhavamo daśabhirbalāḍhyaiḥ || 30 ||

te vīryamuttari samārabhi aramattāḥ
koṭisahasra sugatānabhipūjayanti |
labdhvā samādhi vidu kampayi kṣetrakoṭī
praṇidhīviśeṣu anubhūya guṇākarānām || 31 ||

ityeṣā pañcamī bhūmirvicitropāyakoṭibhiḥ |
nirdiṣṭā sattvasārāṇāmuttamā sugatātmajāḥ || 32 ||

[End of fifth bhūmi's final gathas]

[Beginning of sixth bhūmi's initial gathas]

6 abhimukhī nāma ṣaṣṭhī bhūmiḥ |

upakramagāthāḥ |

caraṇavara śruṇitvā bhūmiśreṣṭhaṃ vidūnāṃ
gagani sugataputrā harṣitāḥ puṣpavarṣī |
maṇiratana udārā ābhayuktā viśuddhā
abhikira sugatasya sādhviti vyāharantaḥ || 1 ||

maruta śatasahasrā harṣitā antarīkṣe
diviya rucira citrā ratnacūrṇā udārāḥ |
abhikira sugatebhyo gandhamālyānulepān
chatradhvajāpatākāhāracandrārdhahārān || 2 ||

marupati vaśavartī sarvadevagaṇena
upari khaga paṭhitvā megha ratnāmayāni |
abhikiriṣu prasannaḥ pūjanārthaṃ jinasya
sādhu sugataputrā vyāharī hṛṣṭacittāḥ || 3 ||

amaravadhusahasrāṇyantarīkṣe sthitāni
gīta ruta manojñā vādyasaṃgītiyuktā |
sarvarutasvarebhyo eva śabdā ravante
jina kṛtu sumanojñaiḥ kleśatāpasya hantā || 4 ||

śūnya prakṛtiśāntā sarvadharmānimittāḥ
khagapathasamatulyā nirvikalpā viśuddhāḥ |
gatisthitivinirvṛttā niṣprapañcā aśeṣā
tathatasama tathatvāddharmatā nirvikalpā || 5 ||

yaiḥ punaranubuddhāḥ sarvadharmeva teṣāṃ
bhāvi tatha abhāve iñjanā nāsti kācit |
kṛpa karuṇa jage ca mocanārthaṃ prayuktā-
ste hi sugataputrā aurasā dharmajātāḥ || 6 ||

dānacari carante sarva hitvā nimittaṃ
śīlasudhṛtacittāṃ ādiśāntā praśāntāḥ |
jagati kṛta kṣamante akṣayā dharmajñānī
viriyabalaupetāḥ sarvadharmāviviktāḥ || 7 ||

dhyānanayapraviṣṭā jīrṇakleśā viśuddhāḥ
sarvaviditavastū ādiśūnyādhimuktāḥ |
jñānakriyabalāḍhyā nityayuktā jagārthaṃ
te hi sugataputrāḥ śāntapāpā mahātmāḥ || 8 ||

īdṛśā rutasahasra bhaṇitvā
khe sthitāḥ sumadhurā surakanyāḥ |
tūṣṇibhūta jinamīkṣi prasannā
dharmagauravaratā marukanyāḥ || 9 ||

vimukticandra abravīdvajragarbhaṃ viśāradam |
kīdṛśākāraniṣpattiḥ pañcamāyāmanantaram || 10 ||

[End of sixth bhūmi's initial gathas]

6 abhimukhī nāma ṣaṣṭhī bhūmiḥ ।

A

vajragarmo bodhisattva āha - yo'yaṃ bhavanto jinaputrā bodhisattvaḥ pañcamyāṃ bodhisattvabhūmau suparipūrṇamārgaḥ ṣaṣṭhīṃ bodhisattvabhūmimavatarati । sa daśabhirdharmasamatābhiravatarati । katamābhirdaśabhiḥ? yaduta sarvadharmānimittasamatayā ca sarvadharmālakṣaṇasamatayā ca sarvadharmānutpādasamatayā ca sarvadharmājātatayā ca sarvadharmaviviktasamatayā ca sarvadharmādiviśuddhisamatayā ca sarvadharmaniṣprapañcasamatayā ca sarvadharmānāvyūhānirvyūhasamatayā ca sarvadharmamāyāsvapnapratibhāsapratiśrutkodakacandrapratibimb anirmāṇasamatayā ca sarvadharmabhāvābhāvādvayasamatayā ca । ābhirdaśabhirdharmasamatābhiravatarati ।।

sa evaṃsvabhāvān sarvadharmān pratyavakṣemāṇo'nusṛjan anulomayan avilomayan śraddadhan abhiyan pratiyan avikalpayan anusaran vyavalokayan pratipadyamānaḥ ṣaṣṭhīmabhimukhīṃ bodhisattvabhūmimanuprāpnoti tīkṣṇayā ānulomikyā kṣāntyā । na ca tāvadanutpattikadharmakṣāntimukhamanuprāpnoti ।।

B

sa evaṃsvabhāvān sarvadharmānanugacchan bhūyasyā mātrayā mahākaruṇāpūrvaṃgamatvena mahākaruṇādhipateyatayā mahākaruṇāparipūrṇārthaṃ lokasya saṃbhavaṃ ca vibhavaṃ ca vyavalokayate ।

C

tasya lokasya saṃbhavaṃ ca vibhavaṃ ca vyavalokayata evaṃ bhavati - yāvatyo lokasamudācāropapattayaḥ sarvāḥ, tā ātmābhiniveśato bhavanti । ātmābhiniveśavigamato na bhavanti lokasamudācāropapattaya iti । tasyaivaṃ bhavati - tena khalu punarime bālabuddhya ātmābhiniviṣṭā ajñānatimirāvṛtā bhāvābhāvābhilāṣiṇo-'yoniśomanasikāraprasṛtā vipathaprayātā mithyānucāriṇaḥ puṇyāpuṇyāneñjyānabhisaṃskārānupacinvanti । teṣāṃ taiḥ saṃskārairavaropitaṃ cittabījaṃ sāsravaṃ sopādānamāyatyāṃ jātijarāmaraṇapunarbhavābhinirvṛttisaṃbhavopagataṃ bhavati । karmakṣetrālayamavidyāndhakāraṃ tṛṣṇāsnehamasmimānapariṣyandanataḥ । dṛṣṭikṛtajālapravṛddhyā ca nāmarūpāṅkuraḥ prādurbhavati । prādurbhūto vivardhate | vivṛddhe nāmarūpe pañcānāmindriyāṇāṃ pravṛttirbhavati | pravṛttānāmindriyāṇāmanyonya(saṃ)nipātataḥ sparśaḥ | sparśasya saṃnipātato vedanā prādurbhavati | vedanāyāstata uttare'bhinandanā bhavati | tṛṣṇābhinandanata upādānaṃ vivardhate | upādāne vivṛddhe bhavaḥ saṃbhavati | bhave saṃbhūte skandhapañcakamunmajjati | unmagnaṃ skandhapañcakaṃ gatipañcake'nupūrvaṃ mlāyati | mlānaṃ vigacchati | mlānavigamājjvaraparidāhaḥ | jvaraparidāhanidānāḥ sarvaśokaparidevaduḥkhadaurmanasyopāyāsāḥ samudāgacchanti | teṣāṃ na kaścitsamudānetā | svabhāvānābhogābhyāṃ ca vigacchanti | na caiṣāṃ kaścidvigamayitā | evaṃ bodhisattvo'nulomākāraṃ pratītyasamutpādaṃ pratyavekṣate ||

D

tasyaivaṃ bhavati - satyeṣvanabhijñānaṃ paramārthato'vidyā | avidyāprakṛtasya karmaṇo vipākaḥ saṃskārāḥ | saṃskārasaṃniśritaṃ prathamaṃ cittaṃ vijñānam | vijñānasahajāścatvāra upādānaskandhā nāmarūpam | nāmarūpavivṛddhiḥ ṣaḍāyatanam | indriyaviṣayavijñāgatrayasamavadhānaṃ sāsravaṃ sparśaḥ | sparśasahajā vedanā | vedanādhyavasānaṃ tṛṣṇā | tṛṣṇāvivṛddhirupādānam | upādānaprasṛtaṃ sāsravaṃ karma bhavaḥ | karmaniṣyando jātiḥ skandhonmajjanam | skandhaparipāko jarā | jīrṇasya skandhabhedo maraṇam | mriyamāṇasya vigacchataḥ saṃmūḍhasya sābhiṣvaṅgasya hṛdayasaṃtāpaḥ śokaḥ | śokasamutthitā vākpralāpāḥ paridevaḥ | pañcendriyanipāto duḥkham | manodṛṣṭinipāto daurmanasyam | duḥkhadaurmanasyabahulatvasaṃbhūtā upāyāsāḥ | evamayaṃ kevalo duḥkhaskandho duḥkhavṛkṣo'bhinirvartate kārakavedakavirahita iti ||

tasyaivaṃ bhavati - kārakābhiniveśataḥ kriyāḥ prajñāyante | yatra kārako nāsti, kriyāpi tatra paramārthato nopalabhyate |

E

tasyaivaṃ bhavati - cittamātramidaṃ yadidaṃ traidhātukam |

F

yānyapīmāni dvādaśa bhavāṅgāni tathāgatena prabhedaśo vyākhyātāni, api sarvāṇyeva tāni cittasamāśritāni | tatkasya hetoḥ? yasmin vastuni hi rāgasaṃyuktaṃ cittamutpadyate tadvijñānam | vastusaṃskāre'smimoho'vidyā | avidyācittasahajaṃ nāmarūpam |

nāmarūpavivṛddhiḥ ṣaḍāyatanam I ṣaḍāyatanabhāgīyaḥ sparśaḥ I sparśasahajā vedanā I vedayato'vitṛptistṛṣṇā I tṛṣṇārtasya saṃgraho-'parityāga upādānam I eṣāṃ bhavāṅgānāṃ saṃbhavo bhavaḥ I bhavonmajjanaṃ jātiḥ I jātiparipāko jarā I jarāpagamo maraṇamiti I I

G

tatra avidyā dvividhakāryapratyupasthānā bhavati I ālambanataḥ sattvān saṃmohayati, hetuṃ ca dadāti saṃskārābhinirvṛttaye I saṃskārā api dvividhakāryapratyupasthānā bhavanti I anāgatavipākābhinirvṛtti ca kurvanti, hetuṃ ca dadati vijñānābhinirvṛttaye I vijñānamapi dvividhakāryapratyupasthānaṃ bhavati I bhavapratisaṃdhiṃ ca karoti, hetuṃ ca dadāti nāmarūpābhinirvṛttaye I nāmarūpamapi dvividhakāryapratyupasthānaṃ bhavati I anyonyopastambhanaṃ ca karoti, hetuṃ ca dadāti ṣaḍāyatanābhinirvṛttaye I

ṣaḍāyatanamapi dvividhakāryapratyupasthānaṃ bhavati I svaviṣayavibhaktitāṃ cādarśayati, hetuṃ ca dadāti sparśābhinirvṛttaye I sparśo'pi dvividhakāryapratyupasthāno bhavati I ālambanasparśanaṃ ca karoti, hetuṃ ca dadāti vedanābhinirvṛttaye I vedanāpi dvividhakāryapratyupasthānā bhavati I iṣṭāniṣṭobhayavimuktānubhavanaṃ ca karoti, hetuṃ ca dadāti tṛṣṇābhinirvṛttaye I tṛṣṇāpi dvividhakāryapratyupasthānā bhavati I saṃrajanīyavastusaṃrāgaṃ ca karoti, hetuṃ ca dadātyupādānābhinirvṛttaye I upādānamapi dvividhakāryapratyupasthānaṃ bhavati I saṃkleśabandhanaṃ ca karoti, hetuṃ ca dadāti bhavābhinirvṛttaye I

bhavo'pi dvividhakāryapratyupasthāno bhavati I anyabhavagatipratyadhiṣṭhānaṃ ca karoti, hetuṃ ca dadāti jātyabhinirvṛttaye I jātirapi dvividhakāryapratyupasthānā bhavati I skandhonmajjanaṃ ca karoti, hetuṃ ca dadāti jarābhinimvṛttaye I jarāpi dvividhakāryapratyupasthānā bhavati I indriyapariṇāmaṃ ca karoti, hetuṃ ca dadāti maraṇasamavadhānābhinirvṛttaye I maraṇamapi dvividhakāryapratyupasthānaṃ bhavati - saṃskāravidhvaṃsanaṃ ca karoti, aparijñānānucchedaṃ ceti I I

H

tatra avidyāpratyayāḥ saṃskārā ityavidyāpratyayatā saṃskārāṇām-anucchedo'nupastambhaśca I saṃskārapratyayaṃ vijñānamiti saṃskārapratyayatā vijñānānāmanucchedo'nupastambhaśca I peyālaṃ...jātipratyayatā jarāmaraṇasyānucchedo'nupastambhaśca I avidyānirodhātsaṃskāranirodha ityavidyāpratyayatābhāvāt-saṃskārāṇāṃ vyupaśamo'nupastambhaśca I peyālaṃ...jāti-pratyayatābhāvājjarāmaraṇasya vyupaśamo'nupastambhaśca I I

I

tatra avidyā tṛṣṇopādānaṃ ca kleśavartmano'vyavacchedaḥ I saṃskārā bhavaśca karmavartmano'vyavacchedaḥ I pariśeṣaṃ duḥkhavartmano'vyavacchedaḥ I pravibhāgataḥ pūrvāntāparānta-nirodhavartmano vyavacchedaḥ I evameva trivartma nirātmakam-ātmātmīyarahitaṃ saṃbhavati ca asaṃbhavayogena, vibhavati ca avibhavayogena svabhāvato naḍakalāpasadṛśam I I

J

api tu khalu punaryaducyate - avidyāpratyayāḥ saṃskārā ityeṣā paurvāntikyapekṣā I vijñānaṃ yāvadvedanetyeṣā pratyutpann-āpekṣā I tṛṣṇa yāvadbhava ityeṣā aparāntikyapekṣā I ata urdhva-masya pravṛttiriti I avidyānirodhātsaṃskāranirodha ityapekṣā-vyavaccheda eṣaḥ I I

K

api tu khalu punastriduḥkhatā dvādaśa bhavāṅgānyupādāya I tatra avidyā saṃskārā yāvatṣaḍāyatanamityeṣā saṃskāraduḥkhatā I sparśo vedanā caiṣā duḥkhaduḥkhatā I pariśeṣāṇi bhavāṅgānyeṣā pariṇāmaduḥkhatā I avidyānirodhātsaṃskāranirodha iti triduḥkhatā-vyavaccheda eṣaḥ I I

L

avidyāpratyayāḥ saṃskārā iti hetupratyayaprabhavatvaṃ saṃskārāṇām I evaṃ pariśeṣāṇām I avidyānirodhātsaṃskāra-nirodha ityabhāvaḥ saṃskārāṇām I evaṃ pariśeṣāṇām I I

avidyāpratyāḥ saṃskārā ityutpādavinibandha eṣaḥ I evaṃ pari-śeṣāṇām I avidyānirodhātsaṃskāranirodha iti vyayavinibandha eṣaḥ I evaṃ pariśeṣāṇām I I

avidyāpratyayāḥ saṃskārā iti bhāvānulomaparīkṣā I evaṃ pari-śeṣāṇām I avidyānirodhātsaṃskāranirodha iti kṣayavyayāvini-vandha eṣaḥ I evaṃ pariśeṣāṇām I I

M

sa evaṃ dvādaśākāraṃ pratītyasamutpādaṃ pratyavekṣate'nulomapratilomaṃ yaduta bhavāṅgānusaṃdhitaśca ekacittasamavasaraṇataśca svakarmāsaṃbhedataśca avinirbhāgataśca trivartmānuvartanataśca pūrvāntapratyutpannāparāntāvekṣaṇataśca triduḥkhatāsamudayataśca hetupratyayaprabhavataśca utpāda-
vyayavinibandhanataśca abhāvākṣayatāpratyavekṣaṇataśca | |

N

tasyaivaṃ dvādaśākāraṃ pratītyasamutpādaṃ pratyavekṣamāṇasya
nirātmato niḥsattvato nirjīvato niṣpudgalataḥ kārakavedakarahitato-
'svāmikato hetupratyayādhīnataḥ svabhāvaśūnyato viviktato'sva-
bhāvataśca prakṛtyā pratyavekṣamāṇasya śūnyatāvimokṣamukham-
ājātaṃ bhavati | |

tasyaivaṃ bhavāṅgānāṃ svabhāvanirodhātyantavimokṣapraty-
upasthānato na kiṃciddharmanimittamutpadyate | ato'sya ānimitta-
vimokṣamukhamājātaṃ bhavati | |

tasyaivaṃ śūnyatānimittamavatīrṇasya na kaścidabhilāṣa utpadyate
anyatra mahākaruṇāpūrvakātsattvaparipācanāt | evamasya apraṇi-
hitavimokṣamukhamājātaṃ bhavati | |

ya imāni trīṇi vimokṣamukhāni bhāvayan ātmaparasaṃjñāpagato
kārakavedakasaṃjñāpagato bhāvābhāvasaṃjñāpagato

O

bhūyasyā mātrayā mahākaruṇāpuraskṛtaḥ prayujyate'pariniṣ-
pannānāṃ bodhyaṅgānāṃ pariniṣpattaye, tasyaivaṃ bhavati –
saṃyogātsaṃskṛtaṃ pravartate | visaṃyogānna pravartate |
sāmagryā saṃskṛtaṃ pravartate | visāmagryā na pravartate | hanta
vayamevaṃ bahudoṣaduṣṭaṃ saṃskṛtaṃ viditvā asya saṃyogasya
asyāḥ sāmagryā vyavacchedaṃ kariṣyāmaḥ, na cātyantopaśamaṃ
sarvasaṃskārāṇāmavirāgayiṣyāmaḥ sattvaparipācanatāyai | |

evamasya bhavanto jinaputrāḥ saṃskāragataṃ bahudoṣaduṣṭaṃ
svabhāvarahitamanutpannāniruddhaṃ prakṛtyā pratyavekṣamāṇasya mahākaruṇābhinirhārataśca sattvakāryānutsargataśca
saṅgajñānābhimukho nāma prajñāpāramitāvihāro'bhimukhībhavaty-

avabhāsayogena | sa evaṃ jñānasamanvāgataḥ prajñāpāramitāvihār-āvabhāsito bodhyaṅgāhārakāṃśca pratyayānupasaṃharati | na ca saṃskṛtasaṃvāsena saṃvasati | svabhāvopaśamaṃ ca saṃskārāṇāṃ pratyavekṣate | na ca tatrāvatiṣṭhate bodhyaṅgāparityaktatvāt | |

P

tasya asyāmabhimukhyāṃ bodhisattvabhūmau sthitasya bodhi-sattvasya avatāraśūnyatā ca nāma samādhirājāyate | svabhāva-śūnyatā...paramārthaśūnyatā...paramaśūnyatā...mahāśūnyatā...saṃpr ayogaśūnyatā...abhinirhāraśūnyatā yathāvadavikalpaśūnyatā sāpekṣaśūnyatā vinirbhāgāvinirbhāgaśūnyatā nāma samādhirājāyate | tasyaivaṃpramukhāni daśa śūnyatāsamādhimukhaśatasahasrāṇy-āmukhībhavanti | evamānimittasamādhimukhaśataśahasrāṇi apra-ṇihitasamādhimukhaśatasahasrāṇyāmukhībhavanti |

Q

tasya bhūyasyā mātrayā asyāmabhimukhyāṃ bodhisattvabhūmau sthitasya bodhisattvasyabhedyāśayatā ca paripūryate | niyatāśayatā-...kalyāṇāśayatā...gambhīrāśayatā...apratyudāvartyāśayatā...apratipra strabdhāśayatā...vimalāśayatā...anantāśayatā...jñānābhilāṣāśayatā...u pāyaprajñāsaṃprayogāśayatā ca paripūryate | |

R

tasyaite daśa bodhisattvāśayāḥ svanugatā bhavanti tathāgatabodhau | apratyudāvartanīyavīryaśca bhavati sarvaparapravādibhiḥ | sam-avasṛtaśca bhavati jñānabhūmau | vinivṛttaśca bhavati śrāvakapraty-ekabuddhabhūmibhyaḥ | ekāntikaśca bhavati buddhajñānābhi-mukhatāyām | asaṃhāryaśca bhavati sarvamārakleśasamudācāraiḥ | supratiṣṭhitaśca bhavati bodhisattvajñānālokatāyām | supari-bhāvitaśca bhavati śūnyatānimittāpraṇihitadharmasamudācāraiḥ | saṃprayuktaśca bhavatyupāyaprajñāvicāraiḥ| vyavakīrṇaśca bhavati bodhipākṣikadharmābhinirhāraiḥ| tasya asyāmabhi-mukhyāṃ bodhisattvabhūmau sthitasya prajñāpāramitāvihāro'ti-riktatara ājāto bhavati, tīkṣṇā cānulomikī tṛtīyā kṣāntireṣāṃ dharmāṇāṃ yathāvadanulomatayā na vilomatayā | |

S

tasya asyāmabhimukhyāṃ bodhisattvabhūmau sthitasya bodhi-sattvasya yathāvatsamāpattiprajñājñānālokatayā prayujyate, prati-pattitaścādhārayati | sa bhūyasyā mātrayā tathāgatadharmakośa-prāpto bhavati | tasya asyāmabhimukhyāṃ bodhisattvabhūmau sthitasya anekān kalpāṃstāni kuśalamūlāni bhūyasyā mātrayā uttaptaprabhāsvaratarāṇi bhavanti I anekāni kalpaśatāni.... I tāni kuśalamūlāni bhūyasyā mātrayottaptaprabhāsvaratarāṇi bhavanti I tadyathāpi nāma bhavanto jinaputrāstadeva jātarūpaṃ vaiḍūryapari-sṛṣṭaṃ bhūyasyā mātrayottaptaprabhāsvarataraṃ bhavati, evameva bhavanto jinaputrā bodhisattvasya asyāmabhimukhyāṃ bodhisattva-bhūmau sthitasya tāni kuśalamūlānyupāyaprajñājñānavicāritāni bhūyasyā mātrayottaptaprabhāsvaratarāṇi bhavanti, bhūyo bhūyaśca praśamāsaṃhāryatāṃ gacchanti I tadyathāpi nāma bhavanto jinaputrāścandrābhā sattvāśrayāṃśca prahlādayati asaṃhāryā ca bhavati catasṛbhirvātamaṇḍalībhiḥ, evameva bhavanto jinaputra bodhisattvasya asyāmabhimukhyāṃ bodhisattvabhūmau sthitasya tāni kuśalamūlānyanekeṣāṃ sattvakoṭinayutaśatasahasrāṇāṃ kleśa-jvālāḥ praśamayanti, prahlādayanti, asaṃhāryāṇi ca bhavanti caturbhirmārāvacaraiḥ I tasya daśabhyaḥ pāramitābhyaḥ prajñā-pāramitā atiriktatamā bhavati, na ca pariśeṣā na samudāgacchati yathābalaṃ yathābhajamānam I iyaṃ bhavanto jinaputrā bodhi-sattvasya abhimukhī nāma ṣaṣṭhī bodhisattvabhūmiḥ samāsa-nirdeśataḥ, yasyāṃ pratiṣṭhito bodhisattvo bhūyastvena sunirmito bhavati devarājaṃ kṛtī prabhuḥ sattvānāmabhimānapratipra-srabdhaye kuśalaḥ sattvānyābhimānikadharmebhyo vinivartayitum I asaṃhāryaśca bhavati sarvaśrāvakaparipṛcchāyāṃ kuśalaḥ sattvān pratītyasamutpāde'vatārayitum I yacca kiṃcit.... I I

abhimukhī nāma ṣaṣṭī bhūmiḥ I I

[Beginning of sixth bhūmi's final gathas]

upasaṃhāragāthāḥ ।

paripūrṇamārgacaraṇā vidu pañcamāyāṃ
dharmānimittata alakṣaṇatā ajātā ।
anutpāda ādipariśuddhyatiniṣprapañcā
bhāvetva jñānamati ṣaṣṭhi samākramanti ।। 11 ।।

dharmā vivikta apratigraha nirvikalpā
māyāsvabhāva dvayabhāvatu viprayuktā ।
anulomayanta avilomanta dharmanetrī
jñānānvitāḥ pravara ṣaṣṭhi samākramanti ।। 12 ।।

tīkṣṇānulomasthita jñānabalopapetāḥ
samudāgamaṃ vibhavu prekṣiṣu sarvaloke ।
mohāndhakāraprabhavaṃ jagasaṃbhavātmā
tasyaiva mohavigamena pravṛti nāsti ।। 13 ।।

vicinanti pratyayakṛtiṃ paramārthaśūnyāṃ
kriya hetupratyayasamajña kriyāvirodhau ।
yāthāvataḥ karakapetakriyāṃ viditvā
vicinanti saṃskṛta ghanābhrasamaṃ nirīham ।। 14 ।।

satyeṣu'jñānu paramārthatu sā avidyā
karmā ca cetanabalena vibhāgaprāptam ।
cittaṃ niśritya sahajaṃ puna nāmarūpam
evaṃmukhā bhavati yāva dukhasya skandhaḥ ।। 15 ।।

te cittamātra ti traidhātukamotaranti
api cā bhavāṅga iti dvādaśa ekacitte ।
saṃrāgu jātu api cittu prabhāvitastu
evaṃ ca saṃbhavakṣayaṃ puna cittabhāgam ।। 16 ।।

kāryaṃ avidyadvaya kurvati mohabhāve
mohebhi hetu vahate puna cetanāyāḥ ।

evaṃ ca yāva jaradhvaṃsanaskandhabhedam
anu sarva duḥkhaprabhavaṃ kṣayataḥ abhāvaḥ || 17 ||

ucchedu no bhavati pratyayatāmavidyā
nocchedyatāpi kara prahāya saṃnirodham |
moho teṣu ca upādānaṃ kleśavartma
karma bhavaṃ ca api cetana śeṣa duḥkhā || 18 ||

mohaṃ tu āyatana saṃskṛtaduḥkha teṣāṃ
sparśaṃ ca vedana sukhādukhatāya duḥkhā |
śeṣānamaṅganapariṇāmaduḥkhavṛddhiḥ
vyuccheda tasya duḥkhatā na hi ātmamasti || 19 ||

adhveṣu pūrvaṃ tamacetanasaṃskṛtasya
vijñāna vedana vivartati pratyutpannam
aparāntu teṣu prabhavo dukhasaṃbhaveyam
āpekṣa cchedu prasaraṃ ca nirīkṣayantaḥ || 20 ||

mohasya pratyayatu saṃbhavate vibandhā
vinibandhanavyayakṣaye sati pratyayānām |
hetośca mūlaprabhavaṃ na tu hetubhedaṃ
vyuparīkṣate ca jina jñāna svabhāvaśūnyam || 21 ||

anuloma mohaprabhavaṃ ca prabhāvataśca
pratilomahetu kṣayato bhava sarvacchedyam |
gambhīrapratyayatamasya sato'sataśca
vyuparīkṣate daśavidhaṃ aniketabuddhiḥ || 22 ||

saṃdhī bhavāṅgatu tathāpi ca karmasthānam
avibhāgatastrividhu vartmani pūrvataśca |
triyahetu duḥkhavibhavā udaya vyayaṃ ca
abhāvato'kṣayata pratyaya ānulomam || 23 ||

evaṃ pratītyasamutpāda samotaranti
māyopamaṃ vitatha vedakarmāpanītam |
svapnopamaṃ ca tathatā pratibhāsa caiva
bālāna mohana marīcisamasvabhāvam || 24 ||

yā eva bhāvana sa śūnyata paṇḍitānāṃ
rati pratyayāna bhavate idamānimittam |
jānitva jātu vitathaṃ praṇidhātu nāsti
anyatra sattvakṛpayā upapadyanti || 25 ||

evaṃ vimokṣamukha bhāvayi te mahātmā
kṛpabuddhi bhūya tatha buddhaguṇābhilāṣī |
saṃyogasaṃskṛtikṛta vyuparīkṣamāṇo
niyatāśayo bhavati naikaguṇopapetaḥ || 26 ||

pūrṇā sahasra daśa śūnyataye samādhī
tatha ānimittavaradaṃ ca vimokṣa tāyī || 27[2] ||

pralhādayanti jagadāśaya candraābhā
vahamānu vāta caturo asaṃhāryaprāptā |
atikramya mārapathamābha jinaurasānāṃ
praśamenti kleśaparitāpa dukhārditānām || 28 (29) ||

iha bhūmideśupagatā marutādhipāste
bhontī sunirmita kṛtāvadhimānaghātī |
yaṃ caiva ārabhiṣu jñānapathopapetā
asaṃhārya śrāvakagatī atikrānta dhīrāḥ || 29 (30) ||

ākāṅkṣamāṇu sugatātmaja vīryaprāptāḥ
koṭīśatasahasrapūrṇa samādhi labdhāḥ |
paśyanti ekakṣaṇi buddha daśaddiśāsu
pratapanti sūrya eva madhyagu grīṣmakāle || 30 (31) ||

gambhīra durdṛśā sūkṣma durjñeyā jinaśrāvakaiḥ |
ṣaṣṭhī bhūmirmahātmānāmākhyātā sugatātmajāḥ || 31 (32) ||

[End of sixth bhūmi's final gathas]

[Beginning of seventh bhūmi's initial gathas]

7 dūraṃgamā nāma saptamī bhūmiḥ |

upakramagāthāḥ |

atha vividharucirameghān marudgaṇo'bhikiriṣu vegaprāptāḥ |
pravyāharanti madhurā girivara śubha prītisaṃpūrṇāḥ || 1 ||

sādhu varatīkṣṇacittā guṇaśatasamupetajñānavaśavartim |
varacaraṇaṃ parituṣṭaṃ jagahitavarapuṇḍarīkāṇām || 2 ||

tada pravaramatulamābhā maheśvarāḥ khegatā naravarasya |
vararuciragandhameghānabhikiri kleśaughamapahartum || 3 ||

pravyāharanti madhuraṃ marudgaṇā harṣakararuciraghoṣāḥ |
paramasulabdhalābhāḥ śrutu yairayu bhūminirdeśaḥ || 4 ||

tūrya madhuraghoṣayukta marukanyāḥ prīṇitamanobhiḥ |
sucarasugatānubhāvādvaracaririyamīdṛśī proktā || 5 ||

sumanī sucaraṇaśreṣṭhaḥ sudānta damakāna lokamahitānām |
atikramya sarvalokaṃ lokacariṃ darśayī sūkṣmām || 6 ||

darśenti kāya vividhān kāyākāyāṃśca dharmatopetāḥ |
śamathaḥ samitivibhakto bhaṇati ghoṣaṃ na cākṣaraṃ ravati || 7 ||

kṣetraśatamākramante pūjenti nāyakān paramapūjiyān |
ātmajanitakṣetrasaṃjñā vidhunitvā jñānavaśavartī || 8 ||

paripācayanti sattvānna cātmaparasaṃjña sarvaśa upenti |
śubha saṃcinanti pravaraṃ na cāpi śubhasaṃcayaniketāḥ || 9 ||

rāgarajadoṣamohaiḥ paśyitva sarvaloka jvalamānān |
varjeti sarvasaṃjñā vīryaṃ varamārabhī kṛpayā || 10 ||

marukanyā devasaṃghāśca pūjentā varasvaram |
tūṣṇīṃbhāvaratāḥ sarve prekṣante puruṣarṣabham || 11 ||

pariṣadviprasanneyamavocat sugatātmajam |
saptamyā bhūmerākārān nirdiśasva guṇākara || 12 ||

[End of seventh bhūmi's initial gathas]

7 duraṃgamā nāma saptamī bhūmiḥ ।

A

vajragarbha āha - yo'yaṃ bhavanto jinaputrā bodhisattvaḥ ṣaṣṭyāṃ bodhisattvabhūmau suparipūrṇabodhisattvamārgaḥ saptamīṃ bodhisattvabhūmimākramati, sa daśabhirupāyaprajñājñānābhinirhṛtairmārgāntarārambhaviśeṣairākramati । katamairdaśabhiḥ? yaduta śūnyatānimittāpraṇihitasamādhisuparibhāvitamānasaśca bhavati, mahāpuṇyajñānasambhāropacayaṃ ca saṃbibharti । nairātmyaniḥsattvanirjīvaniṣpudgalatāṃ ca sarvadharmāṇāmavatarati, caturapramāṇābhinirhāraṃ ca notsṛjati । puṇyadharmocchrayapāramitābhisaṃskāraṃ cābhisaṃskaroti, na ca kiṃciddharmamabhiniviśate । sarvatraidhātukavivekaprāptaśca bhavati, traidhātukaviṭhapanālaṃkārābhinirhāraṃ cābhinirharati । atyantaśāntopaśāntaśca sarvakleśajvālāpagamādbhavati, sarvasattvarāgadveṣakleśajvālāpraśamābhinirhāraṃ cābhinirharati । māyāmarīcisvapnapratibhāsapratiśrutkodakacandrapratibimbanirmāṇabhāvābh āvasvabhāvādvayānugataśca bhavati, karmakriyāvibhaktyapramāṇāśayatāṃ cābhinirharati । ākāśasamakṣetrapathasubhāvitamanāśca bhavati, buddhakṣetraviṭhapanālaṃkārābhinirhāraṃ cābhinirharati । prakṛtidharmakāyatāṃ ca sarvabuddhanāmavatarati, rūpakāyalakṣaṇānuvyañjanaviṭhapanālaṃkārābhinirhāraṃ cābhinirharati ।

anabhilāpyarutaghoṣāpagataṃ ca prakṛtiśāntaṃ tathāgataghoṣamadhimucyate, sarvasvarāṅgavibhaktiviśuddhyalaṃkārābhinirhāraṃ cābhinirharati । ekakṣaṇatryadhvānubodhaṃ ca buddhānāṃ bhagavatāmavatarati, nānālakṣaṇākalpasaṃkhyāvibhāvanāṃ cānupraviśati sattvāśayavibhāvanāya । evirbhavanto jinaputrā daśabhirupāyaprajñājñānābhinirhṛtibhirmārgāntarārambhaviśeṣairbodhisattv aḥ ṣaṣṭhyā bodhisattvabhūmeḥ saptamīṃ bodhisattvabhūmimākrānta ityucyate ।।

B

sa saptamyāṃ bodhisattvabhūmau sthito bodhisattvo'pramāṇāsattvadhātumavatarati । apramāṇaṃ ca buddhānāṃ bhagavatāṃ sattvaparipācanavinayakarmāvatarati । apramāṇaṃ lokadhātumavatarati । apramāṇaṃ ca buddhānāṃ bhagavatāṃ kṣetrapariśuddhimavatarati । apramāṇaṃ ca dharmanānātvamavatarati ।

apramāṇaṃ ca buddhānāṃ bhagavatāṃ jñānābhisaṃbodhim-avatarati | apramāṇaṃ ca kalpasaṃkhyāpraveśamavatarati | apramāṇaṃ ca buddhānāṃ bhagavatāṃ tryadhvānubodham-avatarati | apramāṇaṃ ca sattvānāmadhimuktinānātvaviśeṣam-avatarati | apramāṇaṃ ca buddhānāṃ bhagavatāṃ rūpakāyan-ānātvadarśanamavatarati | apramāṇaṃ ca sattvānāmāśayendriya-nānātvamavatarati | apramāṇaṃ ca buddhānāṃ bhagavatāṃ ghoṣ-odāhārasattvasaṃtoṣaṇamavatarati | apramāṇaṃ sattvānāṃ citta-caritanānātvamavatarati | apramāṇaṃ ca buddhānāṃ bhagavatāṃ jñānaprasarānugamamavatarati | apramāṇaṃ śrāvakayāna-niryāṇāadhimuktinānātvamavatarati | apramāṇaṃ ca buddhānāṃ bhagavatāṃ mārgadeśanāvatāramavatarati | apramāṇaṃ pratyeka-buddhayānasamudāgamaniṣpattimavatarati | apramāṇaṃ ca buddhānāṃ bhagavatāṃ jñānamukhapraveśanirdeśamavatarati | bodhisattvānāṃ bodhisattvacaryāprayogamavatarati | apramāṇaṃ ca buddhānāṃ bhagavatāṃ mahāyānasamudayāvatāranirdeśanām-avatarati ||

C

tasyaivaṃ bhavati - evamapramāṇaḥ khalu punastathāgatānām-arhatāṃ samyaksaṃbuddhānāṃ viṣayo yasya na sukarā saṃkhyā kartuṃ kalpakoṭiśatasahasrairyāvadetāvadbhirapi kalpakoṭiniyuta-śatasahasraiḥ | sarva...viṣayo'smābhiḥ samupasthāpayitavyo-'nābhogato'kalpāvikalpataśca paripūrayitavya iti | sa evaṃ supratyavekṣitajñānābhijñaḥ satatasamitamabhiyuktopāyaprajñā-paribhāviteṣu mārgāntarārambhaviśeṣeṣu supratiṣṭhito bhavaty-avicālyayogena ||

D

sa ekakṣaṇamapi mārgābhinirhārānna vyuttiṣṭhate | sa gacchanneva jñānābhinirhārayukto bhavati | tiṣṭhannapi niṣaṇṇo'pi śayāno'pi svapnāntaragato'pyapagatanīvaraṇaḥ sarveryāpathe sthito'virahito bhavati ebhirevaṃrūpaiḥ saṃjñāmanasikāraiḥ | tasya sarvacitt-otpāde daśānāṃ bodhisattvapāramitānāṃ samudāgamaparipūriḥ samudāgacchati | tatkasmāddhetoḥ? tathā hi sa bodhisattvaḥ sarv-āṃścittotpādānutpannotpannān mahākaruṇāpūrvakān buddha-dharmasamudāgamāya tathāgatajñānāya pariṇāmayati | tatra yaḥ kuśalamūlasya sattvebhya utsargo buddhajñānaṃ paryeṣamāṇasya, iyamasya dānapāramitā | yaḥ praśamaḥ sarvakleśaparidāhānām, iyamasya śīlapāramitā | yā kṛpāmaitrīpūrvagamā sarvasattveṣu kṣāntiḥ, iyamasya kṣāntipāramitā | ya uttarottarakuśaladharmātṛptatayārambhaḥ parākramaḥ, iyamasya vīryapāramitā | yā vipratisāryavisṛtamārgatā sarvajñajñānābhimukhatā, iyamasya dhyānapāramitā | yā sarvadharmāṇāṃ prakṛtyanutpādābhimukhī kṣāntiḥ, iyamasya prajñāpāramitā | yo'pramāṇājñānābhinirhāraḥ, iyamasyopāyakauśalapāramitā | yā sarvaparapravādimārasaṃghairmārgānācchedyatā, iyamasya balapāramitā | yadyathāvatsarvadharmajñānanitīraṇam, iyamasya jñānapāramitā | evamasya bhavanto jinaputrā bodhisattvasya dūraṃgamāyāṃ bodhisattvabhūmau sthitasya imā daśa pāramitāḥ kṣaṇe kṣaṇe paripūryante | evaṃ catvāri saṃgrahavastūni paripūryante, catvāri ca adhiṣṭhānāni, saptatriṃśad bodhipakṣyāśca dharmāḥ, trīṇi ca vimokṣamukhāni, samāsataḥ sarvabodhyaṅgikā dharmāḥ kṣaṇe kṣaṇe paripūryante ||

E

evamukte vimukticandro bodhisattvo vajragarbhaṃ bodhisattvametadavocat - kiṃ punarbho jinaputrā asyāmeva saptamyāṃ bodhisattvabhūmau sthitasya bodhisattvasya sarvabodhyaṅgikā dharmāḥ kṣaṇe kṣaṇe paripūryante, āhosvitsarvāsu daśasu bodhisattvabhūmiṣu? vajragarbha āha - sarvāsu bho jinaputrā daśasu bodhisattvabhūmiṣu bodhisattvasya sarvabodhyaṅgāni kṣaṇe kṣaṇe paripūryante, tadatirekeṇa punarasyāmeva saptamyāṃ bodhisattvabhūmau | tatkasya hetoḥ? iyaṃ bho jinaputrā bodhisattvabhūmiḥ prāyogikacaryāparipūraṇī ca jñānābhijñānacaryākramaṇī ca | api tu khalu punarbho jinaputrāḥ prathamāyāṃ bodhisattvabhūmau sarvapraṇidhānādhyālambena bodhisattvasya sarvabodhyaṅgāni kṣaṇe kṣaṇe paripūryante | dvitīyāyāṃ cittamalāpanayanena | tṛtīyāyāṃ praṇidhānavivardhanatayā dharmāvabhāsapratilambhena ca | caturthyāṃ mārgāvatāreṇa | pañcamyāṃ lokatrayānuvṛtyā | ṣaṣṭyāṃ gambhīradharmamukhapraveśena | asyāṃ tu saptamyāṃ bodhisattvabhūmau sarvabuddhadharmasamutthāpanatayā kṣaṇe kṣaṇe sarvabodhyāṅgāni paripūryante |

F

tatkasya hetoḥ? yāni bodhisattvena prathamāṃ bodhisattvabhūmimupādāya yāvatsaptamī bodhisattvabhūmirityabhinirhṛtāni jñānābhinirhāraprayogāṅgāni, imānyaṣṭamī bodhisattvabhūmimārabhya yāvadatyantaparyavasānamityanābhogena pariniṣpadyante | tadyathāpi nāma bho jinaputrā dvayorlokadhātvoḥ saṃkliṣṭaviśuddhāśayaśca lokadhātorekāntapariśuddhāśayaśca lokadhātorlokāntarikā duratikramā na śakyā yathātathātikramitumanyatra mahābhijñābalādhānāt, evameva bho jinaputra vyāmiśrapariśuddhā bodhisattvacaryāntarikā duratikramā na śakyā yathātathātikramitumanyatra mahāpraṇidhānopāyaprajñābhijñābalādhānāt | vimukticandra āha - kiṃ punarbho jinaputra saptasu bodhisattvabhūmiṣu kleśacaryāsaṃkliṣṭā bodhisattvacaryā pratyetavyā ? vajragarbha āha - prathamāmeva bho jinaputra bodhisattvabhūmimupādāya sarvābodhisattvacaryāpagatakleśakalmāṣā bodhipariṇāmanādhipatyena pratyetavyā | yathābhāgimārgasamatayā, (na ca) tāvatsaptasu bodhisattvabhūmiṣu samatikrāntā kleśacaryetyavācanīyā | tadyathāpi nāma bho jinaputra rājā cakravartī divyaṃ hastiratnamabhirūḍhaścaturo dvīpānākramati, manuṣyaduḥkhadāridryasaṃkleśadoṣāṃśca prajānāti, na ca tairdoṣairlipyate | na ca tāvatsamatikrānto manuṣyabhāvaṃ bhavati | yadā punarmanuṣyāśrayaṃ hitvā brahmalokopapanno bhavati brāhmyavimānamabhirūḍhaḥ, sahasralokadhātumalpakṛcchreṇa paśyatyanuvicarati, brahmapratibhāsaṃ cādarśayati, na ca manuṣya iti prabhāvyate, evameva bhoḥ prathamāṃ bhūmimupādāya bodhisattvaḥ pāramitāyānābhirūḍhaḥ sarvajagadanuvicaran saṃkleśadoṣān prajānāti, na ca tairdoṣairlipyate samyagmārgābhirūḍhatvāt | na ca tāvatsamatikrāntaḥ sarvajagatsaṃkleśadoṣān vaktavyaḥ | saptasu bhūmiṣu sarvaprāyogikacaryāṃ vihāya saptamyā bhūmeraṣṭamīṃ bodhisattvabhūmimavakrānto bhavati, tadā pariśuddhaṃ bodhisattvayānamabhirūḍhaḥ sarvajagadanuvicaran sarvajagatsaṃkleśadoṣān prajānāti, na ca tairdoṣairlipyate samatikrāntatvād lokatriyābhyaḥ | asyāṃ punarbho jinaputra sapyamyāṃ bodhisattvabhūmau sthito bodhisattvo bhūyastvena rāgādipramukhaṃ sarvakleśagaṇaṃ samatikrānto bhavati | so'syāṃ dūraṃgamāyāṃ bodhisattvabhūmau caran bodhisattvo'saṃkleśāniṣkleśa iti vaktavyaḥ | tatkasmāt? asamudācārātsarvakleśānāṃ na saṃkleśa iti vaktavyaḥ | tathāgatajñānābhilāṣādaparipūrṇābhiprāyatvācca na niṣkleśa iti vaktavyaḥ ||

G

so'syāṃ saptamyāṃ bodhisattvabhūmau sthito bodhisattvo'dhyāśayapariśuddhena kāyakarmaṇā samanvāgato bhavati | adhyāśayapariśuddhena vākkarmaṇā adhyāśayapariśuddhena manaskarmaṇā samanvāgato bhavati | ye ceme daśākuśalāḥ karmapathāstathāgatavivarṇitāḥ, tān sarveṇa sarvaṃ samatikrānto bhavati | ye ceme daśa kuśalāḥ karmapathāḥ samyaksaṃbuddhānubhāvitāḥ, tān satatasamitamanuvartate | yāni laukikāni śilpasthānakarmasthānāni yānyabhinirhṛtāni pañcamyāṃ bodhisattvabhūmau, tānyasya sarvāṇyanābhogata evaṃ pravartante | sa ācāryaḥ saṃmato bhavati trisāhasra mahāsāhasralokadhātau, sthāpayitvā tathāgatānarhataḥ samyaksambuddhān, aṣṭamīṃ bhūmimupādāya ca bodhisattvān | nāsya kaścitsamo bhavatyāśayena vā prayogeṇa vā | yāni cemāni dhyānāni samādhayaḥ samapattayo'bhijñā vimokṣāśca, tānyasya sarveṇa sarvamāmukhībhavanti bhāvanābhinirhārākāreṇa | na ca tāvadvipākataḥ pariniṣpannāni bhavanti tadyathāpi nāma aṣṭamyāṃ bodhisattvabhūmau sthitasya bodhisattvasya | asyāṃ saptamyāṃ bodhisattvabhūmau sthitasya bodhisattvasya sarvacittotpādeṣu prajñopāyabhāvanābalaṃ paripūryate | bhūyasyā mātrayā sarvabodhyaṅgaparipūriṃ pratilabhate ||

H

so'syāṃ saptamyāṃ bodhisattvabhūmau sthitaḥ san suvicitavicayaṃ ca nāma bodhisattvasamādhi samāpadyate | suvicintitārthaṃ ca nāma... | viśeṣamatiṃ ca nāma... | prabhedārthakośaṃ ca... | sarvārthavicayaṃ ca... | supratiṣṭhitadṛḍhamūlaṃ ca... | jñānābhijñāmukhaṃ ca... | dharmadhātu(pari)karmaṃ ca... | tathāgatānuśaṃsaṃ ca... | vicitrārthakośasaṃsāranirvāṇamukhaṃ ca bodhisattvasamādhiṃ samāpadyate | sa evaṃpramukhāni mahābhijñājñānamukhāni paripūrṇāni daśa samādhiśatasahasrāṇi bhūmipariśodhikāni samāpadyate ||

I

sa eṣāṃ samādhīnāmupāyaprajñāsupariśodhitānāṃ pratilambhānmahākaruṇābalena cātikrānto bhavati śrāvakapratyekabuddhabhūmim, abhimukhaśca bhavati prajñājñānavicāraṇābhūmeḥ ||

J

tasya asyāṃ saptamyāṃ bodhisattvabhūmau sthitasya bodhisattvasya apramāṇaṃ kāyakarma nimittāpagataṃ pravartate | apramāṇaṃ vākkarma...manaskarma nimittāpagataṃ pravartate suviśodhitamanutpattikadharmakṣāntyavabhāsitam | vimukticandra āha - nanu bho jinaputra, prathamāyāmeva bodhisattvabhūmau sthitasya bodhisattvasya apramāṇaṃ kāyavāṅmanaskarma sarva-

śrāvakapratyekabuddhacaryāṃ samatikrāntaṃ bhavati? vajragarbha
āha - bhavati bho jinaputra | tatpunarbuddhadharmādhyālambana-
māhātmyena, na punaḥ svabuddhivicāreṇa | asyāṃ tu punaḥ
saptamyāṃ bodhisattvabhūmau svabuddhigocaravicāraprati-
lambhādasaṃhāryaṃ śrāvakapratyekabuddhairbhavati | tadyathāpi
nāma bhavanto jinaputrā rājakulaprasūto rājaputro rājalakṣaṇa-
samanvāgato jātamātra eva sarvāmātyagaṇamabhibhavati rāj-
ādhipatyena, na punaḥ svabuddhivicāreṇa | yadā punaḥ sa
saṃvṛddho bhavati tadā svabuddhibalādhānataḥ sarvāmātyakriyā-
samatikrānto bhavati, evameva bho jinaputrā bodhisattvaḥ sahacitt-
otpādena sarvaśrāvakapratyekabuddhānabhibhavatyadhyāśaya-
māhātmyena, na punaḥ svabuddhivicāreṇa | asyāṃ tu saptamyāṃ
bodhisattvabhūmau sthito bodhisattvaḥ svaviṣayajñānaviśeṣa-
māhātmyāvasthitatvātsarvaśrāvakapratyekabuddhakriyāmatikrānto
bhavati | |

K

sa khalu punarbho bodhisattvo'syāṃ saptamyāṃ bodhisattvabhūmau sthito gambhīrasya vivittasyāpracārasya kāyavāṅmanas-
karmaṇo lābhī bhavati | na cottaraṃ viśeṣaparimārgaṇābhiyogam-
avasṛjati | [yena parimārgaṇābhiyogena nirodhaprāptaśca bhavati,
na ca nirodhaṃ sākṣātkaroti | |]

L

vimukticandra āha - katamāṃ bhūmimupādāya bodhisattvo
nirodhaṃ samāpadyate? vajragarbha āha - ṣaṣṭhīṃ bho jinaputra
bodhisattvabhūmimupādāya bodhisattvo nirodhaṃ samāpadyate |
asyāṃ punaḥ saptamyāṃ bodhisattvabhūmau pratiṣṭhito bodhi-
sattvaścittakṣaṇe cittakṣaṇe nirodhaṃ samāpadyate ca vyuttiṣṭhate
ca | na ca nirodhaḥ sākṣātkṛta iti vaktavyaḥ | tena so'cintyena
kāyavāṅmana skarmaṇā samanvāgata ityucyate | āścaryaṃ bho
yatra hi nāma bodhisattvo bhūtakoṭivihāreṇa ca viharati, na ca
nirodhaṃ sākṣātkaroti | tadyathāpi nāma bho jinaputra puruṣaḥ
kuśalo mahāsāgare vārilakṣaṇābhijñaḥ paṇḍito vyakto medhāvī tatr-
opagatayā mīmāṃsayā samanvāgato mahāsāgare mahāyāna-
pātrābhirūḍho vahanakuśalaśca bhavati, vārikuśalaśca bhavati, na ca
mahāsamudre vāridoṣairlipyate, evameva bho jinaputra asyāṃ
saptamyāṃ bodhisattvabhūmau pratiṣṭhito bodhisattvaḥ sarva-
jñajñānamahāsāgarāvatīrṇaḥ pāramitāmahāyānapātrābhirūḍho

bhūtakoṭivihāreṇa ca viharati, na ca nirodhaṃ sākṣātkaroti, (na ca sasṃkṛtātyantavyupaśamavitarkadoṣairlipyate) ||

M

sa evaṃ jñānabalādhānaprāptaḥ samādhijñānabalabhāvanābhinirhṛtayā buddhyā mahatopāyaprajñābalādhānena saṃsāramukhaṃ cādarśayati | nirvāṇasatatāśayaśca bhavati | mahāparivāraparivṛtaśca bhavati | satatasamitaṃ ca cittavivekapratilabdho bhavati | traidhātukopapattiṃ ca praṇidhānavaśenābhinirharati sattvaparipācanārtham | na ca lokadoṣairlipyate | śāntapraśāntopaśāntaśca bhavati | upāyena ca jvalati | jvalaṃśca na dahate | saṃvartate ca buddhajñānena | vivartate ca śrāvakapratyekabuddhabhūmibhyām | buddhajñānaviṣayakośaprāptaśca bhavati | māraviṣayagataśca dṛśyate | caturmārapathasamatikrāntaśca bhavati | māraviṣayagocaraṃ cādarśayati | sarvatīrthyāyatanopagataśca dṛśyate | buddhatīrthyāyatanānutsṛṣṭāśayaśca bhavati | sarvalokakriyānugataśca dṛśyate | lokottaradharmagatisamavasaraṇaśca bhavati | sarvadevanāgayakṣagandharvāsuragaruḍakinnaramahoragamanuṣy āmanuṣyaśakrabrahmalokapālātirekavyū-hālaṃkāraviṭhapanāprāptaśca bhavati | sarvabuddhadharmatimanasikāraṃ ca na vijahāti ||

N

tasyaivaṃ jñānasamanvāgatasya asyāṃ saptasyāṃ dūraṃgamāyāṃ bodhisattvabhūmau sthitasya bodhisattvasya bahavo buddhā ābhāsamāgacchanti...| tāṃśca tathāgatānarhataḥ samyaksaṃbuddhān paryupāsate | teṣāṃ ca sakāśādgauravacitrīkāreṇa satkṛtya dharmadeśanāṃ śṛṇoti, udgṛhṇāti dhārayati | śrutvā ca yathāvatsamāpattiprajñājñānālokena prayujyate | pratipattitaścādhārayati | śāsanasaṃdhārakaśca bhavati teṣāṃ buddhānāṃ mahātmanām | asaṃhāryaśca sarvaśrāvakapratyekabuddhābhisamayaparipṛcchāsu | tasya bhūyasyā mātrayā sattvānugrahāya gambhīradharmakṣāntirviśuddhyati | tasya...anekān kalpāṃstāni kuśalamūlānyuttapyante, pariśuddhyanti, karmaṇyāni ca bhavanti, paryavadānaṃ cāgacchanti | anekāni kalpaśatāni...anekāni kalpakoṭiniyutaśatasahasrāṇi tāni kuśalamūlānyuttapyante, pariśuddhyanti, karmaṇyāni ca bhavanti, paryavadānaṃ cāgacchanti | tadyathāpi nāma bho jinaputrāḥ tadeva jātarūpaṃ sarvaratnapratyuptaṃ bhūyasyā mātrayottaptataraṃ bhavati, prabhāsvarataraṃ bhavati, asaṃhāryataraṃ ca bhavatyanyābhyo bhūṣaṇavikṛtibhyaḥ, evameva bho jinaputrāḥ...tāni kuśalamūlānyupāyaprajñājñānābhinirhṛtāni bhūyasyā mātrayottaptatarāṇi bhavanti prabhāsvaratarāṇi, paryavadātatarāṇi asaṃhāryatarāṇi ca bhavanti sarvaśrāvakapratyekabuddhaiḥ ǀ tadyathāpi nāma bho jinaputrāḥ sūryābhā asaṃhāryā bhavanti sarvajyotirgaṇacandrābhābhiścaturṣu mahādvīpeṣu, sarvasnehagatāni bhūyastvena pariśoṣayanti, sarvaśasyāni paripācayanti, evameva bho jinaputrā...tāni kuśalamūlānyasaṃhāryāṇi bhavanti sarvaśrāvakapratyekabuddhaiḥ, caturviparyāsagatāni ca sarvakleśasnehagatāni bhūyastvena pariśoṣayanti ǀ kleṣāvilāni ca sarvasaṃtānāni paripācayanti ǀ tasya daśabhyaḥ pāramitābhya upāyakauśalyapāramitā atiriktatamā bhavati, na ca pariśeṣā na samudāgacchati yathābalaṃ yathābhajamānam ǀ iyaṃ bho jinaputrā bodhisattvasya dūraṃgamā nāma saptamī bodhisattvabhūmiḥ samāsanirdeśataḥ, yasyāṃ pratiṣṭhito bodhisattvo bhūyastvena vaśavartī bhavati devarājaḥ kṛtī prabhuḥ sattvānāmabhisamayajñānopasaṃhāreṣvaparyantaḥ sarvaśrāvakapratyekabuddhaparipṛcchāsu kuśalaḥ sattvānniyāmamavakrāmayitum ǀ yacca kicit... ǀ ǀ

dūraṃgamā nāma saptamī bhūmiḥ ǀ ǀ

[Beginning of seventh bhūmi's final gathas]

upasaṃhāragāthāḥ |

gambhīrajñāna paramārthapadānusārī
ṣaḍbhūminiścitamatiḥ susamāhitātmā |
prajñāmupāya yugapadyabhinirharanto
bhūmyākramanti vidu saptami caryaśreṣṭhām || 13 ||

śūnyānimittapraṇidhīkṛpamaitrayuktā
buddhānudharma sugatānuga pūjayantaḥ |
jñānena śubhamahapuṇyabalebhyatṛptā-
stāmākramanti vidu saptami bhūmideśam || 14 ||

traidhātukena adhivāsa vivekaprāptāḥ
śāntaśca kleśabalaśāntijagābhikāṅkṣī |
pratibhāsa māya supinādvayadharmacārī
kṛpa darśayanti vidu saptamimākramanti || 15 ||

śodhenti kṣetra khasamāśaya nirvikalpā
jinalakṣanairupāgato'caladharmatāyām |
abhilāpyaghoṣavigatā jagatoṣaṇārthaṃ
kṣaṇajñāna cittasya jināna samosaranti || 16 ||

abhāsaprāpta iti dharma vicārayanti
ākrānta bhūmipravarāṃ jagadarthakārāḥ |
te atra bhūmyasthita sattvacarī anantān
vicinanti karma sugatān niyutāpramāṇān || 17 ||

kṣetrāṃśca naikavidhadharmatha kalpasaṃkhyān
adhimuktiāśaya ca cittavicitradhārān |
triyāṇadeśanamananta samosaranti
asmābhi sattva paripācayitavyametat || 18 ||

ye te jñānanicitā varamārgaprāptā
īryāpathaiścaturbhi prajñamupāyamuktāḥ |

sarvasmi cittakṣaṇi bodhiguṇānuprāptāḥ
paripūrayanti daśa pāramitāpradeśān || 19 ||

sarveṣu mārgakuśalasya ya eṣa dānaṃ
śīlaṃ ca kleśapraśamaṃ kṣamamakṣatitvam |
vīryaṃ ca bhūyu anu uttari ārabhante
mārge acalyataya dhyānaguṇānvitānām || 20 ||

anutpādakṣānti virajā varaprajña śreṣṭhā
parṇāmupāya praṇidhī bhuyu kāṅkṣi lakṣmī |
ato'mardayitva balajñānanitīraṇatvād
evaṃ khu bodhiguṇa sarvakṣaṇenupenti || 21 ||

ālambanātu prathamā guṇapāripūri
dvitīyā malāpanaya ūrdhva vibandhacchedam |
caturthāya mārgu samatākriya pañcamāya
anutpāda āhvaya viduḥ puna ṣaṣṭhavṛttiḥ || 22 ||

iha saptamīmupagatāḥ sakalaṃ guṇāni
praṇidhāna naikavividhānabhinirharanti |
kiṃ kāraṇaṃ yaduta jñānakriyābhyupenti
sā aṣṭamīprabhṛti sarvaviśuddhyupenti || 23 ||

duratikramā dūraṃgamā bahusthānakarmā
kṣetrāntaradvipathameva yathottaranti |
vicaranti saptasu alipta nṛpo yathaiva
mārgasthitā na puna sarvatikrānta dhīrāḥ || 24 ||

yada aṣṭamīmupagatāḥ puna jñānabhūmim
atikrānta cittaviṣaye sthita jñānakarme |
brahmā na pekṣati jagannaramānuṣātmā
evaṃ caranti vidu padmamivā aliptāḥ || 25 ||

atra sthitā vividhakleśamatikramanti
teṣāṃ na kleśacari no ca kṣayo'nuprāptiḥ |
mārgasthitā na tada kleśacariṃ caranti
saṃpūrṇa āśaya jinajña kṣayo na tāvat || 26 ||

ye laukikā vividhaśilpakriyāprayogā
ājāti sarvavidunā sthita śāstrajñāne |
dhyānā abhijña bala bhāvayanto'bhyupenti
bhūyaḥ samādhi vividhānabhinirharanti | | 27 | |

atikrānta śravakacariṃ tatha pratyayānāṃ
sthita bodhisattvacaraṇe vidu apramāṇām |
pūrve hi āśayatayā iha jñānatāyā
nṛpatīsuto yatha vivṛddhabalopapetaḥ | | 28 | |

gāmbhīryatāmupagatā bhuyu ārabhanti
cittaṃ nirodhupagatā na ca sākṣikriyāḥ |
yathā sāgare upagatāḥ sthita yānapātre
pratyakṣa sarva udake na ca yānahāniḥ | | 29 | |

bhūyo upāyabalaprajñavarābhyupetā
durjñeyasarvajagajñānakriyāguṇāḍhyāḥ |
pūjenti buddha niyutā bhuyu śuddhibhāvā
yathā tadvibhūṣaṇavicitritu naikaratnaiḥ | | 30 | |

atra sthitāna vidunāṃ varaprajña ābhā
śoṣenti tṛṣṇasalilaṃ yatha bhāskārābhāḥ |
te atra bhūmyupagatā vaśavartinaśca
bhonti kṛtī kuśala jñānaphalodeśaiḥ | | 31 | |

ākāṅkṣamāṇa dṛḍhavīryabalābhyupetāḥ
koṭīnayūtaśata buddhasahasra pūrṇān |
paśyanti sarvadiśatāsu samāhitatvād
bhūyo'pyataḥ praṇidhiśreṣṭha guṇāprameyāḥ | | 32 | |

durjñeyā sarvalokena vaśipratyekacāribhiḥ |
ityeṣā saptamī bhūmirupāyaprajñaśodhanā | | 33 | |

[End of seventh bhūmi's final gathas]

[Beginning of eighth bhūmi's initial gathas]

8 acalā nāma aṣṭamī bhūmiḥ |

upakramagāthāḥ |

eva śrutva caraṇaṃ viduna śreṣṭhaṃ
devasaṃgha muditā marupatiśca |
bodhisattva bahavo jagaddhitaiṣi
pūjayanti sugataṃ jinasutāṃśca || 1 ||

puṣpamālya rucirā dhvajāpatākā
gandhacūrṇa rucirā ratanavastrā |
chatra naikarucirān maṇipratyuptān
hārameghapravarānabhisṛjanti || 2 ||

manojñaghoṣamadhuraṃ suravandū
mukta naikaturiyapravaranāṭān |
pūjanārthi jinaputra sugatāṃśca
varṇaśreṣṭha munino udāharanti || 3 ||

sarvi darśi vṛṣabhī dvipādaśreṣṭho
darśi buddhaviṣayaṃ jagaddhitārtham |
śabdamegha rucirān pratāḍamānā-
stūryatāla vividhāstada pramuktāḥ || 4 ||

vālakoṭi sugatāḥ śatasahasrā
gaṅgākoṭi nayutā rajaviśiṣṭāḥ |
kṣemamapratisamāḥ pravaraśreṣṭhaṃ
deśayanti vṛṣabhī virajadharmam || 5 ||

preta tirya narakā manujadevāḥ
yakṣa rakṣa bhujagā asurasaṃghā |
....
nānakarmaviṣaye samanubhonti || 6 ||

sarvakṣetraviṣaye dhutarajānāṃ
cakra śreṣṭhapravaraṃ tadanirvṛttam |
deśayanti madhuraṃ sugataghoṣaṃ
saṃjñacitta jagatastatha vicāran || 7 ||

sattvakāyi sugatā vividhakṣetrā
kṣetri sattvapravarāḥ punavipākāḥ |
devamānuṣagatī tatha vicitrā
jñātva sarva sugato bhaṇati dharmam || 8 ||

sūkṣmasaṃjña bhavati vipulakṣetre
vipulasaṃjña bhavati rajanimitte |
evamādi vividhāṃ sugatarddhiṃ
sarvaloka bhaṇato na kṣepayeyuḥ || 9 ||

īddaśaṃ vacamāhātmyaṃ vacitvā madhurasvaram |
praśāntā pariṣatprītā prekṣate vadatāṃ varam || 10 ||

praśānta parṣadaṃ jñātvā mokṣacandro'bravītpunaḥ |
aṣṭamyā bhūmiākārāṃ praveśaṃ ca nidarśaya || 11 ||

[End of eighth bhūmi's initial gathas]

8 acalā nāma aṣṭamī bhūmiḥ |

A

vajragarbho bodhisattva āha - yo'yaṃ bhavanto jinaputrā bodhisattvaḥ saptasu bodhisattvabhūmiṣu sukṛtavicayaḥ prajñopāyābhyāṃ supariśodhitamārgaḥ susaṃbhṛtasaṃbhāraḥ suparibaddhamahāpraṇidhānaḥ adhiṣṭhitatathāgatādhiṣṭhānaḥ svakuśalamūlabalādhānaprāptaḥ tathāgatabalavaiśāradyāveṇikabuddhadharmānugatasaṃjñāmanasikāraḥ supariśodhitādhyāśayasaṃkalpa puṇyajñānabalābhyudgataḥ mahākaruṇākṛpābhyāṃ sarvasattvānutsṛṣṭaprayogaḥ apramāṇajñānapathānugataḥ,

B

sa sarvadharmāṇāmādyanutpannatāṃ ca yathābhūtamavatarati | ajātatāṃ ca alakṣaṇatāṃ ca asaṃbhūtatāṃ ca avināśitāṃ ca aniṣṭhitatāṃ ca apravṛttitāṃ ca anabhinivṛttitāṃ ca abhāvasvabhāvatāṃ ca ādimadhyaparyavasānasamatāṃ ca tathatāvikalpasarvajñajñānapraveśatāṃ ca sarvadharmāṇāṃ yathābhūtamavatarati | sa sarvaśaścittamanovijñānavikalpasaṃjñāpagato'navagṛhītākāśasamo'bhyavakāśaprakṛtito'vatīrṇo'nutpattikadharmakṣāntiprāpta ityucyate ||

C

tatra bhavanto jinaputrā evaṃ kṣāntisamanvāgato bodhisattvaḥ sahapratilambhādacalāyā bodhisattvabhūmergambhīraṃ bodhisattvavihāramanuprāpto bhavati durājñātamasaṃbhinnaṃ sarvanimittāpagataṃ sarvasaṃjñāgrahavyāvṛttamapramāṇam-asaṃhāryaṃ sarvaśrāvakapratyekabuddhaiḥ sarvavivekābhimukhībhūtam | tadyathāpi nāma bhavanto jinaputrā bhikṣurṛddhimāṃścetovaśipāramitāprāpto'nupūrveṇa navamaṃ nirodhaṃ samāpannaḥ sarveñjitamanyanāspanditavikalpāpagato bhavati, evameva bhavanto jinaputrā bodhisattvo'syā aṣṭamyā acalāyā bodhisattvabhūmeḥ sahapratilambhātsarvābhogavigato'nābhogadharmatāprāptaḥ kāyavākcittautsukyāpagataḥ sarveñjitamanyanāspanditavikalpāpagato vipākadharmatāvasthito bhavati | tadyathāpi nāma bho jinaputrāḥ puruṣaḥ suptaḥ svapnāntaragato mahaughaprāptam-ātmānaṃ saṃjānīte | sa tatra mahadvyāyāmautsukyamārabhet-ottaraṇāya | sa tenaiva mahatā vyāyāmautsukyena vibudhyeta | samanantaravibuddhaśca vyāyāmautsukyabhayāpagato bhavet |

evameva bho jinaputrā bodhisattvaścaturmahaughaprāptaṃ sattvakāyaṃ saṃjānāna uttaraṇābhiprāyaḥ sarvajñajñānābhisaṃbodhāya mahadvyāyāmautsukyamārabhate I sa mahāvīryārambhaprāptaḥ samanantaramanuprāpta imāmacalāṃ bodhisattvabhūmiṃ sarvābhogavigato bhavati I tasya sarveṇa sarvaṃ dvayasamudācāro vā nimittasamudācāro vā nābhāsībhavati I tadyathāpi nāma bho jinaputrā brahmalokopapattisthitaḥ kāmāvacarān kleśān na samudācarati, evameva bho jinaputrā bodhisattvo'calāyāṃ bodhisattvabhūmau sthitaḥ sarvacittamanovijñānasamudācārānna samudācarati I sarvabuddhasamudācāramapi...bodhisamudācāramapi...-bodhisattvasamudācāramapi...pratyekabuddhasamudācāramapi...śrā vakasamudācāramapi...nirvāṇasamudācāramapi...arhatsamudācāram api...anāgāmisamudācāramapi...nirvāṇasamudācāramapi...arhatsamu dācāramapi...anāgāmisamudācāramapi...sakṛdāgāmisamudācāramap i...-srotaāpannasamudācāramapi na samudācarati I kaḥ punarvādo laukikān samudācārān samudācariṣyatīti I I

D

tasya khalu bho jinaputra bodhisattvasya evamimāmacalāṃ bodhisattvabhūmimanugatasya pūrvapraṇidhānabalādhānasthitasya buddhā bhagavantastasmin dharmamukhasrotasi tathāgatajñānopasaṃhāraṃ kurvanti I evaṃ cainaṃ bruvanti - sādhu sādhu kulaputra I eṣā paramārthakṣāntirbuddhadharmānugamāya I api tu khalu punaḥ kulaputra yā asmākaṃ daśabalacaturvaiśāradyabuddhadharmasamṛddhiḥ, sā tava nāsti I tasyā buddhadharmasamṛddheḥ paryeṣaṇāya abhiyogaṃ kuru, vīryamārabhasva I etadeva kṣāntimukhaṃ monmokṣīḥ I

E

api tu khalu punaḥ kulaputra kiṃcāpi tvayaivaṃ śāntavimokṣavihāro'nuprāptaḥ, imān punaraśāntānapraśāntān bālapṛthagjanān nānākleśasamudācāraprāptān vividhavitarkopahatamānasān samanvāhara, apekṣasva I

F

api tu khalu punaḥ kulaputra pūrvapraṇidhānamanusmara sattvārthasaṃprāpaṇaṃ jñānamukhācintyatāṃ ca I

G

api tu khalu punaḥ kulaputra eṣā sarvadharmāṇāṃ dharmatā I utpādādvā tathāgatānāmanutpādādvā sthitaivaiṣā dharmatā dharmadhātusthitiḥ yadidaṃ sarvadharmaśūnyatā sarvadharm-ānupalabdhiḥ । naitayā tathāgatā eva kevalaṃ prabhāvyante, sarva-śrāvakapratyekabuddhā api hyetāmavikalpadharmatām-anuprāpnuvanti ।

H

api tu khalu punaḥ kulaputra prekṣasva tāvat tvamasmākaṃ kāyā-pramāṇatāṃ ca jñānāpramāṇatāṃ ca buddhakṣetrāpramāṇatāṃ ca jñānābhinirhārāpramāṇatāṃ ca prabhāmaṇḍalāpramāṇatāṃ ca svar-āṅgaviśuddhyapramāṇatāṃ ca । tathaiva tvamapyabhinirhāram-utpādaya ।

I

api tu khalu punaḥ kulaputra ekastveṣa āloko yo'yaṃ sarvadharma-nirvikalpālokaḥ । īdṛśāstu kulaputra dharmālokāstathāgatānām-aparyantagatā aparyantakṛtā aparyantabaddhāḥ, yeṣāṃ saṃkhyā nāsti, gaṇanā pramāṇamupaniṣadaupamyaṃ nāsti, teṣām-adhigamāya abhinirhāramutpādaya ।

J

api tu khalu punaḥ kulaputra prekṣasva tāvaddaśasu dikṣu apramāṇakṣetratāṃ ca apramāṇasattvatāṃ ca apramāṇadharma-vibhaktitāṃ ca । tatsarvamanugaṇaya । yathāvattayā abhinirhāram-utpādaya । iti hi bho jinaputra te buddhā bhagavanta evaṃbhūmy-anugatasya bodhisattvasya evaṃ pramukhānyaprameyāṇy-asaṃkhyeyāni jñānābhinirhāramukhānyupasaṃharanti, yairjñān-ābhinirhāramukhairbodhisattvo'pramāṇajñānavibhaktito'bhinirhārak armābhiniṣpādayati ।।

K

ārocayāmi te bho jinaputra, prativedayāmi । te cedbuddhā bhagavantastaṃ bodhisattvamevaṃ sarvajñajñānābhinirhāra-mukheṣu nāvatārayeyuḥ, tadevāsya parinirvāṇaṃ bhavetsarva-sattvakāryapratiprasrabdhiśca । tena khalu punarbuddhā bhagavantastasya bodhisattvasya tāvadapramāṇaṃ jñānābhinirhāra-karmopasaṃharanti, yasyaikakṣaṇābhinirhṛtasya jñānābhinirhāra-karmaṇaḥ sa pūrvakaḥ prathamacittotpādamupādāya yāvat-saptamīṃ bhūmipratiṣṭhāmupāgata ārambhaḥ śatatamīmapi kalāṃ nopeti, sahasratamīmapi, śatasahasratamīmapi...peyālaṃ... koṭīniyutaśatasahasratamīmapi kalāṃ nopeti, saṃkhyāmapi, gaṇanāmapi, upamāmapi, upanisāmapi, yāvadaupamyamapi na kṣamate । tatkasya hetoḥ? tathā hi bho jinaputra pūrvamekakāyābhinirhāratayā caryābhinirhāro'bhūt । imāṃ punarbhūmiṃ samārūḍhasya bodhisattvasya apramāṇakāyavibhaktito bodhisattvacaryābalaṃ samudāgacchati । apramāṇaghoṣābhinirhārataḥ apramāṇajñānābhinirhārataḥ apramāṇopapattyabhinirhārataḥ apramāṇakṣetrapariśodhanataḥ apramāṇasattvaparipācanataḥ apramāṇabuddhapūjopasthānataḥ apramāṇadharmakāyānubodhataḥ apramāṇābhijñābalādhānābhinirhārataḥ apramāṇaparṣanmaṇḍalavibhaktyabhinirhārataśca apramāṇānugatena kāyavāṅmanaskarmābhinirhāreṇa sarvabodhisattvacaryābalaṃ samudāgacchatyavicālyayogena । tadyathāpi nāma bho jinaputra mahāsamudragāmī poto'prāpto mahāsamudraṃ sābhogavāhano bhavati । sa eva samanantaramanuprāpto mahāsamudramanābhogavāhano vātamaṇḍalīpraṇīto yadekadivasena mahāsamudre kramate, tatsarvasābhogavāhanatayā na śakyaṃ varṣaśatenāpi tāvadaprameyamanuprāptum । evameva bho jinaputra bodhisattvaḥ susaṃbhṛtamahākuśalamūlasaṃbhāro mahāyānasamudāgamābhirūḍho mahābodhisattvacaryāsāgaramanuprāpto yadekamuhūrtena jñānānābhogatayā sarvajñajñānenākramati, tanna śakyaṃ pūrvakeṇa sābhogakarmaṇā kalpaśatasahasreṇāpi tāvadaprameyamanuprāptum ।।

L

tatra bho jinaputra bodhisattvo'ṣṭamīṃ bodhisattvabhūmimanuprāpto mahatyā upāyakauśalyajñānābhinirhārānābhogaprasṛtayā bodhisattvabuddhyā sarvajñajñānaṃ vicārayan lokadhātusaṃbhavaṃ ca vicārayati, lokadhātuvibhavaṃ ca vicārayati । sa yathā ca lokaḥ saṃvartate, taṃ ca prajānāti । yathā ca loko vivartate,... । yena ca karmopacayena lokaḥ saṃvartate,... । yena ca karmakṣayeṇa loko vivartate,... । yāvatkālaṃ ca lokaḥ saṃvartate, ... । yāvatkālaṃ ca loko vivartate, ... । yāvatkālaṃ ca lokaṃ saṃvṛttastiṣṭhati,... । yāvatkālaṃ ca loko vivṛttastiṣṭhati, taṃ ca prajānāti sarvatra cānavaśeṣataḥ । sa pṛthivīdhātuparīttatāṃ ca prajānāti mahadgatatāṃ ca...apramāṇatāṃ ca...vibhaktitāṃ ca prajānāti । abdhātu... । tejodhātu... । vāyudhātu... । sa paramāṇurajaḥsūkṣmatāṃ ca prajānāti, mahadgatatāṃ ca apramāṇatāṃ ca vibhaktitāṃ ca prajānāti ।

apramāṇaparamāṇurajovibhaktikauśalyaṃ ca prajānāti । asyāṃ ca lokadhātau yāvanti pṛthivīdhātoḥ paramāṇurajāṃsi tāni prajānāti । yāvanti abdhātoḥ... । tejodhātoḥ...। vāyudhātoḥ...। yāvantyo ratnavibhaktayo yāvanti ca ratnaparamāṇurajāṃsi tāni prajānāti । sattvakāya... । kṣetrakāya... । sa sattvānāṃ kāyaudārikatāṃ ca kāyasūkṣmatāṃ ca kāyavibhaktitāṃ ca prajānāti । yāvanti paramāṇurajāṃsi saṃbhūtāni nairayikakāyāśrayatastāni prajānāti । tiryagyonikāyāśrayataḥ... । ...yamalokakāyāśrayataḥ... । ...asuralokakāyāśrayataḥ.... । devalokakāyāśrayataḥ .... । manuṣyalokakāyāśrayataḥ.... । sa evaṃ paramāṇurajaḥprabhedajñānāvatīrṇaḥ kāmadhātusaṃvartaṃ ca prajānāti । rūpadhātuvivartaṃ... । ārūpyadhātuvivartaṃ ca prajānāti । rūpadhātuparīttatāṃ.... ārūpyadhātuparīttatāṃ... । āmadhātuparīttatāṃ ca mahadgatatāṃ ca apramāṇatāṃ ca vibhaktitāṃ ca prajānāti । rūpadhātuparīttatāṃ... ārūpyadhātuparīttataṃ... । kāmadhātuparīttatāṃ ca mahadgatatāṃ ca apramāṇatāṃ ca vibhaktitāṃ ca prajānāti । rūpadhātvārūpyadhātuparīttatāṃ... । traidhātukavicārajñānānugame svabhinirhṛtajñānālokaḥ sattvakāyaprabhedajñānakuśalaḥ kṣetrakāyavibhāgajñānakuśalaśca sattvopapattyāyatanābhinirhāre buddhiṃ cārayati । sa yādṛśī sattvānāmupapattiśca kāyasamudāgamaśca, tādṛśameva svakāyamadhitiṣṭhati sattvaparipācanāya । sa ekāmapi trisāhasramahāsāhasrāṃ lokadhātuṃ spharitvā sattvānāṃ svakāyaṃ vibhaktyadhimuktiṣu tathatvāyopapattaye'bhinirharati pratibhāsajñānānugamanatayā (yathā sattvāḥ paripākaṃ gacchantyanuttarasamyaksaṃbodhivimuktaye) । evaṃ dve vā tisro vā catasro vā pañca vā daśa vā viṃśatirvā triṃśadvā catvāriṃśadvā pañcāśadvā śataṃ vā yāvadanabhilāpyā api trisāhasramahāsāhasrā lokadhātūḥ spharitvā sattvānāṃ svakāyaṃ...peyālaṃ...pratibhāsajñānānugamanatayā । sa evaṃjñānasamanvāgato'syāṃ bhūmau supratiṣṭhita ekabuddhakṣetrācca na calati, anabhilāpyeṣu buddhakṣetreṣu tathāgataparṣanmaṇḍaleṣu ca pratibhāsaprāpto bhavati ।।

M

yādṛśī sattvānāṃ kāyavibhaktiśca varṇaliṅgasaṃsthānārohapariṇāhādhimuktyadhyāśayaśca teṣu buddhakṣetreṣu teṣu ca parṣanmaṇḍaleṣu tatra tatra tathā tathā svakāyamādarśayati । sa śramaṇaparṣanmaṇḍaleṣu śramaṇavarṇarūpamādarśayati । brāhmaṇaparṣanmaṇḍaleṣu brāhmaṇavarṇarūpamādarśayati । kṣatriya...। vaiśya...। śūdra... । gṛhapati... । cāturmahārājika... । trāyastriṃśa... ।

evaṃ yāma... | tuṣita... | nirmāṇarati... | paranirmitavaśavarti... | māra... | brahma... | yāvadakaniṣṭha... | śrāvakavaineyikānāṃ sattvānāṃ śrāvakakāyavarṇarūpamādarśayati | pratyekabuddhavaineyikānāṃ sattvānāṃ pratyekabuddhakāyavarṇarūpamādarśayati | bodhisattva... | tathāgata... | iti hi bho jinaputra yāvanto-'nabhilāpyeṣu buddhakṣetreṣu sattvānāmupapattyāyatanādhimuktiprasarāsteṣu tathatvāya svakāyavibhaktimādarśayati | |

N

sa sarvakāyavikalpāpagataḥ kāyasamatāprāptaḥ (taccāsya kāyasaṃdarśanamakṣūṇamavandhyaṃ ca sattvaparipākavinayāya) sa sattvakāyaṃ ca prajānāti | kṣetrakāyaṃ ca... | karmavipākakāyaṃ ca... | śrāvakakāyaṃ ca... | pratyekabuddhakāyaṃ ca ... | bodhisattvakāyaṃ ca... | tathāgatakāyaṃ ca... | jñānakāyaṃ ca... | dharmakāyaṃ ca... | ākāśakāyaṃ ca prajānāti | sa sattvānāṃ cittāśayābhinirhāramājñāya yathākālaparipākavinayānatikramādākāṅkṣan sattvakāyaṃ svakāyamadhitiṣṭhati | evaṃ kṣetrakāyaṃ karmavipākakāyaṃ...ātmakāyamadhitiṣṭhati | sa sattvānāṃ cittāśayābhinirhāramājñāya yaṃ yameva kāyaṃ yasmin yasmin kāye ākāṅkṣati, taṃ tameva kāyaṃ tasmin tasmin kāye (svakāyaṃ) adhitiṣṭhati | sa sattvakāyānāṃ karmakāyatāṃ ca prajānāti | vipākakāyatāṃ ca... | kleśakāyatāṃ ca... | rūpakāyatāṃ ca... | ārūpyakāyatāṃ ca prajānāti | kṣetrakāyānāṃ parīttatāṃ ca prajānāti, mahadgatatāṃ ca apramāṇatāṃ ca saṃkliṣṭatāṃ ca viśuddhatāṃ ca vyatyastatāṃ ca adhomūrdhatāṃ ca samatalatāṃ ca samavasaraṇatāṃ ca digjālavibhāgatāṃ ca prajānāti | karmavipākakāyānāṃ vibhaktisaṃketaṃ prajānāti | evaṃ śrāvakākāyānāṃ pratyekabuddhakāyānāṃ bodhisattvakāyānāṃ vibhaktisaṃketaṃ prajānāti | tathāgatakāyānāmabhisaṃbodhikāyatāṃ ca prajānāti | praṇidhānakāyatāṃ ca... | nirmāṇakāyatāṃ ca | adhiṣṭhānakāyatāṃ ca | rūpalakṣaṇānuvyañjanavicitrālaṃkārakāyatāṃ ca | prabhākāyatāṃ ca | manomayakāyatāṃ ca | puṇyakāyatāṃ ca | jñānakāyatāṃ ca | dharmakāyatāṃ ca prajānāti | jñānakāyānāṃ suvicāritatāṃ ca prajānāti | yathāvannistīraṇatāṃ ca phalaprayogasaṃgṛhītatāṃ ca laukikalokottaravibhāgatāṃ ca triyāṇavyavasthānatāṃ ca sādhāraṇāsādhāraṇatāṃ ca nairyāṇikānairyāṇikatāṃ ca śaikṣāśaikṣatāṃ ca prajānāti | dharmakāyānāṃ samatāṃ ca prajānāti | avikopanatāṃ ca avasthānasaṃketasaṃvṛttivyavasthānatāṃ ca sattvāsattvadharmavyavasthānatāṃ ca buddhadharmāryasaṃghavyavasthānatāṃ ca prajānāti | ākāśakāyānāmapramāṇatāṃ ca sarvatrānugatatāṃ ca aśarīratāṃ ca avitathānantatāṃ ca rūpakāyābhivyaktitāṃ ca prajānāti ||

O

sa evaṃ kāyajñānābhinirhāraprāpto vaśavartī bhavati sarvasattveṣu | āyurvaśitāṃ ca pratilabhate'nabhilāpyānabhilāpyakalpāyuḥ-pramāṇādhiṣṭhānatayā | cetovaśitāṃ ca pratilabhate'pramāṇ-āsaṃkhyeyasamādhinidhyaptijñānapraveśatayā | pariṣkāravaśitāṃ ca sarvalokadhātvanekavyūhālaṃkārapratimaṇḍitādhiṣṭhāna-saṃdarśanatayā | karmavaśitāṃ ca yathākālaṃ karmavipākādhi-ṣṭhānasaṃdarśanatayā | upapattivaśitāṃ ca sarvalokadhātūpapatti-saṃdarśanatayā adhimuktisaṃdarśanatayā sarvalokadhātubuddha-pratipūrṇasaṃdarśanatayā praṇidhānasaṃdarśanatayā yatheṣṭa-buddhakṣetrakālābhisaṃbodhisaṃdarśanatayā ṛddhisaṃ-darśanatayā sarvabuddhakṣetraṛddhivikurvaṇasaṃdarśanatayā dharmasaṃdarśanatayā anantamadhyadharmamukhāloka-saṃdarśanatayā jñānasaṃdarśanatayā tathāgatabalavaiśārady-āveṇikabuddhadharmalakṣaṇānuvyañjanābhisaṃbodhisaṃdarśanat ayā ||

P

sa āsāṃ daśānāṃ bodhisattvavaśitānāṃ sahapratilambhena acintya-jñānī ca bhavati atulyajñānī ca aprameyajñānī ca vipulajñānī ca asaṃ-hāryajñānī ca bhavati | tasyaivaṃbhūmyanugatasya evaṃ jñānasam-anvāgatasya atyantāgavadyaḥ kāyakarmasamudācāraḥ pravartate, atyantānavadyaśca vāk... | atyantānavadyaśca manaḥsamudācāraḥ pravartate | jñānapūrvaṃgamo jñānānuparivartī prajñāpāramit-ādhipateyo mahākaruṇāpūrvaka upāyakauśalyasuvibhaktaḥ praṇi-dhānasvabhinirhṛtastathāgatādhiṣṭhānasvadhiṣṭhito'pratiprasrabdha sattvārthaprayogo'paryantalokadhātuvibhaktigataḥ | samāsato bho jinaputra bodhisattvasya imāmacalāṃ bodhisattvabhūmimanu-prāptasya sarvabuddhadharmasamudānayanāya kāyavāṅmanas-karmasamudācāraḥ pravartate | sa evamimāmacalāṃ bodhisattva-bhūmimanuprāptaḥ supratiṣṭhitāśayabalaśca bhavati sarvakleśasam-udācārāpagatatvāt | supratiṣṭhitādhyāśayabalaśca bhavati mārgāvi-pravāsitatvāt | mahākaruṇābalasupratiṣṭhitaśca bhavati sattvārthān-utsargatvāt | mahāmaitrībala...sarvajagatparitrāṇatvāt | dhāraṇībala-

...asaṃpramoṣadharmatvāt | pratibhānabala...sarvabuddhadharma-pravicayavibhāgakuśalatvāt | abhijñābala...aparyantalokadhātu-caryāvibhāgakuśalatvāt | praṇidhānabala...sarvabodhisattvakriyān-utsargatvāt | pāramitābala...sarvabuddhadharmasamudānayanatvāt | tathāgatādhiṣṭhānabala...sarvākārasarvajñānābhimukhatvāt | sa evaṃbalādhānaprāptaḥ sarvakriyāśca saṃdarśayati, sarvakriyāsu ca anavadyo bhavatyanupaliptaśca | |

Q

iyaṃ bho jinaputra bodhisattvasya aṣṭamī jñānabhūmiracalety-ucyate'saṃhāryatvāt | avivartyabhūmirityucyate jñānāvivartyatvāt | durāsadabhūmirityucyate sarvajagad-durjñānatvāt | kumārabhūmir-ityucyate anavadyatvāt | janmabhūmirityucyate yathābhiprāyavaśa-vartitvāt | pariniṣpannabhūmirityucyate apunaḥkāryatvāt | pari-niṣṭhitabhūmirityucyate | sukṛtajñānavicayatvāt | nirmāṇabhūmir-ityucyate svabhinirhṛtapraṇidhānatvāt | adhiṣṭhānabhūmirityucyate | parāvikopanatvāt | anābhogabhūmirityucyate pūrvāntābhinir-hṛtatvāt | |

R

evaṃ jñānasvabhinirhṛtaḥ khalu punarbho jinaputra bodhisattvo buddhagotrānugato buddhaguṇaprabhāvabhāsitastathāgat-eryāpathacaryācāritrānugato buddhaviṣayābhimukhaḥ satata-samitaṃ svadhiṣṭhitatathāgatādhiṣṭhānaśca bhavati śakrabrahma-lokapālapratyudgataśca vajrapāṇisatatānubaddhaśca samādhibalān-utsṛṣṭaśca ca apramāṇakāyavibhaktyabhinirhṛtaśca sarvakāyacaryā-balopagataśca mahābhijñāvipākapariniṣpannaśca anantasamādhi-vaśavartī ca apramāṇavyākaraṇapratyeṣakaśca yathāparipavakka-jagadabhisaṃbodhinidarśakaśca bhavati | sa evaṃ jñānabhūmy-anugato mahāyānamaṇḍalānupraviṣṭaḥ suvicāritamahājñānābhijñaḥ satatasamitaṃ pramuktaprajñālokaraśmirasaṅgadharmadhātupath-āvatīrṇo lokadhātupathavibhaktikovidaḥ sarvākāraguṇasaṃ-darśakaḥ svacittotpādavaśavartī pūrvāntāparāntasuvicitajñānaḥ sarvamārapathāvartanavivartanajñānānugataḥ sarvatathāgata-viṣayagocarānupraviṣṭo'paryantalokadhātuprasareṣu bodhisattva-caryāṃ caratyapratyudāvartyayogena | tata ucyate bodhisattvo-'calāṃ bodhisattvabhūmimanuprāpta iti | |

S

tatra bho jinaputra acalāṃ bodhisattvabhūmimanuprāpto bodhisattvaḥ satatasamitamaparyantatathāgatadarśanāvirahito bhavati samādhibalasvabhinirhṛtatvāt I audārikaṃ buddhadarśanapūjopasthānaṃ notsṛjati I sa ekaikasmin kalpe ekaikasmin lokadhātuprasare anekān buddhān, anekāni buddhaśatāni...peyālaṃ...anekāni buddhakoṭīnayutaśatasahasrāṇi satkaroti gurukaroti mānayati pūjayati sarvākārapūjābhinirhāraṃ copasaṃharati I tāṃśca tathāgatān paryupāste, lokadhātuvibhaktipūrvakaṃ ca dharmālokopasaṃhāraṃ pratīcchati I sa bhūyasyā mātrayā tathāgatadharmakośaprāpto'saṃhāryo bhavati lokadhātuparipṛcchānirdeśeṣu I tāni cāsya kuśalamūlānyanekān kalpānuttapyante... I tadyathāpi nāma bho jinaputra tadeva jātarūpaṃ supariniṣṭhitaṃ kuśalena karmāreṇa suparikarmakṛtaṃ jambūdvīpasvāminaḥ kaṇṭhe śirasi vā ābaddhamasaṃhāryaṃ bhavati sarvajambūdvīpakānāṃ sattvānāmābharaṇavikṛtaiḥ, evameva bho jinaputra asyāmacalāyāṃ bodhisattvabhūmau sthitasya bodhisattvasya tāni kuśalamūlānyasaṃhāryāṇi bhavanti sarvaśrāvakapratyekabuddhairyāvatsaptamībhūmisthitaiśca bodhisattvaiḥ I imāṃ ca bhūmimanugatasya bodhisattvasya mahatī prajñājñānaprabhā sattvānāṃ kleśatamāṃsi praśamayati suvibhaktajñānamukhābhinirhāratayā I tadyathāpi nāma bho jinaputra sāhasriko mahābrahmā sāhasra lokadhātuṃ maitryā spharitvā prabhayāvabhāsayati, evameva bho jinaputra bodhisattvo'syāmacalāyāṃ bodhisattvabhūmau sthito yāvaddaśabuddhakṣetraśatasahasraparamāṇurajaḥsamān lokadhātūn mahatā maitryavabhāsena spharitvā sattvānāṃ kleśaparidāhānanupūrveṇa praśamayati, āśrayāṃśca prahlādayati I tasya daśabhyaḥ pāramitābhyaḥ praṇidhānapāramitā atiriktatamā bhavati, na ca pariśeṣāsu na samudāgacchati yathābalaṃ yathābhajamānam I iyaṃ bhavanto jinaputrā bodhisattvasya acalā nāma aṣṭamī bodhisattvabhūmiḥ samāsanirdeśataḥ I vistaraśaḥ punaraparyantakalpanirdeśaniṣṭhāto'nugantavyā I yasyāṃ pratiṣṭhito bodhisattvo bhūyastvena mahābrahmā bhavati sāhasrādhipatiḥ I abhibhūranabhibhūto'nvarthadarśī vaśiprāptaḥ kṛtī prabhuḥ sattvānāṃ sarvaśrāvakapratyekabuddhabodhisattvapāramitopadeśopasaṃhāreṣu asaṃhāryo lokadhātuvibhaktiparipṛcchānirdeśeṣu I yacca kiṃcit... I I

acalā nāma aṣṭamī bhūmiḥ I I

[Beginning of eighth bhūmi's final gathas]

upasaṃhāragāthāḥ |

te bhūmya saptasu viśodhita prajñupāyā
mārgā susaṃbhṛta mahāpraṇidhānabaddhāḥ |
supratiṣṭhitā naravarāḥ kuśalopapetā
jñānābhilāṣi vidu aṣṭamimākramanti || 12 ||

te puṇyajñānupagatāḥ kṛpamaitrayuktā
jñānāpramāṇapathagāḥ khagabuddhikalpāḥ |
śrutadharma niścitabalopagatā maharṣī
kṣāntiṃ labhanti anutpādapraśāntisūkṣmām || 13 ||

ādāvajāta anutpāda alakṣaṇaṃ ca
asaṃbhūtatamavinaṣṭata cāpravṛttam |
bhāvasvabhāvavigatā tathatāvikalpā
mama cittacāravigatāḥ khagatulyakalpāḥ || 14 ||

te eva kṣāntisamanvāgata niṣprapañcā
gambhīracālya vidu śāntavicāraprāptāḥ |
durjñeya sarvajagatārahapratyayaiśca
cittaṃ nimittagrahasaṃjñavibhāvitatvāt || 15 ||

evaṃ sthitānamanucintavikalpa nāsti
bhikṣurnirodhyupagato'paprakalpaprāptaḥ |
svapnoghaprāpta pratibuddha tathāvikalpā
brahmāpure ratisaṅgarahito tathaiva || 16 ||

pūrvādhiṣṭhāna sugatā puna codayanti
eṣā sa kṣānti paramā sugatābhiṣeke |
asmāku jñāna vipulaṃ varabuddhadharmā
te tubhya nāsti ta hi vīryu samārabhāyam || 17 ||

kiṃcāpi śānta tava sarvakileśajvālā
jvalitaṃ niśamya puna kleśagatibhya lokam |

praṇidhāna pūrva smara sattvahitaṃ vicārya
jñānārthi prārthita kriyā jagamokṣahetoḥ || 18 ||

sada eṣa dharmata sthitā tathatāvikalpā
sarveṣu buddhajinaśrāvakapratyayānam |
na hi etinā daśabalāna prabhāvu loke
nānyatra jñānavipulaṃ tribhi adhvasaṅgam || 19 ||

evaṃ tamapratisamā naradevapūjyā
upasaṃharanti bahujñānamukhā vicārān |
jinadharmaniṣpattipraveśamanantapāraṃ
yasyā kalā na bhavate puna bodhicaryā || 20 ||

etāni prāpta vṛṣabhī varajñānabhūmim
ekakṣaṇena spharate diśatāḥ samantān |
jñānapraveśupagatā varabhijñaprāptā
yatha sāgare vahanu mārutayānaprāptaḥ || 21 ||

sābhogacittavigatāḥ sthitajñānakarma
vicinanti kṣetraprabhavaṃ vibhavasthitiṃ ca |
dhātuścatvāri vinibhāgagatāna tāṃśca
sūkṣmaṃ mahadgata vibhakti samosaranti || 22 ||

trisahasri sarvaparamāṇurajo taranti
catvāri dhātu jagakāyi vibhaktitaśca |
ratnā vibhaktiparamāṇu suvargatīṣu
bhinditva jñānaviṣayena gaṇentyaśeṣam || 23 ||

jñāne vibhāvitamanā vidu sarvakāyān
sve kāyi tatra upanenti jagārthahetoḥ |
trisahasra sarva ca spharitva vicitrarūpān
darśenti kāya vividhān tathanantaloke || 24 ||

sūryaṃ śaśiṃ ca vahni māruta antarīkṣe
svakamaṇḍalusya udake pratibhāsaprāptā |
jñānottame sthita tathācaladharmatāyāṃ
jaga śuddhaāśaya vidū pratibhāsaprāptā || 25 ||

yathaāśayaṃ jagata kāyavibhaktitāṃ ca
darśenti sarvapariṣe bhuvi sarvaloke |
vaśipratyayāśraya jinātmajaśrāvakānāṃ
darśenti te sugatakāya vibhūṣitāṅgān || 26 ||

sattvāṃśca kṣetra tatha karmavipāka kāyān
āryāśrayān vividhadharmajñānakāyān |
ākāśakāya vṛṣabhī samatāmupetaṃ
darśenti ṛddhi vividhān jagatoṣaṇārtham || 27 ||

vaśitā daśo vimalajñānavicāraprāptā
anuprāpta jñānakṛta maitrakṛpānukūlāḥ |
yāvacca sarvajinadharmamupādakarmā
trisaṃvaraiḥ susthitameka acalyakalpāḥ || 28 ||

ye cā balā jinasutāna daśa akṣobhyā
tehī upeta avibandhiya sarvamāraiḥ |
buddhairadhiṣṭhita namaskṛta śakrabrahmai-
statha vajrapāṇibalakaiḥ satatānubaddhāḥ || 29 ||

ima bhūmideśupagatā na guṇānamanto
no śakyate kṣayitu kalpasahasrakoṭyaiḥ |
te bhūya buddha niyutān samupāsayante
bhonto utapta yatha bhūṣaṇu rājamūrdhni || 30 ||

ima bhūmideśupagatā vidu bodhisattvā
mahabrahma bhonti sahasrādhipatī guṇāḍhyāḥ |
trayayānadeśana akṣobhyasaṃhāraprāptā
maitrāyanaḥ śubhaprabhā jagakleśaghātī || 31 ||

ekakṣaṇena daśakṣetraśataḥsahasrā
yāvā rajodhātu tattaka samādhyupenti |
paśyanti tattaka daśadiśi sattvasārān
bhūyo ataḥ praṇidhiśreṣṭha vyūha nekāḥ || 32 ||

saṃkṣepa eṣa nirdiṣṭo aṣṭamāyā jinātmajāḥ |

vistaraḥ kalpakoṭībhirna śakyaḥ sarva bhāṣitum || 33 ||

[End of eighth bhūmi's final gathas]

[Beginning of ninth bhūmi's initial gathas]

9 sādhumatī nāma navamī bhūmiḥ ।

upakramagāthāḥ ।

imāṃ bhūmiṃ prabhāṣatā kampitāḥ kṣetrakoṭayaḥ ।
adhiṣṭhānā narendrasya aprameyā acintiyā ।। 1 ।।

ābhāsa rucirā muktāḥ kāyataḥ sarvadarśino ।
tayāvabhāsitāḥ kṣetrāḥ sattvāśca sukhitāstayā ।। 2 ।।

bodhisattvasahasrāṇi antarikṣe sthitāni ca ।
divyātikrāntapūjāya pūjyante vadatāṃ varam ।। 3 ।।

maheśvarā devaputrā vaśavartī praharṣitāḥ ।
nānāprakārapūjābhiḥ pūjenti guṇasāgaram ।। 4 ।।

tato'psaraḥsahasrāṇi harṣitāḥ prīṇitendriyāḥ ।
divyā suyattā saṃgītāḥ śāstu pūjāmajagrayam ।। 5 ।।

tebhyaśca tūryanādebhya anubhāvānmaharṣiṇaḥ ।
īdṛśā rutasahasrā ravantī madhurasvarāḥ ।। 6 ।।

imi sarve jinasutā khilamalavigatā
upagata bhuvi varasuruciracaraṇāḥ ।
jagahita vicarati daśadiśa vṛṣabhī
darśayi jinacari khagasamamanasā ।। 7 ।।

narapuri marupuri bhujagapativiṣaye
viyuha daśadiśi puṇyabalamudīritāḥ ।
tata tu bhuyu jinasuta darśayi atulī
jinasutaprabhava jinanupathaniratā ।। 8 ।।

ekakṣetri acalita sarvakṣetravirajā
anugata jagahita śaśiriva pratibhā ।

sarvaghoṣahānacitta praśamitamanasā
viyahari kṛtaśataśrutipathagiribhiḥ | | 9 | |

yatra sattva hīnacitta dīna mānaniratā-
statra vidu śrāvakācarī deśeti vṛṣabhī |
yatra sattva tīkṣṇacitta pratyayānaniratā-
statra jñāna pratyayāna darśayanti virajā | | 10 | |

ye tu sattvahitamaitramanasā (abhiratās)
tatra tyaṃ(tvaṃ) jinaputrāna darśayanti caraṇam |
ye tu sattva agra śreṣṭha matimānaniratā-
statra amī buddhakāya darśayanti atulam | | 11 | |

māyā yathā māyakāro darśeti jagahite
yāya koṭi naikavidyā sarvabhāvavigatā |
eva vidū buddhasutā jñānamāyaniratā
darśayanti sarvacarī sarvabhāvavigatā | | 12 | |

etādṛśā rutasahasrān bhaṇitva madhurāṃ-
stadā marukanyakā jinaṃ dṛṣṭvā tūṣṇīṃbhūtāḥ |
parṣadviprasanneyamavocatsugatātmajam
aṣṭamāyā bhaṇa ūrdhvaṃ cariṃ saddharmarājinām | | 13 | |

[End of ninth bhūmi's initial gathas]

9 sādhumatī nāma navamī bhūmiḥ |

A

vajragarbho bodhisattva āha - yo'yaṃ bhavanto jinaputrā bodhisattva evamapramāṇajñeyavicāritayā buddhyā bhūyaścottarān śāntān vimokṣānadhyavasyan adhyālambamānaḥ bhūyaścottaraṃ tathāgatajñānaṃ susamāptaṃ vicārayan tathāgataguhyānupraveśaṃ cāvataran acintyajñānamāhātmyaṃ ca pravicinvan dhāraṇīsamādhipravicayaṃ ca pariśodhayan abhijñāvaipulyaṃ cābhinirharan lokadhātuvibhaktiṃ cānugacchan tathāgatabalavaiśādyāveṇikabuddhadharmāsaṃhāryatāṃ ca parikarmayan tathāgatadharmacakrapravartanavṛṣabhatāṃ cānukramamāṇaḥ mahākaruṇādhiṣṭhānapratilambhaṃ cānutsṛjan navamīṃ bodhisattvabhūmimākramati |

B

so'syāṃ sādhumatyāṃ bodhisattvabhūmau sthitaḥ kuśalākuśalāvyākṛtadharmābhisaṃskāraṃ ca yathābhūtaṃ prajānāti | sāsravānāsravadharmābhisaṃskāraṃ ca... | laukikalokottaradharmābhisaṃskāraṃ ca... | cintyācintyadharmābhisaṃskāraṃ ca... | niyatāniyatadharmābhisaṃskāraṃ ca... | śrāvakapratyekabuddhadharmābhisaṃskāraṃ ca... | bodhisattvacaryādharmābhisaṃskāraṃ ca... | tathāgatabhūmidharmābhisaṃskāraṃ ca... | saṃskṛtadharmābhisaṃskāraṃ ca.. | asaṃskṛtadharmābhisaṃskāraṃ ca yathābhūtaṃ prajānāti ||

C

sa evaṃjñānānugatayā buddhyā sattvacittagahanopacāraṃ ca yathābhūtaṃ prajānāti | kleśagahanopacāraṃ ca... | karmagahanopacāraṃ ca... | indriyagahanopacāraṃ ca ... | adhimuktigahanopacāraṃ ca... | dhātugahanopacāraṃ ca... | āśayānuśayagahanopacāraṃ ca... | upapattigahanopacāraṃ ca... | vāsanānusaṃdhigahanopacāraṃ ca... | trirāśivyavasthānagahanopacāraṃ ca yathābhūtaṃ prajānāti |

D

sa sattvānāṃ cittavaimātratāṃ ca yathābhūtaṃ prajānāti | cittavicitratāṃ ca cittakṣaṇalaghuparivartabhaṅgabhaṅgatāṃ ca cittaśarīratāṃ ca cittānantyasarvataḥprabhūtatāṃ ca cittaprabhāsvaratāṃ ca cittasaṃkleśaniḥkleśatāṃ ca cittabandhavimokṣatāṃ ca cittamāyāviṭhapanatāṃ ca cittayathāgatipratyupasthānatāṃ ca yāvadanekāni cittanānātvasahasrāṇi yathābhūtaṃ prajānāti |

E

sa kleśānāṃ dūrānugatatāṃ ca yathābhūtaṃ prajānāti | prayogānantatāṃ ca... | sahajāvinirbhāgatāṃ ca... | anuśayaparyutthānaikārthatāṃ ca... | cittasaṃprayogāsaṃprayogatāṃ ca... | upapattisaṃdhiyathāgatipratyupasthānatāṃ ca... | traidhātukavibhaktitāṃ ca... | tṛṣṇāvidyādṛṣṭiśalyamānamahāsāvadyatāṃ ca... | trividhakarmaṇi dānānupacchedatāṃ ca... | samāsato yāvaccaturaśītikleśacaritanānātvasahasrānupraveśatāṃ ca yathābhūtaṃ prajānāti |

F

sa karmaṇāṃ kuśalākuśalāvyākṛtatāṃ ca... | vijñaptyavijñaptitāṃ ca... | cittasahajāvinirbhāgatāṃ ca... | svarasakṣaṇakṣīṇabhaṅgopacayāvipraṇāśaphalānusaṃdhitāṃ ca... | vipākavipākatāṃ ca... kṛṣṇaśuklākṛṣṇaśuklānekadeśakarmasamādānavaimātratāṃ ca... | karmakṣetrāpramāṇatāṃ ca... | āryalaukikapravibhaktitāṃ ca... | lokottaradharmavyavasthānatāṃ ca... | (sopādānānupādānatāṃ ca... | saṃskṛtāsaṃskṛtatāṃ ca |) dṛṣṭadharmopapadyāparaparyāyavedanīyatāṃ ca... | yānāyānaniyatāniyatatāṃ ca... | samāsato yāvaccaturaśītikarmanānātvasahasrapravibhaktivicayakauśalyaṃ ca yathābhūtaṃ prajānāti |

G

sa indriyāṇāṃ mṛdumadhyādhimātratāṃ ca... | pūrvāntāparāntasaṃbhedāsaṃbhedatāṃ ca... | udāramadhyanikṛṣṭatāṃ ca... | kleśasahajāvinirbhāgatāṃ ca... | yānāyānaniyatāniyatatāṃ ca... | yathāparipavkāparipakvavaineyikatāṃ ca... | indriyajālānuparivartanalaghubhaṅganimittagrahaṇatāṃ ca... | indriyādhipatyānavamardanīyatāṃ ca... | vivartyāvivartyendriyapravibhāgatāṃ ca... | dūrānugatasahajāvinirbhāganānātvavimātratāṃ ca, samāsato yāvadanekānīndriyanānātvasahasrāṇi prajānāti | so'dhimuktīnāṃ mṛdumadhyādhimātratāṃ ca...yāvadanekānyadhimuktinānātvasahasrāṇi prajānāti | sa dhātūnāṃ.... | sa āśayānāṃ.... |

H

so'nuśayānāmāśayasahajacittasahajatāṃ ca.... | cittasaṃprayogatāṃ ca... | viprayogavibhāgadūrānugatatāṃ ca... | anādikālānuddhaṭitatāṃ ca... | sarvadhyānavimokṣasamādhisamāpattyabhijñāprasahyatāṃ ca | traidhātukasaṃdhisunibaddhatāṃ ca | anādikālacittanibandhasamudācāratāṃ ca | āyatanadvārasamudayavijñaptitāṃ ca । pratipakṣālābhādravyabhūtatāṃ ca । bhūmy-āyatanasamavadhānāsamavadhānatāṃ ca । ananyāryamārgasam-uddhaṭanatāṃ ca prajānāti ।

I

sa upapattinānātvatāṃ ca । yathākarmopapattitāṃ ca । niraya-tiryagyonipretāsuramanuṣyadevavyavasthānatāṃ ca । rūpārūpy-opapattitāṃ ca । saṃjñāsaṃjñopapattitāṃ ca । karmakṣetratṛṣṇā-snehāvidyāndhakāravijñānabījapunarbhavaprarohaṇatāṃ ca । nāmarūpasahajāvinirbhāgatāṃ ca । bhavasaṃmohatṛṣṇābhilāṣa-saṃdhitāṃ ca । bhoktukāmabhavitukāmasattvaratyanavarāgratāṃ ca । traidhātukāvagrahaṇasaṃjñāniṣkarṣaṇatāṃ ca prajānāti ।

J

sa vāsanānāmupacārānupacāratāṃ ca... । yathāgatisaṃbandhavāsan-āvāsitatāṃ ca । yathāsattvacaryācaraṇavāsitatāṃ ca । yathākarma-kleśābhyāsavāsitatāṃ ca । kuśalākuśalāvyākṛtadharmābhyāsa-vāsitatāṃ ca । punarbhavagamanādhivāsitatāṃ ca... । anupūrvādhi-vāsitatāṃ ca । dūrānugatānupacchedakleśopakarṣaṇavikārānud-dharaṇavāsitatāṃ ca । dravyabhūtādravyabhūtavāsitatāṃ ca । śrāvakapratyekabuddhabodhisattvatathāgatadarśanaśravaṇasaṃvās avāsitatāṃ ca prajānāti ।

K

sa sattvarāśīnāṃ samyaktvaniyatatāṃ ca prajānāti mithyātva-niyatatāṃ ca । ubhayatvāniyatatāṃ ca... । samyagdṛṣṭisamyagni-yatatāṃ ca mithyādṛṣṭimithyā...niyatatāṃ ca । tadubhayavigamād-aniyatatāṃ ca pañcānantaryānyatamamithyādṛṣṭiniyatatāṃ ca... । pañcendriyasamyagniyatatāṃ ca... । aṣṭamithyātvamithyāniyatatāṃ ca... । samyaktvasamyagniyatatāṃ ca... । apunaḥkāritatāṃ ca... । mātsaryerṣyāghṛṇopacārāvinivṛttyā mithyāniyatatāṃ ca... । āryān-uttaramārgabhāvanopasaṃhārasamyaktvaniyatatāṃ ca... । tad-ubhayavigamādaniyatarāśyupadeśatāṃ ca prajānāti । iti hi bho jinaputra evaṃjñānānugato bodhisattvaḥ sādhumatyāṃ bodhisattva-bhūmau pratiṣṭhita ityucyate ।।

L

so'syāṃ sādhumatyāṃ bodhisattvabhūmau sthita evaṃ caryāvi-mātratāṃ sattvānāmajñāya tathaiva mokṣopasaṃhāramupa-saṃharati । sa sattvaparipākaṃ prajānāti । sattvavinayaṃ ca... । śrāvakayānadeśanāṃ ca । pratyekabuddhayānadeśanāṃ ca । bodhisattvayānadeśanāṃ ca | tathāgatabhūmideśanāṃ ca prajānāti | sa evaṃ jñātvā tathatvāya sattvebhyo dharmaṃ deśayati |

yathāśayavibhaktito yathānuśayavibhaktito yathendriyavibhaktito yathādhimuktivibhaktito yathāgocaravibhāgajñānopasaṃhārataḥ sarvagocarajñānānugamanato yathādhātugahanopacārānugamanato yathāgatyupapattikleśakarmavāsanānuvartanato yathārāśivyavasthānānugamanato yathāyānādhimokṣavimuktiprāptito'nantavarṇarūpakāyasaṃdarśanataḥ sarvalokadhātumanojñasvaravijñāpanataḥ sarvarutaravitaparijñānataḥ sarvapratisaṃvidviniścayakauśalyataśca dharmaṃ deśayati | |

M

so'syāṃ sādhumatyāṃ bodhisattvabhūmau sthitaḥ san bodhisattvo dharmabhāṇakatvaṃ kārayati, tathāgatadharmakośaṃ ca rakṣati |

N

sa dharmābhāṇakagatimupagato'pramāṇajñānānugatena kauśalyena catuḥpratisaṃvidabhinirhṛtayā bodhisattvavācā dharmaṃ deśayati | tasya satatasamitamasaṃbhinnāścatasro bodhisattvapratisaṃvido-'nupravartante | katamāścatasraḥ? yaduta dharmapratisaṃvit arthapratisaṃvit niruktipratisaṃvit pratibhānapratisaṃvit | |

O

sa dharmapratisaṃvidā svalakṣaṇaṃ dharmāṇāṃ prajānāti | arthapratisaṃvidā vibhaktiṃ dharmāṇāṃ prajānāti | niruktipratisaṃvidā asaṃbhedadeśanāṃ dharmāṇāṃ prajānāti | pratibhānapratisaṃvidā anuprabandhānupacchedatāṃ dharmāṇāṃ prajānāti | |

P

punaraparaṃ dharmapratisaṃvidā abhāvaśarīraṃ dharmāṇāṃ prajānāti | arthapratisaṃvidā udayāstagamanaṃ dharmāṇāṃ prajānāti | niruktipratisaṃvidā sarvadharmaprajñaptyacchedanadharmaṃ deśayati | pratibhānapratisaṃvidā yathāprajñaptyavikopanatāparyantatayā dharmaṃ deśayati | |

Q

punaraparaṃ dharmapratisaṃvidā pratyutpannavibhaktiṃ dharmāṇāṃ prajānāti | arthapratisaṃvidā atītānāgatavibhaktiṃ dharmāṇāṃ prajānāti | niruktipratisaṃvidā atītānāgapratyutpannāsaṃbhedato dharmaṃ deśayati | pratibhānapratisaṃvidā ekaikamadhvānamārabhya aparyantadharmālokatayā dharmaṃ deśayati

| |

R

punaraparaṃ dharmapratisaṃvidā dharmaprabhedaṃ prajānāti | arthapratisaṃvidā arthaprabhedaṃ prajānāti | niruktipratisaṃvidā yathārutadeśanatayā dharmaṃ deśayati | pratibhānapratisaṃvidā yathānuśayajñānaṃ deśayati | |

S

punaraparaṃ dharmapratisaṃvidā dharmajñānavibhaktya-saṃbhedakauśalyaṃ prajānāti | arthapratisaṃvidā anvayajñāna-tathātvavyavasthānaṃ prajānāti | niruktipratisaṃvidā saṃvṛtijñāna-saṃdarśanāsaṃbhedatayā nirdiśati | pratibhānapratisaṃvidā para-mārthajñānakauśalyena dharmaṃ deśayati | |

T

punaraparaṃ dharmapratisaṃvidā ekanayāvikopaṃ dharmāṇāṃ prajānāti | arthapratisaṃvidā skandhadhātvāyatanasatyapratītya-samutpādakauśalyānugamamavatarati | niruktipratisaṃvidā sarva-jagadabhigamanīyasumadhuragirinirghoṣākṣarairnirdiśati | prati-bhānapratisaṃvidā bhūyo bhūyo'paryantadharmāvabhāsatayā nirdiśati | |

U

punaraparaṃ dharmapratisaṃvidā ekayānasamavasaraṇanānātvaṃ prajānāti | arthapratisaṃvidā pravibhaktayānavimātratāṃ prajānāti | niruktipratisaṃvidā sarvayānānyabhedena nirdiśati | pratibhāna-pratisaṃvidā ekaikaṃ yānamaparyantadharmābhāsena deśayati | |

V

punaraparaṃ dharmapratisaṃvidā sarvabodhisattvacarijñānacari-dharmacarijñānānugamamavatarati | arthapratisaṃvidā daśabhūmi-vyavasthānanirdeśapravibhaktimavatarati | niruktipratisaṃvidā yathābhūmimārgopasaṃhārasaṃbhedena nirdiśati | pratibhāna-pratisaṃvidā ekaikāṃ bhūmimaparyantākāreṇa nirdiśati | |

W

punaraparaṃ dharmapratisaṃvidā sarvatathāgataikalakṣaṇānu-bodhamavatarati | arthapratisaṃvidā nānākālavastulakṣaṇavibhaṅg-ānugamaṃ prajānāti | niruktipratisaṃvidā yathābhisaṃbodhiṃ vi-bhaktinirdeśena nirdiśati | pratibhānapratisaṃvidā ekaikaṃ dharmapadamaparyantakalpāvyavacchedena nirdiśati | |

X

punaraparaṃ dharmapratisaṃvidā sarvatathāgatavāgbalavaiś-arādyabuddhadharmamahākaruṇāpratisaṃvitprayogadharmacakrān upravartamānasarvajñajñānānugamaṃ prajānāti | arthapratisaṃvidā caturaśītisattvacaritasahasrāṇāṃ yathāśayaṃ yathendriyaṃ yathā-dhimuktivibhaktitastathāgataghoṣaṃ prajānati | niruktipratisaṃvidā sarvasattvacaryāsaṃbhedatastathāgataghoṣānuraveṇa nirdiśati | pratibhānapratisaṃvidā tathāgatajñānaprabhācaryāmaṇḍal-ādhimukttyā dharmaṃ deśayati ||

Y

sa evaṃ pratisaṃvidā jñānābhinirhārakuśalo bho jinaputra bodhisattvo navamīṃ bodhisattvabhūmimanuprāptastathā-gatadharmakośaprāpto mahādharmabhāṇakatvaṃ ca kurvāṇaḥ arthavatīdhāraṇīpratilabdhaśca bhavati | dharmavatī...| jñānābhi-nirhāravatī...| avabhāsavatī...| vasumatīdhāraṇī...| sumatidhāraṇī...| tejodhāraṇī... | asaṅgamukhadhāraṇī... | ananta... | vicitrārthakośa... | sa evamādīnāṃ dhāraṇīpadānāṃ paripūrṇāni daśadhāraṇīmukh-āsaṃkhyeyaśatasahasrāṇi pratilabhate | tathā asaṃkhyeyaśata-sahasrānugatenaiva svarāṅgakauśalyena tāvadapramāṇānugatenaiva pratibhānavibhaktimukhena dharmaṃ deśayati | sa evam-apramāṇairdhāraṇīmukhāsaṃkhyeyaśatasahasrairdaśasu dikṣu aprameyāṇāṃ buddhānāṃ bhagavatāṃ sakāśāddharmaṃ śṛṇoti | śrutvā ca na vismārayati | yathāśrutaṃ ca apramāṇavibhaktita evaṃ nirdiśati ||

Z

sa ekasya tathāgatasya sakāśāddaśabhirdhāraṇīmukhāsaṃkhyeya-śatasahasrairdharmān paryavāpnoti | yathā caikasya, evamapary-antānāṃ tathāgatānām | sa praṇidhānamātreṇa bahutaraṃ samyak-saṃbuddhasakāśāddharmamukhālokaṃ saṃpratīcchati, na tveva mahābāhuśrutyaprāptaḥ śrāvakaḥ śrutodgrahaṇadhāraṇīprati-labdhaḥ kalpaśatasahasrodgrahaṇādhiṣṭhānena | sa evaṃ dhāraṇī-prāptaśca bhavati pratibhānaprāptaśca dharmasāṃkathyaṃ saṃ-niṣaṇṇaḥ sarvāvatīṃ trisāhasramahāsāhasralokadhātuṃ spharitvā yathāśayavibhaktitaḥ sattvebhyo dharmaṃ deśayati dharmāsane niṣaṇṇaḥ | dharmāsanaṃ cāsya tathāgatānabhiṣekabhūmiprāptān bodhisattvān sthāpayitvā sarvato viśiṣṭamapramāṇāvabhāsaprāptaṃ bhavati | sa dharmāsane niṣaṇṇa ākāṅkṣan ekaghoṣodāhāreṇa sarvaparṣadaṃ nānāghoṣarutavimātratayā saṃjñāpayati | ākāṅkṣan nānāghoṣanānāsvarāṅgavibhaktibhirājñāpayati | ākāṅkṣan raśmimukhopasaṃhārairdharmamukhāni niścārayati | ākāṅkṣan sarvaromakūpebhyo ghoṣānniścārayati | ākāṅkṣan yāvattrisāhasramahāsāhasrāyāṃ lokadhātau rūpāvabhāsāstebhyaḥ sarvarūpāvabhāsebhyo dharmarutāni niścārayati | ākāṅkṣan ekasvararutena sarvadharmadhātuṃ vijñāpayati | ākāṅkṣan sarvarutanirghoṣeṣu dharmarutamadhitiṣṭhati | ākāṅkṣan sarvalokadhātuparyāpannebhyo gītāvādyatūryaśabdebhyo dharmarutaṃ niścārayati | ākāṅkṣan ekākṣararutātsarvadharmapadaprabhedarutaṃ niścārayati | ākāṅkṣan anabhilāpyānabhilāpyalokadhātvaparyantataḥ pṛthivyaptejovāyuskandhebhyaḥ sūkṣmaparamāṇurajaḥprabhedata ekaikaparamāṇurajonabhilāpyāni dharmamukhāni niścārayati | sacettaṃ trisāhasramahāsāhasralokadhātuparyāpannaḥ sarvasattvā upasaṃkramya ekakṣaṇalavamuhūrtena praśnān paripṛccheyuḥ, ekaikaśca teṣāmapramāṇarutavimātratayā paripṛcchet, yaṃ caikaḥ sattvaḥ paripṛcchenna taṃ dvitīyaḥ, taṃ bodhisattvaḥ sarvasattvarutapadavyañjanamudgṛhṇiyāt | udgṛhya caikarutābhivyāhāreṇa teṣāṃ sarvasattvānāṃ cittāśayān paritoṣayet (yāvadanabhilāpyalokadhāturpayāpannā vā sattvā upasaṃkramya ekakṣaṇalavamuhūrtena praśnān paripṛccheyuḥ, ekaikaśca teṣāmapramāṇarutavimātratayā paripṛcchet, yaṃ caikaḥ paripṛcchenna taṃ dvitīyaḥ, taṃ bodhisattva ekakṣaṇalavamuhūrtenaiva sarvamudgṛhya ekodāhāreṇaiva sarvānājñāpayet | yāvadanabhilāpyānapi lokadhātūn spharitvā yathāśayendriyādhimuktitaḥ sattvebhyo dharmaṃ deśayati | dharmasāṃkathyaṃ niṣaṇṇaśca tathāgatādhiṣṭhānasaṃpratyeṣakaḥ sakalena buddhakāryeṇa sarvasattvānāṃ pratyupasthito bhavati | sa bhūyasyā mātrayā evaṃ jñānāvabhāsapragrahaṇamārabhate | sacedekasmin vālāgraprasare yāvantyanabhilāpyeṣu lokadhātuṣu paramāṇurajāṃsi tāvantastathāgatāstāvadapramāṇaprāpteṣveva parṣanmaṇḍaleṣu dharmaṃ deśayeyuḥ | ekaikaśca tathāgatastāvadapramāṇaprāptebhyaḥ sarvasattvebhyo nānātvato dharmaṃ deśayet, ekaikasmiṃśca sattvāśayasaṃtāne tāvadapramāṇameva dharmopasaṃhāramupasaṃharet | yathā caikastathāgataḥ parṣanmaṇḍale tathā te sarve tathāgatāḥ | yathā caikasmin vālāgraprasare tathā sarvasmin dharmadhātau | tatrāsmābhistādṛśaṃ smṛtivaipulyamabhinirhartavyaṃ yathaikakṣaṇena sarvatathāgatānāṃ sakāśāddharmāvabhāsaṃ pratyeṣemahi ekarutāvyatirekāt | yāvanti ca tāni yathāparikīrtitāni parṣanmaṇḍalāni nānānikāyadharmapravaṇaika-paripūrṇāni, tatrāsmābhistādṛśaṃ prajñāvabhāsaviniścayaprati-bhānaṃ pariśodhyaṃ yadekakṣaṇena sarvasattvān paritoṣayet, kiṃ punariyatsu lokadhātuṣu sattvāni ||

sa imāṃ sādhumatīṃ bodhisattvabhūmimanuprāpto bodhisattvo bhūyasyā mātrayā rātriṃdivamananyamanasikāraprayukto bhūtvā buddhagocarānupraviṣṭastathāgatasamavadhānaprāpto gambhīra-bodhisattvavimokṣānuprāpto bhavati | sa evaṃjñānānugato bodhi-sattvaḥ samāhitastathāgatadarśanaṃ na vijahāti | ekaikāsmiṃśca kalpe'nekān buddhān, anekāni buddhaśatāni...anekāni buddhakoṭi-nayutaśatasahasrāṇi... | dṛṣṭvā ca satkaroti gurukaroti mānayati pūjayati | audārikena buddhadarśanena pūjopasthānaṃ notsṛjati | tāṃśca tathāgatān praśnān paripṛcchati | sa dharmadharaṇīnirdeś-ābhinirjāto bhavati | tasya bhūyasyā mātrayā tāni kuśalamūlāny-uttaptatamānyasaṃhāryāṇi bhavanti | tadyathāpi nāma bho jina-putrāstadeva jātarūpamābharaṇīkṛtaṃ supariniṣṭhitaṃ kuśalena karmāreṇa rājñaścakravartina uttamāṅge kaṇṭhe vā ābaddham-asaṃhārya bhavati sarvakoṭṭarājānāṃ cāturdvipakānāṃ ca sattvānāmābharaṇavikṛtaiḥ, evameva bho jinaputrā bodhisattvasya asyāṃ sādhumatyāṃ bodhisattvabhūmau sthitasya tāni kuśala-mūlāni mahājñānāloka suvibhaktānyuttapyante, asaṃhāryāṇi bhavanti sarvaśrāvakapratyekabuddhairadharabhūmisthitaiśca bodhisattvaiḥ | tasya sā kuśalamūlābhā sattvānāṃ kleśacitta-gahanānyavabhāsya tata eva vyāvartate | tadyathāpi nāma bho jina-putrā dvisāhasriko mahābrahmā sarvasmin dvisāhasrike lokadhātau gahananimnopacārānavabhāsayati, evameva bho jinaputrā bodhi-sattvasya asyāṃ sādhumatyāṃ bodhisattvabhūmau sthitasya sā kuśalamūlābhā sattvānāṃ kleśacittagahanānyavabhāsya tata eva vyāvartate | tasya daśabhyaḥ pāramitābhyo balapāramitā atirikta-tamā bhavati, na ca pariśeṣāsu na samudācarati yathābalaṃ yathā-bhajamānam | iyaṃ bhavanto jinaputrā bodhisattvasya sādhumatī nāma navamī bodhisattvabhūmiḥ...mahābrahmā bhavati mahābala-sthāmaprāpto dvisāhasrādhipatirabhibhūḥ...pāramitopadeśeṣv-asaṃhāryaḥ sattvāśayaparipṛcchānirdeśaiḥ | yacca kiṃcit... ||

sādhumatī nāma navamī bhūmiḥ ||

[Beginning of ninth bhūmi's final gathas]

upasaṃhāragāthāḥ |

te apramāṇabalabuddhi vicārayantaḥ
susūkṣmajñānaparamā jagatā durjñeyā |
tatha guhyasthāna sugatāna samosaranto
bhūmiṃ kramanti navamīṃ jagato'rthakarīm | | 14 | |

te dhāraṇīmukhi samādhisamāhitāgrā
vipulā abhijñā api kṣetrapraveśanantam |
balajñānaniścayamapi jinu dhairyasthānaṃ
praṇidhīkṛpāśayavidū navamotaranti | | 15 | |

te atra bhūmyanugatā jinakośadhārī
kuśalāśca dharmakuśalāśca avyākṛtāśca |
ye sāsravā api ca laukika ye ca āryā-
ścintyā acintiya vidū anubuddhyayanti | | 16 | |

niyatāṃśca dharmaniyatāṃ pravicārayanti
trayayānasaṃpadakriyā paritārayanti |
bhūmidharma yathāadhimukti pracārataśca
abhisaṃskaronti yatha lokya tathotaranti | | 17 | |

te evajñānanugatā varasūkṣmabuddhī
sattvāna cittagahanaṃ parimārgayanti |
(cittaṃ vicitrakṣaṇavartanivartatāṃ ca)
cittaṃ anantaprabhavaṃ sada otaranti | | 18 | |

kleśānanādina prayogasahāyatāśca
ye paryutthānanuśayā gatisaṃdhitaśca |
tatha karmapraveśa vicitravibhaktitaśca
hetū niruddhaphalanāśa samotaranti | | 19 | |

indriya yā mṛdukamadhya udārataśca
saṃbhedapūrvamaparānta samotaranti |

adhimukti naika vividhā śubha āśubhataśca
catvāri āśīti sahasra samotaranti | | 20 | |

dhātūpraveśa jaga bhāvitakleśadṛṣṭī
gahanaṃ gatā anavarāgra acchedataśca |
ye āśayā anuśayā sahajapracārī
cittāsamosṛta nibaddha accheda tanti | | 21 | |

cittaṃ yathā anuśayā na ca dravyabhūto
na ca deśasthā na ca vipravasanti āśayā |
durheya dhyānaviṣayānabhivartiyāśca
chedaśca mārga vinayena na cānyamasti | | 22 | |

upapatti ṣaḍgati vibhaktipraveśataśca
snehaṃ ca tṛṣṇamavidyāndhaka karmakṣetrā |
vijñānabījasahajāṅkuranāmarūpaṃ
traidhātuke anavarāgra samotaranti | | 23 | |

te vāsanāgati kileśa ca karma cittā
suvihāratāya na punargatisanta kāmā |
rāśitribhirniyatasattva samotaranti
dṛṣṭīnimagnamapi jñāna samotaranti | | 24 | |

evaṃ visaraṇagatāḥ sthita atra bhūmyāṃ
sarvasattva āśaya yathendriya yādhimuktiḥ |
teṣāmarthe dharmavibhakti prakāśayanti
pratisaṃvidarthakuśalāḥ pratibhā nirukti | | 25 | |

te dharmabhāṇaka gatī anuprāpta (sthānaṃ)
siṃhariṣabhanibhā girirājakalpāḥ |
abhipravarṣanti madhuramamṛtasya varṣaṃ
bhujagendrasāgara yathā anupūrayanti | | 26 | |

hitārthajñānakuśalāstatha dharmatāyāṃ
sarvaṃ niruktyanugatāḥ pratibhānaprāptāḥ |
te dhāraṇī daśa asaṃkhyasahasra labdhā
dhāranti dharma yatha (sāgara varṣadhārī) | | 27 | |

evaṃ ca dhāraṇiviśuddhisamādhiprāptā
ekakṣaṇena daśabuddhasahasra dṛṣṭāḥ ।
śravaṇena dharmaratanaṃ ca nideśayanti
(ekaikamaṇḍalaviśuddhisvarāṅgagatāḥ) ।। 28 ।।

vyohārate trisahasramahalokadhātuṃ
pariśeṣa sattva vividhāstrayaratanebhyaḥ ।
toṣenti sarva yathaindriyaāśayāśca
catudvīpasāgara varṣā sama modayanti ।। 29 ।।

(bhūyottariṃ guṇinu vīrya samārabhante)
cittaanti vālaprasara asmi sucetanantāḥ ।
deśeyu dharma sugatāḥ puna nānasattvaṃ
śrutvā dharema yatha sarvada (bījadhārī) ।। 30 ।।

(yāvatakā) jagadiha praviśanti sattvāḥ
(te sarva ekapariṣanmaṇḍale niṣaṇṇāśca) ।
eṣāṃ ca ekakṣaṇi sarvi samotaritvā
ekāṃ rutena imi tarpayitavya sarve ।। 31 ।।

(atra sthitā naramaruttama dharmarājā)
bhontī dharmairjinasutāḥ paricālayanti ।
rātriṃdivaṃ sada jinaiḥ śamathānuprāptā
gambhīra śānta sthita jñānavimokṣadhīrā ।। 32 ।।

(te'nekabuddhaniyutān paryupāsayante)
bhontī uttapta paṇu (pāṇḍu) cakravartaḥprabhāvā ।
tasya kleśagahanāni prabhā samājya
brahmaṇo va dvisahasrikalokadhātuḥ ।। 33 ।।

(atra sthitā guṇadharā) mahabrahmaloke
bhontī (triyānadeśanaṃ viditānubhāvā ।)
yaṃ caivamārabhati sarvajagaddhitāya
sarvajñajñānupagatā guṇajñānaprāptā ।। 34 ।।

(kṣetrāpramāṇaparyāpanna) ekā rajāgre

kṣaṇi eki (tattakasamādhi u)penti dhīrāḥ ǀ
(dṛṣṭvā sarve diśi jināṃśca vacaḥ śṛṇonti)
tato vikurvi praṇidhānanvitāpramāṇāḥ ǀǀ 35 ǀǀ

ityeṣā navamī bhūmirmahājñānavicāriṇā ǀ
gambhīrā durdṛśā sūkṣmā nirdiṣṭā sugatātmajāḥ ǀǀ 36 ǀǀ

[End of ninth bhūmi's final gathas]

[Beginning of tenth bhūmi's initial gathas]
10 dharmameghā nāma daśamī bhūmiḥ ।

upakramagāthāḥ ।

eva śrutva caraṇamanuttamaṃ
śuddhavāsanayutāḥ praharṣitāḥ ।
antarīkṣasthita prīṇitendriyāḥ
pūjayanti sugataṃ tathāgatam ।। 1 ।।

bodhisattvanayutā acintiyā
antarīkṣagatiprāptiharṣitāḥ ।
gandhamegha atulān manomayān
dhūpayanti sattvakleśaghātinaḥ ।। 2 ।।

devarāja vaśavarti prīṇito
antarīkṣa trisahasrakoṭibhiḥ ।
vastrakaiḥ samakarī sagauravā
bhrāmayanti rucirān varān śatam ।। 3 ।।

apsarā bahava prīṇitendriyāḥ
pūjayanti sugataṃ sagauravāḥ ।
tūryakoṭinayutāḥ pravāditā
evarūpa ravuyukta rāvataḥ ।। 4 ।।

ekakṣetra sugato niṣaṇṇakaḥ
sarvakṣetri pratibhāsa darśayī ।
kāyakoṭi vividhā manoramā
dharmadhātuvipulān spharitvana ।। 5 ।।

ekaromu sugatasya raśmayo
niścaranti jagakleśa śāmyati ।
śakyu (kṣetra-raja-dhātu'pi) kṣayī
tasya raśmigaṇanā tvajānitum ।। 6 ।।

keci buddhavaralakṣaṇaṃ viduḥ

paśyayanti varacakravartinaḥ |
anyakṣetravaracarya uttamāṃ
śodhayanti dvipadendra dṛśyate || 7 ||

(tuṣitāyatanaprāpta nāyako)
cyavamānu caṃkramāṇa dṛśyate |
garbhaprāpta bahukṣetrakoṭiṣu
jāyamāna kvaci kṣetra dṛśyate || 8 ||

niṣkramanta jagahetu nāyako
budhyamāna puna bodhimuttamām |
(dharmacakravartanirvṛtāgato)
dṛśyamāna buddhakṣetrakoṭiṣu || 9 ||

māyakāra yatha vidyaśikṣito
jīvikārtha bahukāya darśayī |
tadva śāstu varaprajñaśikṣito
sarvakāyabhinihartu (sattvana) || 10 ||

śūnya śānta gatadharmalakṣaṇā
antarīkṣasamaprāptadharmatām |
buddhaśāstu paramārthatattvataṃ
darśayī pravarabuddhagocaram || 11 ||

yatha svabhāvu sugatānagocarā
sarvasattva tatha prāpta dharmatām |
lakṣalakṣa samalakṣa tādṛśā
sarvadharma paramārthalakṣaṇāḥ || 12 ||

ye tu jñāna sugatāna arthiṃke
kalpakalpaparikalpavarjitam |
bhāvabhāvasamabhāvabuddhayaḥ
kṣipra bheṣyati nareśa uttamāḥ || 13 ||

īdṛśān rutasahasrān bhaṇitva madhurasvarāḥ |
marukanyā jinaṃ lokya tūṣṇībhūtāḥ śame ratāḥ || 14 ||

prasannaṃ parṣadaṃ jñātvā mokṣacandro viśāradaḥ ।
vajragarbhaṃ tridhāpṛcchajjinaputraṃ viśāradam ।। 15 ।।

daśamī saṃkramantānāṃ kīdṛśaṃ guṇagocaram ।
nimittaprātihāryāṃśca sarvamākhyā(hi) parikrama ।। 16 ।।

atha khalu vajragarbho bodhisattvo daśadiśaṃ vyavalokya sarvāvatīṃ parṣadaṃ vyavalokya dharmadhātuṃ ca vyavalokayan sarvajñatācittotpādaṃ ca saṃvarṇayan bodhisattvaviṣayamādarśayan caryābalaṃ pariśodhayan sarvākārajñatāsaṃgrahamanuvyāha ran sarvalokamalamapakarṣayan sarvajñajñānamupasaṃharan acintyajñānaniryūhamādarśayan bodhisattvaguṇān prabhāvayan evameva bhūmyarthaṃ prarūpayamāṇo buddhānubhāvena tasyāṃ velāyāmimā gāthā abhāṣata -

[End of tenth bhūmi's initial gathas]

10 dharmameghā nāma daśamī bhūmiḥ ।

A

vajragarbho bodhisattva āha - yo'yaṃ bhavanto jinaputrā bodhisattva evamapramāṇajñeyavicāritayā buddhyā yāvannavamī bodhisattvabhūmiriti suvicitavicayaḥ suparipūrṇaśukladharmaḥ paryantasaṃbhāropacayopacitaḥ suparigṛhītamahāpuṇyajñānasaṃbhāraḥ mahākaruṇāvaipulyādhigataḥ lokadhātuvibhaktivaimātryakovidaḥ sattvadhātupraviṣṭagahanopacāraḥ tathāgatagocarapraveśānugatasaṃjñāmanasikāraḥ balavaiśāradyabuddhadharmādhyālambanānugataḥ sarvākārasarvajñajñānābhiṣekabhūmiprāpta ityucyate ।।

B

tasya khalu punarbhavanto jinaputrā evaṃjñānānugatasya bodhisattvasya abhiṣekabhūmisamāpannasya vimalo nāma samādhirāmukhībhavati । dharmadhātuvibhaktipraveśaśca nāma । bodhimaṇḍālaṃkāravyūhaśca nāma । sarvākāraraśmikusumaśca nāma । sāgaragarbhaśca nāma । sāgarasamṛddhiśca nāma । ākāśadhātuvipulaśca nāma । sarvadharmasvabhāvavicayaśca nāma । sarvasattvacittacaritānugataśca nāma । pratyutpannasarvabuddhasaṃmukhāvasthitaśca nāma bodhisattvasamādhirāmukhībhavati । tasaivaṃpramukhāni daśa samādhyasaṃkhyeyaśatasahasrāṇyāmukhībhavanti । sa tān sarvān samādhīn samāpadyate ca vyuttiṣṭhate ca, samādhikauśalyānugataśca yāvatsamādhikāryaṃ tatsarvaṃ pratyanubhavati । tasya yāvaddaśasamādhyasaṃkhyeyaśatasahasrāṇāṃ paryante sarvajñajñānaviśeṣābhiṣekavānnāma bodhisattvasamādhirāmukhībhavati ।।

C

yasmin samanantarābhimukhībhūte daśatrisāhasraśatasahasrāparyantapramāṇaṃ mahāratnarājapadmaṃ prādurbhavati sarvākāraratnapratyarpitaṃ sarvalokaviṣayasamatikrāntaṃ lokottarakuśalamūlasaṃbhūtaṃ māyāsvabhāvagocarapariniṣpannaṃ dharmadhātusuvyavasthitāvabhāsaṃ divyaviṣayasamatikrāntaṃ mahāvaiḍūryamaṇiratnadaṇḍamatulyacandanarājakarṇikaṃ mahāśmagarbhakesaraṃ jāmbūnadasuvarṇāvabhāsapatramaparimitaraśmisaṃkusumitaśarīraṃ sarvapravararatnapratyuptagarbhamaparyantamahāratnajālasaṃchannaṃ paripūrṇadaśatrisāhasraśatasahasraparamāṇurajaḥsamamahāratnapadmaparivāram । tadanugatastadanurūpaśca tasya bodhisattvasya kāyaḥ saṃtiṣṭhate | sa tasya sarvajñajñāna-viśeṣābhiṣekavataḥ samādheḥ sahapratilambhāttasminmahāratna-rājapadme niṣaṇṇaḥ saṃdṛśyate | samanantaraniṣaṇṇaśca sa bodhi-sattvastasmin mahāratnarājapadme, atha yāvanti tasya mahāratna-rājapadmasya mahāpadmāni parivāraḥ prādurbhūtaḥ, tāvanto bodhisattvā daśadiglokadhātusaṃnipatitāstaṃ bodhisattvamanu-parivārya teṣu mahāratnapadmeṣu niṣīdanti | ekaikaśca teṣāṃ daśa samādhiśatasahasrāṇi samāpadyate tameva bodhisattvaṃ nirīkṣa-māṇaḥ ||

D

samanantarasamāpanne ca tasmin bodhisattve teṣu ca bodhisattveṣu niravaśeṣam, atha sarvalokadhātusaṃprakampanaṃ bhavati | sarv-āpāyapratiprasrambhaṇaṃ ca, sarvadharmadhātvavabhāsakaraṇaṃ ca, sarvalokadhātupariśodhanaṃ ca, sarvabuddhakṣetranāmadheya-rutānanuravaṇaṃ ca, sarvasabhāgacaritabodhisattvasaṃnipātanaṃ ca sarvalokadhātudevamanuṣyatūryasaṃgītisaṃpravādanaṃ ca sarvasattvasukhasaṃjananaṃ ca sarvasamyaksaṃbuddhācintya-pūjopasthānapravartanaṃ ca sarvatathāgataparṣanmaṇḍala-vijñāpanaṃ ca bhavati | tatkasya hetoḥ? tathā hi bho jinaputrāstasya bodhisattvasya samanantaraniṣaṇṇasya tasmin mahāratnarājapadme adhastāccaraṇatalābhyāṃ daśaraśmyasaṃkhyeyaśatasahasrāṇi niścaranti | niścarya daśadiśamavīciparyantān mahānirayān-avabhāsayanti | nairayikānāṃ sattvānāṃ sarvaduḥkhāni pratipra-srambhayati | jānumaṇḍalābhyāṃ daśa...daśadiśaṃ sarvatiryagyoni-bhavanānyavabhāsayanti, sarvatiryagyoniduḥkhāni ca praśamayanti | nābhimaṇḍalād daśa...sarvayamalokabhavanāni avabhāsayanti, sarvayamalaukikānāṃ sattvānāṃ duḥkhāni ca praśamayanti | vāma-dakṣiṇābhyāṃ pārśvābhyāṃ...manuṣyāśrayān...manuṣya... | ubhābhyāṃ pāṇibhyāṃ devāsurabhavanāni...devāsura... | aṃsābhyāṃ...śrāvakayānīyāśrayānavabhāsayanti, dharmāloka-mukhaṃ copasaṃharanti | pṛṣṭhato grīvāyāśca...pratyekabuddh-āśrayānavabhāsayanti, śāntisamādhimukhanayaṃ copasaṃharanti | mukhadvārād...prathamacittopādamupādāya yāvannavamīṃ bhūmimanuprāptān bodhisattvānavabhāsayanti, prajñopāya-kauśalyanayaṃ copasaṃharanti | ūrṇākośāddaśaraśmyasaṃkhyeya-śatasahasrāṇi niścaranti, niścarya daśasu dikṣu sarvamārabhavan-ānyavabhāsya dhyāmīkṛtya abhiṣekabhūmiprāptān bodhisattvān avabhāsya tatkāyeṣvevāstaṃ gacchanti | uparyuttamāṅgāt paripūrṇadaśatrisāhasrāsaṃkhyeyaśatasahasraparamāṇurajaḥsamā raśmayo niścaranti, niścarya daśasu dikṣu dharmadhātupramāṇānyākāśadhātuparyavasānāni sarvatathāgataparṣanmaṇḍalānyavabhāsya daśākāraṃ lokaṃ pradakṣiṇīkṛtya uparikhagapathe sthitvā mahāraśmijālamaṇḍalāni kṛtvā uttaptaprabhāsaṃ nāma mahattathāgatapūjopasthānaṃ sarvatathāgatānāmanupravartayanti | tasya pūjopasthānasya prathamacittotpādamupādāya yāvannavamībhūmyanupravartitam tathāgatapūjopasthānaṃ... | tataḥ khalvapi mahāraśmijālamaṇḍalādyāvatī daśasu dikṣu niravaśeṣasarvadharmadhātvantargatā puṣpaprajñaptirvā gandhadhūpamālyavilepanacūrṇacīvaracchatradhvajapatākāvastrābharaṇamaṇiratnaprajñaptirvā, tato'tiriktatarāḥ sarvalokaviṣayasamatikrāntā lokottarakuśalamūlasaṃbhārādhipatyābhinirvṛttāḥ sarvākāraguṇasaṃpannā acintyanirvāṇādhiṣṭhānādhiṣṭhitā nānāvyūhamahāratnavarṣā iva ekaikatathāgataparṣanmaṇḍale mahāmeghā ivābhipravarṣanti sma | tāṃ ca ye sattvāḥ pūjāṃ saṃjānante, te sarve niyatā bhavantyanuttarāyāṃ samyaksaṃbodhau | evaṃrūpaṃ pūjopasthānaṃ pravartya tā raśmayaḥ punareva sarvāvanti tathāgataparṣanmaṇḍalānyavabhāsya daśākāraṃ lokaṃ pradakṣiṇīkṛtya teṣāṃ tathāgatānāmarhatāṃ samyaksaṃbuddhānāmadhastātkramataleṣu astaṃ gacchanti | tatasteṣāṃ tathāgatānāṃ teṣāṃ ca bodhisattvānāṃ viditaṃ bhavati - amuṣmin lokadhātuprasare evaṃcaryānugato bodhisattvo'bhiṣekakālaprāpta iti | tatra bho jinaputrā daśabhyo digbhyo'paryantebhyo lokadhātuprasarebhyo'prameyāsaṃkhyeyāparyantā bodhisattvā yāvannavamībodhisattvabhūmipratiṣṭhitā āgatya taṃ bodhisattvamanuparivārya mahatīṃ pūjāṃ kṛtvā tameva bodhisattvaṃ nirīkṣamāṇā daśa samādhiśatasahasrāṇi samāpadyante | abhiṣekabhūmiprāptānāṃ ca bodhisattvānāṃ kāyebhyaḥ śrīvatsālaṃkārādvajrasvastikāt sarvamāraśatruvijayo nāmaikaikā mahāraśmirdaśaraśmyasaṃkhyeyaśatasahasraparivārā niścarati, niścarya daśadiśo'vabhāsya aparyantāni prātihāryāṇi saṃdarśya tasya bodhisattvasya śrīvatsālaṃkāre vajrasvastika evāstaṃ gacchati | samanantarādastamitāyāśca tasyā raśmyāḥ śatasahasraguṇottarā tasya bodhisattvasya balasthāmābhivṛddhiḥ prajñāyate ||

E

atha khalu bho jinaputrāḥ sarvajñatābhijñāvatyo nāma raśmayasteṣāṃ tathāgatānāmarhatāṃ samyaksaṃbuddhānāmūrṇākośebhyo niścarantyasaṃkhyeyaoparivārāḥ | tāḥ sarvāsu daśasu dikṣu aśeṣataḥ sarvalokadhātūnavabhāsya daśākāraṃ lokaṃ pradakṣiṇīkṛtya mahānti tathāgatavikurvitāni saṃdarśya bahūni bodhisattvakoṭiniyutaśatasahasrāṇi saṃcodya sarvabuddhakṣetraprasarān ṣaḍvikāraṃ saṃprakampya sarvāpāyacyutigatyupapattīḥ praśamya sarvamārabhavanāni dhyāmīkṛtya sarvatathāgatābhisaṃbodhivibuddhabuddhāsanānyupasaṃdarśya sarvabuddhaparṣanmaṇḍalavyūhaprabhāvaṃ nidarśya dharmadhātuparamānākāśadhātuparyavasānān sarvalokadhātūnavabhāsya punarevāgatya taṃ sarvāvantaṃ bodhisattvaparṣatsaṃnipātamuparyuparipradakṣiṇīkṛtya mahāvyuhānnidarśya tā raśmayastasya bodhisattvasyottamāṅge'staṃ gacchanti | tatparivāraraśmayaśca tathā saṃnipatitānāṃ teṣāṃ bodhisattvānāṃ śirassvantardhīyante sma | samanantarasaṃnipatitābhiśca tābhī raśmibhiste bodhisattvā apratilabdhapūrvāṇi daśa samādhiśatasahasrāṇi pratilabhante | tāśca raśmayastulyakālaṃ tasya bodhisattvasyottamāṅge nipatitā bhavanti | sa ca bodhisattvo'bhiṣikta ityucyate samyaksaṃbuddhaviṣaye | daśabalaparipūryā tu samyaksaṃbuddha iti saṃkhyāṃ gacchati | tadyathāpi nāma bho jinaputrā yo rājñaścakravartinaḥ putro jyeṣṭhaḥ kumāro›gryamahiṣīprasūtaścakravartirājalakṣaṇasamanvāgato bhavati, taṃ rājā cakravartī divye hastisauvarṇe bhadrapīṭhe niṣādya, caturbhyo mahāsamudrebhyo vāryānīya, upariratnavimānena dhāryamāṇena mahatā puṣpadhūpagandhadīpamālyavilepanacūrṇacīvaracchatradhvajapatākātūryatālāvacarasaṃgitivyūhena sauvarṇaṃ bhṛṅgāraṃ gṛhītvā tena vāriṇā taṃ kumāraṃ mūrdhanyabhiṣiñcati | samanantarābhiṣiktaśca rājā kṣatriyo mūrdhabhiṣikta iti saṃkhyāṃ gacchati | daśakuśalakarmapathaparipūryā tu cakravartīti saṃjñāṃ pratilabhate | evameva bho jinaputrāḥ samanantarābhiṣikto bodhisattvastairbuddhairbhagavadbhirmahājñānābhiṣekābhiṣikta ityucyate | samyaksaṃbuddhābhiṣekeṇa daśabalaparipūryā tu samyaksaṃbuddha iti saṃkhyāṃ gacchati | ayaṃ bho jinaputrā bodhisattvasya mahājñānābhiṣeko yasyārthe bodhisattvo'nekāni duṣkaraśatasahasrāṇyārabhate | sa evamabhiṣikto›prameyaguṇajñānavivardhito dharmameghāyāṃ bodhisattvabhūmau pratiṣṭhita ityucyate ||

F

so'syāṃ dharmameghāyāṃ bodhisattvabhūmau pratiṣṭhito bodhisattvo dharmadhātusamudāgamaṃ ca yathābhūtaṃ prajānāti I kāmadhātusamudāgamaṃ ca yathābhūtaṃ prajānāti I rūpadhātusamudāgamaṃ ca yathābhūtaṃ prajānāti I ārūpyadhātusamudāgamaṃ ca yathābhūtaṃ prajānāti I lokadhātusamudāgamaṃ ca yathābhūtaṃ prajānāti I sarvasattvadhātusamudāgamaṃ ca yathābhūtaṃ prajānāti I vijñānadhātusamudāgamaṃ ca yathābhūtaṃ prajānāti I saṃskṛtāsaṃskṛtadhātusamudāgamaṃ ca yathābhūtaṃ prajānāti I ākāśadhātusamudāgamaṃ ca yathābhūtaṃ prajānāti I bhūtābhūtadeśanāṃ ca yathābhūtaṃ prajānāti I nirvāṇaṃ ca yathābhūtaṃ prajānāti I dṛṣṭikleśasamudāgamaṃ ca yathābhūtaṃ prajānāti I lokadhātupravṛttinivṛttisamudāgamaṃ ca yathābhūtaṃ prajānāti I śrāvakacaryāsamudāgamaṃ ca yathābhūtaṃ prajānāti I pratyekabuddhacaryāsamudāgamaṃ ca yathābhūtaṃ prajānāti I bodhisattvacaryāsamudāgamaṃ ca yathābhūtaṃ prajānāti I

tathāgatabalavaiśāradyāveṇikabuddhadharmarūpakāyadharmakāya samudāgamaṃ ca yathābhūtaṃ prajānāti I sarvākārasarvajñajñānasamudāgamaṃ ca yathābhūtaṃ prajānāti I abhisaṃbodhidharma-cakrapravṛttisaṃdarśanasamudāgamaṃ ca yathābhūtaṃ prajānāti I samāsataḥ sarvadharmapraveśavibhaktiniṣṭīrṇasamudāgamaṃ ca yathābhūtaṃ prajānāti I sa evaṃjñānānugatayā buddhyā uttari sattvakāyanirmāṇaṃ ca yathābhūtaṃ prajānāti I kleśakāyanirmāṇaṃ ca yathābhūtaṃ prajānāti I dṛṣṭikṛtanirmāṇaṃ ca... lokadhātunirmāṇaṃ ca...dharmadhātunirmāṇaṃ ca...śrāvakanirmāṇaṃ ca...pratyekabuddhanirmāṇaṃ ca...bodhisattvanirmāṇaṃ ca...tathāgatanirmāṇaṃ ca...sarvanirmāṇakalpākalpatāṃ ca yathābhūtaṃ prajānāti I sarvabuddhādhiṣṭhānaṃ ca...dharmādhiṣṭhānaṃ ca...saṃghādhiṣṭhānaṃ ca...karmādhiṣṭhānaṃ ca kleśādhiṣṭhānaṃ ca...kālādhiṣṭhānaṃ ca...praṇidhānādhiṣṭhānaṃ ca...pūjādhiṣṭhānaṃ ca...caryādhiṣṭhānaṃ ca...kalpādhiṣṭhānaṃ ca...jñānādhiṣṭhānaṃ ca prajānāti I sa yānīmāni tathāgatānāmarhatāṃ samyaksaṃbuddhānāṃ sūkṣmapraveśajñānāni yaduta caryāsūkṣmapraveśajñānaṃ vā, cyutyupapattisukṣmapraveśajñānaṃ vā, janmasūkṣmapraveśajñānaṃ vā, abhiniṣkramaṇasūkṣmapraveśajñānaṃ vā, abhisaṃbodhisūkṣmapraveśajñānaṃ vā, vikurvaṇasukṣmapraveśa-

jñānaṃ vā, dharmacakrapravartanasūkṣmapraveśajñānaṃ vā, dharmadeśanāsukṣmapraveśajñāna vā, dharmavistarasūkṣmapraveśajñānaṃ vā, āyuḥpramāṇādhiṣṭhānajñānaṃ vā, varṇarūpakāyasaṃdarśanajñānaṃ vā, sarvasattvavinayātikramaṇajñānaṃ vā, sarvalokadhātuspharaṇajñānaṃ vā, sarvasattvacittacaritavyavalokanajñānaṃ vā, ekakṣaṇe tryadhvavyavalokanajñānaṃ vā, pūrvāntāparāntaniravaśeṣajñānaṃ vā, sarvasattvacittacaritanānātvasamantajñānaṃ vā, tathāgatabalavaiśāradyabuddhadharmācint ya-
jñānaṃ vā, tathāgataparinirvāṇajñānaṃ vā, śāsanādhiṣṭhānasaddharmasthitijñānaṃ vā, evaṃpramukhānyaprameyāsaṃkhyeyāni tathāgatānāṃ sukṣmapraveśajñānāni, tāni sarvāṇi yathābhūtaṃ prajānāti | sa yānīmāni tathāgatānāmarhatāṃ samyaksaṃbuddhānāṃ guhyasthānāni yaduta kāyaguhyaṃ vā vāgguhyaṃ vā cittaguhyaṃ vā kālākālavicāraṇāguhyaṃ vā bodhisattvavyākaraṇaguhyaṃ vā sattvasaṃgrahanigrahaguhyaṃ vā vineyotsādanāvasānaguhyaṃ vā yathākālāvavādānuśāsanādhyupekṣaṇaṃ vā yānanānātvavyavasthāpanaguhyaṃ vā sattvacaryendriyavibhaktiguhyaṃ vā sattvakarmakriyāvatāraguhyaṃ vā bodhisattvacaryendriyavibhaktiguhyaṃ vā caryābhisaṃbodhisvabhāvaprabhāvānubodhiguhyaṃ vā svabhāvābhisaṃbodhyadhiṣṭhānaguhyaṃ vā avatārottāraṇaguhyaṃ vā ākarṣaṇasaṃpreṣaṇaguhyaṃ vā sthānacaṃkramaṇaniṣadyāśayyāsanasaṃdarśanaguhyaṃ vā āhāraparibhogakāyopakaraṇapratisevanaguhyaṃ vā bhāṣitatūṣṇīṃbhāvadhyānavimokṣasamādhisamāpattisaṃdarśanaguhyaṃ vā, evaṃpramukhānyaprameyāsaṃkhyeyāni tathāgatānāṃ guhyasthānāni, tāni sarvāṇi yathābhūtaṃ prajānāti | sa yānīmāni tathāgatānāṃ kalpapraveśasamavasaraṇajñānāni yaduta ekakalpāsaṃkhyeyakalpasamavasaraṇatā | asaṃkhyeyakalpaikakalpasamavasaraṇatā | saṃkhyeyakalpāsaṃkhyeyakalpasamavasaraṇatā | asaṃkhyeyakalpasaṃkhyeyakalpasamavasaraṇatā | cittakṣaṇakalpasamavasaraṇatā | kalpacittakṣaṇasamavasaraṇatā | kalpākalpasamavasaraṇatā | akalpakalpasamavasaraṇatā | sabuddhakakalpābuddhakakalpasamavasaraṇatā | abuddhakakalpasabuddhakakalpasamavasaraṇatā | atītānāgatakalpapratyutpannakalpasamavasaraṇatā | pratyutpannakalpātītānāgatakalpasamavasaraṇatā | atītakalpānāgatakalpasamavasaraṇatā | anāgatakalpātītakalpasamavasaraṇatā | dīrgha-

kalpahrasvakalpasamavasaraṇatā | hrasvakalpadīrghakalpa-
samavasaraṇatā | sarvakalpeṣu saṃjñākṛtasamavasaraṇatā | sarva-
saṃjñākṛteṣu kalpasamavasaraṇatā | evaṃ pramukhānyapra-
meyāṇyasaṃkhyeyāni kalpapraveśasamavasaraṇāni, tāni sarvāni
yathābhūtaṃ prajānāti | sa yānīmāni tathāgatānāmarhatāṃ samyak-
saṃbuddhānāmavatārajñānāni yaduta vālapathāvatārajñānaṃ vā
paramāṇurajovatārajñānaṃ vā buddhakṣetrakāyābhisaṃbodhyavatārajñānaṃ vā sattvakāyacittābhisaṃbodhyavatārajñānaṃ vā
sarvatrānugatābhisaṃbodhyavatārajñānaṃ vā vyatyastacarisaṃ-
darśanāvatārajñānaṃ vā anulomacarisaṃdarśanāvatārajñānaṃ vā
pratilomacarisaṃdarśanāvatārajñānaṃ cintyācintyalokavijñeya-
vijñeyaṃ carisaṃdarśanāvatārajñānaṃ vā śrāvakavijñeyapratyeka-
buddhavijñeyabodhisattvavijñeyatathāgatavijñeyacarisaṃdarśanāvat
ārajñānaṃ vā, tāni sarvāṇi yathābhūtaṃ prajānāti | iti hi bho jina-
putrā aprameyaṃ buddhānāṃ bhagavatāṃ jñānavaipulyam-
apramāṇamevāsyāṃ bhūmau sthitasya bodhisattvasyāvatārajñānam
| |
G
sa khalu punarbho jinaputrā bodhisattva evamimāṃ bodhisattva-
bhūmimanugato'cintyaṃ ca nāma bodhisattvavimokṣaṃ pratilabhate
| anāvaraṇaṃ ca nāma viśuddhivicayaṃ ca nāma samantamukh-
āvabhāsaṃ ca nāma tathāgatakośaṃ ca nāma apratihatacakrānu-
gataṃ ca nāma tryadhvānugataṃ ca nāma dharmadhātugarbhaṃ ca
nāma vimuktimaṇḍalaprabhāsaṃ ca nāma aśeṣaviṣayagamaṃ ca
nāma bodhisattvavimokṣaṃ pratilabhate | iti hi bho jinaputrā imān
daśa bodhisattvavimokṣān pramukhān kṛtvā aprameyāsaṃkhyeyāni
bodhisattvavimokṣamukhaśatasahasrāṇi bodhisattvo'syāṃ
daśamyāṃ bodhisattvabhūmau pratiṣṭhitaḥ pratilabhate | evaṃ
yāvatsamādhiśatasahasrāṇi dhāraṇīśatasahasrāṇi abhijñābhinirhāra-
śatasahasrāṇi pratilabhate | jñānālokaśatasahasrāṇi vikurvaṇaśata-
sahasrāṇi prasaṃvinnirhāraśatasahasrāṇi upāyaprajñāvikrīḍitaśata-
sahasrāṇi gambhīradharmanayapraveśaśatasahasrāṇi mahākaruṇ-
āvegaśatasahasrāṇi bodhisattvavaśitāpraveśaśatasahasrāṇi prati-
labhate | |
H
sa evaṃjñānānugatayā buddhyā apramāṇānugatena smṛtikauśalyena
samanvāgato bhavati | sa daśabhyo digbhyo'prameyāṇāṃ

buddhānāṃ bhagavatāṃ sakāśādekakṣaṇalavamuhūrtenā apramāṇān mahādharmāvabhāsān mahādharmālokān mahādharmameghān sahate saṃpratīcchati svīkaroti saṃghārayati । tadyathāpi nāma bho jinaputrāḥ sāgaranāgarājameghavisṛṣṭo mahānapskandho na sukaro'nyena pṛthivīpradeśena soḍhuṃ vā saṃpratyeṣituṃ vā svīkartuṃ vā saṃdhārayituṃ vā anyatra mahāsamudrāt, evameva bho jinaputrā ye te tathāgatānāṃ bhagavatāṃ guhyānupraveśā yaduta mahādharmāvabhāsā mahādharmālokā mahādharmāmeghāḥ, te na sukarāḥ sarvasattvaiḥ sarvaśrāvakapratyekabuddhaiḥ prathamāṃ bhūmimupādāya yāvannavamībhūmipratiṣṭhitairapi bodhisattvaiḥ, tān bodhisattvo'syāṃ dharmameghāyāṃ bodhisattvabhūmau sthitaḥ sarvān sahate saṃpratīcchati svīkaroti saṃdhārayati । tadyathāpi nāma bho jinaputrā mahāsamudra ekasyāpi mahābhujagendrasya mahāmeghān sahate...dvayorapi trayāṇāmapi yāvadaparimānāṇāmapi bhujagendrāṇāmekakṣaṇalavamuhūrtenāprameyān mahāmeghān sahate... । tatkasya hetoḥ? apramāṇavipulavistīrṇatvānmahāsamudrasya । evameva bho jinaputrā asyāṃ dharmameghāyām bodhisattvabhūmau pratiṣṭhito bodhisattva ekasyāpi tathāgatasya sakāśādekakṣaṇa...dvayorapi trayānāmapi yāvadaparimānāṇāmapi tathāgatānāṃ sakāśādekakṣaṇa... । tata ucyata iyaṃ bhūmirdharmamegheti ।।

vimukticandro bodhisattva āha - śakyaṃ punarbho jinaputra saṃkhyāṃ kartuṃ kiyatāṃ tathāgatānāmantikebhyo bodhisattvaikakṣaṇa...? vajragarbho bodhisattva āha - na sukarā bho jinaputra saṃkhyā kartu gaṇanānirdeśena - iyatāṃ tathāgatānāmantikebhyo bodhisattvaikakṣaṇa... । api tu khalvaupamyaṃ kariṣyāmi । tadyathāpi nāma bho jinaputra daśasu dikṣu daśabuddhakṣetrānabhilāpyakoṭiniyutaśatasahasraparamāṇurajaḥsamāsu lokadhātuṣu yāvat sattvadhātuniravaśeṣayogena saṃvidyate । tata ekaḥ sattvaḥ śrutagrahaṇadhāraṇīpratilabdho bhavettathāgatānāmupasthāuyako mahāśrāvako›gryaḥ śrutadharāṇām । tadyathāpi nāma bhagavato vajrapadmottarasya tathāgatasyārhataḥ samyaksaṃbuddhasya mahāvijayo nāma bhikṣurevaṃrūpeṇa śrutakauśalyabalādhānena sa ekaḥ sattvaḥ samanvāgato bhavet । yathā ca sa ekaḥ sattvastathā niravaśeṣāsu sarvāsu lokadhātuṣu te sarve sattvāḥ samanvāgatā bhaveyuḥ । yaccaikenodgṛhītaṃ syānna dvitīyena । tatkiṃ manyase bho jinaputra bahutaraṃ teṣāmaprameyāpramāṇaṃ vā śrutakauśalyaṃ bhavet? vimukticandro bodhisattva āha - bahu bho jinaputra apramāṇaṃ tatteṣāṃ sarvasattvānāṃ śrutakauśalyaṃ bhavet । vajragarbho bodhisattva āha - ārocayāmi te bho jinaputra, prativedayāmi । yaṃ dharmameghāyāṃ bodhisattvabhūmau pratiṣṭhito bodhisattva ekakṣaṇalavamuhūrtenaikasyaiva tāvattathāgatasya sakāśāddharmadhātutryadhvakośaṃ nāma mahādharmāvabhāsālokameghaṃ sahate... । yasya mahādharmāvabhāsālokameghasaṃdhāraṇakauśalyasya tat pūrvakaṃ śrutakauśalyaṃ...kṣamate । yathā caikasya tathāgatasya sakāśāttathā daśasu dikṣu yāvanti tāsu pūrvikāsu lokadhātuṣu paramāṇurajāṃsi saṃvidyante, tāvatāṃ samyaksaṃbuddhānāṃ tato›pi bhūya uttari aprameyāṇāṃ tathāgatānāṃ sakāśādekakṣaṇalavamuhūrtena dharmadhātutryadhvakośaṃ nāma mahādharmāvabhāsālokameghaṃ sahate... । tata ucyata iyaṃ bhūmirdharmamegheti ।।

punaraparaṃ bho jinaputra dharmameghāyāṃ bodhisattvabhūmau pratiṣṭhito bodhisattvaḥ svapraṇidhānabalādhānato mahākṛpākaruṇāmeghaṃ samutthāpya mahādharmāvabhāsagarjanamabhijñāvidyāvaiśāradyavidyudvidyotitaṃ mahāraśmimārutasamīritaṃ mahāpuṇyajñānaghanābhrajālasaṃdarśanaṃ vividhakāyaghanāvartasaṃdarśanaṃ mahādharmanirnādanaṃ namuciparṣadvidrāvaṇamekakṣaṇalavamuhūrtena daśasu dikṣu yāvanti tāsu lokadhātuṣu tāni paramāṇurajāṃsi saṃvidyante tāvanti lokadhātukoṭinayutaśatasahasrāṇi spharitvā tebhyo'pi bhūyo'prameyāṇi lokadhātukotinayutaśatasahasrāṇi spharitvā mahāmṛtakuśaladhārābhipravarṣaṇena yathāśayataḥ sattvānāmajñānasamutthitāḥ sarvakleśarajojvālāḥ praśamayati । tata ucyata iyaṃ bhūmirdharmamegheti ।।

punaraparaṃ bho jinaputra dharmameghāyāṃ bodhisattva ekasyāmapi lokadhātau tuṣitavarabhavanavāsamupādāya cyavanācaṃkramaṇagarbhasthitijanmābhiniṣkramaṇābhisaṃbodhyadhyeṣaṇamahādharmacakrapravartana-mahāparinirvāṇabhūmiriti sarvatathāgatakāryamadhitiṣṭhati yathāśayeṣu sattveṣu yathāvaineyikeṣu, evaṃ dvayorapi yāvadyāvanti tāsu lokadhātuṣu paramāṇurajāṃsi saṃvidyante, tato'pi bhūyo'prameyeṣu lokadhātukoṭiniyutaśatasahasreṣu tāni paramāṇu... vaineyikeṣu ।।

I

sa evaṃjñānavaśitāprāptaḥ suviniścitamahājñānābhijña ākāṅkṣan saṃkliṣṭāyā lokadhātoḥ pariśuddhatāmadhitiṣṭhati | pariśuddhāyā lokadhātoḥ saṃkliṣṭatāmadhitiṣṭhati | saṃkṣiptāyā lokadhātor-vistīrṇatāmadhitiṣṭhati | vistīrṇāyāḥ saṃkṣiptatāmadhitiṣṭhati | evaṃ vipulamahadgatāpramāṇasūkṣmaudārikavyatyastāva-mūrdhamatalādīnāṃ sarvalokadhātūnāṃ vṛṣabhatayānantam-abhinirhāramadhitiṣṭhati | ākāṅkṣan ekasmin paramāṇurajasyekām-api lokadhātuṃ sarvāvatīṃ sacakravālaparikhāmadhitiṣṭhati | tacca paramāṇurajo na vardhayati tāṃ ca kriyāmādarśayati | dve'pi tisro-'pi catasro'pi pañcāpi yāvadanabhilāpyāpi lokadhāturekasmin paramāṇurajasi sarvāḥ sacakravālaparikhā adhitiṣṭhati | ākāṅkṣan ekasyāṃ lokadhātau dvilokadhātuvyūhamādarśayati | ākāṅkṣan yāvadanabhilāpyalokadhātuvyūhamādarśayati | ākāṅkṣan ekaloka-dhātuvyūhaṃ dvayorlokadhātvorādarśayati | yāvadanabhilāpyāsu lokadhātuṣvādarśayati | ākāṅkṣan yāvadanabhilāpyāsu lokadhātuṣu yaḥ sattvadhātustamekasyāṃ lokadhātau saṃdadhāti, na ca sattvān viheṭhayati | ākāṅkṣan ekasyāṃ lokadhātau yāvān sattvadhātus-tamanabhilāpyāsu lokadhātuṣu saṃdadhāti... | ākāṅkṣan anabhil-āpyalokadhātugatān sattvānekavālapathe saṃdadhāti... | ākāṅkṣan ekavālapathe ekaṃ sarvabuddhaviṣayavyūhamādarśayati | ākāṅkṣan yāvadanabhilāpyān sarvākārabuddhaviṣayavyūhānā-darśayati | ākāṅkṣan yāvantyanabhilāpyāsu lokadhātuṣu paramāṇu-rajāṃsi tāvata ātmabhāvānekakṣaṇalavamuhūrtena nirmimīte | ekaikasmiṃśca ātmabhāve tāvata eva pāṇīn saṃdarśayati | taiśca pāṇibhirdaśasu dikṣu buddhapūjāyāṃ prayujyate | ekaikena ca pāṇinā gaṅgānadīvālikāsamān puṣpapuṭāṃsteṣāṃ buddhānāṃ bhagavatāṃ kṣipati | yathā puṣpāṇāmevaṃ gandhānāṃ mālyānāṃ vilepanānāṃ cūrṇānāṃ cīvarāṇāṃ chatrāṇāṃ dhvajānāṃ patākānāmevaṃ sarvavyūhānām | ekaikasmiṃśca kāye tāvantyeva śirāṃsi adhitiṣṭhati | ekaikasmiṃśca śirasi tāvatīreva jihvā adhi-tiṣṭhati | tābhisteṣāṃ buddhānāṃ bhagavatāṃ varṇaṃ bhāṣate | citt-otpāde ca daśadikpharaṇaṃ gacchāti | cittakṣaṇe cāpramāṇā abhi-saṃbodhīryāvanmahāparinirvāṇāvyūhānadhitiṣṭhati | apramāṇa-kāyatāṃ ca trayadhvatāyāmadhitiṣṭhati | svakāye cāpramāṇānāṃ buddhānāṃ bhagavatāmaprameyān buddhakṣetraguṇavyūhān-adhitiṣṭhati | sarvalokadhātusaṃvartavivartavyūhāṃśca svakāye-

'dhitiṣṭhati । sarvā vātamaṇḍalīścaikaromakūpādutsṛjati । na ca sattvān viheṭhayati । ākāṅkṣaṃścaikāmapskandhaparyantaṃ lokadhātumadhitiṣṭhati । tasyāṃ ca mahāpadmamadhitiṣṭhati । tasya ca mahāpadmasya prabhāvabhāsavyūhena anantā lokadhātūḥ spharati । tatra ca mahābodhivṛkṣamādarśayati । yāvatsarvākāravaropetaṃ sarvajñānatvaṃ saṃdarśayati । svakāye daśadiṅmaṇividyuccandrasūryaprabhā yāvatsarvāvabhāsaprabhā adhitiṣṭhati । ekamukhavātena caikaikasyā diśaḥ pratidiśamanantā lokadhātūḥ kampayati, na ca sattvānuttrāsayati । daśadiśaṃ ca vātasaṃvartanīṃ tejaḥsaṃvartanīmapsaṃvartanīmadhitiṣṭhati । sarvasattvāṃśca ākāṅkṣan yathābhiprāyaṃ rūpāśrayālaṃkṛtānadhitiṣṭhati । svakāye ca tathāgatakāyamadhitiṣṭhati । tathāgatakāye ca svakāyamadhitiṣṭhati । tathāgatakāye svabuddhakṣetramadhitiṣṭhati । svabuddhakṣetre ca tathāgatakāyamadhitiṣṭhati । iti hi bho jinaputra dharmameghāyāṃ bodhisattvabhūmau pratiṣṭhito bodhisattva imāni cānyāni cāprameyāsaṃkhyeyāni ṛddhivikurvaṇakoṭinayutaśatasahasrāṇyādarśayati । ।

J

atha khalu tasyāḥ parṣadaḥ keṣāṃcidbodhisattvānāṃ keṣāṃciddevanāgayakṣagandharvāsuragaruḍakinnaramahoragaśakrabrahmal okapālamaheśvaraśuddhāvāsānāmetadabhavat - yadi tāvadbodhisattvasyaivamapramāṇa ṛddhyabhisaṃskāragocaraḥ, tathāgatānāṃ punaḥ kiṃrūpo bhaviṣyatīti ? atha khalu vimukticandro bodhisattvastasyāḥ parṣadaścittāśayavicāramājñāya vajragarbhaṃ bodhisattvametadavocat - saṃśayitā bateyaṃ bho jinaputra parṣat । sādhu, asyāḥ saṃśayacchityarthaṃ kiṃcinmātraṃ bodhisattvavyūhaprātihāryaṃ saṃdarśaya । atha khalu vajragarbho bodhisattvastasyāṃ velāyāṃ sarvabuddhakṣetrakāyasvabhāvasaṃdarśanaṃ nāma bodhisattvasamādhiṃ samāpadyate । samanantarasamāpanne vajragarbhe bodhisattve sarvabuddhakṣetrakāyasvabhāvasaṃdarśanaṃ bodhisattvasamādhim, atha tāvadeva sā sarvāvatī bodhisattvaparṣat sā ca devanāgayakṣaśuddhāvāsaparṣad vajra-garbhasya bodhisattvasya kāyāntarībhūtamātmānaṃ saṃjānīte sma, tatra ca buddhakṣetramabhinirvṛtaṃ saṃjānīte sma । tasmiṃśca buddhakṣetre ye ākāravyūhāste na sukarāḥ paripūrṇayāpi kalpakoṭyā prabhāvayitum । tatra ca bodhivṛkṣaṃ daśatrisāhasraśatasahasraviṣkambhaskandhaṃ paripūrṇatrisāhasrakoṭivipulāpramāṇaviṭapodviddhaśikharaṃ tadanurūpaṃ ca tasmin bodhimaṇḍe siṃhāsanavaipulyaṃ tatra sarvābhijñāmatirājaṃ nāma tathāgataṃ bodhimaṇḍavaragataṃ samapaśyat । iti hi yāvantastatra vyūhāḥ saṃdṛśyante te na sukarāḥ paripūrṇayāpi kalpakoṭyā prabhāvayitum । sa idaṃ mahāprātihāryaṃ saṃdarśya tāṃ sarvāvatīṃ bodhisattva-parṣadaṃ tāṃ ca devanāga... śuddhāvāsaparṣadaṃ punareva yathā-sthāne sthāpayāmāsa । atha khalu sā sarvāvatī parṣadāścaryaprāptā tūṣṇīṃbhūtā tameva vajragarbhaṃ bodhisattvaṃ nidhyāyantī sthit-ābhūt । atha khalu vimukticandro bodhisattvo vajragarbhaṃ bodhi-sattvametadavocat - āścaryamidaṃ bho jinaputra, adbhutaṃ yāvad-acintyopamasya samādhernimeṣavyūhaprabhāvaḥ । tatko nāmāyaṃ bho jinaputra samādhiḥ? vajragarbho bodhisattva āha – sarva-buddhakṣetrakāyasvabhāvasaṃdarśano nāmāyaṃ bho jinaputra samādhiḥ । vimukticandro bodhisattva āha - kaḥ punarbho jinaputra asya samādhergocaraviṣayavyūhaḥ ? vajragarbho bodhisattva āha – ākāṅkṣan bho jinaputra bodhisattvo'sya samādheḥ suparibhāvita-tvādgaṅgānadīvālikāsamalokadhātuparamāṇurajaḥsamāni daśa buddhakṣetrāṇi svakāye ādarśayet, ato vā bhūya uttari । īdṛśānāṃ bho jinaputra bodhisattvasamādhīnāṃ dharmameghāyāṃ bodhi-sattvabhūmau sthito bodhisattvo bahūni śatasahasrāṇi pratilabhate । tena tasya bodhisattvasya yāvad yauvarājyaprāptairapi bodhi-sattvaiḥ sādhumatībodhisattvabhūmau pratiṣṭhitairna sukaraḥ kāyaḥ kāyakarma vā jñātum । na sukarā vāgvākkarma vā jñātum । na sukaraṃ mano manaskarma vā jñātum । na sukararddhirjñātum । na sukaraṃ tryadhvavilokitaṃ jñātum । na sukaraḥ samādhigocarānu-praveśo jñātum । na sukaro jñānaviṣayo jñātum । na sukaraṃ vimokṣavikrīḍitaṃ jñātum । na sukaraṃ nirmāṇakarma vā adhi-ṣṭhānakarma vā prabhākarma vā prabhākarma vā jñātum । na sukaraṃ yāvatsamāsataḥ kramotkṣepanikṣepakarmāpi jñātum । yāvat yauvarājya...। evamapramāṇā bho jinaputra iyaṃ dharma-meghā bodhisattvabhūmiḥ samāsanirdeśataḥ । vistaraśaḥ punar-asaṃkhyeyakalpaśatasahasranirdeśāparyantākārato draṣṭavyā ।।

vimukticandro bodhisattva āha - kidṛśo bho jinaputra tathāgata-gocaraviṣayapraveśo yatredaṃ bodhisattvānāṃ caryāviṣayādhi-ṣṭhānamevamaopramāṇam? vajragarbho bodhisattva āha – tadyath-āpi nāma syādbho jinaputra kaścideva puruṣaścaturdvīpikāyā loka-dhātordvau trīn vā kolāsthimātrān pāṣāṇān gṛhitvaivaṃ vadet –

kiyatī nu khalu sā pṛthivīdhāturaparyantāsu lokadhātuṣu itaḥ pāṣāṇebhyo mahadgatatayā vā pramāṇatveneti? īdṛśamidaṃ mama tvadvacanaṃ pratibhāti । yastvamapramāṇajñāninām tathāgatānāmarhatāṃ samyaksaṃbuddhānāṃ dharmatāṃ bodhisattvadharmatayā tulayasi । api tu khalu punarbho jinaputra yathā cāturdvīpikāyā lokadhātoḥ parīttā pṛthivīdhāturyā udgṛhītāpramāṇāvaśiṣṭā, evameva bho jinaputra asyā eva tāvaddharmameghāyā bodhisattvabhūmeraprameyān kalpānnirdiśyamānāyāḥ pradeśamātraṃ nirdiṣṭaṃ syāt, kaḥ punarvādastathāgatabhūmeḥ । ārocayāmi te bho jinaputra, prativedayāmi । ayaṃ me tathāgataḥ purataḥ sthitaḥ sākṣībhūtaḥ । sacedbho jinaputra daśasu dikṣu ekaikasyāṃ diśi aparyantalokadhātuparamāṇurajaḥsamāni buddhakṣetrāṇyevaṃbhūmiprāptairbodhisattvaiḥ pūrṇāni bhaveyuryathekṣuvanaṃ vā naḍavanaṃ vā veṇuvanaṃ vā tilavanaṃ vā śālivanaṃ va, teṣāmaparyantakalpābhinirhṛto bodhisattvacaryābhinirhāratathāgatasyaikakṣaṇajñānaprasṛtasya tathāgataviṣayasya... । iti hi bho jinaputra evaṃjñānānugato bodhisattvastathāgatādvayakāyavākcitto bodhisattvasamādhibalaṃ ca notsṛjati buddhadarśanapūjopasthānaṃ ca karoti । sa ekaikasmin kalpe'paryantāṃstathāgatān sarvākārābhinirhārapūjābhiḥ pūjayati । audārikānugatayā pūjayā teṣāṃ ca buddhānāṃ bhagavatāmadhiṣṭhānāvabhāsaṃ saṃpratīcchati । sa bhūyasyā mātrayā asaṃhāryo bhavati dharmadhātuvibhaktiparipṛcchānirdeśaiḥ । anekān kalpānanekāni kalpaśatāni...anekāni kalpakoṭinayutaśatasahasrāṇi । tadyathāpi nāma bho jinaputra divyakarmārakṛtaṃ mahābharaṇopacāraṃ mahāmaṇiratnapratyuptaṃ vaśavartino devarājasyottamāṅge kaṇṭhe vā āvaddhamasaṃhāryaṃ bhavati tadanyairdivyamānuṣyakairābharaṇavibhūṣaṇopacāraiḥ, evameva bho jinaputra bodhisattvasyemāṃ daśamīṃ dharmameghāṃ bhodhisattvabhūmimanuprāptasya te bodhisattvajñanopacārā asaṃhāryā bhavanti sarvasattvaiḥ sarvaśrāvakapratyekabuddhaiḥ prathamāṃ bodhisattvabhūmimupādāya yāvannavamīṃ bodhisattvabhūmimanuprāptairbodhisattvaiḥ । asyāṃ ca bodhisattvabhūmau sthitasya bodhisattvasya jñānavabhāsaḥ sattvānāṃ yāvatsarvajñajñānāvatārāya saṃvartate›saṃhāryastadanyairjñānāvabhāsaiḥ । tadyathāpi nāma bho jinaputra maheśvarasya devarājasyābhā atikrāntā bhavati sarvopapattyāyatanāni, sattvānāṃ ca kāyāśrayān prahlādayati, evameva bho jinaputra bodhisattvasya asyāṃ daśabhyāṃ dharmameghāyāṃ bodhisattvabhūmau sthitasya jñānābhā asaṃhāryā bhavati sarvaśrāvakapratyekabuddhaiḥ prathamāṃ bodhisattvabhūmimupādāya yāvannavamībodhisattvabhūmipratiṣṭhitairbodhisattvairyāvatsarvajñajñānadharmatāyāṃ ca sattvān pratiṣṭhāpayati | sa khalu punarbho jinaputra bodhisattva evaṃjñānānugato buddhairbhagavadbhistryadhvajñānaṃ ca saṃśrāvyate | dharmadhātuprabhedajñānaṃ ca sarvalokadhātuspharaṇaṃ ca sarvalokadhātvavabhāsādhiṣṭhānaṃ ca sarvasattvakṣetradharmaparijñānaṃ ca sarvasattvacittacaritānupraveśajñānaṃ ca sarvasattvayathākālaparipākajñānaṃ ca vinayānatikramaṇaṃ ca sarvadharmapravicayavibhaktijñānakauśalyaṃ ca samāsato yāvatsarvajñajñānāpramāṇatāṃ ca saṃśrāvyate | tasya daśabhyaḥ pāramitābhyo jñānapāramitā atiriktatamā bhavati, na ca pariśeṣāsu na samudāgacchati yathābalaṃ yathābhajamānam | iyaṃ bho jinaputra bodhisattvasya dharmameghā nāma daśamī bodhisattvabhūmiḥ samāsanirdeśataḥ | vistaraśaḥ punarasaṃkhyeyāparyantakalpanirdeśaniṣṭhāto'nugantavyā | yasyāṃ pratiṣṭhito bodhisattvo bhūyastvena maheśvaro bhavati devarājaḥ kṛtī prabhuḥ sattvānāṃ sarvaśrāvakapratyekabuddhabodhisattvapāramitopadeśeṣvasaṃhār yo dharmadhātuvibhaktiparipṛcchānirdeśaiḥ | yacca kiṃcit... ||

dharmameghā nāma bodhisattvabhūmirdaśamī ||

[Beginning of tenth bhūmi's final gathas]

upasaṃhāragāthāḥ ।

śamadamaniratānāṃ śāntadāntāśayānāṃ
khagapathasadṛśānāmantarīkṣasamānām ।
khilamanavidhutānāṃ mārgajñāne sthitānāṃ
śṛṇuta cariviśeṣān bodhisattvāna śreṣṭhān ।। 17 ।।

kuśalaśatasahasraṃ saṃciyā kalpakoṭyā
buddhaśatasahasrān pūjayitvā maharṣīn ।
pratyayajinavaśīṃścāpūjayitvā anantān
sarvajagatahitāyā jāyate bodhicittam ।। 18 ।।

vratatapatapitānāṃ kṣāntipāraṃgatānāṃ
hiriśiricaritānāṃ puṇyajñānodgatānām ।
vipulagatimatīnāṃ buddhajñānāśayānāṃ
daśabalasamatulyaṃ jāyate bodhicittam ।। 19 ।।

yāva jina triyadhvā pūjanārthāya pūjaṃ
khagapathapariṇāmaṃ śodhanaṃ sarvakṣetram ।
samyaganugatārthe yāvatā sarvadharmān
mokṣa jagata arthe jāyate bodhicittam ।। 20 ।।

pramuditasamutīnāṃ dānadharmāratānāṃ
sakalajagahitārthe nityamevodyatānām ।
jinaguṇaniratānāṃ sattvarakṣāvratānāṃ
tribhuvanahitakārye jāyate bodhicittam ।। 21 ।।

akuśalaviratānāṃ śuddhaśīlāvratānāṃ
vrataniyamaratānāṃ śāntasaumyendriyāṇām ।
jinaśaraṇagatānāṃ bodhicaryāśayānāṃ
tribhuvanahitasādhyaṃ jāyate bodhicittam ।। 22 ।।

anugatakuśalānāṃ kṣāntisauratyabhājāṃ
viditaguṇarasānāṃ tyaktamānotsavānām ।

nihitaśubhamatīnāṃ dāntusaumyāśayānāṃ
sakalahitavidhāne jāyate bodhicittam || 23 ||

pracalitaśubhakāryā dhīravīryotsahā ye
nikhilajanahitārthe prodyayāmāna siṃhāḥ |
avirataguṇasādhyā nirjitakleśasaṃghā
jhaṭiti manasi teṣāṃ jāyate bodhicittam || 24 ||

susamavahitacittā dhvastamohāndhakārā
vigalitamadamānā tyaktasaṃkliṣṭamārgāḥ |
śamasukhaniratā ye tyaktasaṃsārasaṅgā
jhaṭiti manasi teṣāṃ jāyate bodhicittam || 25 ||

vimalakhasamacittā jñānavijñānavijñā
nihatanamucimārā vāntakleśābhimānāḥ |
jinapadaśaraṇasthā labdhatattvārthakā ye
sapadi manasi teṣāṃ jāyate bodhicittam || 26 ||

tribhuvanaśivasādhyopāyavijñānadhīrāḥ
kalibalaparihāropāyavidyarddhimantaḥ |
sugataguṇasamīhā ye ca puṇyānurāgāḥ
sapadi manasi teṣāṃ jāyate bodhicittam || 27 ||

tribhuvanahitakāmā bodhisaṃbhārapūrye
praṇihitamanasā ye duṣkare'pi caranti |
avirataśubhakarmaprodyatā bodhisattvāḥ
sapadi manasi teṣāṃ jāyate bodhicittam || 28 ||

daśabalaguṇakāmā bodhicaryānuraktā
vijitakalibalaughāstyaktamānānuṣaṅgāḥ |
anugataśubhamārgā labdhadharmārthakāmā
jhaṭiti manasi teṣāṃ jāyate bodhicittam || 29 ||

iti gaṇitaguṇāṃśā bodhicaryāścarantu
jinapadapraṇidhānāḥ satsamṛddhiṃ labhantu |
triguṇapariviśuddhā bodhicittaṃ labhantu
triśaraṇapariśuddhā bodhisattvā bhavantu || 30 ||

daśa pāramitāḥ pūrya daśabhūmīśvaro bhavet |
bhūyo'pi kathyate hyetacchruṇutaivaṃ samāsataḥ || 31 ||

bodhicittaṃ yadāsādya saṃpradānaṃ karoti yaḥ |
tadā pramuditāṃ prāpto jambūdvīpeśvaro bhavet || 32 ||

tatrasthaḥ pālayan sattvān yathecchāpratipādanaiḥ |
svayaṃ dāne pratiṣṭhitvā parāṃścāpi niyojayet || 33 ||

sarvān bodhau pratiṣṭhāpya saṃpūrṇā dānapāragaḥ |
etaddharmānubhāvena saṃvaraṃ samupācaret || 34 ||

samyakśīlaṃ samādhāya saṃvarakuśalī bhavet |
tataḥ sa vimalāṃ prāptaścāturdvīpeśvaro bhavet || 35 ||

tatrasthaḥ pālayan sattvān akuśalanivāraṇaiḥ |
svayaṃ śīle pratiṣṭhitvā parāṃścāpi niyojayet || 36 ||

sarvān bodhau pratiṣṭhāpya saṃpūrṇaśīlapāragaḥ |
etaddharmavipākena kṣāntivratamupāśrayet || 37 ||

samyakkṣāntivrataṃ dhṛtvā kṣāntibhṛtkuśalī bhavet |
tataḥ prabhākarīprāptastrayastriṃśādhipo bhavet || 38 ||

tatrasthaḥ pālayan sattvān kleśamārganivāraṇaiḥ |
svayaṃ kṣāntivrate sthitvā parāṃścāpi niyojayet || 39 ||

sattvān bodhau pratiṣṭhāpya kṣāntipāraṃgato bhavet |
etatpuṇyavipākaiḥ sa vīryavratamupāśrayet || 40 ||

samyagvīryaṃ samādhāya vīryabhṛt kuśalī bhavet |
tataścārciṣmatīprāptaḥ suyāmādhipatirbhavet || 41 ||

tatrasthaḥ pālayan sattvān kudṛṣṭisaṃnivāraṇaiḥ |
samyagdṛṣṭau pratiṣṭhāpya bodhayitvā prayatnataḥ || 42 ||

svayaṃ vīryavrate sthitvā parāṃścāpi niyojayet |
sarvān bodhau pratiṣṭhāpya vīryapāraṃgato bhavet || 43 ||

etatpuṇyavipākaiśca dhyānavrataṃ samāśrayet |
sarvakleśān vinirjitya samādhisuṣṭhito bhavet || 44 ||

samyag dhyānaṃ samādhāya samādhikuśalī bhavet |
tataḥ sudurjayāprāptaḥ saṃtuṣitādhipo bhavet || 45 ||

tatrasthaḥ pālayan sattvān tīrthyamārganivāraṇaiḥ |
satyadharmaṃ pratiṣṭhāpya bodhayitvā prayatnataḥ || 46 ||

svayaṃ dhyānavrate sthitvā parāṃścāpi niyojayet |
sarvān bodhau pratiṣṭhāpya dhyānapāraṃgato bhavet || 47 ||

etatpuṇyavipākaiśca prajñāvratamupāśrayet |
sarvamārān vinirjitya prajñābhijñasamṛddhimān || 48 ||

samyakprajñāṃ samādhāya svabhijñākuśalī bhavet |
tataścābhimukhīprāptaḥ sunirmitādhipo bhavet || 49 ||

tatrasthaḥ pālayan sattvān abhimānanivāraṇaiḥ |
śūnyatāsu pratiṣṭhāpya bodhayitvā prayatnataḥ || 50 ||

svayaṃ prajñāvrate sthitvā parāṃścāpi niyojayet |
sarvān bodhau pratiṣṭhāpya prajñāpāraṃgato bhavet || 51 ||

etatpuṇyavipākaiśca sa supāyavrataṃ caret |
sarvaduṣṭān vinirjitya saddharmakuśalī bhavet || 52 ||

sa supāyavidhānena sattvān bodhau niyojayet |
tato dūraṃgamāprāpto vaśavartīśvaro bhavet || 53 ||

tatrasthaḥ pālayan sattvānabhisamayabodhanaiḥ |
bodhisattvaniyāmeṣu pratiṣṭhāpya prabodhayan || 54 ||

tatropāye svayaṃ sthitvā parāṃścāpi niyojayet |

sarvān bodhau pratiṣṭhāpya hyupāyapārago bhavet | | 55 | |

etatpuṇyānubhāvaiśca supraṇidhimupāśrayet |
mithyādṛṣṭiṃ vinirjitya samyagdṛṣṭikṛtī budhaḥ | | 56 | |

supraṇihitacittena samyagbodhau pratiṣṭhitaḥ |
tataścāpyacalāprāpto brahmā sāhasrikādhipaḥ | | 57 | |

tatrasthaḥ pālayan sattvān triyānasaṃpraveśanaiḥ |
lokadhātuparijñāne pratiṣṭhāpya prabodhayan | | 58 | |

supraṇidhau svayaṃ sthitvā parāṃścāpi niyojayet |
sarvān bodhau pratiṣṭhāpya praṇidhipārago bhavet | | 59 | |

etatpuṇyānusāraiśca balavratamupāśrayet |
sarvaduṣṭān vinirjitya saṃbodhau kṛtaniścayaḥ | | 60 | |

samyagbalasamutsāhaiḥ sarvatīrthyān vinirjayet |
tataḥ sādhumatīprāpto mahābrahmā bhavet kṛtī | | 61 | |

tatrasthaḥ pālayan sattvān buddhayānopadarśanaiḥ |
sattvāśayaparijñāne pratiṣṭhāpya prabodhayan | | 62 | |

svayaṃ bale pratiṣṭhitvā paraṃścāpi niyojayet |
sarvān bodhau pratiṣṭhāpya balapāraṃgato bhavet | | 63 | |

etatpuṇyavipākaiśca jñānavratamupāśrayet |
caturmārān vinirjitya bodhisattvo guṇākaraḥ | | 64 | |

samyag jñānaṃ samāsādya saddharmakuśalī bhavet |
dharmameghāṃ tataḥ prāpto maheśvaro bhavet kṛtī | | 65 | |

tatrasthaḥ pālayan sattvān sarvākārānubodhanaiḥ |
sarvākāravare jñāne pratiṣṭhāpya prabodhayan | | 66 | |

svayaṃ jñāne pratiṣṭhitvā parāṃścāpi niyojayet |
sarvān bodhau pratiṣṭhāpya jñānapāraṃgato bhavet | | 67 | |

etatpuṇyānubhāvaiśca daśabhūmīśvaro jinaḥ |
sarvākāraguṇādhāraḥ sarvajño dharmarāḍ bhavet || 68 ||

iti matvā bhavadbhiśca saṃbodhipadalabdhaye |
daśapāramitāpūryai caritavyaṃ samāhitaiḥ || 69 ||

tathā bodhiṃ śivāṃ prāpya caturmārān vijitya ca |
sarvān bodhau pratiṣṭhāpya nirvṛtiṃ samavāpsyatha || 70 ||

etatcchrutvā parijñāya caradhvaṃ bodhisādhane |
nirvighnaṃ bodhimāsādya labhadhvaṃ saugatāṃ gatim || 71 ||

[End of tenth bhūmi's final gathas]

[Beginning of parīndanāparivartaḥ's gathas]

11 parīndanāparivartaḥ ।

upakramaḥ ।

etāstāḥ khalu punarbho jinaputrā daśa bodhisattvabhūmayaḥ samāsato nirdiṣṭāḥ sarvākāravaropetasarvajñajñānānugatā draṣṭavyāḥ । tasyāṃ velāyāmayaṃ trisāhasramahāsāhasro lokadhātuḥ ṣaḍvikāraṃ prākampat । vividhāni ca puṣpāṇi viyato nyapatan । divyamānuṣyakāni ca tūryāṇi saṃpravāditānyabhūvan । anumodanāśabdena ca yāvadakaniṣṭhabhuvanaṃ vijñaptamabhūt ।।

atha tasmin samaye bhagavāṃstān vimukticandrapramukhān sarvān bodhisattvānāmantrya evamādiśat - imāmahaṃ mārṣā asaṃkhyeyakalpakoṭīnayutaśatasahasrasamudānītāmanuttarāṃ samyaksaṃbodhiṃ yuṣmākaṃ haste parindāmi anuparindāmi paramayā parindanayā । tadyūyaṃ sarve svayaṃ caivamimaṃ dharmaparyāyaṃ dhārayata, parebhyaśca vistareṇa saṃprakāśayata । saṃkṣepānmārṣā yadi tathāgataḥ kalpasthitikenāyuḥpramāṇena rātriṃdivamadhitiṣṭhamāno'sya dharmaparyāyasya varṇaṃ bhāṣate, naivāsya dharmaparyāyasya varṇaparyanto bhavet, na ca tathāgatapratibhānakṣayo bhavet । yathā tathāgataśīlasamādhiprajñāvimuktijñānadarśanamapramāṇamaparyantam, evameva mārṣā ya imaṃ dharmaparyāyamudgrahīṣyati dhārayiṣyati vācayiṣyati likhiṣyati likhāpayiṣyati paryavāpsyati pravartayiṣyati, parṣanmadhye ca vistareṇa saṃprakāśayiṣyati - anena cittena kathamamī sattvā evamudāradharmasya lābhinaḥ syuriti śraddhayā satkṛtya śrāvayiṣyanti śroṣyanti ca yoniśo manasi bhāvayiṣyanti ca । pustakalikhitaṃ kṛtvā gṛhe dhārayiṣyati satkariṣyati gurukariṣyati mānayiṣyati pūjayiṣyati । amātsaryacittatayā asya dharmaparyāyasya varṇaṃ bhāṣitvā likhanāya vācanāya svādhyayanāya pūjanāya darśanāya dāsyati, teṣāmapi nāsti puṇyaparyantaḥ ।।

atha khalu bhagavānasyaiva dharmaparyāyasya bhūyasyā mātrayā anuparindanārthaṃ tasyāṃ velāyāmimā gāthā abhāṣata –

sattvā dṛṣṭā ye mayā buddhadṛṣṭyā
te'rhantaḥ syuḥ śāriputreṇa tulyāḥ |
tāṃ cetkaścitpūjayetkalpakoṭyā
tulyān gaṅgāvālukābhiryathaiva || 1 ||

pratyekabuddhāya tu yaśca pūjāṃ
kuryādahorātramapi prahṛṣṭaḥ |
mālyaprakāraiśca tathāmbaraiśca
tasmādayaṃ puṇyakṛto viśiṣṭaḥ || 2 ||

sarve'pi pratyekajinā yadi syu-
stān pūjayet kaścidihāpramattaḥ |
puṣpaiśca gandhaiśca vilepanaiśca
kalpānanekān śayanānnapānaiḥ || 3 ||

ekasya yaścaiva tathāgatasya
kuryāt praṇāmamapi caikavāram |
prasannacitto'tha vadennamo'rhan
tasmādidaṃ śreṣṭhataraṃ ca puṇyam || 4 ||

buddhā bhaveyuryadi sarvasattvā-
stān pūjayet yaśca yathaiva pūrvam |
divyaiśca puṣpairatha mānuṣaiśca
kalpānanekān bahubhiḥ prakāraiḥ || 5 ||

yaścaiva saddharmavilopakāle
tyaktvā svakāyaṃ ca tathātmajīvam |
dadyādahorātramidaṃ hi sūtraṃ
viśiṣyate puṇyamidaṃ hi tasmāt || 6 ||

yasyepsitaṃ pūjayituṃ jinendrān
pratyekabuddhānapi śrāvakāṃśca |
dṛḍhaṃ samutpādya sa bodhicittam
idaṃ sadā sūtravaraṃ dadātu || 7 ||

rājā hyayaṃ sarvasubhāṣitānāṃ

so'bhudgataḥ sarvatathāgatānāma |
gṛhe sthitastasya tathāgataḥ sa
tiṣṭhedidaṃ yatra hi sūtraratnam || 8 ||

prabhāṃ sa prāpnoti śubhāmanantām
ekaṃ padaṃ vādi śatīhayaśca |
na vyañjanād grasyati nāpi cārthād
dadāti yaḥ sūtramidaṃ parebhyaḥ || 9 ||

anuttarāsau naranāyakānāṃ
sattvo na kaścit sadṛśo'sya vidyate |
bhavetsamudreṇa samaśca so'kṣayaḥ
śrutvā hi yo dharmamimaṃ prapadyate || 10 ||

[End of parīndanāparivartaḥ's gathas]

11 parīndanāparivartaḥ |

A

imāstāḥ khalu punarbho jinaputrā daśa bodhisattvabhūmayaḥ samāsanirdeśato nirdiṣṭāḥ | vistaraśaḥ punaraparyantakalpa-nirdeśaniṣṭhāto'nugatavyāḥ | yā atītānāgatapratyutpannairbuddhair-bhagavadbhirbhāṣitāśca bhāṣiṣyante ca bhāṣyante ca, tāḥ khalu punarbho jinaputra, etā daśa bodhisattvabhūmayaḥ sarvākārasarva-jñajñānānugatā draṣṭavyā anupūrvābhimukhatvāt | tadyathāpi nāma bho jinaputra anavataptahradaprabhavaṃ pravahadvāri caturbhir-mahānadīsrotomukhairjambūdvīpaṃ saṃtarpya akṣayaṃ bhūyo vivṛddhamaprameyāṇāṃ sattvānāmupakārībhūtaṃ yāvanmahā-samudramarpayati, tacca vāri ādita eva mahāsāgarābhimukham, evameva bho jinaputra bodhicittamahāhradaprabhavaṃ pravahat kuśalamūlavāri mahāpraṇidhānanadīsrotomukhaiścaturbhiḥ saṃ-grahavastubhiḥ sarvasattvadhātu saṃtarpya akṣayaṃ bhūya uttari vivṛddham aprameyāṇāṃ sattvānāmupakārībhūtaṃ yāvatsarvākāra-sarvajñajñānamahāsamudramarpayati | tacca kuśalamūlavāri ādita eva sarvajñatāmahāsāgarābhimukham ||

B

tāḥ khalu bho jinaputra etā daśa bhūmayo buddhajñānaṃ pratītya prajñāyante | tadyathāpi nāma bho jinaputra mahāpṛthivīṃ pratītya daśa mahāratnaparvatarājāḥ prajñāyante | tadyathā himavān parvatarājo gandhamādano vaidalya ṛṣigiriryugaṃdharo'śvakarṇa-girirnimiṃdharaścakravālaḥ ketumān sumeruśca mahāparvatarājaḥ | tara bho jinaputra tadyathāpi nāma himavān parvatarāja ākaraḥ sarvabhaiṣajyajātīnāmaparyantaḥ sarvabhaiṣajyajātigrahaṇatayā, evameva bho jinaputra pramuditāyāṃ bodhisattvabhūmau sthito bodhisattva ākaro bhavati sarvalaukikakāvyaśāstramantravidy-āsthānānāmaparyantaḥ sarvalaukikakāvyaśāstramantravidyopāyena | tadyathāpi nāma bho jinaputra gandhamādano mahāparvatarāja ākaraḥ sarvagandhajātīnāmaparyantaḥ sarvagandhajātigrahaṇena, evameva bho jinaputra vimalāyāṃ bodhisattvabhūmau sthito bodhi-sattva ākaro bhavati sarvabodhisattvaśīlasaṃvaracāritragandhānām-aparyantaḥ sarvabodhisattvaśīlasaṃvaracāritragandhasaṃgrahaṇena | tadyathāpi nāma bho jinaputra vaidalyo mahāparvatarājaḥ śuddho ratnamaya ākaraḥ sarvaratnajātīnāmaparyantaḥ sarvalaukikaratnajātigrahaṇena, evameva bho jinaputra prabhākaryāṃ buddhabhūmau sarvalaukikadhyānābhijñāvimokṣasamādhisamāpattīnām, aparyantaḥ sarvalaukikadhyānābhijñāvimokṣasamādhisamāpattīnām, aparyantaḥ sarvalaukikadhyānābhijñāvimokṣasamādhisamāpattiparipṛcchānirdeśaiḥ | tadyathāpi nāma bho jinaputra ṛṣigirirmahāparvatarājaḥ pañcābhijñānāmṛṣīṇāmaparyantaḥ pañcābhijñarṣigaṇanayā, evameva bho jinaputra arciṣmatyāṃ buddhabhūmau sarvamārgāmārgāntarāvatāranirdeśaviśeṣajñānānāmaparyantaḥ sarvamārgāmārgāntaraviśeṣajñānaparipṛcchānirdeśaiḥ | tadyathāpi nāma bho jinaputra yugaṃdharo mahāparvatarājaḥ sarvayakṣamaharddhikānāmaparyantaḥ sarvayakṣamaharddhikagaṇanayā, evameva bho jinaputra sudurjayāyāṃ buddhabhūmau sarvābhijñarddhivikurvaṇaprātihāryāṇāmaparyantaḥ sarvābhijñarddhivikurvaṇaprātihāryaparipṛcchānirdeśaiḥ | tadyathāpi nāma bho aśvakarṇagirirmahāparvatarājaḥ sarvaphalajātīnāmaparyantaḥ sarvaphalajātigrahaṇena, evameva bho jinaputra abhimukhyāṃ buddhabhūmau pratītyasamutpādāvatāranirdeśānāmaparyantaḥ śrāvakaphalābhisamayaparipṛcchānirdeśaiḥ | tadyathāpi nāma bho jinaputra nimiṃdharo nāma mahāparvatarājaḥ sarvanāgamaharddhikānāmaparyantaḥ sarvanāgamaharddhigaṇanayā, evameva bho jinaputra dūraṃgamāyāṃ buddhabhūmau upāyaprajñānirdeśānāmaparyantaḥ pratyekabuddhaphalābhisamayaparipṛcchāanirdeśaiḥ | tadyathāpi nāma bho jinaputra cakravālo nāma mahāparvatarājaḥ vaśībhūtānāmaparyanto vaśībhūtagaṇanayā, evameva bho jinaputra acalāyāṃ buddhabhūmau sarvabodhisattvavaśitābhinirhārāṇāmaparyanto lokadhātuvibhaktiparipṛcchānirdeśaiḥ | tadyathāpi bho jinaputra ketumān nāma mahāparvatarājaḥ asuramaharddhikānāmaparyanto'suramaharddhikagaṇanayā, evameva bho jinaputra sādhumatyāṃ buddhabhūmau sarvasattvapravṛttinivṛttijñānopacārāṇāmaparyantaḥ sarvajagatsaṃbhavavibhavaparipṛcchānirdeśaiḥ | tadyathāpi bho jinaputra sumerurmahāparvatarājaḥ sarvadevamaharddhikānāmaparyantaḥ sarvadevamaharddhikagaṇanayā, evameva bho jinaputra dharmameghāyāṃ buddhabhūmau tathāgatabalavaiśaradyāveṇikabuddhadharmāṇāmaparyanto buddhakāyasaṃdarśanaparipṛcchānirdeśaiḥ | yathā khalu punarime bho jinaputra daśa mahāratnaparvatā mahāsamudrasaṃbhūtā mahāsamudraprabhāvitāḥ, evameva bho jinaputra imā api daśa bhūmayaṃ sarvajñatāsaṃbhūtāḥ sarvajñatāprabhāvitāḥ ||

C

tadyathāpi bho jinaputra mahāsamudro daśabhirākāraiḥ saṃkhyāṃ gacchatyasaṃhāryatayā | katamairdaśabhiḥ? yaduta anupūrvanimnataśca mṛtakuṇapāsaṃvāsataśca anyavārisaṃkhyātyajanataśca ekarasataśca bahuratnataśca gambhīraduravagāhataśca vipulāpramāṇataśca mahābhūtāvāsataśca sthitavelānatikramaṇataśca sarvameghavārisaṃpratyeṣaṇātṛptitaśca, evameva bho jinaputra bodhisattvacaryā daśabhirākāraiḥ saṃkhyāṃ gacchatyasaṃhāryatayā | katamairdaśabhiḥ ? yaduta pramuditāyāṃ bodhisattvabhūmau anupūrvamahāpraṇidhānābhinirhāranimnataḥ | vimalāyāṃ bodhisattvabhūmau dauḥśīlyamṛtakuṇapāsaṃvāsataḥ | prabhākaryāṃ bodhisattvabhūmau laukikaprajñaptisaṃkhyātyāgataḥ | arciṣmatyāṃ bodhisattvabhūmau buddhabhedyaprasādaikarasataḥ | sudurjayāyāṃ bodhisattvabhūmau apramāṇopāyābhijñālokakriyābhinirhārabahuratnataḥ | abhimukhyāṃ bodhisattvabhūmau pratītyasamutpādapratyavekṣaṇaduravagāhagāmbhīryataḥ | dūraṃgamāyāṃ bodhisattvabhūmau buddhipravicayakauśalyavipulāpramāṇataḥ | acalāyāṃ bodhisattvabhūmau mahāvyūhābhinirhārasaṃdarśanamahābhūtāvāsataḥ | sādhumatyāṃ bodhisattvabhūmau gambhīravimokṣajagaccaritayathāvatprativedhasthitavelānatikramaṇ ataḥ | dharmameghāyāṃ bodhisattvabhūmau sarvatathāgatadharmāvabhāsamahāmeghavārisaṃpratyeṣaṇātṛptitaḥ ||

D

tadyathāpi bho jinaputra mahāmaṇiratnaṃ yadā daśa ratnagotrāṇyatikramya abhyutkṣiptaṃ ca bhavati kuśalakarmārasuparitāpitaṃ ca suparipiṇḍitaṃ ca supariśodhitaṃ ca suparyavadāpitaṃ ca sunirviddhaṃ ca ratnasūtrasvāviddhaṃ ca uccavaiḍūryamaṇiratnadaṇḍadhvajāgrāvaropitaṃ ca sarvāvabhāsapramuktaṃ ca rājānujñātaṃ ca bhavati, tadā sarvasattvānāṃ sarvaratnasaṃgrahāya pratyupasthitaṃ bhavati, evameva bho jinaputra yadā bodhisattvānāṃ sarvajñatāratnacittotpādo daśāryaratnagotrāṇyatikramyotpanno bhavati dhūtaguṇasaṃlekhaśīlavratatapaḥsuparitāpitaśca dhyānasamādhisamāpattisuparipiṇḍitaśca mārgāṅgākārasupariśodhitaśca upāyābhijñāsuparyavadāpitaśca pratītyasamutpādasunirviddhaśca upāyaprajñāvicitraratnasūtrasvāviddhaśca vaśitāmahāvaiḍūryamaṇiratnadaṇḍadhvajāgrāvaropitaśca sattvacaritapratyavekṣaṇaśrutajñānāvabhāsasaṃprayuktaśca tathāgatadharmarājasamyaksaṃbuddhajñānābhiṣekānugataśca bhavati, tadā sarvasattvānāṃ sarvabuddhakāryaratnasaṃgrahāya pratyupasthito bhavati, tadā ca sarvajña ityākhyāyate ||

E

ayaṃ khalu punarbho jinaputra bodhisattvacaryāsamudānayanaḥ sarvākārasarvajñajñānaguṇasaṃcayo dharmamukhaparivarto nānavaropitakuśālamūlānāṃ sattvānāṃ śravaṇāvabhāsamāgamiṣyati || vimukticandro bodhisattva āha - yeṣāṃ punarbho jinaputra ayaṃ sarvākārasarvajñajñānaguṇasaṃcayo dharmamukhaparivartaḥ śravaṇāvabhāsamāgamiṣyati, te kiyatā puṇyopacayena samanvāgatā bhaviṣyanti? vajragarbho bodhisattva āha – yāvān bho jinaputra sarvajñajñānasya prabhāvastāvān sarvajñatācittotpādasaṃgrahālambanātpuṇyopacayaḥ syāt | yāvān sarvajñatācittotpādasaṃgrahālambanataḥ puṇyopacayastāvānevāsya dharmamukhaparivartasyābhimukhaḥ puṇyopacayo'nugantavyaḥ | tatkasya hetoḥ? na hi bho jinaputra śakyaṃ anyatra bodhisattvena ayaṃ sarvākārasarvajñajñānaguṇasaṃcayo dharmamukhaparivartaḥ śrotuṃ vā adhimoktuṃ vā pratyetuṃ vā udgrahītuṃ vā dhārayituṃ vā saṃdhārayituṃ vā | kaḥ punarvādo bhāvanākāraprayogodyoganiṣpādaneṣu? tasmāttarhi bho jinaputra sarvajñajñānamukhānugatāste saṃdhārayitavyāḥ, ye imaṃ sarvajñajñānaguṇasaṃcayadharmamukhaparivartaṃ śropyati, śrutvā cādhimokṣyante, adhimucya cādhārayiṣyanti, bhāvanākāreṇa prayokṣyante || atha khalu tasyāṃ velāyāṃ buddhānubhāvena dharmatāpratilambhena ca daśadiglokadaśabuddhakṣetrakoṭiparamāṇurajaḥsamā lokadhātavaḥ ṣaḍvikāramaṣṭādaśamahānimittamakampanta prākampanta saṃprākampanta | acalan prācalan saṃprācalan | avedhanta prāvedhanta saṃprāvedhanta | araṇan prāraṇan saṃprāraṇan | akṣumyan prākṣubhyan saṃprākṣumyan | agarjan prāgarjan saṃprāgarjan | divyāśca puṣpagandhamālyameghā abhiprāvarṣan | divyāśca vastrameghā divyāścūrṇameghā divyā ratnameghā divyā ābharaṇameghā divyā chatrameghā divyā dhvajameghā divyā patākāmeghā abhiprāvarṣan | divyaṃ ca sūryacakrātmabhāvamaṇḍalamaṇirājasumerumeghavarṣamabhiprāvarṣan | divyaṃ ca sarvarutaravitavādyamaṇirājasumerumeghavarṣamabhiprāvarṣan | divyaṃ ca jāmbūnadakanakavarṇaprabhāmaṇḍalamaṇirājasumerumeghavarṣamabhiprāvarṣan I divyāśca tūryatālāvacarasaṃgītimeghā nadanti sma I divyasamatikrāntāḥ sarvajñatābhūmyabhiṣṭavasaṃgītimeghā nadanti sma I yathā cāsyāṃ lokadhātau cāturdvīpikāyāṃ paranirmitavaśavartino devarājasya vimāne maṇiratnagarbhaprāsāde, tathā sarvalokadhātuṣu daśa diśaḥ spharitvā iyameva dharmadeśanā sarvatraiva pravartate sma I ...daśabhyo digbhyo daśabuddhakṣetrakoṭiparamāṇurajaḥsamānāṃ lokadhātūnāṃ pareṇa daśabuddhakṣetrakoṭiparamāṇurajaḥsamā bodhisattvā āgacchanti daśadiśaṃ spharantaḥ I te ca āgatyaivamāhuḥ - sādhu sādhu bho jinaputra, yastvamimāṃ bodhisattvabhūmidharmatāṃ sūcayati I vayamapi bho jinaputra sarve vajragarbhasamanāmakā eva vajraśrīnāmikābhyo nānālokadhātubhya ihāgatā vajradhvajanāmakānāṃ tathāgatānāmantikebhyaḥ I sarvāsu ca tāsu lokadhātuṣu iyameva dharmadeśanā pravartate buddhānubhāvena evaṃrūpāsveva parṣatsu I ebhireva padairebhireva vyañjanairebhireva niruktairetamevārthamabhilaṣadbhiranūnamanadhikamanatiriktam, te vayaṃ bho jinaputra sākṣībhūtā buddhānubhāvenemāṃ parṣadaṃ saṃprāptāḥ I yathā ca bho jinaputra vayamimāṃ lokadhātuṃ saṃprāptāstathā ca daśasu dikṣu sarvalokadhātuṣvekaikasyāṃ lokadhātau cāturdvīpikāyāṃ paranirmitavaśavartibhavane vaśavartino devarājasya vimāne maṇiratnagarbhaprāsāde saṃprāptā iti I I idamavocadvajragarbho bodhisattvo mahāsattvo'bhyanujñātastathāgatena I āttamanāḥ sā ca sarvāvatī bodhisattvaparṣat sā ca devanāga...śuddhāvāsaparṣad bhagavāṃśca paranirmitavaśavartiṣu deveṣu viharannacirābhisaṃbuddho dvitīye saptāhe vaśavartino devarājasya vimāne maṇiratnagarbhe vajragarbhasya bodhisattvasya bhāṣitamabhyanandann-iti I I iti parīndanāparivarto nāmaikādaśaḥ I I iti śrībodhisattvacaryāprasthāno daśabhūmīśvaro nāma mahāyānasūtraratnarājaḥ samāptaḥ I I

Sanskrit Text Endnotes

1. Use of this Sanskrit text here is by the kind permission of Dr. Miroj Shakya, Project Coordinator, Digital Sanskrit Buddhist Canon Project and Rare Buddhist Sanskrit Manuscript Preservation Project, University of the West, Rosemead, CA. Sandhi-compliant line breaks were added in-house by Kalavinka Press.
2. Although not noted in the DSBC text's numbering, apparently the last half of verse 27 and all of verse 28 have been lost from the Sanskrit. I have appended the original numbering of each remaining verse in parentheses.

About the Translator

Bhikshu Dharmamitra (ordination name "Heng Shou" – 釋恆授) is a Chinese-tradition translator-monk and one of the earliest American disciples (since 1968) of the late Guiyang Ch'an patriarch, Dharma teacher, and pioneer of Buddhism in the West, the Venerable Master Hsuan Hua (宣化上人). He has a total of 33 years in robes during two periods as a monastic (1969–1975 & 1991 to the present).

Dharmamitra's principal educational foundations as a translator of Sino-Buddhist Classical Chinese lie in four years of intensive monastic training and Chinese-language study of classic Mahāyāna texts in a small-group setting under Master Hsuan Hua (1968–1972), undergraduate Chinese language study at Portland State University, a year of intensive one-on-one Classical Chinese study at the Fu Jen University Language Center near Taipei, two years of course work at the University of Washington's Department of Asian Languages and Literature (1988–90), and an additional three years of auditing graduate courses and seminars in Classical Chinese readings, again at UW's Department of Asian Languages and Literature.

Since taking robes again under Master Hua in 1991, Dharmamitra has devoted his energies primarily to study and translation of classic Mahāyāna texts with a special interest in works by Ārya Nāgārjuna and related authors. To date, he has translated more than fifteen important texts comprising approximately 150 fascicles, including most recently the 80-fascicle *Avataṃsaka Sūtra* (the "Flower Adornment Sutra"), Nāgārjuna's 17-fascicle *Daśabhūmika Vibhāśa* ("Treatise on the Ten Grounds"), and the *Daśabhūmika Sūtra* (the "Ten Grounds Sutra"), all of which are current or upcoming Kalavinka Press publications.

Kalavinka Buddhist Classics

(www.kalavinkapress.org)

Fall, 2019 Title List

Meditation Instruction Texts

The Essentials of Buddhist Meditation

A marvelously complete classic *śamathā-vipaśyanā* (calming-and-insight) meditation manual. By Tiantai Śramaṇa Zhiyi (538–597).

Six Gates to the Sublime

The early Indian Buddhist meditation method involving six practices used in calming-and-insight meditation. By Śramaṇa Zhiyi

Bodhisattva Path Texts

On Generating the Resolve to Become a Buddha

On the Resolve to Become a Buddha by Ārya Nāgārjuna
Exhortation to Resolve on Buddhahood by Patriarch Sheng'an Shixian
Exhortation to Resolve on Buddhahood by the Tang Literatus, Peixiu

Letter from a Friend - The Three Earliest Editions

The earliest extant editions of Ārya Nāgārjuna's *Suhṛlekkha*:
Translated by Tripiṭaka Master Guṇavarman (*ca* 425 CE)
Translated by Tripiṭaka Master Saṇghavarman (*ca* 450 CE)
Translated by Tripiṭaka Master Yijing (*ca* 675 CE).

Marvelous Stories from the Perfection of Wisdom

130 Stories from Ārya Nāgārjuna's *Mahāprājñāpāramitā Upadeśa.*

Nāgārjuna's Guide to the Bodhisattva Path

The *Bodhisaṃbhāra Treatise* with abridged Vaśitva commentary.

The Bodhisaṃbhāra Treatise Commentary

The complete exegesis by the Indian Bhikshu Vaśitva (*ca* 300–500).

Nāgārjuna on Mindfulness of the Buddha

Ch. 9 and Chs. 20–25 of Nāgārjuna's *Daśabhūmika Vibhāṣā*
Ch. 1, Subchapter 36a of Nāgārjuna's *Mahāprājñāpāramitā Upadeśa.*

Nāgārjuna on the Six Perfections

Chapters 17–30 of Ārya Nāgārjuna's *Mahāprājñāpāramitā Upadeśa.*

A Strand of Dharma Jewels (Ārya Nāgārjuna's *Ratnāvalī*)

The earliest extant edition, translated by Paramārtha: *ca* 550 CE

The Ten Bodhisattva Grounds

Śikṣānanda's translation of The Flower Adornment Sutra, Ch. 26

The Ten Grounds Treatise
Nāgārjuna's 35-chapter *Daśabhūmika Vibhāṣā*

The Ten Grounds Sutra
Kumārajīva's translation of the *Daśabhūmika Sūtra*

Vasubandhu's Treatise on the Bodhisattva Vow
By Vasubandhu Bodhisattva (*ca* 300 CE)